Justice mis

POSTMODERN THEORY

Series editor:

THOMAS DOCHERTY
School of English, Trinity College Dublin

A series which openly and rigorously confronts the question of the postmodern in contemporary debates, and which boldly proposes a refiguration of what is understood as 'the modern' in all its forms: aesthetic and political, cultural and social, material and popular.

Other titles in the series include:

Jarring witnesses: Modern fiction and the representation of history
ROBERT HOLTON

Modern wasteland to postmodern wilderness
RODNEY GIBLETT

POSTMODERN THEORY

Justice miscarried
Ethics and aesthetics in law

COSTAS DOUZINAS AND
RONNIE WARRINGTON

HARVESTER WHEATSHEAF

New York   London   Toronto   Sydney   Tokyo   Singapore

First published 1994 by
Harvester Wheatsheaf
Campus 400, Maylands Avenue
Hemel Hempstead
Hertfordshire, HP2 7EZ
A division of
Simon & Schuster International Group

Typeset in 9½/12 pt Melior
by Photoprint, Torquay

Printed and bound in Great Britain by Biddles Ltd,
Guildford and King's Lynn

British Library Cataloguing in Publication Data

A catalogue record for this book is available
from the British Library

ISBN 0–7450–1635–9 (pbk)

1 2 3 4 5   98 97 96 95 94

For Alethea, Phaedra and Sibylla

Contents

Acknowledgements

A large number of friends and colleagues helped in the writing of this book. We would like to mention Alexandra Bakalaki, Viv Brown, Yifat Hachamovitch, Alan Hunt, Bernard Jackson, Les Moran, Peter Rush, David Sugarman and Alison Young. Shaun McVeigh has been a constant source of criticism and ideas. Peter Goodrich has provided inimitable and manic inspiration, obscure historical evidence, great stories and esoteric Latin maxims. Thomas Docherty was a continuous source of support at every stage of writing and an exemplary editor. Finally we would like to thank Jackie Jones and Alison Stanford at Harvester Wheatsheaf for their great editorial work and patience, and Justin Dyer for his meticulous and elegant copy editing.

An earlier version of Chapter 6 was published in *Law and Critique*, Vol. II, no. 2 (1991).

1

The return of ethics to law

I

An apparent paradox characterises contemporary law. While the legal system is going through one of its periodic crises, jurisprudence is enjoying a notable return to theory and a renewed interest in the role of value and principle in law. The crisis of law can be described as a crisis of legal form and a demand for an ethics. The theoretical turn is related to the crisis; its most interesting examples adopt a hermeneutical approach and are ethically motivated. They are attempts to 're-moralise' the operations of the legal system. Crisis in this context indicates a *krinein*, a turning to new directions in both law and jurisprudence, rather than a pending and prophesied catastrophe.

To begin with the crisis of legal form: in outline this concerns a complementary process of increasing juridification of social and private fields and of privatisation or deregulation of hitherto public areas of concern and provision. This double move has turned the traditional divide and boundary between public and private areas of action and regulation, upon which much of modern law rests, into an elastic line of passage, communication and osmosis. Administrative law, to take an obvious case, keeps extending its scope to an increasing number of previously domestic areas. This regulatory colonisation does not seem to represent or pursue any inherent logic, overarching policy direction or coherent value system. Policy considerations differ between family law and planning or between criminal justice and the regulation of official secrecy, privacy and data protection. Even worse, contradictory policies appear to motivate regulatory

1

practices in each area. Nevertheless, each sphere is experiencing the increasing colonisation of the social by legalised relations of power.

This development goes hand in hand with a limited amount of privatisation and deregulation. Privatisation does not return utilities and services to the logic of the private realm; rather, it hives off aspects of state regulation and places them in the hands of formally private interests acting in a public capacity. Both sides of this double extension and mutation in the governance of society seem to underuse the deontic logic of rules. Rules as normative propositions which prescribe criteria of right and wrong action are general and abstract, they anticipate and describe broad types of factual situations and ascribe legal entitlements and obligations to wide categories of (legal) subjects. Regulatory practices, on the other hand, are detailed, specific and change in accordance with the vagaries of the situation and the contingencies of the administrative environment; they distribute benefits, facilities and positions according to policy rather than entitlement; they construct small-scale institutions; they assign variable and changing roles to subjects; they plan local and micro-relations; and they discipline people and agencies by arranging them along lines of normal behaviour. Regulatory norms normalise.

In the midst of these changes, the signs of collapse of the legal expressions of the public/private divide are increasing. The distinction between rule and discretion, the hallowed basis of the rule of law ideal, is gradually becoming anachronistic as rule-makers couch their delegations of authority to administrators in wide terms, while administrators adopt policies, guidelines and rules to structure the exercise of discretion and protect themselves from challenge. Legislative and regulatory systems are adopted to promote transient, provisional and local policy objectives with no immediate or obvious link with wider social policy. Policy has become visible throughout the operation of law-making and administration; in many instances policy- and rule-making are delegated to experts, who fill the gaps according to the latest claims of scientific knowledge (Cotterrell 1992). Law appears at its most imperialistic at the precise moment when it starts losing its specificity.

No area is now immune from state intervention; but as law is disseminated throughout society its form becomes detailed and full of discretion, its sources multiple and diffused, its aims unclear, unknown or contradictory, its effects unpredictable, variable and uneven. All the key themes of legal systematicity are weakened. Sovereignty is gradually being replaced by performativity and the sovereign by international and supranational institutions; rule and normativity are replaced by normalisation, value by discretion and the legal subject by administratively assigned roles and competencies. The law is expanding but at the price of assuming the characteristics of contemporary society, thus becoming open, decentred, fragmented, nebulous and multiform. State powers, never as separate as constitutionalism suggested, are becoming fused. Public functionaries, who often belong institutionally to the redefined 'private' realm, become all three, policy-initiators, rule-makers and dispute-solvers. Outside the trappings of central power, beyond Whitehall, Westminster and the superior courts, law is increasingly law because it calls itself law. Law's legitimacy at street level is primarily based on its ability to mobilise the icons and symbols of legality. Additionally, acts of power acquire the character of legality if they are backed by the force of state institutions. If, as has been argued, society no longer exists, law has contributed to its demise by shifting the boundaries of a fragmented sociality and by rapidly retreating from its traditional 'natural' terrain.

It is at this crucial point that jurisprudence has turned its attention to hermeneutics, semiotics and literary theory as an aid to the ailing enterprise of positivism. This appeal to hermeneutics can be seen as a last desperate attempt to present the law as a closed and coherent system. But the hermeneutic turn also expresses a deeply felt need for a return to morality. The jurisprudence of positivism had based the legitimacy of law on the formalism of legality and the consequent decline in the relevance of ethical considerations. Using the strict distinction between fact and value, positivists from Kelsen to Hart had tried to exclude or minimise the influence of moral values and principles in law. The effort was motivated by cognitive-epistemological and political considerations. A 'science' or an analytics of law could only be founded on observable, objective phenomena, not on subjective and relative values. Rules and norms, despite their obvious logical variance from constative statements and their ontological difference from the phenomenal world, were transformed into quasi-hard facts and became the source and object of 'legal science'. This purified science of norms preoccupied itself with questions of validity and presented the law as a coherent, closed and formal system guaranteed internally through the logical interconnection of norms and externally through the rigorous rejection of all non-systemic matter such as content, value, historical provenance or empirical context.

The political dimension of the exclusion of morality should be sought in the modern experience of relativism and pluralism of values and the fear of nihilism (Goodrich 1986). Law is presented as the answer to the irreconcilability of value and as the most perfect embodiment of human reason. Private law turns social conflict into technical disputes and entrusts their resolution to public experts and the technicians of rules and procedures. Public law imposes constitutional limits and normative restrictions upon the organisation and exercise of state power. The logic of rules depersonalises power and structures discretion by excluding subjective value; it restricts choice in the application of law by administrators and judges. The distrust of administrative discretion and of judicial creativity; the antipathy towards administrative tribunals, legal pluralism and non-judicial methods of dispute resolution; the insistence on the declaratory role of statutory interpretation and the 'strictness' of precedent; the emphasis on the 'literal' rule of interpretation which allegedly allows the exclusion of subjective preference and ideological disposition – all these are key components of the rule of law as the law of rules and at the same time the diverse facets of the attempt to rid the law of ethical considerations. The positivist understanding and explanation of the operation and majesty of law is logically and politically premised on the absence of morality. Indeed, the law as a whole is presented as a moral enterprise because it excludes morality from its operation.

But the early 1990s witnessed an overwhelming call for a return to ethical values and moral principles throughout public life. In no other area was the anxiety of morality experienced more than in law. We outline in section II of this chapter some of the recent gross inadequacies and failings of the common law, as described and prescribed by positivist jurisprudence, which contributed to the widespread public unease about the state of the legal system. Nevertheless, the difficulties in re-imagining moral theory and making justice the proper and main concern of legal action, after repeated pronouncements about the intrinsic separation of the two, are daunting. Let us map briefly the problems facing contemporary jurisprudence.

The positivistic emphasis on formal rules and normativity appears unrealistically naïve in the new era of legal hyper-inflation. In addition, the evidence supporting the realist and critical legal thesis about the indeterminacy of legal interpretation and justification has become unanswerable from within traditional legal theory. The importation of hermeneutics, semiotics and literary theory in jurisprudence was motivated, therefore, by the urgent need to correct the descriptively inadequate and morally impoverished theory of law as exclusively rules and to re-inscribe morality in law. The new hermeneutical jurisprudence insists that the law is a valuable source of meaning, and that it means values. We may disagree as to the meaning of any particular statute or precedent, we may even accept that judicial reasoning and justification can legitimately lead to conflicting directions, but it is agreed, as a minimum, that law is about interpreting texts, that in some special way it is a form of literary exercise (see section IV below). We can therefore abandon the *Grundnorm* and the rule of recognition for the meaning of meaning; we can replace or supplement the technical rules of legal reasoning with the protocols of interpretation or with the study of rhetorical tropes and hermeneutical criteria; we can approach the texts of law through the law of text.

There is no doubt that this literary and hermeneutical turn gave legal theory a new lease and a long-lost sense of excitement. But another effect was to make morality an integral element of law, and in particular of judicial interpretation. The new jurisprudence of meaning responded to the highly topical demand and ethics became part and justification of the newly discovered interpret-ative character of the legal enterprise. But there is a catch. To take Dworkin's well-respected hermeneutical theory, the operation of law is presented as necessarily embodying and following moral values and principles. The notorious 'right answer' to legal problems presupposes for its existence and discovery an interpret-ative practice that reads the legal texts of the community as a single and coherent scheme animated by the principles of 'justice and fairness and procedural process in the right relation' (Dworkin

1986, p. 404). A similar position can be found in Boyd White's (1990) theory of justice as translation (see Chapter 5 below). Against the positivist lack of interest in morality, the interpretative scholars assert that the law is all morality and that judicial interpretation presupposes or leads to an ethics of legal reading.

Undoubtedly, the law is interpretation and interpretation is the life of law. The law follows principles and furthers values. But there is more to it: before and after the meaning-giving act, law is force. Statutes, judgments and administrative decisions act upon people and impose patterns of behaviour, attitudes and, ultimately, sanctions. Law's meaning coerces and legal values constrain. This all-important aspect of the legal operation, fully acknowledged by the early positivists, was underplayed later by Hart (1961) and became extinct in recent hermeneutics. In the enthusiasm for the semantic component, the law is presented as exclusively textual and ethical.

We are thus faced with a new paradox: power relations and practices proliferate and penetrate deep into the social, often taking a loose and variable legal form. Their common characteristics are few: an often extremely tenuous derivation from the legislative power and, more importantly, their link with the increasingly empty referent 'law' which bestows upon them its symbolic and legitimatory weight. If, for positivism, the 'law is the law', in the sense of law's existence and certification according to internal criteria of validity, the underlying idea becomes now fully radicalised. Power relations are law if and when they succesfully attach to themselves the predication 'legal', or law is everything that succeeds in calling itself law. But the most advanced legal theory ignores these accelerating developments and continues to be preoccupied, like classical political philosophy, with sovereignty and right, representation and delegation, integrity and 'right answers'; it examines almost exclusively the case law of appellate courts, the most formal and centralist expression of the legal system which is becoming increasingly unrepresentative of the whole system. If positivism fails to understand the moral substance of law, apologetic hermeneutics becomes even more unrealistic by neglecting power or reducing and subsuming it under the operations of legal *logos*. But *auctōritas est potestas non veritas*.

It is at this juncture that critical legal theory must intervene.

The hermeneutical and moral turn in jurisprudence is welcome; but the moral substance of law must be argued and fought for rather than simply assumed. Furthermore, in order to understand justice, the specifically legal facet of morality, we must link it with law's force. A postmodern jurisprudence must abandon the key premises of amoral positivism and of all too moral but power-less hermeneutical jurisprudence. But is such a jurisprudence possible?

The allegations against current alternative readings are well known: postmodernism and deconstruction are at least indifferent and at worst destructive of ethics and politics; they have shown knowledge to be so many facets of value, thus undermining the ability to found the ethical response; they have tediously repeated that texts accept an infinite number of interpretations, thus disqualifying any promise of a politics based on hermeneutical consensus; they have attacked the dialectic of subject and object, original and copy, inside and outside, thus weakening the claim of the sovereign self to stand in judgment in a community of reason. And as all reality has been reduced to the playful ruses of an aberrant and undecidable textuality, a night of reason in which 'all cows are black', responsibility has allegedly gone on permanent retirement. But recently poststructuralist philosophy has addressed the question of justice. We should examine more closely the moral turn in postmodern theory and its implications for jurisprudence. In order to do so, we need to understand something of the causes of postmodernism's turn to morality, ethics and justice.

II

One way of characterising the first phase of postmodernism, if the periodisation that this implies can be accepted, is that part of its main initial intellectual claim was oppositional. Postmodernism opposed the certainties of modernity and the 'truths' of Enlighten-ment thinking. Above all, postmodernism questioned the possibi-lity of a pure expression of a human 'essence'. This notion was supposedly guaranteed by thought's unmediated access to an inner authentic and whole self, and passed through self's immediate manifestations, speech and its accompanying gesture. But the belief that 'man' 'progressed' by the mechanism of a doubting subject applying scientific method to produce knowledge no longer carried conviction. This 'new' insight gave postmodernism part of its initial impetus.

This first phase, the phase of radical doubt, produced a contradictory politics; some saw it as deeply conservative (Habermas 1985), others as oppositional, transgressive and liberating (Foster 1985). The more conservative forms, especially in some of their openly celebratory versions, as practised particularly in the United States, went the whole way. Sure there are no truths, or 'Truth', science does not provide a model for all human thought, etc. But this recognition means no politics either. If politics is the free and willing attempt to 'improve society', it is inevitably based on one or more obscure and almost megalomaniac claims. But the essence of man, economic systems, laws of history, laws of gods, dialectical progression of forces and classes, binding social contracts etc., are all the junk of murky, indeed fearful, minds, minds that are frightened if they do not have some foundational certainty to underpin every aspect of existence. All previous grand systems of total and all-encompassing reason and explanation are recognised as simply the misguided aspirations of thought still not free from the mystical yearnings of the ancients, medievals and moderns for some ultimate ground in God, truth, or whatever.

By contrast, for the neopragmatists what matters is the democratic polity, from Athens to Chicago, in which things tick along in the chatter of conversations. Changes take place, of course, but experience shows that most, or perhaps all, social transformations are either the result or the cause of changes in our conversational modes. There is nothing else; transformations in society are simply impossible, or, in terms of the politics of the 1980s, there is 'no alternative'. Bourgeois democracy becomes a sort of mock-Hegelian final result, and the end of history arrives. We can all relax into the success that modern democracy brings and sensibly try to solve its problems without resorting to eternal verities, which are as real as fairies.

On the other side was the radical tinge of postmodernism: in architecture, literature, painting, but perhaps most significantly literary criticism, the realisation that there were no truths led to the experience of unprecedented freedom. In literary criticism especially, but to a small, perhaps surprising, extent even in legal studies, the chains were off and the reader could be abandoned to the pleasures of textual meanderings, a sort of textual liberation. Texts had no authors, or if they did, any intentions ascribed to them were probably invented and certainly unnecessary; the reader was invited to indulge in the fast and loose of play. The reader's imagination, combined with whatever textual possibilities the particular subject of discussion seemed to permit, encouraged and invited a new and at times delightful form of free expression. It was not a free-for-all: literary criticism always respected the text itself. But infinite possibilities seemed to open before this newly liberated consumer of the word. The death of the author suggested that, potentially, the same fate might be meted out to author-ity itself.

The two sides, then, shared certain beliefs: no privileging of supposed authorial intentions; interpretative creationism in the reading of texts, which elevated (even flattered) the importance of the reader; the impossibility of predetermined fixed meanings anchored in texts by authors, circumstances or history. But whilst the one side accepted this as a confirmation of the sound basis of the world and as a justification for the exploitation of the system by some at the expense of many, the other side was not so sure. The dethroning of 'truth' and 'certainty' was of no value to them if they could not somehow act upon these new non-truths in order to alter what they perceived to be the wretched state of things. If 'grand narratives', as social theory became known, were suspect, that called not for the abandonment of practice but for 'better' praxis.

In particular, the question of values returned to stalk the discussion. It was all very well to slide around in the joys of textual analysis, but to what can this lead? Are all values equal, and if not, what standards are there to judge differences? How can choices be made? The notion that 'Reason' or 'reason' is no longer relevant, was never something that deconstruction took seriously. But the charge that there was no way of dealing with reason's demands, since it was impossible to determine to which specific result reason pointed, needed urgent political and theoretical responses. If all values were equal, or if, in the slightly milder version, there was no privileged way of determining which values were more significant than others, then there was the danger of slipping into totalitarianism, or at least of having no means of criticising it. Attempts to argue for free choice, local communities and respect for the validity of individual or small-scale solutions meant that there semed no sensible way of disempowering certain ideas, almost no matter how horrendous their implications. The urgent task was therefore to start to re-explore the ethical dimensions, to find methods of distinguishing between the flippant and the fundamental, the worthless and the worthwhile, without in any way reinstating the modernist claims to the power of authority.

To turn to our own concerns, developments in the relation between law and politics allowed the question of justice to be reinserted into critical discussion around law. What apparently had been for so long ignored suddenly seemed urgently and obviously pressing: how was it that the law had managed to establish its credentials by the very act of eliminating most, if not all, substantial considerations of justice? Law seemed to embody modernity's supreme god of rationality in the most perfect form; from a medieval set of somewhat mystical practices, law had transformed itself into a sort of idealised Enlightenment occupation which, in the terms of some apologists, represented the model for all other types of endeavour. Indeed, law worked by translating and incorporating all other activities into its own rationalist and near-perfect procedures. But this rush to modernity had swamped any substantive notions of justice which the law was supposed to embody. More than in any other discipline, such issues are back on the agenda of law.

III

This turn to substantive values coincides with a particular crisis in the legal system. Traditionally, the Establishment, especially in its specifically English manifestation, had assumed that the common law legal system was the greatest gift from God to the Empire, the manna that heaven had granted the chosen people. Having garnered and refined the crop, the English then bountifully spread it throughout the world with a confidence that came from the combination of military might and economic growth. (The legacy of Empire and the common law in many parts of Africa and Asia needs no elaboration.)

But as the conquerors retreated to home base, one thing remained solid in a changing world: the confidence of the English

Establishment, especially amongst those who knew best, that is, judges and lawyers, that the common law was the finest system of dispensing justice. It is only a few years ago that the merest threat to change a minor aspect of the system (the hierarchical relationship between barristers and solicitors) forced the then Lord Chief Justice, in a staggering example of 'the insolence of office', to utter some of the most absurd remarks about the quality and near perfection of the existing constitutional arrangements and system of justice, since one of his even more notorious predecessors, Judge Jeffreys, went about hanging and flogging poor wretches for supposedly threatening the same glorious institutions. On the whole, most of the legal establishment, whilst not quite so convinced that heaven was still represented in the common law as currently practised with all its purity, has always considered that there is nothing to match the English system of dispensing justice. God may have been shunted into a siding, but as long as the common law stayed on the rails the world was still a good place.

How quickly things have changed in the estimation of many, including many lawyers. The most stark manifestation is the disquiet amongst bench, Bar and public that has surrounded the notorious miscarriage of justice cases that came to light during the late 1980s and are still being revealed in the 1990s. As is well known, it turned out that many innocent people had been jailed wrongly; furthermore, they had found it necessary to fight for years to get the political authorities and the courts to reconsider the prosecution evidence (frequently manifestly perjured) on the basis of which they were wrongly convicted. Even when they had overcome all the hurdles that the system threw in their way before they were permitted to present their argument, the courts at first insisted that there could be nothing done wrong by the system and its representatives and that therefore the innocents must be guilty. The list of gross miscarriages of justice seems by no means closed. All this acted as a shock to the profession and beyond. The evidence that the legal system was failing in the most far-reaching and radical manner spoke volumes.

But the well-publicised and repeated convictions of the innocent, as a result of the complicity or at least complacency of the legal system in the criminal activity of the state prosecuting authorities, was only one of the blows to the confidence of the law. Many other instances of monumental failings have continued to pursue the legal system. Without listing them all, the reader might summarily be reminded of some of the loud and continuing cries of professional foul that have been raised in the last few years. The appalling condition of life in prisons, both for those actually convicted and for the innocent (those on remand awaiting trial) causes continuing concern, and receives publicity periodically when inmates rebel and riot. The government's Chief Inspector of Prisons (himself a judge) repeatedly issues reports condemning the inhuman state of prisons. If the conditions for adult detainees were not bad enough, the revelation that homes for the most vulnerable members of society, dispossessed and unwanted children, have repeatedly been found to be places where the young are physically and mentally abused has shocked even government ministers. 'The law's delay', always legendary, has now become so pressing on both the civil and the criminal side that even the current Lord Chief Justice has called on the government to recognise that justice delayed is justice denied, and provide the funds for more judges to be appointed so that the waiting time for cases to be heard can be reduced.

But access to justice will be affected even more by the government's proposals (first announced in their current form in autumn 1992) drastically to reduce the numbers who will be eligible for legal aid. It is well known that most people simply cannot afford to go to court, and unless the legal aid system is saved then the problem of justice for the majority of people goes away, almost literally. 'Plea bargaining' (the process where counsel and judge get together prior to a trial and the judge indicates in chambers the amount by which he or she would consider reducing the defendant's penalty if he or she were to plead guilty, thus avoiding the expense of trial) is causing a degree of disquiet and was commented upon in July 1993 by the Royal Commission on Criminal Justice headed by Lord Runciman. Plea bargaining is not supposed to take place, as the Court of Appeal banned it; and yet everyone connected with the criminal justice system knows it happens. Indeed, without plea bargaining the whole criminal court system would break down under the weight of pending cases. To much 'surprise', what was supposed to be the open, fair system of public hearing, where the defendant at least gets his or her 'day in court', turns out to be a process of grubby dealing by the lawyers.

Then there is the institutionalised racism; this has been pretty evident in the legal profession for years, and there is still no sign of an appointment of someone from an ethnic minority to the High Court Bench, though there are now a small number of (token?) appointments of non-white males to the lower branches of the judiciary and there has been a conspicuous appointment of a meagre handful of women to some of the higher courts. There are persistent and distressing allegations of discriminatory treatment of black defendants by both police and courts. Racial discrimination seems endemic at the Bar itself. This is now so bad that students from minority backgrounds are sufficiently incensed by the treatment they receive at the hands of the Bar's education authorities that they are taking judicial review proceedings against the Inns of Court's own Law School, alleging racial discrimination in the process of qualifying at the Bar.

If these and other glaring lapses at home are not enough to throw doubt upon the hallowed practices of the common law and its claim to be the best and fairest in the world, then there are the interfering foreigners; time after time over the last twenty years, the British government has been taken to the European Commission and Court of Human Rights and found to be deficient in its practices. It seems that the common law does not even provide the minimum standards of protection recognised by those inferior systems in Europe, which take for granted certain levels of regard for the individual as against the state.

These and other examples showing the blatant failure to do 'justice', as the legal system is supposed to understand and operate that term, are depressingly familiar. The Establishment's critics are not lacking arguments to demonstrate the now heavily exposed shortcomings of the system, and concerned practising and academic lawyers can and will argue for improvements, real and cosmetic. For most lawyers, however, the system is basically sound; there are defects, but these should and could be remedied to bring the system back to its own proper standards. Many solutions present themselves and appear quite sensible to the profession itself. For example, police officers can be supplied with codes of ethical conduct to which they 'must' adhere (a practice which the police themselves have proposed to introduce); courts can vow to listen more carefully to the defendant's evidence and perhaps more suspiciously to the prosecution's; the Runciman Royal Commission examined several aspects of the law and proposed improvements to prevent any future manifest wrongful convictions, though the experience of the results of the earlier Commission, itself convened as a result of miscarriages of justice, is cautionary; indeed, the most discussed and controversial change in the law, following the Runciman Commission's report, was the abolition of the right to silence, a rather odd reform considering that the reason for setting up the review of the criminal justice system was the wrongful conviction of people, based mainly on their uncorroborated confessions. The government can 'promise' to fund courts and litigants properly; the process of plea bargaining can either be outlawed (again) or made public, with the defendant at least being properly advised of the rights that are being traded for a lesser tariff; those who run children's homes can be more carefully 'vetted' and supervised; the Bar Council can try to stamp out racial discrimination within its institutional practices; the Lord Chancellor could actually appoint non-whites and non-males to higher judicial offices; the Home Secretary can continue to promise to improve the state of prisons and the conditions under which those awaiting trial are held. In general, even the most conservative elements of the legal profession would agree that the requirements of procedural justice need to be respected, and insofar as justice is denied, delayed or perverted, then at least some remedies are not too difficult to enumerate and seem fairly obvious.

IV

But for critical legal scholars, the issues go beyond instant remedies and solutions. There have always been pressing problems with particular aspects of social arrangements, and no shortage of reformers anxious to deal with the effects of each particular ill as it manifested itself. Critical theory since Kant, and certainly since Marx, has been concerned with something more, some comprehensive idea or reason which explains not just one particular difficulty or evil but a whole range of them. Such critics, looking for universal causes, have always sought universal solutions to go with them. And though it may seem strange to modern understandings, where lawyers are generally regarded as overpaid drones with little intellectual interest or ambition, it was often the lawyers who were regarded as being at the forefront of the drive to universalise, to lift the horizon of inquiry beyond the immediate issues. It is true that the most ambitious and scholarly of lawyers, the real successors to 'Renaissance man', were often marginalised or excluded. But despite this marginalisation, the attempt to raise law beyond the day-to-day struggle presented an image of what might have been and created symbols that shadow the icons of power and practices of the institution. Some of the major continental intellectuals of early modern France and Germany were lawyers who were not just concerned with the next case and the next fee. As Foucault put it, the great civil lawyers of the eighteenth century opposed the autocratic state and, for many, symbolised the 'universal intellectual': 'The man of justice, the man of law, he who opposes to power, despotism, the abuses and arrogance of wealth, the universality of justice and the equity of an ideal law' (Foucault 1979, p. 43). Present-day critical lawyers, themselves largely side-lined and sometimes excommunicated, have realised that to abandon the terrain of critique means to leave the ground free for those who abuse power. In an age when the grand narratives of modernity have been seen as totalitarian and oppressive as much as liberating and enlightening, the challenge for critique is not just to find quick-fix solutions to immediate problems (important though this work is) but to reconstruct the practice of moral evaluation, and to reinvent the art of political judgment. The sense of outrage that greets some of the blatant injustices of the legal system must be related to the recognition of the rather startling divorce that modernity introduced, between law and ethics, legality and morality, justice as process and justice as substance.

That modernity played such a large trick is not, perhaps, so surprising. In the Europe of the nineteenth century, a crude model of science often held sway and infected many aspects of scholarly inquiry. What mattered were 'facts', while judgment, compassion, humanity, morality, a concern for others, for the weak, oppressed and disposessed, could be relevant only after the results of scientific enquiry had been established, and could not be the cause or the mainsprings of progress, economic, scientific or intellectual. A recognition of the failures of modernity in this regard was a force promoting the breakdown of intellectual certainty which we have already cursorily sketched and one of the reasons for the growing interest in theories loosely headed 'postmodern'.

But the discovery of textual 'indeterminacy', exciting and liberating as that was, still left unanswered the persistent and troubling question: if texts could be read to mean more than one thing, how could authorised meanings be challenged? If it were really true that 'anything goes', then Hegel and Pope were correct after all: 'in erring Reason's spite/ One truth is clear, Whatever is, is RIGHT.' In other words, if there could be many readings out of one text, and therefore out of any particular form of conducting human affairs (themselves texts in many senses, including the notorious one given by Derrida), there was no way of saying what was 'right'. In which case the arguments for not disturbing the accepted order of things, for pretending slavishly to follow precedent (the lawyer's dream, the citizen's nightmare), became overwhelming. If one person's reading was as good as another's, any existing way of doing things must be acceptable. And given the inherent dangers of change, how could alterations in the way things were done be justified?

As we outlined in section II, it was against this background that the 'leftist' tendency of postmodernism, especially in its academic form, heavily influenced as it was by deconstruction, was faced with the next move: how to link the excitement of deconstructive readings with the immediate practical ethical reconstructive readings which, to some at least, seemed so glaringly necessary as to be beyond argument. In particular, in law, it has become 'obvious' that the patching of the system is insufficient. Some relating of law to justice, to the 'good' in either its Aristotelian rationalistic sense, or its more mystical Platonic sense, has become pressing and indeed has been taken up by some critical legal scholars.

The impasse that was raised for legal theory specifically was how to recognise that there is more to law than instant judgments in instant cases, and that the need to re-establish an ethical element for law and justice is not contradicted by the freedoms revealed by deconstructive reading practices. To put it differently, the task was to find grounds for arguing that there can be an ethical substance for law, without reproducing the discredited essential-ism of Enlightenment thinking.

One way for the lawyers to proceed was, somewhat ironically, by a sort of 'back to basics', to return to what lawyers had always done best, reading (Norris 1988). Lawyers have always been 'textualists'; in the real world and in the academy, lawyers must read texts with an exacting eye. Both those who are drafting documents (statutes, regulations, judgments, contracts, conveyances, wills, etc.) and those who interpret them when something goes wrong (lawyers and judges) must be the most discriminating of readers. Disputes about the placing of humble punctuation marks can still make all the difference between the success and failure of cases. So, in a sense, when the deconstructionists started to urge 'close readings' they were only asking literary critics to do what the lawyers had always done. But what deconstructive readings also did was to extract implications for close readings well beyond anything within most laywers' imaginative powers. Deconstruction played a major part in questioning the certainties of modernity because its practitioners carefully reread some of the foundational texts of the Enlightenment (especially Rousseau, Kant and Hegel) and raised one rather disturbing implication from their inquiries: that on the evidence (the lawyers would at least like that) the certainties that these founding texts had always been thought to create were simply not available. Not only did these texts not mean what had passed for years as accepted wisdom, it might be rather hard to determine what, if anything, these texts were trying to do at all. It was not that texts suddenly became 'meaningless'; that would be plain silly. It was that meaning, far from being authorised, was contestable. Indeed, for reasons partly related to the inherent instability of linguistic expression (that is, contrary to the wisdom of structuralism), texts could often be read explicitly against the grain of 'authorised' readings without in any way doing violence to the actual linguistic artefacts in question.

For us, these new readings must go beyond critique, beyond exposing the 'noble lie' of authorised and totalising meanings. The challenge is to articulate a theory of ethical action upon which a practice of justice can be built which itself would not reproduce the totalising tendencies that deconstruction so correctly challenged. In this book, we turn to a philosophy of 'otherness' to attempt this construction in the wake of deconstruction. Whilst we expound in more detail what a philosophy of otherness will entail in Chapter 4 and throughout, we can summarily state here that we take Derrida's political and ethical work, together with the intervention of Levinas, as beginning on this delicate task. Levinas argues that a fundamental consideration of the other must always be undertaken prior to the ethical decision, indeed to any decision; the other in the nakedness of the face always presents herself to us as the irreducible, sometimes inexpressible, ethical demand: 'consider me before you act.' And the consideration that is required by this 'total' demand is always to be accounted for prior to any thought of self or own.

The problem with this, as Critchley (1992) points out, is that this ethical propriety only speaks of a one-to-one relation where 'the other' presents itself in all her immediate powerlessness. The question becomes how to generalise this ethical basis from individual, possibly even parochial, concentration to a generalised theory of social action which can take us into the realm of politics as justice. Levinas achieves this vital transition by reinstating the 'third'; that is, by reminding readers, politicians, judges and citizens that our ethical duty to the other is always situated in a context where more than two people are involved. The third, then, is symbolic of the social, of the whole; our ethical responsibility to act justly is part of a setting in which all ethical actions beyond that between a Crusoe and a Man Friday take place. The responsibility for just actions in relation to the other becomes a responsibility for just actions amongst all others, and in this way an otherwise potentially overwhelming burden is mitigated. Levinas gets beyond an almost primitive (and, as we shall indicate in section v of this chapter, and especially in Chapters 2 and 4, a pre-ontological) relationship to allow for the development of a theory of justice by reminding us that the concern for the other is always set in a context of concern for all others.

Our own construction recognises the need to extend the theory of otherness beyond the one-to-one relationship but does not just accept the implications of Levinas's (somewhat problematic) suggestion that the recognition of the social context of actions gets beyond the potentially impossible demands that the premise of the other might seem to make. It is by accepting the all-pervasive aspect of legal adjudication in the modern world that we recognise that a philosophy of otherness never simply concerns merely a cosy 'one-to-one' relation. We hope that this aspect will emerge more clearly from some of the later chapters in this book.

V

In the remainder of this introductory chapter we outline the issues with which we deal in order to establish our own position, which we can now epitomise as follows: the law often acts unjustly. Unjust actions should not be tolerated. But in order to change the legal climate from one where substantive notions of justice are regarded as extraneous to the operation of the system, we make the simple claim that the law, if not founded on just, ethical principles, is not acceptable. The ethical substance on which we base the claim for a re-creation of the notion of justice is the philosophy of otherness. Although a more detailed exposition of this philosophy comes later, we can summarily state that ethical action is based on a non-fixed relation between self and other. The other is neither the self's *alter ego*, nor its reflection or extension, nor its dialectical partner. The other, for us, is always what comes first in any ethical system. The other, though never fully knowable, always precedes, surprises and above all calls upon us to consider her before ethical or legal decisions are taken.

In Levinas's analysis, the sign of the other in all her vulnerability is the face. Because the face is unique, it can never be reduced to an image or reflection of some pre-existing Platonic substance or essence of self. It is an expression without an essence and in its very existence the face asks us, and therefore the law, not to judge on the basis of some pre-existing, totalising and denigrating image of a (legally constructed) essence. The demand of the suffering other is the non-essential essence which the legal system needs to recognise in order to merit its necessary but currently absent claim to do justice.

To put it simply, the point is not to return to a privileged, modernist, foundationalist fallacy. There is no point in dethroning truth, or labour or science (if this is what the combined forces of cultural postmodernism and philosophical deconstructionism have done) only to substitute an essentialist notion of *the other*. If we were to do this, then not only would we be returning to a modernist orthodoxy, we would also destroy the very ethical sensitivity to the other that Levinas tries to remember and revitalise. If the other were to be categorised in terms of an essence of 'otherness', that essence could only be a reflection of the self. To construct an essence of otherness is to destroy the respect for the

other, something the law frequently does, sometimes quite
ruthlessly, as we demonstrate in Chapter 6. An awareness of
otherness cannot determine the attributes of the other, but it
recognises that there will always be aspects of every other that we
cannot know. Its unfathomable depths call upon us to respect it, in
its nonessentialisable difference. In the Levinas idiom, otherness
is therefore not a foundational idea in the Enlightenment sense. It
is an essential unknowable 'demanding' our attention, respect and
love, and, as we start to explain in Chapter 2, this non-demanding
demand precedes our own consideration of self-preservation and
of being.

In Chapter 2, we turn directly to the most superb exposition of
the origins of the ethical demand that can found this non-
foundation of law in western literature, Sophocles' *Antigone*. In
this supreme, moving and most powerful drama we find not just
the launch of a western literary tradition (the relationship between
the individual and society) but the commencement of the legal
correlation of this relation, the respective roles of positive and
natural law. Indeed, we would argue that Antigone herself is as
significant for the foundation of justice as her father, Oedipus, was
for the foundation of psychoanalysis. But the play has generally
been taken to turn on the dispute between the eternal (in Antigone
as representative of natural law) and the state (in Creon as
representative of positive law); this aspect of the issues is well
known and has been endlessly discussed. Of more interest,
however, we find in the play a recognition of what comes before
the law; that is what was there both before human laws as we know
them were established or natural law was thought of, a claim that
calls us and demands our recognition irrespective of any particular
legal code which might be assumed to bind. Antigone answers the
call of the other not just because she wants to, or thinks it
advisable or politically expedient or legally correct, but because
she must. 'Yes! he is my brother. . . . I must bury him.' In the
dreadful plight in which Antigone finds herself, both respecting
and rejecting the 'legitimate' code, we find the call of the other and
its relationship to all laws unequivocally seeking attention.
Antigone puts into action a law of law that demands a hearing
before the law, in either its positive or natural manifestations and
is formulated, before Plato put into circulation a concept of being
in which the self in its selfishness is central both in epistemology

and in ethics. That is to say, Antigone places the ethical before the ontological. She powerfully and movingly articulates a call that, despite the mental and physical threats of Creon and his cronies, she cannot get out of her head the call of the other; in this case of her dead brother in his corporeal specificity. For her, it is a call that comes before the law is set down. For us, it provides the 'must' of a contemporary theory of justice.

In Chapter 3, we leave the direct call of Antigone and examine an alternative ethical tradition, this time one that appears different from the standard form of legal interpretation we now take for granted, casuistry. Although we reject the orthodox religious foundation of casuistical reasoning, we recognise that there is here a form, sometimes connected directly to orthodox legal interpretation, sometimes running alongside it, that also tries to understand the individual's fate and face in the light of the specific situation, and does not just purport to operate on the basis of general laws. One way of summarising our work is to make the rather startling claim that for law's empire to reincorporate the demand of justice, without which any claim to respect is forfeited, it must listen to the call of Antigone and therefore acknowledge the eternal other in every situation, and practise a refined casuistry in order to take account of the specifics of the unique individual.

In Chapter 4, we pull together the strands of the argument. We here try to explain why the strong ethical call that we found in *Antigone*, a call that precedes any specific legal exposition, is something we cannot ignore. We trace a number of 'heterodox' strands in ethics that have been repressed in modernist moral philosophy, from Aristotle to Hegel and Kant through to Levinas and Derrida and make them the underpinning for a postmodern theory of justice. Such a theory that meets the urgent ethical demand in law must answer Antigone's call and must incorporate the casuists' realisation that universal laws can only achieve justice if they give way to the uniqueness of the individual who comes before the law.

Chapter 5 examines two recent theories of legal interpretation, by Boyd White and by Cornell, that try to take seriously the question of otherness and of the good in law. White argues that the law, as the most important and extensive form of conversation of the modern western world, must hear the claims of those outside standard legal discourses and practices. Cornell argues that by recognising the claims of otherness in law and outside it, we can move beyond the limits of conventional legal analysis of both the positivists and critical legal scholars. But both these texts, though particularly the second, also raise a question which we have already touched on, namely how to determine between different people, causes and values, in a word between the various others? It is all very well respecting the other in the way Chapter 4 suggests, but if the other is a murderer or a mugger, a rapist or a racist, how is consideration to be given without some form of approval? How are values simultaneously to be respected and condemned? In part, this question relates to the problem of situating the respect for an other within the social context of many others, to which we have already referred, but it is also a problem in its own right. Whilst our first text finds a solution by returning to the fundamentals of republicanism in order to answer this difficulty, thus weakening the basis of an argument purporting to respect the other, our second text approaches the problem far more rigorously by combining a philososphy of otherness with an open declaration of support for some values and a rejection of unacceptable ones. We will suggest, however, in the end, that this attempt is also unsatisfactory. However, in criticising both these exemplary and blindingly honest struggles to take further the notion of otherness in law, we sharpen our own critique of current alternative theories of justice within law and recognise some of the shortcomings of our own position.

In the remaining chapters of the book, we move from the elaboration of a general ethical plea that should inform a theory of justice to the more concrete implications of our analysis; we try to provide specific examples of what a reading informed by the call of Antigone and a secularised casuistry might involve. We start with the particularity of legal reports, and analyse directly how the law treats those beyond its physical and geographical borders, the pure outsiders; we then turn to the more abstract level of love poetry in which legal domination is seen to work its insidious effects well beyond its supposed remit. Finally, we examine an aspect of a most abstract form of art, painting, in which once again we find the law in its imperialistic mode denying the rights of all but those to whom its established tradition and power have determined shall receive its blessing.

To start with the paradigmatically legal, in Chapter 6 we look at that category of rank outsiders, those who are the most explicit example in law of 'otherness', refugees, as they have been recently treated by the highest English courts. The cases we analyse show why a theory that respects the difference of the other has become urgent. The tendency of the common law, whether in its pure positivistic manifestations, or even in its softer humanistic guises, is always to reduce the outsider to the insider. The insider, represented by the judge, who himself represents the eternal wisdom of the common law, always knows what the outsider feels because the outsider is only the same as the insider stripped of the sophisticated responses that the insider, the judge, is able to make. The other, as outsider, can always be reduced to the comprehensible insider by being made to conform to the vision the supreme insider, the judge, expects of everyone else. It therefore follows that the standards of the judge are also applicable to the refugee, and if on these criteria the judge feels no need to protect the refugee, then the refugee can be sent back to persecution and probably devastation with a good conscience. The suffering face of the outsider is 'translated' into the reasonable man of the common law and on this basis is found not to be suffering at all, not to be in need of the very protection that the law is supposed to provide for the weak and the disadvantaged. The other becomes self and in the process her destruction is assured. As Europe continues to tear itself apart in demonic religious, racist and nationalistic wars, nothing illustrates more dramatically the need for a Levinasian sensitivity to the requirements of the totally different, non-reducible other than the case of refugees.

Having seen the treatment of the outsider in the pure genre of legal texts, that is, in case reports (nothing is more legal than a law report), we then generalise the argument in our next 'case' study. We now try to show how legal imperialism extends its insidious grasp beyond the routine application evidenced in the law reports and how it takes hold of other literary forms. In Chapter 7, we take a well-known sonnet (nothing is more literary than a sonnet) and show how relationships as apparently basic, even natural, as sexual encounters can be overdetermined and destroyed by the totalising tendency of law's empire. The ethics of a deconstructive reading reveals both the impoverishment of standard hermeneutical and critical readings and the possibility of a transcendence for which an ethical reading of a law/love poem can prepare the

ground. The Sonnet demonstrates that the law's failure to respect
the other of love leads to the destruction of others, lovers, and self.

Having moved from the arena of case reports to the genre of
literature, we then turn to the pure genre of art (nothing is more
artistic than a painting) as expounded by its practitioner and
theorist Sir Joshua Reynolds. Here, we find an apparent expression
of artistic integrity actually determined to exclude the other, those
outside the established province of 'Art'. Furthermore, we show
how a quasi-legal analysis is used to excuse and justify the
brutality of the exercise. Reynolds draws on the common law in
order to maintain the inside/outside distinction. But as even his
best efforts fail, despite the seeming legal rigour of the argument,
we show how a theory of justice demands an ethics of reading in
the realm of the aesthetic that takes seriously the call of the other,
those the law systematically tries to exclude, and how an
aesthetic-legal theory can itself be made subject to the demands of
justice for which this book argues.

If postmodernism is entering a new end of century phase, then a
rekindling of respect for the very human values that law ought to
represent is part of the wider movement towards ethical awareness
in critical theory. Whether or not lawyers ever were really
concerned with universal human values, as Foucault and others
have assumed, there is a pressing need for critical legal scholars to
join the debate in order to ensure that the values of the universal
and the human in all their differences and vulnerability can be
represented in the necessary development that law must undergo
in order to regain self-respect. In the meantime, practising law,
without an overwhelming desire to do justice, remains a dangerous destabilising and dehumanising form of *Antigone* without the
princess and of casuistry without the humanism.

2

Antigone's Dikē

The mythical foundations of justice

I

Of all the masterpieces of the classical world – and I know them and you should and you can – the Antigone *seems to make the most magnificent and satisfying work of art of its kind.*

Hegel, *Aesthetics*

New 'Antigones' are being imagined, thought and lived now; and will be tomorrow.

Steiner, *Antigones*

Where is the site of law's emergence? Where does law come from? Whence does it draw its power? Our inquiry will attempt to trace the 'question of law': of law's origins and of its value, of law's validity and force. The question is haunted, persecuted by two ghosts. The more recent but in another sense the most ancient answers to the name of Heidegger, the recorder of the closure of metaphysics and of the death of jurisprudence. The other, Antigone, from whose grave jurisprudence emerges but never leaves, is the more ancient but also the most contemporary. We will follow the advice of the two spectres in our attempt to approach the law of law.

We shall start where we should, at the start. We shall start on the 'should' on the 'must'; on the ground for this 'should', the ground of law, what Hegel calls the ethical substance *Sittlichkeit*. At the very beginning of Sophocles' *Antigone*, the tragic heroine states her own 'must' in the most categorical way. Antigone will defy the command of her uncle, King Creon, and will bury the corpse of her brother, Polynices. There is no equivocation, no ambiguity, no hesitation in Antigone's voice in the face of the

25

disreputable death of her brother or Creon's law, only an immediate and unquestioning acceptance of the 'should', an unwavering assumption of responsibility:

ISMENE: You cannot mean . . . to bury him? Against the order?
ANTIGONE: Yes! He is my brother . . .
      I **must** bury him myself . . .
ISMENE: Then go if you **must**
      wild, irrational as you are. (44–6, 71; 98–9; emphasis added)[1]

We cannot remain indifferent in the face of the wild irrational force of this 'must'. Where does it come from? To attempt an answer to the question of law, we turn to the tragedy as it comes to us through the thick matter of commentary and interpretation, philological and philosophical, that has covered Antigone's face like a wedding veil and sepulchral curtain. But why turn to *Antigone*? What is the relevance of a text written in Athens in the fifth century BC for our understanding of law?

Greek tragedy has been for centuries the meeting point of philosophy, literature and ethics, of reason, form and law. Tragedy, Nietzsche's 'philosophical opus *par excellence*', has been the testing ground of the Odyssey of Spirit for Hegel, of unconscious desire for Freud and Lacan and of the primordial memory of Being for Heidegger. And according to Steiner, amongst the great works of world literature, no one 'has elicited the strengths of philosophic and poetic interest focused on Sophocles' *Antigone*' (1986, p. 103). We cannot read *Antigone* today without repeating or refuting these powerful interpretations. We are caught in a dialectic of acceptance or rejection that is condemned to circle around Hegel's Antigones in their incorporation of the agonistic form of the tragedy if not in their substantive claims. And as Hegel busily hovered throughout the meandering excursions of the spirit around the text of Sophocles, we, too, seem condemned to Antigone's law; both to the law of the text of *Antigone* and to the law that Antigone so clearly hears right from the start of her tragic action.

---

[1] The translations of *Antigone* used in this and the following chapter are based on the Penguin editions (Sophocles 1947 and 1984). The line numbers in the text refer to the classical edition by Jebb (1966). Some translations have been altered to bring the text closer to the original Greek and emphasise the legal concerns and vocabulary of the play.

Interestingly, while philosophy has consistently turned to tragedy as the ground of the dialectic and to *Antigone* in order to understand the nature of the law and of law's power, jurisprudence has been very sparing in its examination of the tragedy, perhaps because 'it would be idle to suppose that one has anything new to contribute to the commentaries on the confrontations between conscience and state in *Antigone*' (Steiner 1986, p. 247). Jurisprudence textbooks usually refer to *Antigone* in passing, in the chapter on natural law.[2] They present the tragedy as an early statement of the potential conflict between a superior source of duty and the law of the state. Antigone is the 'first great heroine of civil resistance, almost the leader or inspirator of a resistance movement against tyranny' (Weinreb 1987, p. 21). And as most jurisprudence improbably presents modern conceptions of natural law as the outcome and perfection of an unbroken, continuous history that started with the Greeks, *Antigone* gets a statutory mention alongside Aristotle and the Stoics. But this is merely to attribute to *Antigone* a certain foundational status without attempting to listen to her call. Despite the imprudent neglect of jurisprudence, the praise of philosophy should alert us to the importance of *Antigone* for the moral unconscious of law. *Oedipus Tyranos* and the myth of Oedipus have been recognised as key texts for the understanding of psyche and identity. The daughter of Oedipus, Antigone, must be similarly acknowledged as the mythic foundation of thought and action concerning *physis* and *nomos*, *nomos* and *dikē*, law and justice.

The presence of these myths is so pervasive in our culture that only a sense of misplaced arrogance and originality have stopped us from acknowledging the 'repetitive and epigonal character of our consciousness and expression' (Steiner 1986, p. 113). Heidegger agrees:

all progressivist and evolutionary anthropology is false. The beginning is the strangest and the mightiest. What comes after that is not a development but flattening that results from mere spreading out. . . . Historical knowledge is an understanding of the mysterious character of this beginning. If anything it is knowledge of mythology. (1961, p. 155)

---

[2] Amongst many references in passing to the play, see D'Entreves (1970, p. 14), Lloyd and Freeman (1985, p. 100 fn. 5), Posner (1988).

But the origins to which Heidegger is referring are not some idealised, Greek 'childhood of man' that was perfected in his western maturity. Instead Heidegger speaks of the leap, both original and final, in which man founded himself by finding himself, we will argue, before the 'other' who put to him the first, continuing and last ethical command which lays the philosophical foundations of law.

In our quest for the (ethical) law of law, we will conduct three readings of *Antigone*: the juridical, the dialectical-speculative and the ontological. But each will be 'deconstructed' by being directed to the question of law and justice. The juridical reading will show the impossibility of a *nomos* with(out) *dikē*; the dialectical will reveal the universal and the (legal) system devoured by the singular; finally, the ontological will show how ethics comes before the destiny of Being and ontology and brings the law to the question of justice. Let us repeat our claim that *Antigone* is as important for the exploration of the origins and force of the law as Freud believed that *Oedipus* was for the understanding of the psyche.

*   *   *

At the start of the play, the two daughters of Oedipus are in conversation. Antigone tells Ismēnē of the latest catastrophe to visit the house of Laius and Labdacus. Creon has issued a decree prohibiting the burial of their brother, Polynices, and threatens disobedience with death. Both Polynices and his brother, Eteocles, perished in the battle for Thebes. Eteocles, the defender of the city, was given the full funeral honours of a dead hero; but Creon's edict was that the traitor, Polynices, should be left unburied. As a result his soul will be unable to enter Hades. Antigone tells her sister that she will defy the King's proclamation and tries to involve her in the act. Ismēnē is not prepared to challenge the law and tries to reason with Antigone. Antigone, fearless and determined, despairs at her sister's indecisiveness and sets off to bury Polynices on her own.

Creon then proclaims his vision of politics based on utilitarian calculation and pragmatic compromise. He announces his harsh edict and informs the Thebans that he has posted sentinels to guard the corpse. He is interrupted by a terrified soldier who comes to announce a 'miracle'; Polynices' corpse has been covered by a film of dust, but no one was seen carrying out the libation. The Chorus suspects divine intervention, but Creon is convinced that it is the work of political conspirators and accuses the guard of complicity, threatening terrible punishments.

Antigone is brought before Creon by the guard who caught her in the act of burying Polynices. Antigone freely admits her guilt and appeals to the eternal laws of the gods who ordain that the dead should be properly buried in order to travel from this world to Hades. Creon condemns her to be buried alive. The King's son, Antigone's fiancé, Haemon, tries to convince his father that Antigone's action was holy and her life should be spared. Creon sees in his pleadings the work of a feeble mind, infatuated by love and unable to reason. Incensed by his son's disobedience that threatens both paternal and political authority, he confirms Antigone's sentence.

Teiresias, the blind seer, tells the King he has received terrible omens. The gods will not accept his sacrifices, which is why a plague is tormenting Thebes. The carrion of Polynices' corpse that the beasts bring into the city has polluted the temples. As the signs of divine anger multiply, Creon relents. He will save Antigone from her grave and bury the corpse. But fate has ordained differently. When Creon arrives at the burial site, Antigone has killed herself. Haemon, who has followed her, mad with anger and remorse, attacks his father and kills himself. Creon returns to Thebes to hear the final part of his family's destruction; his wife Eurydice, on hearing the news, is overcome with grief and she, too, commits suicide on the family altar. The houses of Creon and of Oedipus have been destroyed.

II

Is there anyone who doesn't evoke *Antigone* whenever there is a question of a law that causes conflict in us even though it is acknowledged by the community to be a just law?   Lacan, *Ethics of Psychoanalysis*

Unusually for tragedy, *Antigone* has 'a double centre of gravity' (Goheen 1951, p. 97). The tragedy progresses through the clearly defined conflict of the two protagonists, Antigone and Creon. Their

arguments, principles and actions in relation to the moral and
political issues and dilemmas involved are sharply distinguished
and are presented consistently from two diametrically opposed
perspectives. As a result some of the most influential readings of
Antigone have treated the tragedy as the manifestation of a series
of underlying conflicts of value and standpoint that move the
action inexorably towards its doom-laden conclusion. The trend
started with Hegel's influential philosophical interpretation and
has been repeated in many critical readings.

In general terms, philosophy has treated oppositions of principle or concept either as the inevitable preparatory steps towards
their eventual dialectical synthesis or, as eternally circulating and
irreconcilable antitheses that constitute the subterranean 'grammar' of action. To be sure, conceptual oppositions invite or inhabit
axiological hierarchies in which one side is superior to the other. If
Creon and Antigone are the human embodiments of a double
perspective, inescapably bound to each other, the attribution of
guilt and responsibility for the monstrous catastrophe that befalls
all main characters by the end of the tragedy becomes the key
question in the interpretation of *Antigone*. If the two protagonists
are masks of a fatal conflict, the question of the supremacy of one
of the antagonistic principles, of 'who is right' has correctly
dominated the commentaries.

Many principles have been proposed as the key organising
oppositions of the conflict.[3] But it is the attitude of the protagonists
to law that receives one of the clearest presentations and has
dominated the critical literature. It is a question of law, justice and
punishment.

CREON: Now, tell me – not in many words but briefly –
did you know that an edict (*kērychthenta*) had forbidden this?
ANTIGONE: Of course I knew it; it was public (*emphanē*).
CREON: And did you dare to transgress these laws (*nomous*)?

---

[3]A strong tradition of reading *Antigone* in terms of juridical contrasts and binary
oppositions finds its best representative in the works of the American classicist
Charles Segal, who is strongly influenced by Lévi-Strauss. Segal (1964) is followed
by a magisterial study of tragedy (Segal 1981); see also Segal (1986). The themes of
justice and law and their conflict, exemplified by Antigone and Creon, are treated as
key interpretative principles in classical philology. See, amongst others, Bowra
(1944, Chap. 3), Lloyd-Jones (1971, Chap. v), Whitman, (1951, Chap. 5) and
Winnington-Ingram (1980, Chap. 5).

ANTIGONE: It wasn't Zeus, not in the least,
  who made this proclamation (kēryxas) – not to me.
  Nor did that Justice (Dikē), dwelling with the gods
  beneath the earth, ordain such laws (nomous) for men.
  Nor did I think your edicts (kērygmata) had such force
  that you, a mere man, could override
  the great unwritten and certain laws of the gods
  (agrapta kasphalē theōn nomima).
  They are alive, not just today or yesterday:
  they live forever, and no one knows
  when they were first legislated. (446–57)

A strict dichotomy is established. The divine proclamations of
Zeus and the laws of the chthonic gods of the Underworld are
juxtaposed to the *nomos* or *kērygma* of the *polis*. Divine law is
unwritten, certain and eternal; as unwritten it is felt and acted
upon by those who receive its call. It lives in the actions of people
rather than in public proclamations. Its *certainty* does not invite
interpretation but immediate obedience that does not calculate the
consequences. To die before her time carrying out her duty is, for
Antigone, a 'gain', *kerdos* (464). Finally, *ta theōn nomima* are
everlasting; they exist before and beyond the time of political
institutions and of human machinations and devices like writing.
The world of heaven and of Hades intrude upon history as
disturbances of temporality and rationality. The timelessness of
their commands is a permanent challenge to the timeliness of the
laws and institutions that establish the boundaries of the *polis*.

At the other end stand the *nomoi* of the *polis* legislated by the
rightful King.[4] Creon's law is man-made, secular and civic; it is the
basis of all civilising values of the *polis* and the cause of its
salvation. There is no greater test for a man than 'rule and law-
giving', *archais te kai nomoisin* (177) and Creon boasts that he has
passed it: his *nomoi* guard the city's greatness (191). It is in his first
speech to the Chorus, which parallels Pericles' funeral oration to
the Athenians, that Creon sets out the general principles of the
democratic state, always threatened by enemies external and
within. Polynices, a traitor who attacked his city and family,

---

[4] The semantic range of *nomos* in classical Greece is quite varied and covers a large
number of normative systems from universal laws of nature to specific and local
customs. Ostwald (1969, Chap. 2) counts twelve separate meanings. See also section
VII below.

deserves the cruellest punishment. Creon's edict is presented as a straightforward application of the general law of state necessity:

I could never stand by silent,
watching destruction march against our city, putting safety to rout,
nor could I ever make that man a friend of mine
who menaces our country. Remember this:
our country is our safety.
Only while she voyages true on course
can we establish friendships, truer than blood itself. Such are my laws
(nomoisi).
They make our city great. (184–91)

Creon's words sound no different from any other leader's in the midst of strife and war. The Chorus thoroughly agrees with him:

It's true your word is law (nomō de chrēsthai)
and you can legislate
both for the living and the dead. (213–14)

The Chorus has no kind words for Antigone until much later in the play when the displeasure of the gods at Creon's impiety becomes clear. To understand the impact of the developing conflict for the *phronimous andres* of the Chorus, we should compare the contrasting positions with the dominant political and ethical theories of classical Greece.

For the Athenians of the fifth century, the *polis* is both spatially and metaphorically the focus of man's civilising influence. Aristotle in his *Ethics* presents the city as the median place between the world of the gods above and of the animals (zōa) below. Civic virtue can only develop in the institutions of the *polis* and man can overcome his animality (zōon) only when he belongs to the city (politikon), the topos between divinity and bestiality. Thucydides reports that the Athenians prided themselves for being law-abiding (II.37.3.) and Euripides believes that it is the enactment of laws that distinguishes Greeks from barbarians (Euripides 1963: Medea 536–7; 1971: Bacchae 881–2). In the Crito (Plato 1969), Socrates is visited by his old friend Crito in his prison where he is awaiting execution. Crito has prepared his master's escape. Socrates, in a dream-like encounter with the Laws of Athens, is reminded that a state cannot survive if individuals disobey the laws. To the argument that unjust laws may be disobeyed, the personified Laws respond that under their binding contract Socrates agreed to obey the laws at all times. Their authority should not be undermined, because they protect the state, which is holier than mother and father (*ibid.*, p. 91).

To Athenian ears, therefore, Creon's opening speech, with its moving references to the paramount importance of the salvation of the ship of state, would not have sounded very different from Socrates' argument or from Pericles' *Epitaphios* (Funeral Oration). The great rhetor Demosthenes is reported to have used part of Creon's address in defending his own case against Aeschines, whom he attacked for abandoning these great principles in his political life (*De Falsa Legatione* XIX.247; Santirocco 1986, p. 183). Despite some fanciful interpretations of the tragedy (Whitman 1951, p. 90), the Greek citizen, Aristotle's *zōon politikon*, knows that his salvation and well-being depend on the safety of the *polis*, which should not be easily gainsaid.

As the action unfolds, however, Creon's attitude gradually changes. First, he identifies the law, *nomos*, with his own pronouncements (449, 481), which are declared equivalent with earth, the 'highest goddess', and the temples (284–7). In his confrontation with his son, Haemon, Creon claims absolute obedience for his laws:

> But that man the city places in authority,
> his orders must be obeyed, in small things and large,
> in just and unjust (*dikaia kai t'enantia*). (667–9)

There is no greater evil than *anarcheia* proclaims the King (672). But when his arguments fail to alter Haemon's position, the desperate Creon abandons his earlier high-minded claims and asserts that the city belongs to him (738). It has been argued that this change of attitude turns Creon from a legitimate king to a demagogue and a tyrant who will soon forfeit whatever sympathy still lay with the Chorus. But this is by no means the opinion of the jurisprudential commentators and certainly not of Hegel. For Posner, it would be a 'mistake, to think Creon a monster who gets his just deserts'. He is confronted 'by a blunt challenge to his authority, and the authority of law, by a woman who speaks with uncompromising self-righteousness rather than asking for mercy'. It is a 'no win' situation for Creon and the play is 'his tragedy as well as Antigone's' (Posner 1988, 111, 112; cf. Knox 1984, whom Posner quotes approvingly). Despite his harsh pronouncements, many see Creon as representative of the 'rigour of human law, – neither restricted by absence of higher law, nor intensified by a personal desire to hurt' (Jebb 1966, p. xxxvii).

But if the two protagonists, Creon and Antigone, seem to have totally antagonistic conceptions of law, the same appears to be true in relation to their attitudes to *dikē*, justice. In Creon's vocabulary *dikē* is an attribute of civic rule closely associated with positive law and *dikaios* is the obedient and virtuous citizen (208, 400). On two occasions, the expression *dounai dikēn* (to give or to do justice) identifies *dikē* with judicial procedure, the administration of justice and punishment (228, 303).[5] Creon, however, is not totally impervious to the claims of divine justice; in his opening address he appeals to Zeus as witness to the justice of his rule and as protector of Thebes. But as the confrontation with Antigone and her claim to follow divine law intensifies, he distances himself from godly appellations and claims supreme validity for his own edicts. Creon distinguishes between the law-abiding man, *dikaios*, and the claims of Zeus (658–61). He demands obedience for both his just and unjust laws (665–7); he identifies justice with his laws (744) and uses the word *dikē* pejoratively to signify feud, conflict (742). Finally, he denounces Teiresias as a lover of injustice, *tádikēin philon* (1059). In Creon's enlightened and secular humanism, civic order and the rule of law are the highest principles. They subsume all reasonable religious claims and try to turn them to advantage, according to the principles of political utilitarianism and state necessity. To deny the civilising influence of the law is the greatest crime, but at the same time Creon seems to prepare his own downfall in not recognising the proper rights of the gods.

By contrast, Antigone's *dikē* is divine in provenance and private in operation. Dikē is personified, an infernal goddess who dwells with the gods below (451) and ordains what is due to the dead (94) and to gods (459–60). Dikē's commands are specific, they are addressed individually and privately to the elect rather than to the whole *polis*; she who receives the *nomous* of Hades (519) is immediately obliged to answer with deeds, irrespective of personal interest or the consequences of her action (538–43). The

---

[5] The jurisprudence of modernity too identifies justice with judicial procedure. See Chapters 4 and 6 below.

responsibility of the recipient of the law is original and unique
(908, 914) and forces her to action. It cannot be shared after the
deed through the expression of sympathy or a merely verbal
undertaking of responsibility. Ismēnē cannot join in Antigone's
punishment as she did not answer the call of Dikē (542–7).

Antigone is not indifferent to the interests of the state. She
believes that her fellow citizens support her action and would do
so publicly but for the fear of reprisals from Creon (519), an
assertion repeated by Haemon. She would not have acted against
the wishes of the *polis* if the dead were a husband or son (905–7);
but the call of the dead brother and the law of the chthonic Dikē
exceptionally makes her disobey. She has received her own law
and she is acting upon it of her own free will. As a consequence
she will suffer a fate no other mortal has ever known: she will be
buried alive. She is *autonomos*, says the awe-struck Chorus (821).

On the few occasions that legal literature has turned to
Antigone, it is this dichotomy that has been mostly discussed. It is
presented as the first clear statement of the conflict between
natural and positive law; the law that comes from the Gods, let us
call it provisionally *dikē* (justice) against the law of the state
(*nomos*). In this interpretation, *Antigone* inaugurates the eternal
confrontation at the heart of normativity. She splits the ethical
substance at its very start between a divine and a secular
component, the unwritten and the written, the eternal and the
temporary. The two poles are placed in their unceasing circulation
and create an economy of conflict and of revolving hierarchies,
which is none other than the history of law and of law's
consciousness, jurisprudence.

III

Like Hegel, we have been fascinated by Antigone, by this unbelievable
relationship, this powerful liaison without desire, this immense impossible
desire that could not live, capable only of overturning, paralysing, or exceeding
any system and history, of interrupting the life of the concept, of cutting off its
breath, or better, what comes down to the same thing, of supporting it from
outside or underneath a crypt.   Derrida, *Glas*

There is, however, a second, parallel narrative of the tragedy,
which deeply affected Hegel. Antigone stands for the principle of

family, for the realm of the private, of individuality and love. Repeatedly she reminds both her sister Ismēnē and Creon of her familial duty to her brother, which in some instances appears ordained by the 'unwritten laws' but more often is presented as the result of Antigone's *philia* (love, loyalty, affection and kinship). She and Ismēnē are the only survivors from the house of Oedipus. In her moving soliloquy, before she is led to the tomb, Antigone recounts how she carried out the funeral rites on her father and mother and her other brother Eteocles. Her duty now finally extends to Polynices.

> And even if I die in the act, a good death
> I will lie loved with the one I love (*philē philou*) . . .
> If I had allowed
> my own mother's son to rot, an unburied corpse
> that would have been agony . . .
> Not ashamed for a moment
> to honour my brother, my own flesh and blood. (72–7)

No death is nobler than that imposed for burying her *philtatos* dearest brother (81, 503, 512, 517). She will bury Polynices both because he is a brother and out of the deepest affection for him. Throughout the play, Antigone uses the language of love and of family-kinship as demanding of her with equal force to defy the law of the *polis*.

Antigone stands for the rights of the *genos*, of blood lineage. As the sister, she is the kinswoman who has the duty to perform the burial rites necessary for her kin to enter the netherland, the dark region of Hades. The origin of her duty and her affection is the common womb from which she and Polynices have emerged. There are repeated references to the womb as the place that establishes a primordial bond. From the first striking line of the play, Antigone appeals to the strong link of kinship morality. She calls Ismēnē 'my sister my own dear sister' and uses an uncommon word for sister (*autadelphos*) which emphasises the sisters' relation through the *delphys*, womb. Her brothers and sisters are *adelphoi, homogastrioi* (co-uterine), *homosplanchnoi* (of the same belly); *philia* is a blood kinship.

Creon, on the contrary, from his first speech, defines *philia* in terms of civic obedience and political friendship (182–3):

> Only while our city voyages true on course can we establish friendships,
> truer than blood itself. (188–90)

Blood friendship must be subordinated to the salvation of the city. Moreover, Creon reminds Antigone, the two brothers, despite their common descent, found themselves the worst of enemies and killed each other in battle. The commonality of blood was destroyed by the bloodshed.

> Miserable wretches who, born from one father and mother,
> levelled double-conquering spears against one another and so won, both of them,
> a common share in death . . .
> The foe (echtros) is never a friend (philos) – not even in death. (143–6)

Antigone's answer is perhaps the most famous line in all tragedy:

> I was not born to hate but to love (symphilein). (522–3)

Against Creon's distinctions and discriminations, Antigone allies nature to her own idea of love. She will purify the miasma (170–2) and heal the infectious division of the house of Oedipus by re-uniting the two brothers in Hades and following them there. Antigone stands anti the genos or gonos. She compensates for the curse of her house, that turned mother and son into husband and wife, father and offspring into brothers and sisters, in other words she stands for the basic laws and taboos of womb integrity. But she also stands against the family because her maiden betrothal with death virtually ensures the destruction of her father's line. If her act renounces hatred for love and law for the justice of the gods, at the same time it denies love for the sake of death and adopts the undifferentiated dikē of Hades against the luminous distinctions of new(born) life.

Antigone, therefore, is both for and against the family. Her name alone should alert us to the excessive formalism of the 'structuralist' or 'jurisprudential' readings of Antigone. Their confrontations and reversals, oppositions and syntheses provide too neat and formal readings of the text. Characters and principles, actions and words do not stand ready formed, closed and totally opposed to each other. Ambiguity, conflict and tension exist both within all main characters and concepts of the tragedy as well as between them. This tension is all too apparent at the level of the legal terms and institutions that form the background against which the action takes place.

Language generally, and legal discourse in particular, is a battleground for the protagonists who use the same legal concepts with profoundly different meanings. Take, for example, the key term *nomos*, the law. Its semantic field is beset with extreme ambiguity. For Antigone, *nomos* is the religious law, the ancient and unwritten customs of family, kinship and Hades. For Creon, *nomos* is the edict of the King, his *kērygma*, promulgated in his sovereign speech (*kēryttein*: to announce, pronounce). *Nomos*, of course, derives from *nemein*, regular attribution fixed by custom but also territorial attribution fixed by pastorage.[6] The fecundity of the term allows both uses to co-exist even though they are totally contradictory. As a result the protagonists misunderstand each other and accelerate the conflict. The famous *stichomythia* between Creon and Antigone on the meaning of law is a good example of the *dialogue des sourds*, the repeated monologues of the protagonists. Language, the contested terrain, is both the means of and a barrier to communication.

But the sharp contrasts between antagonistic laws and principles, all too easily identified by jurisprudence, are soon upset. Creon, for whom *nomos* is the edict of the state enunciated in his authoritative commands, comes to meet the laws of those forces that do not follow his rationalism. These laws are not promulgated in speech (*logos*) nor are they the products of reason (*logos*). He is reminded of the law of fate and of the gods connected with the unleashing and punishment of wanton boastfulness (*atē*). 'Nothing that is vast enters into the life of mortals without a curse' (614). The wonderful power that lies at the centre of all human greatness (352ff.) carries with it the violence of destruction, linking unbreakably the greatest and basest in man. The law of *eros* next, of love and sexual passion, is inescapable by mortal men and immortal gods alike (786–90) and is enthroned on the side of the eternal laws (799). Love makes people forget and disobey the orders of state law, as it did with Haemon whose infatuation with Antigone wrecked the royal court. Finally, as the scale of destruction of his own home becomes clear, Creon has to acknowledge the existence and validity of the *kathestōtas nomous*, the laws established by powers beyond his sovereignty (1113-4) which are indispensable to the well-ruled city, *eunomousa polin*.

---

[6] See further section IX below for Heidegger's understanding of *nomos*.

Too late, responds the Chorus. Creon 'saw *dikēn*' at last, but not in
time to save himself and his *oikos* (1270).

But Antigone, too, comes to experience a Dikē different from
that of the underground gods she cherishes. In her last exchanges
with her fellow citizens, as she tries to understand her fate and
solicit sympathy, the Chorus explains:

> You went too far, the last limits of daring –
> smashing against the high throne of Dikē. (853–5)

Dikē forbids the suppliants to come too close; there is a point after
which no further advance to the throne of Dikē is allowed.
Antigone rushes forward nevertheless; but she stumbles, smashes
herself against the throne and falls. We can never know *dikē* fully.
Justice forbids and she forbids herself. Antigone teaches that to
come close to Dikē, we must launch ourselves, attempt to
transcend self and the law and experience the inevitable fall. But
the throne of Dikē is high, it belongs, in other words, to the
Olympian gods of daylight and rationality. For the first time, the
possibility that she, too, may have miscalculated in attributing
exclusive significance to one set of laws enters Antigone's mind.
This doubt eventually engulfs her in mortal ambiguity as she is led
to her grave. The gods, for whose law she is suffering the
ignominious fate of the living corpse, do not seem to acknowledge
her resolution or to support her martyrdom.

> What law of the mighty gods (*daimonōn dikēn*) have I transgressed?
> Why look to the heavens any more, tormented as I am?
> Whom to call, what comrades now? Just think
> my reverence only brands me for irreverence!
> Very well: if this is the pleasure of the gods,
> once I suffer my doom I shall come to know my sin.
> But if these men are wrong, let them suffer
> nothing worse than they mete out to me –
> these masters of injustice! (921–8)

This is an awesome combination of defiance of the unjust justice of
the law, of abandonment in the face of the unknown wishes of the
gods and of extreme agony. The Dikē she has appealed to
throughout remains uncommunicative and the law she gives to
herself as *autonomos* may still turn out to be unjust. Antigone
accepts that the law – her own and Creon's – will take its course
and will not allow her to know before her terrible death whether

she is pious or sinful. The law metes out its punishment before we know fully its command, like the infernal machine in Kafka's *Penal Colony*, which physically inscribes the law and their crimes on the backs of the convicts, who will learn their transgression in their punishment.

Antigone goes to her death 'pious out of impiety' (924), a criminal whose crime has been the most holy (74). She is a tragic and heroic *persona* on whose corporeal body, law and *dikē*, the highest and the lowest will play out to the end both their catastrophic antithesis and eternal symbiosis (Whitman 1951). And if this is the law, it is given to the solitary person in unpredictable fashion and is never beyond doubt. But the wavering of ethical solitude is only temporary. The terrible law can only be fully known after it has taken its course. And it is the fate of Antigone, the *isothea* of Hölderlin, to take this course and defy both earthly and godly powers. This simultaneous acceptance and defiance of both laws fascinated Hegel. Antigone's sacrifice would lead the antagonistic principles to their sublation and transcendence. Can we escape Hegel's reading, or are we forever condemned to reading the history of the law from the perspective of the dialectic?

IV

The celestial Antigone. The most resplendent figure ever to have appeared on earth.   Hegel, *Lectures on the Philosophy of Religion*

Hegel's commentaries on *Antigone* are part of a long series of philosophical readings and translations. Small changes in emphasis separate his early attempts to understand and translate the unique genius of the classical Greek *polis* (Hegel 1975a) from his mature rendering of the theory of tragedy in *Lectures on the Philosophy of Religion* (1988) and *Aesthetics* (1975b). In between stands the *Phenomenology of Spirit* (1977). As the dialectic moves in its inexorable path and the spirit journeys upwards sublating and transcending its more concrete formulations on its way to full self-consciousness, Antigone turns out to be a most valued fellow traveller for Hegel. In the *Phenomenology*, Antigone herself is mentioned sparingly; but the tragedy forms the backdrop of the work, as Hegel debates with Athena the first and most perfect manifestation of the spirit (1977, pp. 261, 284). It is a remarkable incorporation of poetry in philosophy and a major source of understanding the key issues, conventions and laws of hermeneutics (Pietercil 1978).

Hegel's interest in Greek tragedy is linked with his diagnosis of the social and philosophical condition of modernity. Kant had inaugurated philosophically the modern obsession with the split between subject and object, and the fragmentation of self and the world. The main philosophical task of German Romanticism was to heal the rift and assert again the oneness of existence. The early Romantics had tried to overcome the fissure by declaring the priority of one or the other of its poles. Hegel's answer was to internalise and historicise the split. The fragmentation of modernity is conceived as a necessary stage in the Odyssey of Western Spirit towards self-consciousness. The key oppositions of modernity are therefore the expression of an ongoing conflict, an *agōn* internal to our existence and the inescapable condition of our consciousness. Thought, consciousness and the spirit are action, a continuous struggle. The spirit must fight a civil war against its own alienation and must recognise itself in and return to itself through its other. It is only through this *emphilios polemos* (war of friends) that the spirit gathers and sublates the fragments in the totality of history. Against what he saw as Kant's moral formalism, Hegel claims that freedom and the possibility of ethical life are intrinsically linked, indeed that they are the outcome of the initially split existence within the organic community. But the condition of ethical life, *Sittlichkeit*, the ethical substance as realised in the state, is necessarily tragic.

The development of the dialectic brings the key concerns and categories of tragedy to bear upon the jurisprudence and the law of the age. In the *Philosophy of Right* (1967), the movement to the absolute Spirit, Reason's self-consciousness, is presented in the usual triurnal progression but in explicitly legal terms; from abstract, formal right to the morality (*Moralität*) of Kantianism, finally to *Sittlichkeit*. Abstract right, both as law and morality, is the immediate, undifferentiated unity of the universal. As such it has formal existence but no determinate content, while its key concept, personality, exists only in the abstract. Human will is absolutely free but its only content is to relate self to itself, thus turning self into a person. This abstract personality can only be legal; the abstract capacity of the *persona* is to have legal rights and duties and thus to form the basis of the laws of property, contract and crime. The first moment, the *thesis*, of the dialectical process to the Spirit is determined by the key categories of Roman law (Hegel 1967, pp. 37–40).

The passage from right to morality involves differentiation and concretisation. The bare, abstract universality of will, personality and formal right are now turned into individual subjectivity. The subject becomes aware of his freedom, as he stands against the world presented to his will. In *Moralität*, I am free not only in the immediate external thing and my right to it, but also in myself and my subjectivity. In this inner sphere, it is intention and purpose that count, as they stand at the bar of the good, of universal morality. But the good should not remain internal to conscience. It must be realised in the external world as its universal end. In morality, however, the two fields remain still formal and unmediated; moral conscience, in its Kantian abstract form, faces the Good, the universal essence of freedom, as two sides external to each other. The Good has no content nor has it become yet a concrete part of subjectivity. The subject has finally entered the stage of the world but his morality is still abstract.

It is in the third moment of ethical life, or *Sittlichkeit*, that formal right and morality are finally absorbed, sublated and cancelled. The differentiated universal with its objective and subjective moments is superseded by the concrete synthesis of universal and particular. The abstract good and human conscience, which were kept apart in morality, now come together and are realised in the actions of concrete individuals. The ethical life is freedom become concrete, the unity of subject and object and of content and form; it constrains 'subjective opinion and caprice' (*ibid.*, p. 105) not as an externally imposed law but as the living good experienced and practised by each citizen. The individual can realise freedom and fulfilment only in and through the ethical order; virtue *is* 'the ethical order reflected in the individual character' (*ibid.*, pp. 107, 109). Unlike the abstract universality of right and the formal subjectivity of morality, in ethical life 'right and duty coalesce, and by being in the ethical order a man has rights in so far as he has duties, and duties in so far as he has rights' (*ibid.*, p. 109).

The concrete embodiment of this ethical substance is posited without hesitation: it is the 'valid laws and institutions' (*ibid.*, p. 105); and again in the *Phenomenology*, 'this Spirit can be called the human law, because it is essentially in the form of a reality that is conscious of itself. In the form of universality it is the *known* law, and the prevailing custom' (Hegel 1977, pp. 267–8). The institutions of the ethical life impose their order on the individual. But unlike the alien order of natural objects which 'conceal their rationality under a cloak of contingency and exhibit it in their utterly *external* and *singularised* way' (Derrida 1990, p. 12; original emphasis), the law of *Sittlichkeit* is the Spirit become historical institution. This is then the movement of the Spirit: from right to morality to the ethical life and in institutional terms from family to civil society to the state. The movement is full of internal and external confrontations and contradictions which are gradually absorbed in the inexorable sublation and transcendence of the opposites. Freedom and the possibility of ethical life are intrinsically linked, indeed they are the outcome of the split existence within the form of the organic community. The condition of ethical life, the ethical substance as realised in the state, is necessarily tragic.

Political philosophers and economists have understandably emphasised the conflict between civil society and the state from the huge Hegelian edifice. And yet the key opposition is that between family and state. The state is the embodiment of positive law, the expression of the principles of generality, equality and legality. Family, on the other hand, is law's other, it stands for concreteness and individuality, for emotion, love and death. The dialectical path to *Sittlichkeit* is split between the demands of the political realm and those of private right, the main aim of which is the preservation of family. This split takes its concrete form in the life and actions of individuals. The first principle of existentialism states that existence is the translation of potential being into action and deed. Consciousness, knowledge and self-consciousness are only acquired in the passage from potentiality to actuality; thought and action are united in the life and existential acts of the individual. The ethical substance enters history through the authentic actions of persons who answer the call of the law.

State action dresses itself in the most pure form of ethicality, the universal. Thus two aspects of the ethical, the substantive and the formal, find themselves in continuous and inevitable conflict. In *Sittlichkeit* each law contains its negation. 'Each of the opposites in which the ethical substance exists contains the entire substance, and all the moments of it contents' (Hegel, 1977, p. 268). The Spirit has finally reached consciousness. Both laws are conscious of themselves and of their opposite and consciousness is 'on the one hand ignorant of what it does, and on the other knows what it does' (*ibid.*, p. 266). When individual authentic action violates the law, the subject both knows and does not know the wrongness of her acts. Against such actions the state will try to impose its own abstract logic and to suppress the ethical command. In the most extreme cases, the conflict will become destructive, as abstract state formalism meets suicidal individual autonomy unprepared to accept any external arbitration as to its rights and obligations. Antigone is one such authentic person: she answers the inner voice, acquires self-consciousness and thus realises the ethical substance. In her action absolute ethicity becomes actual and historical. But in this translation, as the absolute enters the finite and temporal to help Being move towards unification, it suffers a dissension, a dehiscence. The ethical substance is split into a human and divine component; and the concrete human being, whose action becomes the medium and *organon* of the descent of Spirit, is caught in an inescapable conflict and is destroyed. The care and burial of the dead is a key area of conflict between temporal and eternal law, the terrain on which Antigone will become the plaything and promoter of Spirit's progress and homecoming.

The family *qua* family has as its object the absolutely singular. Family love is addressed to the beloved purely for his existence, for who he is and not for what he does. In the consciousness of the family, its member is the most concrete and unique person, an *individualised particularity*, and it is this singularity that makes him worthy of family's ontological valuation. The state, on the other hand, is interested in the citizen's actions and assesses him for what he does. In particular, the pagan state demands that its citizens risk their lives and die for the universal cause of personal and state recognition. And as these actions can be performed by many people, the citizen is a *generalised individuality*.

For Hegel, of course, the ethical purpose of the family is to prepare man, *vir*, for a life of virtue and virility in the community, to transform him from *homme* into *citoyen* and install him in the service of universality and citizenship. Family, the place of the individual and the private, fulfils its role by educating men to renounce family's principle of privacy and love and by teaching them to adopt the public life of state and the spirit. Family's *telos* is to sacrifice itself for the *polis*, renounce its own function and existence in the same way that the universal devours and transcends the particular. State and family are as opposed as earth and the Underworld, their respective principles as those of Zeus and Hades. A young man on his way out from the privacy of the family but who has not yet fully entered the public realm is compared with a dead man, someone who like Polynices is on Hades' boat, between this world and the Underworld, in passage and in need of the rites of passage to succeed in the transition. The corpse of the dead man becomes the symbolic ground of the most acute conflict. Death is the work of family and families busy themselves around death. The wedding present that men offer their brides, their most 'singular gift', is their corpse.

Pure singularity: neither the empiric individual that death destroys, decomposes, analyses, nor the rational universality of the citizen, of the living subject. What I give as a present to the woman, in exchange for the funeral rite, is my own absolutely proper body, the essence of my singularity. (Derrida 1986a, pp. 143–4)

The dead body, freed of its potential for action, has no use for the state; family women will return it to earth and help it join the undifferentiated community of death. Antigone, Mary Magdalene, the waking women of Mani exercise the primordial law of womanhood, which is also the law of gods and the ethical demand of the beloved dead.

Hegel is quite explicit: the family achievement no longer concerns the living but the dead, 'the individual who, after a long succession of separate disconnected experiences, concentrates himself into a single completed shape, and thus raises himself out of the unrest of the accidents of life into the calm of simple universality.' But because it is only as a citizen that he is actual and substantial, 'the individual, so far as he is not a citizen but belongs to the family, is only an unreal impotent shadow' (Hegel 1977, p. 270). Antigone will purify and bury the dead brother, as required by the law of family and woman. Indeed for Hegel, death, the philosophical function of family, creates the greatest duty when it falls on the sister to return her brother to family and earth. But in obeying the law she will also raise Polynices to the status of the universal law, she will unblock his passage to the community (of dead) and she will join him there herself. But there is more: the sepulchre and the stēlē inscribed with man's proper name, his singular property, do not just protect man's body from non-conscious nature. They also suppress the unconscious desire of those who have survived death, the women themselves, always a step before or a step after death. 'The family wants to prevent the dead one from being "destroyed" and the burial place violated by this desire' (Derrida 1986a, p. 144). The law of singularity, 'divine, feminine, family, natural, nocturnal' (ibid., p. 146), is internally fissured to protect against both itself and its other, the state: a necessary protection because the state does not recognise women's rights.

Creon condemns Polynices' corpse for his acts, the only thing that concerns the state. Similarly, Antigone must die because she knowingly commits a crime. Creon must threaten the family principle with death to sustain his rule; but, at the same time, as the life, property and labour of the community belong to and are exercised in the family, state law must recognise and protect them. The state depends on and is threatened by individuality if it degenerates into anarchy and by private property if it becomes untrammelled self-interest. To prevent the singular devouring the universal, the government must 'from time to time shake [people] to their core by war. . . . By this means . . . individuals are made to feel by government in the labour laid on for them, their lord and master, death' (Hegel 1977, pp. 272, 273). Death, the province of gods and family, is used to defend the supremacy of state law. Each one of the two laws carries death as its work and its limit. Death, the inner limit attached to both conflicting principles, becomes also the sign of transcendence of the antagonism and the symbol of the dialectic.

Thus, while the state must try to absorb the activity of family and direct it towards its aims and policies, it cannot extend itself beyond a certain limit because the very existence of the family upon which the state bases itself will be threatened. The division between the domains of private and public exemplifies and is one layer or moment of the wider speculative conflict between the *Absolute* and the contingent, or the *Universal* and the singular.

In the pagan World this conflict is inevitable and has no solution: Man cannot renounce his Family, since he cannot renounce the Particularity of his Being; nor can he renounce the State, since he cannot renouce the Universality of his Action. And thus he is always and necessarily *criminal*, either toward the State or toward the Family. And that is what constitutes the *tragic* character of pagan life. (Kojève 1969, pp. 61–2; original emphasis)

Antigone is the symbol of criminality. She knows the law, unlike Oedipus, and she publicly violates it without remorse or regrets. 'The ethical consciousness is more complete, its guilt more inexcusable, if it knows beforehand the law and the power it opposes, if it takes them to be violence and wrong, to be ethical merely by accident, and, like Antigone, knowingly commits the crime' (*ibid.*, p. 284). As a symbol of pure criminality, Antigone must be punished by law, 'the manhood of community'. But at the same time, in defying the law, to defend the principle of family, Antigone abandons the realm of the private. She rejects Creon's angry appeal that the brothers should be differentiated according to their actions, and makes a public principle out of her private devotion to the singular need of the traitor. Antigone thus reverses the order of priority and dependence between state and family and installs the ontological principle of love at the heart of the community of action. In dying for love, Antigone becomes law; her irony and passion inscribe themselves in the midst of the disembodied sobriety of the universal.

Since the community only gets an existence through its interference with the happiness of the Family, and by dissolving [individual] self-consciousness into the universal, it creates for itself in what it suppresses and what at the same time is essential to it an internal enemy – womankind in general. Womankind – the everlasting irony [in the life] of the community – changes by intrigue the universal end of the government into a private end, transforms its universal property of the state into a possession and ornament for the family. Woman in this way turns to ridicule the earnest wisdom of mature age which, indifferent to purely private pleasures and enjoyments, as well as to playing an active part, only thinks of and cares for the universal. (Hegel 1977, p. 288)

There is a third dichotomy, therefore, that *engenders* and *encircles* the conflict between human and divine law and between state and family: woman versus man, 'womankind in general' against the 'manhood of the community'. For Creon, Antigone has been 'mad all her life', she represents 'anarchy', the 'rabble'. 'It's very important to keep women disciplined', says Creon. Men should never lose their 'sense of judgment over a woman'.

> We must defend the men who live by law
> never let some woman triumph over us.
> Better fall from power if fall we must
> at the hands of a man – never be rated
> inferior to a woman, never. (675–80)

Creon's principle is patriarchal and misogynous. But his paternal line comes to a violent end when he attempts to lure his son and heir away from mother and beloved. Haemon, he of the blood (*haima*), chooses the womb of the grave and the blood wedding with Antigone. Haemon reverses his father's priorities: he allies with women and their domain and brings down the manly dark and luminous world of the father. Antigone, on the other hand, welcomes her womanly function and the principle of femininity. She does not waver in her commitment to the crime and its punishment. But she repeatedly laments the fact that death will take her a maiden, unbetrothed and childless. The law of woman and family demands the burial of the brother, but in so doing leads her inexorably to her own burial ground and the renunciation of womanhood. In acting as a woman and following the law of singularity, she destroys the law by preventing its fulfilment in motherhood. Her unspeakably powerful love brings all possibility of love to an end. Antigone, in consciously renouncing the bond of conjugality, enters a diabolical pact:

> O tomb, my bridal-bed, my house, my prison
> cut in the hollow rock, my everlasting watch! . . .
> And now he leads me off, a captive in his hands,
> with no part in the bridal-song, the bridal-beds
> denied all joy of marriage, raising children. (891–3; 916–18)

It has been argued by feminist writers that Antigone's willingness to die for her brother's 'political honour' is the ultimate betrayal of womanhood. Irigaray, for example, has claimed that

if Antigone gives proof of a bravery, a tenderness, and an anger that free her energies and motivate her to resist that outside which the city represents for her, this is certainly because she has digested the masculine. At least partially, at least for a moment. . . . And her work in the service of another, of the male Other, ensures the ineffectiveness of a desire that is specifically her. (1985, pp. 220, 225)

But is it true that Antigone 'attaches no importance' to her own wishes and that Polynices' 'public, universal, male honour takes precedence over her own private, individual, female destiny' (Chanter 1991, p. 141)? The recognition of the polemical symbiosis of the conflicting principles leads these writers to reverse the Hegelian order and to claim that the male/universal pole necessarily subordinates and eventually eliminates the female/individual. But Antigone does not allow us to stabilise the law. Her action is moved by unlimited love and by the feminine duty to care for the integrity of womb, family and earth. It is as woman, in her specificity as sister, maiden and future mother, that Antigone chooses her horrible task.

Creon, too, in bringing death to Antigone, violates the law of gods and family and causes the fated destruction of his family and his own descent into ontological nothingness. The law, committed to the most abstract formalism, must still recognise love. Such conflicts, turns and catastrophes are for Hegel the inevitable stations on the road to Spirit's self-consciousness. The principles of the two protagonists are only partial and one-sided and they must be transcended and unified.

The opposition of the ethical powers to one another, and the process whereby individualities enact these powers in life and deed, have reached their true end only in so far as both sides undergo the same destruction. . . . The victory of one power and its character, and the defeat of the other side, would thus be only the partial, the unfinished work which progresses steadily till equilibrium is attained. It is in the equal subjection of both sides that absolute right is first accomplished, that the ethical substance – as the negative force consuming both parties, in other words, omnipotent and righteous Destiny – makes its appearance. (Hegel 1977, p. 285)

Destiny brings destruction as a result of the protagonists' limitations. Both have raised the principle of their existence, individuality and universality respectively, to exclusive arbiters of morality and law. From their one-sided perspective they will experience their destruction as the inexplicable decree of an irrational fate. But at the same time, the conflict between the two ethical forces will move on to a higher plane as the rights of both state and family, of universality and particularity, will come closer to recognition.

In the *Lectures on the Philosophy of Religion*, Hegel moves to a more formalised presentation of the conflict.

The collision between the two highest moral powers is enacted in plastic fashion in that absolute *exemplum* of tragedy, *Antigone*. Here, familial love, the holy, the inward, belonging to inner feeling, and therefore known also as the law of the nether gods, collides with the right of the state. Creon is not a tyrant, but actually an ethical power. Creon is not in the wrong. He maintains that the law of the state, the authority of the government, must be held in respect, and that infraction of the law must be followed by punishment. Each of these two sides actualises only one of the ethical powers, and has only one as its content. This is their one-sidedness. The meaning of eternal justice is made manifest thus: both attain injustice because they are both one-sided, but both also attain justice. Both are recognised as valid in the 'unclouded' course and process of morality (*Sittlichkeit*). Here both possess their validity, but an *equalised validity*. Justice only comes forward to oppose one-sidedness. (Hegel 1988, pp. 353–4; original emphasis)[7].

But neither the Hegelian sublation nor the juridical prioritisation of one or other pole captures the complexity of *Antigone*. Law's genesis is not the outcome of a symmetrically distributed bipolarity of singular and feminine against universal and masculine, nor is its history their empirically evolving synthesis. The two laws fight each other and split the 'ethical substance', but not

as two solid volumes or surfaces, identical to themselves, homogeneous in themselves. Each law is fissured, notched in its inside, and already by the labour of the other within it. . . . Each law had to take into account, record the calculus of the opposite law. (Derrida 1986a, p. 147)

But more than that: the borderline between the two laws, their line of separation and of contact, is appropriately the netherland between *cosmos* and Hades. Both laws mark and are marked by death. From the very beginning of law, or of what we have been calling rather unclearly the 'must' of the 'ethical substance', death is launched as the paradoxical force of self-preservation of family and the state. There is death in law, and violence beyond language. If *Antigone* is the foundation of western law and jurisprudence, her stone is a burial stone that engulfs and engorges the two

---

[7] Translation amended by Steiner (1986, p. 37).

corpses of female and male law. It is this sepulchral quality of law that makes Walter Benjamin say that there is 'something rotten in law' (1978, p. 286). What is rotting are the corpses of Polynices and Antigone. This spectral element, this ghost entombed in law, has been called by some 'the undecidable'. To look for what puts the law into circulation, we must explore the ground of Antigone's crypt beyond the system.

V

What does one find when one opens *Antigone*? The first thing one finds is Antigone.   Lacan, *Ethics of Psychoanalysis*

Philia and *eros*, kinship and love, form the constant background of *Antigone*. They and death are the inescapable forces that will never be conquered. Blood and lineage are key registers in Antigone's resistance and are linked with divine law. But what about love as *eros*? What is the relationship between law, justice and *eros*? The focal point for our reading is the famous Ode to Love of the third *stasimon*. Haemon has failed to make his father change his mind. Their initially polite conversation deteriorated into outright confrontation and an exchange of insults. Haemon's threat that his father 'will never set eyes on his face again' and Creon's pronouncement of the terrible death that awaits Antigone are still echoing. And at this rather unlikely moment in the action, the Chorus sings one of the most moving poems to love ever to have been written: *Eros anikate machan*, love never conquered in battle (781).

The Ode starts with an invocation of Eros' invincibility and ends with an appeal to the goddess of love, *amachos*, unconquerable Aphrodite. Neither mortals nor the gods can escape the power of love; but beware, love's power can be destructive. It sets blood relations into fatal struggle, it twists the minds of the just and warps them towards injustice and ruin (793). And all along Eros is enthroned in sway beside the law, presiding over the magistracies of the eternal laws (*tōn megalōn paredros en' archais thesmōn*) (796).

The Ode is commonly interpreted as a commentary on the disrespectful outburst of Haemon against his father. Eros has taken over and has metamorphosed him from loyal son to rebellious love-torn youth. But in what sense is love seated in judgment next to the 'eternal and unwritten laws'? What is this close relationship between love and justice? To sketch an answer to this question we must both return to and forget, temporarily, the Hegelian interpretation. Antigone is not just the kinswoman, nor is she solely answering in her self-sacrificial determination the command of the gods. She is in love and she devotes her life to her beloved.[8] There is something unsettling in Antigone's reference to love. Antigone, an incestuous product of the greatest illegitimacy, the bastard daughter of the most bastard family in mythology, comes to save the law and the city out of deep affection for her beloved brother. There are repeated indications of sexual passion and intimacy. Polynices is not just *philos*, kin, but *philtatos*, the lover. In her desperate attempt to explain her motives to Ismēnē, Antigone claims that the greatest joy and reward for her action is that 'she will lie with him' (73). It is this unbelievably strong love that animates the most controversial part of the tragedy, Antigone's 'casuistry' (904–20). It is the second place in which law and love are explicitly and closely connected, and if accepted as sound, it can be taken as a commentary on and explanation of the great

---

[8] The theme of sisterly love obsessed the nineteenth century and became a potent philosophical metaphor for the Romantics. Plato speaks in the *Republic* of a musical *eros* that links the soul with the ideas of the good and the beautiful and in the *Symposium* he claims that *eros* brings the partners into the perfect unison of oneness (1955). But for the Romantics, the rift at the centre of existence, Heidegger's homelessness of Being, is radically internalised and inescapable. Narcissistic introvertion and the ultimate unison and consummation of love in joint ecstatic death were proposed as possible answers to self-alienation by the Romantics, but found wanting. As Kierkegaard insisted, the incorporation of otherness in erotic ecstasy leads to a deeper estrangement and fragmentation in the centre of being. The Platonic oneness is a chimera.

The brother–sister relationship, however, seems more promising. It brings together the two primordial aspects of split Being, man and woman, but it avoids the alienation of sexuality. The tormented – and almost exclusively male – psyche of Romantic and idealist modernity reflects in the mirror of the sister and uniquely finds in her not its own image but 'a perfectly concordant but autonomous counterpart' (Steiner 1986, pp. 12–19). Sisterhood is the principle of identity in difference. For the Romantic imagination, the sister represents the essence of womanhood and of the most perfect and passionate, because prohibited, love. Sisterly love transcends carnal eroticism towards a harmonious co-habitation of spiritual *agapē* and intimate affinity. Thus, Antigone's *synaimon* becomes a privileged symbol of the Romantic consciousness.

unwritten and eternal laws that Antigone so often invokes. The passage appears in the middle of the last threnody of Antigone just before she is led away to her grave.

There is something other-worldly in the whole lament. It opens with the great cry

O tomb, my bridal-bed – my house, my prison
cut in the hollow rock, my everlasting watch. (891–3)

and is addressed throughout to her dead *philoi*, her family, and her beloveds with whom she will soon be united. The appeals for sympathy to the Thebans and the quarrel with Creon are now at an end. The coldness of the tomb is already upon her, darkness has spread its wings; she addresses her father and mother and her two brothers, Eteocles and Polynices, in the second person singular. She is before them and they are her only and last hope that her sacrifice will not be in vain. The arguments are at an end; this is the midnight, the deathbed hour, when the extremities of existence and nothingness appear and no solace can be had in the crippled powers of reason.

The reservations of the Chorus and the absence of divine signs have sown their doubt in her heart. No sacrifice is worse than a sacrifice for the wrong reasons. Antigone explains to her kin how she performed loyally the burial rites for all of them and then, both in internal confession and in prayer, turns to Polynices:

Never I tell you,
if I had been the mother of children
or if my husband died, exposed and rotting –
I'd never have taken this ordeal upon myself,
never defied our people's will. What law (*nomou*),
you ask, is my warrant for what I say?
A husband dead, there might have been another.
A child by another too, if I had lost the first.
But mother and father both lost in the halls of
Death, no brother could ever bloom for me.
For this law alone I held you first in honour. (905–15)

Antigone will defy the state because Polynices is her beloved brother; she would not have buried a husband or son in flagrant defiance of the law of blood. She goes on to confound her 'bizarre', 'disturbing' argument with an even greater assault on the presumed principles of logic, consistency and publicity. Husband and sons can be replaced if they perish; but the brother of dead parents is irreplaceable, and this makes her duty to him paramount.

Few problems of tragedy have been discussed more than the question of the authenticity of these lines.[9] Both stylistic and narrative arguments have been used to discredit the passage. The most important is the argument of inconsistency. Antigone has allegedly stated clearly the principle of divine justice according to which burial rites should be paid to the dead by the living, a duty that falls first and foremost upon their relatives. Her action has been consistent with this principle until the end. She now advances a motive that is wholly 'unworthy' of her, a casuistical argument of great moral dubiousness. The unwritten divine law on burial rites makes no distinction between friend and foe and demands the 'same rites for all'; the blood relationship requires equal treatment for the whole family. And yet in these few lines, Antigone totally redefines the law and the nature of her duty. As Jebb puts it, she suddenly abandons 'the immovable basis of her action – the universal and unqualified validity of the divine law' (1966, p. 259). This is further exacerbated by the 'primitive sophism' that turns the uniqueness of the dead brother into a principle of ethical action, bringing the tragedy 'perilously close to bad comedy' (Steiner 1986, p. 50). Even those who defend the passage, do so rather shamefacedly.[10] There is, however, one incontrovertible piece of evidence in favour of the authenticity of the passage. Aristotle, in the *Rhetoric*, written c. 338 BC and less than a century after the death of Sophocles, cites the disputed passage and quotes almost verbatim the two most controversial lines about the irreplaceability of the brother. He advises an advocate defending an improbable action because of the character

---

[9] In 1821, August Jacob claimed that the passage was spurious; in 1824, Boeckh pronounces the lines authentic; the most accomplished scholiast of Sophocles, Sir Richard Jebb, reviews the debate and comes down strongly in favour of the lines being interpolated (Jebb 1966, pp. 164, 258–63; Steiner 1986, p. 50). 'I would give a great deal if some talented scholar could prove that those lines were interpolated, not genuine', Goethe is reported to have said to his friend Eckermann (Knox 1984, p. 46). An army of philologists, philosophers and critics have tried desperately to satisfy Goethe's request.

[10] Steiner, a most careful reader of the literature, concludes that Antigone, now on the edge of the abyss and in the throes of extreme existential solitude, is forced by the enormity of the situation to reach for this 'shallow but momentarily dazzling rhetorical ingenuity which marked her father's style' (1986, p. 280).

traits of his client to give immediately a reason 'as in the example that Sophocles gives, that from *Antigone*' (Aristotle, 1991, 3.16, p. 254). Aristotle's use of the passage should have alerted its detractors. Admittedly, Aristotle himself initially finds the argument of Antigone hard to believe because of her character, but he is eventually fully satisfied with its rhetorical justification. The authenticity of the passage is not disputed or even mentioned,[11] nor does Aristotle, with his keen critical eye for inconsistency of character, think that the argument lowers the overall aesthetic effect or credibility of the action.

Despite Aristotle's praise of the passage, every stylistic anomaly and peculiarity of composition has been explored to give support to what is in the main an ethical argument. Jebb woefully admits at the end of his exhaustive review of the controversy that 'Goethe's wish [that the lines are inauthentic] can never be fulfilled' (1966, p. 263). Indeed, if anything, critical opinion has on the whole moved since the nineteenth century towards accepting the authenticity of the passage, using in the main historical and anthropological evidence as to the role of women in archaic burial rites (Knox 1984, pp. 46–51). The question remains however, as to the reasons that have directed some of the finest philological minds to what always looked a rather impossible task. After all, even if it were 'proved' that the lines do not come from Sophocles but from his son 'Iophon or some other sorry poet' (Jebb 1966, p. 164), it is still true that at least since the fourth century BC the tragedy has been accepted and is performed with the interpolation which has become part of the canonical text.

Undoubtedly this controversy has been one of the clearest instances where the values of the interpreter are imposed upon the text in such extreme fashion so as to justify the excision of whole passages which contradict the opinions and expectations of the reader. The logic of the 'best argument' (Dworkin 1983, 1986) is taken to its absurd conclusion and demands that the text be discarded if it does not accord with the interpretative axiology. And this axiology broadly coincides with what we could call the modern attitude to morality and legality, Kant's law of law. The Kantian undertones of the detractors are evident in Jebb's striking

---

[11] See *The Poetics* (Aristotle 1920, p. 62) for his criticism of *Iphigenia in Aulis* in relation to this type of problem.

description of the problem. Antigone's casuistry abandons the 'universal unqualified validity of the divine law' (Jebb 1966, p. 259). Ethical action can only be based upon and apply to a law that is general, universal and unqualifiedly valid, in other words a law that has all the formal qualities of the categorical imperative. And as Hegel's critique of Kant has shown, such a law can only have formal qualities. Its substance is utterly empty, the law prescribes and at the same time prescribes itself, conceals its demand in the luxurious robes of its transcendental validity (Hegel 1975a; Taylor 1977, Chap. xiv; A. Wood 1990, Chaps 8 and 9). Hegel based his historical critique of Kantianism on *Sittlichkeit*, the ethical substance of classical Greece and in particular on *Antigone's* contrast between state and family. Indeed, if anything, the ethics of Greece is based on a substantive concept of the good rather than a procedural conception of right and validity (see MacIntyre 1981; Prior 1991, Chap. 1; and Chap. 4 below). However, the Hegelian critique of the empty character of the universal form, problematic as it is in parts, has not entered the extensive literature on lines 904–20. And as Antigone retreats to the horizon of universality, Rousseau and Kant rule.

It appears, therefore, that the natural law of modernity calls upon *Antigone* as one of its first authoritative statements and then proceeds to read into the original the predilections of the moderns. Ethics is turned into legality, morality into the following of the universal law; the basic conflict of the jurisprudential readings between the law of the state and divine law is abolished as both laws appear as instances of the same formal principle and the action of both protagonists as deviation from and perversion of the law.

And yet there is another reading that both respects the historical and textual integrity of *Antigone* and justifies its position as a key document in the history of western ethics and law and as the law's unconscious. But in order to approach it we must forget, if we can, our tradition which identifies ethics with universal form and moral action with obedience to the law. In this reading, the force of the demand to bury the irreplaceable brother, which moves Antigone to her mad sacrifice, is not a violation of the law but, on the contrary, the ground upon which all law arises. This archaic source of duty responds to the concrete call and demand of the most unique and singular person. 'Antigone's position represents the radical limit that affirms the unique value of his being without reference to any content, to whatever good or evil Polynices may have done, or to whatever he may have been subjected to' (Lacan 1992, p. 279). Polynices' request and Antigone's response stand before the Platonic division of good and evil, or the Kantian distinction between right and wrong. The uniqueness of the relationship and the liminality of the demand gather and apply the irresistible force that Antigone feels. Whatever is repeated or repeatable, on the other hand, loses its urgent character and lowers the expectation of absolute obedience. And if repetition is the life of the law, can we not argue that the law and repetition rise on the ground of unrepeatability and that the singular comes always *before* the universal, in both senses of before?

The uniqueness of the demand is determined by the singular corporeality, the incarnate presence of the individual who arises in our field of vision and puts the demand. When speaking to Polynices, Antigone addresses him as *kasignēton kara*, beloved head, face, of my brother (899). Three times in the tragedy Antigone speaks to her siblings face to face: to Ismēnē in the first line and to Eteocles and Polynices in the disputed passage. In all three they are called *kara*, head or face. It is Polynices' head, in its beloved physicality, suspended between the earth from which he has departed and Hades where he cannot arrive without the love of Antigone, that gave her the 'law whereby I held you first in honour' (914–15). The reference to the beloved head reminds us of Antigone's physical longing to lie with her brother, 'her own' as she calls him to Ismēnē (48). The ethical demand arises not out of a form or an idea but out of desire, in a somatic encounter and through the *epiphany* of a head in need.

And if the ethical demand rises concretely in the meetings of heads and bodies, its structure is not dissimilar to that of the unconscious and its action bestows its singularity upon its addressee who answers its request. Antigone is Hegel's eternal sister who follows the law of singularity, femininity and the unconscious, but who also has a presentiment of the ethical. Her ethicity is a response to a necessary contingency: it is the death of the parents that makes the brother unique and turns the unconscious desire into the law of desire, this internally fissured law which demands that Antigone protect Polynices both from her own law and from that of the state. Similarly, if the ethical

substance is the union of the opposites, of man and woman, of consciousness and the unconscious, of universal and singular, of state
and divine law, Antigone shows that the pleasure of copulation
and of the concept(ion) never fully arrives and that, *contra* Hegel,
the law of reason and man will be judged in the (nocturnal) light of
desire and woman. Indeed, although Hegel adored the play, in
making *Antigone* fit his overall scheme he failed to grasp fully
Antigone's desire for death. In the Hegelian universe the conflicting principles between family and state, individual and community must be reconciled. But as Lacan somewhat cuttingly asks: 'I
just wonder what the reconciliation of the end of *Antigone* might
be' (1992, p. 249).

Antigone obeys the law, but the law she obeys is not just some
universally valid rule; its command is the outcome of an
overwhelming desire created in the unrepeatable encounter with
the suffering (br)other. Antigone's 'transcendental surfeit' is not to
be found in her *pleromatic* existence but in her standing for and
before (*anti*) the other. In some traditions this incarnate other as
the absolute alien and the most proximate is the earthly face of
God. It could be that Antigone is an *antitheos* after all, whose
ethical action is constitutively and necessarily a casuistry.[12]

---

[12] There is at least one interpretation of *Antigone*, Hölderlin's *Antigona*, his
magnificent translation and rewriting of Sophocles (R. B. Harrison 1975; Lacoue-
Labarthe 1978), that adopts against the various Kantianisms the position that
Antigone's majesty lies exactly in her absolute and unrepeatable singularity.
Hölderlin's Antigone stands against Creon's formalism as the spirit of 'formless-
ness'; against his principle of law as 'lawless'; against his civic and utilitarian
humanism as 'aorgic', Apollonian fire and Dionysian pathos. A dialectical conflict of
such proportions occurs during revolutions and other such key turning points in
history and leads to the creation of a radically new social condition. The agents that
represent and act out the combat of the two antagonistic worlds are both deeply
religious but experience the divine from opposed perspectives.
Creon is near to God; Antigone is the *antitheos* 'who comports herself as if against
God, in a godly sense'. Sophocles' Antigone called herself 'pious out of impiety' and
Hölderlin transforms this into her ontological principle. She is a holy sinner and
heretic, a demon saint who rebels against God possessed by the Holy Ghost, a great
martyr of negative theology. Her ' "lawlessness" is a divinely inspired judiciousness.
It enacts an espousal of absolute and also of historically evolving justice which not
only exceeds legalism and the statutory but is in inevitable antithesis to them. The
letter of the law (Creon) is challenged by the primal spirit and nascent future of the
law (Antigone)' (Steiner 1986, pp. 82–3).
The challenge of the *antitheos* will force history – the references to the French

VI

The boastful words of the proud are paid in full
with mighty blows of fate, and at last
those blows will teach the chastened prudence (*phronein*)

Chorus

Let us summarise the jurisprudential and speculative stages of our reading. *Antigone* concerns the unfolding of a series of conceptual juxtapositions, embodied and represented by the two diametrically opposed protagonists. The key conflict may be that between divine and human law, or between law and justice, family and state or individual and society; but its narrative presentation always follows the same path. The antagonists judge and are

---

Revolution and its Jacobin spirit are obvious – but will also lead through the fury unleashed to her destruction. Too much of the divine spirit has entered the holy criminal, whose authority emanates from the eternal, unwritten, wild primacy of Being and the world of the dead. These two primordial sources of energy will compel her to join battle with the gods and she will perish in the wrestling of the *isotheoi*.

This most forceful rendering of *Antigone* is the one that captured, for the Romantic imagination, the solitary struggle of those blessed souls who, almost single-handedly against laws and institutions, change the river of history. For an era obsessed with revolution, terror and the romantic image of Napoleon as a philosopher-emperor, it gave the impetus for myriad interpretations of classical tragedy suited to the maelstrom of modernity. Against the philologists' quest for an Antigone dressed in the grey colours of a rainy Köningsberg morning, we are offered a resplendent, awe-inspiring, blinding image whose majestic superhuman fury comes closer to our picture of St Juste and Lenin than to that of a fearful, lonely maiden on her way to a dreadful death.

Aesthetically pleasing as Hölderlin's interpretation is, it leaves us with a certain uneasiness. His answer to the question of law is to confront Kantian legalism with a totally self-determining legislative power that draws its vitality and force exclusively from its transgression of the established law. In Kantianism, the law is to be found by the individual and the *polis* positing their will according to a principle of universal legislation; law's subjects both legislate and obey their own law. In *Antigona*, the *antitheos* is a counter-legislator, a singular individual who possesses, however, all the claims to universality and absolute obedience of her collective counterpart. *Antigona* gives the law as much as Creon, although hers is the law of absolute self-determining singularity while his is of formal generality.

We have already glimpsed a third source of law that we can call the ethical source proper. Antigone obeys the law and as such she differs from the revolutionary *antitheos*. But the law she obeys is irreducibly unique.

themselves judged by their opponent and by the critic. The critic may find for Antigone or – rarely – for Creon or may with Hegel treat both as equivalent forces that must be destroyed and incorporated in the higher ethical community. We can read the two opponents as irreconcilable principles or as steps in the dialectic, but in both cases we are asked to shadow the action of the tragedy and sit in judgment, in the same way that Creon and Antigone sit in judgment on each other. The juridical presentation will always sharpen the issues, abstract the action and present the conflicts in simple terms of right and wrong, of legal evidence and procedure and of a final verdict. Antigone thus turns into a legal drama, both in its action and in the hermeneutical principle it imposes upon its reader. This most exquisite work of literature becomes a legal document;[13] its judgment is not aesthetic but practical. Kant has the last laugh after all. The faculties may be slightly mixed but the law stays intact.

But is there any other position, outside the partialities of the protagonists and beyond the Hegelian circle? To start exploring this possibility we must abandon the conflict of concepts and turn to the action of the tragedy. After all, the character and quality of practical judgments depend on complex considerations of motive and circumstance, of free-will and determination; their aesthetic presentation in Antigone is successful because it protects and presents the compexity of (ethical) life.[14] This complexity is partly due to the fact that, as we saw, the two protagonists are defined against their opponent only to find the opposition in the middle of their own existence. But additionally, as the action unfolds, they and we are faced with a multiplying gathering of forces and circumstances that deny the juridical and conceptual oppositions upon which the tragedy depends. We already encountered the work of death and desire. It is to a closer examination of these imponderables that our reading now turns.

The tragic action is organised around the burial of the dead.[15]

---

[13] See, likewise, our discussion in Chapter 7.

[14] As one critic put it: 'the interest and power of the Antigone lie in the tangled issues which are unravelled in it' (Bowra 1944, p. 66).

[15] A number of anthropologically informed philologists have recently tried to explain Antigone in terms of the conflict between archaic matrilinear kinship, evidenced in death rituals, and the new patriarchal power established in Athens around the sixth century BC. There is historical evidence that Solon had tried to

Creon orders Polynices' corpse to be left unburied 'carrion for the birds and dogs to tear, an obscenity for the city to behold' (68). But he cannot claim like King David:

This day will the Lord deliver thee in my hand; and I will smite thee; and I will give the carcasses of the host of the Philistines this day unto the fowls of the air, and to the wild beasts of the earth, that all the earth may know that there is a God in Israel. (1 Sam. 17.46)

No such absolute power over the enemy has been acknowledged in Greek thought; but, more importantly, Creon is a representative of the Athenian Enlightenment, and of the power of rational thought and institutions to civilise and organise the world. His power is based on *kratos*, authority, *bia*, power or violence, and *logos*. His references to the gods are not many; initially they sound opportunistic and hypocritical but they soon become mockingly dismissive. Antigone, on the other hand, in her unwavering commitment to the *philoi*, kin and beloved, to the eternal laws of *dikē*, and to the rights of death, appears to stand for primordial forces untamed by the power of *logos*.[16]

---

restrict the encroachment of death and death rituals upon the life of Athens by lowering the tone of burials. Some evidence also exists that the refusal to bury an enemy was not considered automatically a blasphemy against the gods. But while such studies shed some light on historical aspects of the tragedy, they cannot explain the fascination that Antigone has exerted upon philosophy and literature for twenty-five centuries. Historical explanation and philosophical reduction are only partial perspectives, only preparatory for our turn to the text and (its) law.

[16] The history of Greek rationalism has been explored by classical historians and philologists and we will only mention a few issues relevant to our discussion here. At the end of the Archaic Age in the Ionian coast in the sixth century and in Athens in the fifth century BC, the dominant archaic world-view came under attack, exemplified by the extreme rationalism and pragmatism of the Sophists, of whom Creon becomes in the course of the play a *reductio ad absurdum*.

The Enlightenment started when the naturalness of the 'Inherited Conglomerate' of religious and political ideas came unstuck. When people stop communicating with the earth and the gods in a sacramental and mystical fashion and posit the divine as an external reality which may be objective and superior or man-made and relative, reason enters history. Hecataeus found mythology and the Homeric epics funny. Xenophanes, a key early influence, thought they were morally suspect; he ridiculed the various processes of divination and accepted the cultural construction and specificity of religion. When Xenophanes said that 'if the ox could paint a picture, his god would look like an ox', he predated the rationalism of Feuerbach and Marx by twenty-four centuries. Between those early pioneers and Aristotle's exploration of the relation between *nomos* and *physis* in the *Ethics*, the first age of

The complex dilemmas and conflicts that move the action are expressions of the fatal intertwining of the power of reason with its manifold others. Pivotal in this respect stands the first choral *stasimon*, the famous Ode on Man, a superb celebration of the civilising power and achievements of human reason and craft.[17] Man, the most wonderful, awesome, terrible of all creatures has used his powers to invent sailing, agriculture, animal husbandry, the building of shelters and of cities and he has crowned his achievements with the creation of laws and institutions. He has taught himself language and the power of thought and wisdom, *phronēma*, which have become the two great foundations of human essence. The Ode presents an early and powerful expression of the anthropocentric belief in the gradual but inexorable human progress through the irresistible conquest and rationalisation of ever-expanding fields and forces.

Creon's political philosophy is a somewhat bowdlerised version of the Ode's secular rationalism. For Creon, the laws and policies of the state are man-made, they purport to increase the happiness of the citizens and their wisdom can only be judged empirically after they have taken their course. There is no limit to human power and control. Man's character as much as the earth

---

rationalism in the West had reached perfection and the belief in the ever-expanding power of reason to colonise all parts of life became dominant.

Protagoras, the key Sophist in the realm of political rationalism, believed that virtue could be taught and if the laws were freed from the remnants of archaic stupidity an unprecedented level of civilised life could be achieved. In the eponymous dialogue both he and Socrates adopt the intellectualist and utilitarian position that if we know what is good for us we would act on it (Plato 1981, *Protagoras*, 352a–e). They both share an early utilitarianism according to which the good is what is profitable for the individual; their main difference is that for Protagoras virtue is installed through processes of socialisation while Socrates thinks that virtue can become the subject matter of *epistēmē* and teaching. Plato, too, even as late in his life and development as the *Laws*, the most secular of his works, seems to have held on to the Socratic opinion that no one commits a sin if he knows about it. Yet Socrates was by no means an unadulterated rationalist. He believed in dreams and oracles and followed an unexplained 'inner voice'. References to Socrates' beliefs in supernatural forces and signs are plentiful: Plato (*Apol.* 33c and 21b; *Crito* 44a); Xenophon (*Anabasis* 3.1.5). See also Dodds (1951, pp. 182–7, 212–13) and Sallis (1991, Chap. 4).

[17] Heidegger said that if the whole of the Greek philosophy and literature was lost and only this Ode was saved, it would be possible to reconstruct all the basic principles of the Greek spirit from it.

can be ploughed and shaped by his upbringing and family (93); good judgment is the most precious gift, and lack of wisdom, mē phronein, the worst affliction (1050–1). Creon, like Aristotle, does not accept that the gods reason differently from man; to know man is to know god and fate. He abhors the prospect that women might acquire public power and he denies the existence of any form of distinctly female rationality except madness. Finally, he does not accept that family ties should make any difference in the way rational men conduct their affairs.

> Never! Sister's child or closer in blood
> than all my family clustered at my altar . . .
> she'll never escape, she and her blood sister
> the most barbaric death. (486–9)

Creon's favourite word is symmetros (for example, 154); the concept of symmetry permeates the discourse of rationality. It is a juridical symmetry of higher and lower principles, where reason triumphs over madness, male over female, age and experience over youth, right over wrong (281, 719ff., 1088). Creon's values may be unpalatable to some contemporary critics but his hermeneutical principles have dominated the literature and display a lack of 'deep awareness of the complexity within the human realm' (Segal 1964, p. 51).

Unlike Creon's simple utilitarianism, the Ode's celebratory sentiments are soon confronted with the darker side of human endeavour. Tragedy holds a mirror to the psyche and the world which refutes philosophy's unrealistic intellectualism. Each one of the optimistic statements is soon found wanting. The earth and the beasts appear in the Ode as resource and object of man's civilising intervention. His incomparable skills and devices, mēchanes, and the instruments of his technē have tamed nature. But this exploitative attitude is soon challenged. When Haemon tries to make his father change his mind, he sees nature as an example of harmony, its forces yielding to superior forces and adjusting to natural rhythms. The domesticated animals on the other hand become metaphors for wild non-rational untamed forces: birds and horses change into symbols of violence and passion, dogs and birds bring carrion torn from the corpse and pollute the city. Finally, the last choral song that celebrates Dionysus presents an image of nature totally at odds with that of the Ode: a nature whose god and personification is Bacchus, a mystical and orgiastic nature, possessed by sacred rage and breathing fire.

Next, the Ode boasts that man taught himself language, thought (*phronēma*) and the mood of legality that creates cities (*astynomous orgas*) (354–5). Creon, too, has an instrumental theory of language and legal communication: he sees language as a tool of the sovereign and a medium for the pronouncement of laws in clear, indisputable terms. But soon this view of language is profoundly challenged. In very few works of literature is the active 'performative' work of language more lethally in evidence. If the Antigone–Creon exchange has been described as a dialogue of the deaf, the Haemon–Creon dispute is one of the greatest word battles in literature. As the pace increases and insults are hurled like stones, we feel the physical ferocity of speech. The dark prophesies and the murderous curses, the shrieking wails and the monstrous cries of Teiresias' birds are paralleled to the frenzied language of mad barbarians (427, 999–1002, 1296, 1304–5). Haemon's attack is conducted in a monstrous eagle-like scream; the curse on the house of Oedipus is 'madness of language and frenzy of mind' (*phrenōn Erinys*) (603–4). And when Creon's world collapses at the end, this exponent of the instrumental use of transparent *logos* is reduced to incoherent screams and cries which, to this day, convey the dread of supreme existential catastrophe: *io, io, aiai, aiai, oimoi, oimoi, pheu, pheu* (1283–4, 1290, 1294, 1300, 1306). Language has turned from instrument of rule and dividing line between man and beast to lethal weapon; from repository of *logos*, to *epiphany* of madness. The Ode itself had already expressed doubt as to the all-conquering power of reason when it came to the greatest human achievement, law and justice. In law and politics, success is the hardest.[18] Man comes 'now to good, now to evil'; when he keeps human law and divine justice he is high in the city, *hypsipolis*, but he becomes stateless, *apolis*, if he acts with rashness and stubbornness. This passage,

---

[18] Protagoras in the myth recounted in the eponymous dialogue insists on the paramount importance for the city but also the great difficulty in keeping justice and respect for law. Men owe their progress and the establishment of cities to the laws and Zeus orders them 'to kill as a disease in the city the man who cannot partake of decency and justice' (Plato 1981, *Protagoras* 322c–d). See also Plato (1969a, *Crito*; 1969b, *Apology*).

too, has become the subject of much controversy. Some see this fear of daring as a condemnation of Antigone's action by the 'little man'; Heidegger disagrees.[19] Creon, in any case, will soon discover that laws and institutions, as much as individuals, are beset by forces beyond reason.

Finally to *phronēma*; this is a key concept throughout the tragedy and, alongside language, the outcome of man's self-teaching and the mainspring of his greatness.[20] *Phronein* is usually translated as thought or wisdom. The Aristotelian *phronēsis* or prudence has been presented in the history of western ethics as an alternative to deductive, code-based forms of morality and as the second great school to claim an exclusive or predominantly rational foundation for practical judgments.[21] The importance of *phronēma* for the Chorus is paramount. Its *exodus* at the end of the play formulates the moral of the tragedy as follows:

Prudence (*phronein*) is the supreme part of happiness
and reverence towards the gods must be safeguarded.
The boastful words of the proud are paid in full
with mighty blows of fate, and at last
those blows will teach the chastened prudence (*phronein*). (1348–53)

The poem starts and finishes with *phronein*; *Antigone* is about practical wisdom, about the way in which *phronein* leads individual and city to happiness, about the nature and components of *phronein*, and finally about thought's relation to action. But the word has another meaning that refers to the darker recesses of the psyche. *Phrenes* are states of mind, sane or mad, good or evil, *Dionysiacally* phrenetic or cynically ataraxtic, passionately active or apathetically passive. *Pathos*, passion, happens to the individual and is not of her own choosing. For Aristotle, someone impassioned is like being asleep, drunk or mad (Aristotle 1976, pp. 232–3; cf. Dodds 1951, Chaps VI and VII). *Phronein* is about self-

[19] No doubt a good example of jurisprudential criticism: see Bowra (1944, pp. 85–7) and Whitman (1951, pp. 87–90); but cf. Heidegger (1961) and section IX below; Steiner (1986, pp. 254–63).
[20] Paul Ricoeur has recently emphasised the importance of *phronēsis* for the understanding of tragedy in general and *Antigone* in particular. However, he misses the second meaning of the term that refers to the non-rational springs of human action. (See Ricoeur 1992, pp. 240–9.)
[21] See further Chapter 4 below.

determination and rational decision-making; *phrenes* or *thumos*, on the other hand, are the seat of *atē* and *daimon*, the supernatural and god-given in Homer or more generally the unexplainable and non-rational springs of human action. These may be the outcome of a family curse that passes on to the offspring; of divine or secular madness; of wine-taking or sexual passion; or of fate. But whatever their provenance, there is always a residue of non-rational motivation of action that shadows the claims of reason to ground political and ethico-legal obligations. As with all reformations and counter-reformations, the relative position and strength of autonomous and heteronomous action, of 'innocent guilt' and 'pious impiety', lies at the heart of the Greek Enlightenment.

When Teiresias is told by Creon that lack of *phronein* is the greatest mischief, he responds, in one of those telling and magnificent semantic reversals that sustain the play's tension, by using the 'state of mind' sense of the word and warning Creon that he himself suffers from a disease of the mind, a *nosos* of the *phrenes*. The Chorus repeats the diagnosis when Creon, dejected and suicidal, returns from the grave; he suffers from lack of judgment (1243) and his action is madness (1260). Finally, Creon himself, the great exponent of *phronēsis*, makes the connection: his woes are the result of the sins of a darkened soul, *phrenōn dysphronōn hamartemata* (1262). Similarly, the word used to celebrate the law-making temper, *orgai*, is later used to express manic anger (280, 875, 766). Both thought and un-thought, *logos* and *pathos*, Eros, Dionysus and Thanatos, lie behind human action.

Tragedy triumphed as an art-form for a brief period in the fifth century BC. That was the era of the Parthenon, of Pericles' Funeral Oration and of the Platonic system, some of the most superb examples of reason's all-conquering power in the arts, the institutions and thought. Few epochs in western civilisation have surpassed the magnificent achievements of the golden century. And yet there is full recognition of the force of the unknown and the unthought, of what is not amenable to reason and must remain untheorised even though its determining power in human affairs is inescapable.[22] Human action is never sufficient on its own without

---

[22] The two classical studies of the non-rational determinations of human action are Dodds (1951) and Vernant and Vidal-Naquet (1990, Chaps II and III).

the supportive intervention of the gods. And while the actor hopes and prays that the gods are on his side, their *thesphata* (oracles) are opaque. Apollo in Delphi, according to Heraclitus, *oute legei oute kryptei, alla sēmainei*, neither speaks nor hides but gives signs (fragment 93, quoted in Heidegger 1961, p. 170). In this early semiotics, human action is always caught in the divine ambiguity of an equivocal semiosis.

There are two sides to every action, one controlled by man, the other open to unpredictable and horrible machinations. Action is always a gamble that may misfire terribly and destroy the actor who appeared at first in full control of his decision. The outcome of the wager will not be known before it has run its course and has been recorded on both human and divine registers. These two registers, however, are inseparable; they are brought together in human action, the hinge upon which the divine and human, determination and freedom, come together, often with catastrophic results. This is, of course, the recognition of Medea: 'I know what wickedness I am about to do; but the *thumos* is stronger than my purposes, *thumos*, the root of man's worse acts' (Euripides 1963, 1078–80). The most famous formulation of this apparent paradox is Phaedra's resigned recognition that we know and recognise the good and the proper, but we fail to act on it. Euripides, the Socratic poet who, according to Nietzsche, destroyed tragedy through his rationalism, uninterested as he is in the metaphysical nature of man's *daimon*, is fully aware, like Kierkegaard, of the clear distinction between a good argument and action based on it. The last line of *Antigone* sums it up well: it is fate and the great disasters in life that teach man *phronēsis*, not just reason and the schools.

VII

To act or not to act and tempt fate?   Pelasgus, *Suppliants*

Because we suffer we acknowledge we have erred.   *Antigone*

Our reading so far has helped us understand some of the conflicts and convergences that underpin law's action. But it does not answer our first question: where does the call of the 'must' come from? The Hegelian interpretation, which we have shadowed, implies that there is a higher law – strictly speaking, according to Antigone, a chthonic, infernal law, the lowest of all the underground laws – which regulates the asymmetrical distribution of forces and principles narrated in the *Aesthetics* and the *Phenomenology of Spirit*. But how does this unknown 'law of laws' work, that puts both justice and law, singular and universal, male and female in their polemical co-circulation, and whence does it emerge? *Antigone* gives this low law a strict name: *moira*, fate or destiny:

CHORUS: The force of destiny is a terrible mysterious wonder
   (*moiridia tis dynasis deina*)
   neither wealth nor armies, towered cities nor ships
   black hulls lashed by the salt
   can save us from that force. (951–3)

sing the Thebans as Antigone is led to her grave. And Creon accepts the awful truth of the triple death with a resigned 'you can't fight the force of destiny' (1106).

What is immediately striking is the stroke of fate. Destiny has invincible force, *dynamis*, both wonderful and terrible, *deina*, an epithet that the Ode on Man has already used to describe man's marvelous and strange power, *deinotaton*. It is the all-powerful destiny which has given man his strong overpowering qualities. We are here close to the mythical anthropology that allies man and the world. But *moira* is part of a wider set of concepts and deities, Themis, Horai, *nomos* and Dikē, that bring us close to the mythological roots of the ethical and legal bond. We will examine briefly these roots and explore the links between destiny and law.

Themis, usually translated as 'right', is the most archaic of the terms associated with the order of things (Harrison 1977). She is next in order of importance to the all-powerful Gaia and occasionally, as in *Promētheus Bound*, she is herself the personification of earth and a prophet. While gods come and go, Themis is eternal and certain and, like the gē, lives below and above all of them. The Homeric *athemistoi* Cyclops are barbarians because they have no customs and conventions that bind them and no *agora*, a forum to argue out their common affairs. With the development of the *polis*, Themis becomes identified with the institutions of the *agora*. Initially diffuse and vague but binding as habit and usage, Themis becomes later the goddess of conventions and customs and, in the *polis*, of law and justice. But Themis exists before the particular shapes of gods or laws and before religion; she is the stuff, the substratum, upon which religion is based. Themis is the original orderliness of gods and men in archaic mythology and social structure, the law of law and the ground upon which the primordial force of obligation to the other is felt. She is the representation of the 'mystery, the thing greater than man, the power not himself that makes for righteousness [and] the pressure of that unknown ever incumbent force' (*ibid*., p. 490). Themis is the mother of the *Horai* or seasons: Dikē, Eunomia and Eirēnē, Peace.

Dikē, a female deity too, is a livelier and less abstract Themis, the order of life and the world, before she becomes the personification of right and justice. While Themis is social order, Dikē, as Heidegger reminded us (see section IX of this chapter), is the way of every thing, of streams and beasts, of stars and men, the regular course of the whole universe. As one of the seasons, she regulates the moves of celestial bodies and personifies the cyclical return of all things and forces. Parmenides says that Dikē guards the gates of Day and Night and she is often linked with the Moirai or fates. In Hesiod's *Works and Days*, Dikē is a maiden whom men attack and drag from her path for evil purposes. Like Antigone, Dikē is an incorruptible virgin who is violated by unjust men. The second major difference between mother and daughter is that Themis belongs to Zeus and the earth while Dikē is associated with Hades and the Underworld, a strong connection we encountered in *Antigone*. The cyclical rhythm will take the living and earthly to the dead and chthonic; mother earth will have to die in order to rise again as in the myth of Dēmēter and Persephonē and of Orpheus and Eurydi(c)kē, the Wide-Justice. Dikē in Hades holds the wheel of fortune that brings forward and completes the necessary motion of all things extant. The first association of Dikē with vengeance, which later led to her identification with justice derives from a pejorative and fearful interpretation of the image of the wheel of *tychē* which inescapably leads to Hades. Dikē is therefore always Eurydikē, wide and plural in its connotations and references. If she is the personification and symbol of justice, she is also woman, the way of all nature and things and people, she is fortune and fate, the rights and the rites of death, the ground of righteousness, finally Heidegger's overpowering force.

Then there is *nomos*, law (Havelock 1978: Jaeger 1947; Ostwald 1969). In classical Athens, *nomos* is the most secular of the three cognate terms. But its relation to *physis* and *dikē* is complex. According to a Heraclitus fragment, *nomos* exists only if it is in conformity with the divine order. The Sophists, however, severed the link between *dikē* and *nomos*. *Nomos* is seen as man-made, a human imposition upon chaotic nature. The boldest of Sophists, Callicles and Thrasymachus, claim that nature is in a state of permanent war and that *nomos*, by imposing its arbitrary order, is a violator of *physis* and a 'despot on mankind' (Plato 1955, pp. 74–102). Plato, too, while refuting the claims of the Sophists in the *Laws*, accepts that *nomos* is man-made and artificial. The so-called 'unwritten laws' must be taken into account by the legislature but they are not laws properly speaking. Aristotle in his *Rhetoric* distinguishes between *idios nomos*, the particular laws of each community partly written and partly customary and unwritten, and *koinos nomos*, the common law of nature (Aristotle, 1950b, I.13.2) and considers Antigone's 'unwritten laws' part of the latter. He thus provides the link between *Antigone* and the modern versions of natural law. In the process *dikē* has changed, from the inherent order, comeliness and regularity of all things, into a set of normative principles that exist against and above the world of nature and of human existence, while *nomos* became increasingly identified with the public promulgations of the city.

Let us finally turn to Dikē's sister, Moira, or destiny. Moira is originally a share or portion, a 'helping' of food. Homer usually speaks of a single *moira* which is the natural apportionment of each person, our assignment or lot, without giving any moral connotation to the term. When Homer personifies Moira, he shows her spinning, most importantly spinning the thread of human life at birth (1961, p. 209). This original apportionment of life remains an important attribute of fate's power and is repeatedly referred to in *Antigone* (461, 895, 987). Indeed the originally single Moira was later divided at Delphi into the two goddesses of birth and death. They were fully personified by Hesiod, who called them daughters of Night or of Zeus and Themis, like the Horai, and named them Clōthō, the spinning fate, Lachēsis, the one who assigns a person's fate, and Atropos, she who cannot be avoided.

In classical Greece, *moirai* appear always in the plural rather than as a single overarching 'destiny' or 'providence'. Their personification is incomplete and Dodds (1951, Chap. 1) argues that other chthonic deities, the Erinyes, are the personal agents who fulfil *moira*.

> The moral function of the Erinyes as ministers of vengeance derives from the primitive task of enforcing a *moira* which was at first morally neutral, or rather, contained by implication both an 'ought' and a 'must' which early thought did not clearly distinguish. (*ibid.*, p. 8)

This troubled relationship between fate, the Furies and man helps us decipher the gnomic sayings of Medea and Phaedra about thought and action and Antigone's dark appellations to Dikē and the eternal laws.

Aeschylus' trilogy *The Oresteia* discusses the role of Erinyes, the Furies, in human action. Orestes is ordered by Apollo, the male god of light and reason, to avenge the murder of his father Agamemnon by his mother Clytemnēstra. Orestes kills his mother and is set upon by the Furies, old and dark goddesses, who, like Antigone's Dikē, protect the earth and the blood lines. The last play, *Eumenides*, a euphemism for the Furies, revolves around the trial of Orestes before the Athenean *agora*. The Furies ask for Orestes' punishment while Apollo defends him. Some of the familiar conflicts of *Antigone* are found here too. Apollo is a relatively recent arrival and a novice in relation to the Furies, the daughters of Gaia, who represent the old matrilineal order. The trial ends with a majority of judges finding against Orestes. But Athena's casting vote in favour of the defendant ties the outcome and as a result of procedural rules Orestes goes free. The Furies wail and threaten terrible punishments. But Athena, who sets up the *Areios Pagos*, the symbolic institution of the new and secular legal order, consoles them. The tied vote was in no way a humiliation; they will continue to be revered and every newborn child will be given to their protection.

'There are cases where Fear (*deinon*) is useful and should be enthroned in the heart permanently, as it is its vigilant guardian', say the Furies (Aeschylus 1953, *Eumenides*, p. 153, v. 516–8; translation altered). Athena fully agrees; she establishes them opposite Zeus *agoraios* as part of the new legal institution. *Philia* and *peithō*, persuasion through argument, are not enough to keep the city together. Fear and terror, the *deinon*, should not be driven outside the walls of the city (*ibid.*, pp. 159–60, v. 690–9). And at the end Athena herself, the wise androgynous maiden, born out of the head of Zeus, comes to praise the Erinyes who have the power to rule men and give songs to some and tears to others (ibid., p. 168, v. 930, 954–5). Law and political authority are based on violence and force, bia, on rational argument and gentle persuasion and on sacred powers, ordained by Moira and Dikē and enforced by the Erinyes.

But if the Moirai and the Furies preside over law and the institution, they are also crucially involved with the mainsprings of human action as part of its 'double determination'. It can be argued that the key to the understanding of the great tragedies is the creative tension between destiny and choice in which the tragic hero finds himself. Take, for example, the myth of the Atreides as represented by Aeschylus in Iphigenia in Aulis and Agamemnon. Agamemnon, the King of the Greeks, is told by the divine Chalcas that, in order to raise the wind necessary to sail the fleet to Troy, he must sacrifice his daughter, Iphigenia, on the orders of the goddess Artemis. In Aeschylus, though not in other versions of the story, Agamemnon cannot avoid or escape this heinous and fatal crime. Zeus demands that the Greek alliance destroy Troy and Artemis makes it clear that for the expedition to start the maiden must be sacrificed. Agamemnon acts under a double divine constraint (anankē, necessity) and he cannot be judged culpable. But at the same time, the King accepts his role in the unfolding of destiny and fervently desires the murder of his daughter, if that is what will fill the sails of his ships. 'If this sacrifice, this virginal blood, is what binds the winds, it is permitted to desire it fervently, most fervently', Agamemnon repeats three times (Aeschylus 1953, Agamemnon, p. 41, v. 214–18). The Chorus, faced with this willed but involuntary crime, proclaims that the King 'made himself the accomplice of a capricious destiny' (ibid., p. 40, v. 186–8). Similarly, when the Homeric Agamemnon apologises to Achilles for stealing his concubine, he claims that he did not cause the act 'but Zeus and my moira and the Erinyes who walks in the darkness; they put wild atē in my understanding, on that day I took Achilles' prize from him arbitrarily. What could I do? Deity will always have its way' (Iliad XIX. 86ff.).

The tragic hero lives a double existence. On the one hand, his actions are predetermined and in this sense he cannot be seen as a free agent. But that does not mean lack or disclaiming of culpability. Agamemnon, after his elaborate defence, offers ample compensation to Achilles precisely because his action was caused by forces beyond his control. The clouding of understanding is interpreted in Homer predominantly as divine intervention. In the tragedies, while *moira* retains its archaic reference to arbitrary and unpredictable processes, it now acquires a new meaning that becomes dominant in Euripides. Destiny is now a partially intelligible process, a just claim to retribution for a willing course of action which will inevitably lead to crime. This is the context for Oedipus and his daughter, the willing victim and the innocent guilty of a 'pious impiety'.

Oedipus is an example of this ambiguous logic between free-will and imposed destiny. In killing his father and marrying his mother, unknowingly and unwillingly, he becomes the puppet of an evil *daimon*, who makes him transgress unwittingly the key taboos of family and society. His blood and lineage (*genos*) are cursed, he defiles and condemns to extinction everything he touches. But when he finds out, Oedipus willingly accepts his responsibility; he takes his eyes out, abandons Thebes and becomes a scapegoat (*pharmakos*), a semi-divine whose grave will bestow blessing upon the city of Athens which welcomed him from his wandering exile. What animates the action is the tension between action and pathos, free-will and predetermination, autonomy and the tragic body. The hero obsessively pursues his inquiry as to the identity of Laius' killer and willingly moves towards the final revelation and judgment; yet throughout the action the basis of this judgment lies elsewhere, in the original transgression of his progenitor, Labdacus, and in the defilement of the bodies of his parents. His final success, in discovering the King's killer, is also his own destruction; the recognition that he himself is the parricide and husband of his mother. That *hamartema* (sin, transgression) has been inscribed on the bodies of Oedipus and his kin. The body will be re-integrated in the divine order through its mutilation and the destruction of all his descendants.

The tragic hero desires (*boulēsis*) the outcome of his action and deliberates (*bouleusis*) as to the best means to bring about the desired outcome. In this he is not far removed from the legal subject in modern criminal law whose responsibility depends on *mens rea*, foreseeability, calculation of the result and acceptance (or recognition) of the consequences. But in choosing and in acting, the tragic hero places himself in the hands of unknown and uninterpretable forces which involve his actions in a fatal plot and invest them with a meaning that remains opaque until destiny has completed its course. 'If this is the pleasure of the gods, after I have suffered my doom, I will come to know my sin' (925-6), cries Antigone.

> CHORUS: And throughout the future, late and soon
> as throughout the past, your law destiny prevails:
> nothing great and vast enters the lives of mortals
> without the power of unreason (*atē*). (611–4)

> Sooner or later, evil seems good
> to the one whose state of mind (*phrenes*)
> god leads to unreason (*atē*) or greatness
> and only for the briefest of time
> is he free of fate as punishment (*atē*). (622–5)

This is the law of destiny; its demands are unknown and we can only learn it through transgression and the visitation of terrible woes. *Moira* puts unreason, *atē*, in us and punishes us for acting on it. But we acquire our freedom and singularity in desiring fervently and unto death this unknown law of destiny. Antigone becomes *autonomos* and *autognotos* (875), she who gives herself the law that she has found and known, in accepting that we can never fully know and predict fate's edicts. Thus, the tragic actor is autonomous and willing her acts and belongs to a higher register at work at the very heart of her decisions, which makes her both human and part of a fatal scheme. She is both culpable and a plaything in the hands of the gods. Human and divine nature, means and ends, are totally opposed to each other but are inseparable and intermingled, and in the tension created the hero becomes both author and victim of her own actions. Antigone, in burying Polynices and in calmly choosing death, answers destiny's call unflinchingly. But, as she repeatedly says, she does not know what this law ordains, what its immutable edicts are, other than what it asks of her, here and now, before the brother's corpse.

> Who knows what the rules are among the dead? (521)

Destiny is the universal law, the law behind the law. It encircles

and entombs, like Antigone's mausoleum, all life. We have
encountered already the invincible laws of gods, of eros and of
death. But destiny is the primordial force and 'nothing can be
exempt'. Its force leads both to ruin and to greatness; its content is
unknown. But it is unknown only in its universality 'among the
dead'. Antigone learns and acts her destiny, as does Creon, after
the forceful entreaties of Teiresias have opened his eyes. The
knowledge of destiny comes in the force of a command, a 'must'
that rises in the encounter with the other. Their different reactions
to this command will determine their respective ends. Creon will
accept the force of destiny as a totally heteronomous and blind
force that man cannot understand or control, as irrational and evil.
He accepts that he has erred, but the mistake itself is the outcome
of divine and fateful intervention. At the end, he is utterly
destroyed, a living corpse for whom life is the worst punishment.
Destiny's force leads to ruin if its power is not heeded.

The Chorus thinks that something similar is happening to
Antigone. She comes from a doomed house and she carries in her
the curse of her father that both makes her act and destroys her.
But Antigone sings her fate and destiny and only briefly despairs.
Her greatness lies exactly in her willing acceptance of destiny, of
love and death. But the earlier analysis gives us a new understanding of the force of destiny and of the process of individuation. Most
translations of the famous *stichomythia* between Antigone and
Creon on the source of law make lines 450–3 mean that as Creon's
edict was not given by Zeus or chthonic Dikē, Antigone could
disobey it. And yet there is a different translation, grammatically
not unacceptable: 'it was neither Zeus nor Dikē that ordered me to
do *this*', that is, to disobey the law. Antigone follows her own law.
And it is her lack of fear and love of death that make her
autonomous and, eventually for the Chorus, an object of wonder
and awe. Her *amor fati* is guided by the – cruel – fate of love.

VIII

I was not born to hate but to love.   *Antigone*

While repeated indications of desire and sexual love form the
background of Antigone's obedience to Dikē, her eros is monstrous; she is besotted with *thanatos*, and will be betrothed with

Hades and death. For Hegel as for Nietzsche and Heidegger, death
is an existential yardstick; its recognition and acceptance as the
inescapable horizon of being is the *differentia specifica* of the
human species. *Antigone* is full of references to the momentous
linking of the primordial forces of love and death. Antigone, we
are told, is in love with the impossible and with death (90, 220).
The Chorus's Ode on Eros is immediately preceded by Creon's
accusation that Antigone is devoted to Hades (776–780). The Ode's
praises to maddening *eros* are followed by the announcement that
the maiden is making her way 'to the bridal vault where all are laid
to rest' (821–2) and her own moving:

I go to wed the lord of the dark lake (*Acheronti nympheuso*). (816)

Antigone consummates her passionate and destructive love with
her *philtatoi* in death; her affection for Polynices but also for the
unlucky Haemon, caught in the maelstorm of forces larger than life
and death, will be fulfilled in the burial and wedding chamber of
Hades:

MESSENGER: And there he lies, body enfolding body
   he has won his bride at last, poor boy,
   not here but in the houses of the dead. (1240–1).

This is not the *eros* of Platonic harmony, nor the Hegelian familial
love that unites the spouses and sublates them in the coming son.
There is no gain to be made from it against Creon's enlightened
utilitarianism, according to which there must be return for all
investment (93). Antigone's *eros* is pure expenditure, a gift with no
return, Sappho's 'elemental force of nature, a whirlwind running
down the mountains' (fragment 47LP, quoted in Segal 1981,
p. 198). It belongs to an *oiko-nomē* of monstrosity.

But what is Antigone's desire? We must ask both questions
implied in the double genitive. What does Antigone want and
what do we want of Antigone? Does she follow the law of family
and the gods, of the symbolic Order, or does she act out her desire
for Polynices? I hear what she says and what she asks of me but
what does she really want? What does the woman want? This is
the question that Creon asks of her and Freud was to repeat. Creon
is convinced that there is a dislocation between Antigone's
demand and act and her desire. Within the framework of his
political rationalism, Antigone can only act for gain or as part of a
conspiracy to overthrow him. The only alternative is that she is

'mad', that a permanent and unbridgeable gap has developed between her locution (what she says) and her illocution (what she aims at), a state that psychoanalysis examines under the name of hysteria. A dangerous political rebel or an unhinged hysteric?

Antigone's answer is: 'I was not born to hate but to love.' In Lacanian theory love has the character of fundamental deception:

We try to fill out the unbearable gap of 'Che vuoi?', the opening of the Other's desire, by offering ourselves to the Other as object of its desire. ... The operation of love is therefore double; the subject fills in his own lack by offering himself to the Other as the object filling out the lack in the Other – love's deception is that this overlapping of two lacks annuls lack as such in a mutual completion. (Žižek, 1989, p. 116)

Antigone's sacrifice is the sign of absolute love. She offers herself to Polynices in order to complete his passage and fill in his lack and at the same time she removes herself from the commotion of activity and passion onto the plane of pure desire and existence.

It has been repeatedly observed that Antigone's character does not develop during the tragedy.[23] From the first scene to the end she remains committed to her act, although she occasionally wavers about its justifications. Neither Creon nor we can know for certain Antigone's object of desire. The only thing we know is that Antigone desires and that she will always act on her desire. But the acting appears secondary. Her calm serenity intimates a saintly passivity, an ontological aloofness: she is already elsewhere, her inscrutable desire is a state of being rather than an act. Her desire is a death drive; in desiring she becomes a deathbound being but 'she will not give way on her desire'. Creon's utilitarianism makes him unable to understand this 'bizarre' calculation and he finally adopts the 'female madness' alternative. But that makes her even more dangerous in his eyes. Her stubborn persistence to death, her frightening ontological ruthlessness which exempts her from the 'circle of everyday feelings and considerations, passions and fears' (Žižek 1989, p. 117), turns her into a symbol of sedition. In desiring unto death, Antigone challenges the symbolic order of state law and male authority and becomes a rebel in the name of desire.

---

[23] Though it should be observed that 'character development' as understood in later western tradition is not necessarily the object of Greek tragedy.

Creon's repeated refusals of god, family ties, love and the dead, on the other hand, are necessary aspects of all rationalist politics. They are part of a considered 'politics of forgetting' that every *polis* must use in order to ban what questions the legitimacy of the institution. This memorial politics – and all discourse of rational legitimation is necessarily in part a Periclean funeral oration – turns the imponderable powers that threaten the city into past, memory and recitation. It transcribes them into a well-organised narrative that re-presents and thus transcends the fearful past presence; and in putting them into *logos* it encloses them into a singular and familiar order of argument and persuasion. Our repeated and memorised myths help us elevate and remove the terrible predicaments of life, and forget the pain of the event.

Creon is a master of the strategy of forgetting and concealing through denial and memorisation. The temporal order he refers to is finite; the repeated past comes to the service of the future through a temporality that is linear and quantitative, rationally organised and mastered. His time and the time of state and legality cannot answer to eternity or the time of the event. The function of the time of repetition and of memory is therapeutic. Their representations aim to make, forget and sublate what is alien to self and the alien itself and thus heal the wound that the abyss opens in the psyche and the social bond. But what was never a presence in the homogeneous time of *logos*, cannot be fully represented and cannot be banned and forgotten. The abyssal always returns, as Creon finally learns.

Antigone belongs to a different temporality. Her measure is not a natural life-time. It is a gain to die before her time, she says to Creon, and she adds to Ismēnē that her soul has died a long time ago (461, 559). Always, forever, eternity: these are the temporal markers of her existence. The sequential time of law and institutions that binds generations through calculations of gain and the totalising time of history have intruded upon Antigone's timelessness and have upset the cyclical rhythm of earth and blood that pre-exists and survives the writing of the law. But Antigone's infinite temporality does not appeal just to the time of nature, *physis*, but also to the timelessness of *dikē*. It is the laws presided over by Dikē, unwritten and everlasting, the laws of Hades, that Antigone gladly follows (456, 76).

This time of *dikē*, which is opposed to the finite time of the institution, but is not simply the time of nature, could be paralleled with the unsettling of temporal sequence that psycho-analysis diagnoses in the work of the unconscious. Antigone has suffered an original excitation, Freud's unconscious affect, that has disturbed the psychic apparatus but has not been 'experi-enced'. It will only surface and be acted upon later in an action that will 'remember' the original blow, which, however, was never recorded as a memory and was thus always a forgotten. Freud speaks of this parasite of the psyche which has entered uninvited and unacknowledged as 'the prehistoric, unforgettable other person who is never equalled by anyone later' (Freud, quoted in Lyotard 1990, p. 45). Freud has Oedipus in mind; but Antigone, too, is a timeless recorder of the forgotten unforgettable as she acts out her desire. Antigone's devotion to Polynices is the outcome of a mad, immemorial desire that has been inscribed into her before and outside of the time of institutions and laws. Her action is the unconscious affect in the house of Being of a stranger who has never entered it. An originary seduction has taken place, the self has been taken hostage by the primordial other whose desire is an excessive overflowing and an inexorable command. In this approach the conflict would be between the passion for the brother that emanates from recesses of the psyche not open to the operations of reminiscence and *logos* and the unspeakable wrong against the love object that the institution commits. Can there be a law that emanates from this dark region of desire and challenges the legality of the city and the work of repression of the family? Psychoanalytic theory has been associated with such an ethics that incorporates the tragic necessity of our desire and the fatal love and excessive passion of femininity. For this law, which is unwritten and eternal but also the most unique and singular, the social bond is not just about good and evil or about right and wrong. Its time is neither that of natural eternity nor of historical totality, but the infinite time of the event; in this diachronous time, *that* 'there is' comes before *what* 'there is'.

Finally, if this is Antigone's desire, what is the reason for our own fascination with Antigone? Could it be that Antigone's attraction must be sought in the stubborn way she has been pursuing her desire to die coupled with her utter inscrutability? Our own desire for Antigone is based on this impossibility to know fully what the other wants from us and turn her demand into law.

We cannot identify with Antigone, with her calm persistence until death that challenges the law, and we are left with an inescapable 'Che vuoi?' But if this is the case, we could argue that *dikē*, as the justice of the law, arises on the ground of this question without answer, on the ground of the sphinx-like enigma of the inscrutable desire of Antigone. To use psychoanalytic terminology, justice is a 'fantasy', a frame we construct to explain away the unknown desire of the other but which at the same time constitutes and organises our own lack and desire for the other. As Žižek puts it, '*desire itself is a defence against desire*: the desire structured through fantasy is a defence against the desire of the Other, against this "pure" trans-phantasmic desire (i.e. the "death drive" in its pure form)' (1989, p. 118; original emphasis).

In this interpretation, *dikē* is not a goddess Antigone appeals to, and even less is she the promised equity of the institution. On the contrary, it is not Antigone who follows justice but justice is the creation of Antigone. Justice is the fantasiacal screen that philosophers, poets and lawyers have erected to shield themselves from the question of the desire of the other. The question of justice can only arise for us on the burial ground of Antigone. It is her death that first alerts us to the desire for the other in the midst of the law, to the unique and contingent character of the demand of the other, that is, to the reasons that make justice both necessary and impossible: we can only negotiate our own desire for the other through our fantasies of justice, but the radical dissymetry, the abyss of the other's desire and of the 'Che vuoi?' will always leave behind a remainder for which neither the law nor fantasy can fully account. In her own excessive love for her brother and death, Antigone may be the eternal reminder of an abyss that enfolds and enforces all law.

IX

How could man ever have invented the power which pervades him, which alone enables him to be man?

Language is the primordial poetry in which a people speak being.
Heidegger, Introduction to Metaphysics

As we approach the clearing and the (burial) ground on which the law emerges, we should remind ourselves that the question of an 'originary ethics' and of the law of law is haunted by Heidegger's spectre, in the same way that (Heidegger's) law is fascinated by Antigone's tomb. Heidegger claims that Antigone's first *stasimon*, the Ode on Man, alongside Hölderlin's translation, could provide the basis of western metaphysics. In his *Introduction to Metaphysics*, Heidegger uses the Ode as a foundational text of ontology; his detailed interpretation is an attempt to cut through the impoverished post-Platonic philosophical language of false oppositions between Being and thought and Being and ought and go back to the beginning, the originary opening, in which Being presented and opened itself into the multiplicity of beings.

Heidegger believed that the Greek spirit and language of the pre-Socratics was in close proximity to the truth (*alētheia*, unconcealment) of Being. The poetic thinkers, Anaximander, Heraclitus, Parmenides, and the thinking poets, Homer, Aeschylus and Sophocles, were still able to understand and express in language the way in which the historical Being-there, *Dasein*, of the Greeks was created. They still possessed a *logos*, language, with the original capacity of truthful nomination and unconcealment of the being of Being and the essence of man. Language could both 'say' this essence and show it; its inner structure and grammar, its syntactic and semantic clarity and archaic etymology could unconceal the structure of Being. Indeed in its various uses, grammatical modes and interpretations of the copula 'to be', Greek poetry and philosophy opened the main avenues of western existence and knowledge. Like the radiant sun of Apollo and Attica, archaic *logos* both lit and revealed the Being of beings and blinded and concealed *Dasein* when it eventually degenerated into solidified and referential discourse.

This primordial power to perceive, name and bring forward *alētheia*, the truth in unconcealment of Being, was soon lost in the various Platonisms which distinguished the sensory from the suprasensible and attributed priority to the latter in its diverse permutations, from the Platonic world of forms to the Christian afterworld, Nietzsche's Platonism for the masses. The pre-Socratics still 'speak Being' and Heidegger turns to their obscure fragments with unprecedented interpretative violence to glimpse the original clearing of Being, the ground on which the consciousness of existence emerged and was articulated in language and myth. It is a glimpse of the unity of existence before Plato and metaphysics, and a genealogy of the great divides that fissured the wholeness of Being.

For Heraclitus and Parmenides, Being is *physis*, the power that emerges in its permanent presence against becoming. The original meaning of *logos* again, before it became discourse and language and even later reason and logic, is to gather, collecting and collectedness, both putting things together and marking them apart in their specificity. *Physis* and *logos* are aspects of Being, they are united in Being's common totality. For modernity and Kantianism, *physis* is objective while *logos qua* thought belongs to the subject. Heidegger could not disagree more fundamentally: the separation between Being and beings is not a transcendental but a thoroughly historical question, indeed the essence of history which is also the essence of man.

The gathering together of *logos* maintains the common bond of all beings in a belonging together of antagonisms. For Heraclitus, the essence of man is first manifested in *polemos*, war, in which men were separated from gods and the two were put forward in their being. The first glimpse of humanity is when we see man struggle with the various beings in the world 'striving to bring them into their being, i.e. into limit and form, that is to say, when he projects something new (not yet present), when he creates original poetry, when he builds poetically' (Heidegger 1961, p. 144). To exemplify this poetical creation of beings in their being through human action and to appreciate fully the closest that man came to understanding Being and his essence, Heidegger turns to the Ode on Man.

CHORUS: Numberless wonders, terrible wonders walk the world
    but none the match of man
    (*polla ta deina koûden anthrōpou deinoteron pelei*). (332)

Man is the strangest, *deinotaton* – a word which in its ambiguity expresses both the extreme reaches and the abyssal depths of Being. Man is the most *deinon* in the sense of the terrible, the 'overpowering power' terrifying and awe-inspiring; but he is also the violent one, violence is of his Being. In his fundamental violence he uses power against overpowering. Man's strangeness, the basic trait of his uncanny essence, is that he always violently abandons the familiar and the secure for the strange and overpowering. But in this endless and violent fleeing to the unknown he becomes *pantoporos aporos* and *hypsipolis apolis*. He opens and follows myriad paths on his flight from home, *poros*, but he is cast out of all of them. He achieves his essence in and out and for the *polis*, historically. *Polis* is the time and place where the paths meet, the site of *Dasein*. But his political action that makes him the highest in the city leaves him also without site, city and place, alien and lonely as he must first create the ground and order of his own creation.

Having outlined the basic design of man, the strangest, most wonderful and terrifying of beings, Heidegger now looks closer at the poem to hear man's Being unfold through the verses. The conquest of the sea and the earth, of animals and birds that opens the Ode are not just descriptions of man's activities: they are an outline of his overpowering being that brings both his and all other beings into their own Being. We have to turn to the pre-Socratics and *Antigone* because, against the evolutionism of modernity, man's beginning reflected there is the strangest and the mightiest of events. It is this original leap into overpowering wandering and alienation that makes man *deinotatos*; 'what comes afterward is not development but the flattening that results from mere spreading out' (Heidegger 1961, p. 155). We must return to *Antigone*, and our poets and philosophers, these 'shepherds of Being', have been returning to her, because modernity, like Odysseus, suffers from the unquenchable nostalgia of the exile and the wanderer: the pain, *algos*, for the day of homecoming, *nostos*, of coming back to the original clearing of Being, before the great scissions of our age.

The second strophe of the Ode names the elements of the overpowering powers: language, thought, passion, laws and buildings rule man and must be taken up by him as he launches into his ever-new ventures.

CHORUS: And speech and thought, quick as the wind
  and the mood and mind for law that rules the city
  all these he has taught himself
  and shelter from the arrows of the frost
  when there is rough lodging under the cold clear sky
  and the shafts of lashing rain –
  ready resourceful man! Never without resources
  never an impasse as he marches on the future –
  only Death, from Death alone he will find no rescue. (354–61)

'But how could man have invented the power which pervades him, which alone allows him to be a man?' asks Heidegger (p. 156) and offers his own translation, which clearly diverges from the accepted both syntactically and semantically.

And he has found his way
to the resonance of the word,
and to wind-swift all-understanding,
and to the courage to rule over cities.
He has considered also how to flee
from exposure to the arrows
of unpropitious weather and frost.
Everywhere journeying, inexperienced and
without issue, he comes to nothingness.
Through no flight he can resist
the one assault of death,
even if he has succeeded in cleverly evading
painful sickness.

Heidegger reads the key term *elidaxato*, against received opinion and its dictionary value, to mean not that man has invented and taught himself language, thought and laws, but that he has found his way towards their overpowering order and there found himself. As soon as man departs into being, he finds himself in language. Language, this uncanny thing, speaks man; its overpowering power helps him speak and create the violent words and acts through which he breaks out into his myriad paths and breaks and subjects his world into its manifold beings. The beginning of language is a mystery; it arose in the violent overpowering of power of originary, archaic poetry and philosophy in which the Greeks spoke Being. The original work of language is not a *semiurgy* but a *demiurgy*. Mastering the violence of language makes man; through speech and understanding he tames and orders the powers of the world and moves into them as the violent creator of beings and history. But all violence shatters against one thing, a limit that surrounds and delimits man's creative violence: death. Shattering against the uncanniness of death is of the essence of being. But it is not the fact of death that is shattering, not the exit itself, but the exitlessness which is proper to *Dasein*, its innermost and necessary possibility. The opening is the admission to the exit, the exitless exit. For Heidegger, being moves to death, death is the necessary possibility and *telos* of *Dasein*. Everything that enters life begins to die, and the certain but indeterminate imminence of death, of *Dasein*'s demise, is *Dasein*'s ownmost possibility and the signpost of its individuation. The *logos* gathers the supreme antagonism, the struggle of life and death, which is the intrinsic togetherness and possibility of Being.

The third strophe brings together the two meanings of *deinon* and their interrelation in the *deinotaton*. *Deinon* as man's violent power is evident in knowledge and art (*technē*); these look beyond the familiar and cause beings to present themselves and stabilise in their Being. *Technē* is the fundamental characteristic of man, and the work of art allows everything to come forward and shine in its Being. *Deinon* as the overpowering power, on the other hand, is evident in the fundamental *dikē*, the proper order and governing structure of Being against which the violence of speech and act will break out and break up. *Technē* confronts *dikē* as man sails into the order of Being, violently tears it assunder using his power against its overpowering dispensation and brings forth the existence of beings. *Dikē* is the overpowering order, *technē* the violence of knowledge. But the overpowering order can never be overcome fully and tosses man *pantoporos*, all-resourceful and everywhere-going, back from pathbreaking to *aporia*, lack of passage and resource, from the greatest glory to the basest infamy and catastrophe.

The *violent one*, the creative man, who sets forth into the un-said, who breaks into the un-thought, compels the un-happened to happen and makes the unseen appear – this violent one stands at all times in venture. . . . In venturing to master being, he must risk the assault of the non-essent, *mē kalon*, he must risk instability, disorder, mischief. The higher the summit of historical being-there, the deeper will be the abyss, the more abrupt the fall into the unhistorical, which merely thrashes around in issueless and placeless confusion. (Heidegger 1961, p. 161)

Now Heidegger proceeds to the final reading of the poem, a paradigmatic presentation of his combined ontology and hermeneutics and his own act as *deinotatos*. To move to the essence of *Antigone*'s text, the reader must abandon the arrogant 'scientific interpretation' and must use interpretative violence to show 'what does not stand in the words and is nevertheless said' (*ibid.*, p. 162). What lies between the lines is the writing of disaster. The

possibility of catastrophe has an ontological permanence. The fall
into disaster is a fundamental tenet that exists in waiting before
every act or word, an inescapable condition of human existence,
caught and created as it is in the conflict and oscillation between
power and overpowering, the violence of knowledge, art and deed
and the order of the world. Man cultivates and guards the familiar,
home, *polis* and hearth only 'to break out of it and let what
overpowers break in' (*ibid.*, p. 163). The violent one desires the
new and unprecedented and abandons all help and sympathy to
fulfil the call of Being; but to achieve his humanness he knows of
no peace and reconciliation, no permanent success and status. 'To
him disaster is the deepest and broadest affirmation of the
overpowering' (*ibid.*). The greatness of the Greeks was to understand the suddenness and uniqueness of Being that forcefully
revealed itself as *physis*, *logos* and *dikē*, and to respond to its
awesome overpowering in the only way that could bring forward
beings out of Being, that is, violently.

In this example of Heideggerian hermeneutical ontology, we are
offered a good insight into the place of ethics in law. Indeed,
despite the strong emphasis in *Antigone* on *nomos* and *dikē*,
Heidegger gives only a general outline of the mythological position
of *dikē* and scarcely mentions the repeated references to *nomos* in
the Ode on Man and throughout the tragedy. We will return to
them shortly, but let us first situate their role in Heideggerian
ontology in order to understand what is at stake in this 'lawless'
reading of *Antigone*.

In the *Letter on Humanism* (1977), Heidegger explicitly
addressed the relationship between ontology and ethics. In Homer,
ēthea are the dwelling places of animals; if the animal cannot
return to its habitus its order has been violated. Heidegger defines
ethics, according to this original meaning of *ēthos*: 'ethics ponders
the abode of man.' Original ethics is a 'thinking which thinks the
truth of Being as the primordial element of man, as the one who
eksists' (*ibid.*, p. 235). The task of 'fundamental ontology', as
defined in *Being and Time* (1962) is to ponder the truth and
presence of Being. It follows that ontology does not need the
supplement of an originary ethics, as they both share the same
field and their aim is to approach the joint clearing on which they
emerge.

Human laws, ethical codes and rules are assigned by Being's

dispensation, which conditions and determines the substance of law. Law itself, nŏmos, like ethics, has a homonym, nomŏs, the original meaning of which is very similar to ēthos. This latter nomŏs refers to the pastures of horses and to the wandering of animals randomly searching for grazing fields. The word later becomes associated with possession and regular usage of pasturage but also with division and distribution, with both habit and accepted practice and nomadic and disordered spreading out. Heidegger exploits these connections in what has been seen as an argument for the primacy of ontology over ethics.

> In Greek to assign is nemein. Nomos is not only law but more originally the assignment contained in the dispensation of Being. Only the assignment is capable of dispatching man into Being. Only such dispatching is capable of supporting and obligating. Otherwise all law remains merely something fabricated by human reason. (ibid., pp. 238–9)

In the Heideggerian idiom, nŏmos is what is assigned or allotted to us by the 'sending', the letter dispatched by Being, before it comes to mean law and rule. It is not philosophy's job to 'legislate' ethics, nor to busy itself with specific laws, principles and ethical commands, the ethics of law and justice of the moral philosophers. Its task is rather to concentrate on the destiny and truth of Being and to trace the demand for an ethics and its various answers back to its primordial linkage with the dispatch of Being. The 'truth of Being' is the way a people 'dwells', the combination of knowledge, art and political arrangements and their historical understanding of the world, gods and themselves. In this sense, ontological thinking abandons the futile and conflicting debates of the moralists in order to understand the fundamental constellation within which human life is organised in each epoch, and which is the historical realisation of the primordial Being and ethos.

The demand for an ethics betrays the naïve position that ethics can be made to measure. The dispatch and allotment of Being, our lot and destiny, is the shape of our historical existence, our bond to our form of life. This bond cannot be of our making alone; it is not that impoverished to have been 'fabricated by human reason'. We found ourselves thrown in it, in medias res, answering its call. Its force lies in the 'demand placed on the individual to assume his place within his society, to answer the call of Being in his time' (Caputo 1987, p. 247). The thinker must not heed demands that come from elsewhere; he must concentrate on answering the call of destiny, abide by the dispensation of Being.

It is this and similar arguments that have been used to suggest that fundamental ontology is a denigration of ethics. We should immediately add, however, that the Heideggerian injunction is itself a strong law. Indeed Heidegger repeatedly gives an ethical tone to the demand that we abide by the destiny of Being, the only way of a fitting life. But 'if this commandment has an ethical meaning, it is not that it belongs to the *domain* of the ethical, but in that it ultimataly authorises every ethical law in general' (Derrida 1978, p. 80). In other words, the Heideggerian injunction is not the law of rules, principles and codes, or the ethics of Derrida's 'ethical domain'. It is rather the law of law, before and outside ethics as discipline, the force that puts into circulation and authorises all extant laws. The law of law is the 'equivalent to what Heidegger calls law as the assignment of the dispensation of Being' (Bernasconi 1987, p. 125). In this reading, destiny imposes an ethical demand that could even be called the originary ethic; but the answer to it cannot take the form of a code or a collection of principles and rules. It is the very refusal to issue an ethical code that abides by the ethical demand. 'To follow rules is to uproot oneself from dwelling. To provide ethical directives is to condemn to the everyday the person who adopts them' (*ibid.*, p. 134). We can now appreciate the importance of Heidegger's reading of *Antigone* and of reading *Antigone contra* Heidegger; this reading can be used as the testing ground for the relationship between Being and ethics, the site of the originary ethics and of the law of law.

The key trope and strategy through which Heidegger claims the primacy of ontology over ethics is the presentation of *dikē* as the primordial orderliness of the world and of *nomos* as our share in it. *Dikē* is not justice but the overpowering structure of Being; it emerges and shines in its permanent presence as *physis* and is gathered together in its collectedness as *logos*, which unites oppositions while keeping their tension. *Physis, logos* and *dikē*, object and subject, law and justice are aspects of the essential unity of Being. Man's *technē*, violent knowledge, attacks *dikē*, and in this original event and reciprocal relation, man ceases to be at home and both home and the alien are disclosed. In his violent naming and acting, the manifold of beings and his own historical being-there are made manifest and are shattered in the catastrophe that lurks before every achievement as its existential precondition.

At first glance it looks as if Heidegger's ontological ethics is identical to Antigone's call and follows closely from *dikē*'s unconscious. And yet something troubling remains. The *hypsipolis*, Heidegger's violent one, according to the Ode on Man, honours both the laws of the land (*nomous chthonos*), and the justice of gods (*theōn t'enorkon dikan*). If man comes into his historical being in the conflict between the violence of knowledge and deed (*technē*) and the overpowering order of the world (*dikē*), *dikē* is split right from the start. But what is the nature of this split? This primordial division cannot be between a mere jurisprudential 'is' and 'ought'. Their separation will come about only at a later 'fallen' stage, heavily influenced by Plato. In Platonism, Being and thought are sharply distinguished; thought becomes dominant while Being is defined as an essence and an idea. But as the good is the idea of ideas, and Being consists in ideas, Being comes into opposition to the good that stands beyond Being and acts as its model. Thus, it is only after the forgetfulness of Being has set in and Being has been defined as an idea that the 'ought' of moral systems arises and opposes itself to Being. The road to the strict modern split between 'is' and 'ought' and object and subject has been opened; it will come to its full and dogmatic fruition in Kant. But, according to Heidegger, *Antigone* still speaks the unity in antagonisms of Being and it is here that we should seek the ground of the law.

If *dikē* is the way of the world, the stuff out of which the basic distinctions of morality, religion and law emerge, it is the *nomos* of *nemein* the earth that confronts and divides *dikē* and brings into the open the human being-there. *Nemein* means dividing, breaking up, sending away in many directions, without pattern, structure or aim. The *nomos* of Being is a nomadic assignation. In this version destiny is not belonging but exile, the Oedipal destiny of the blind wanderer, of the stranger in the house of Being. The truth of Being and of *nomos/ēthos* is from the very start many conflictual, warring truths. The letter the Being sends is unwritten but follows the law of writing. It is never fully present in a historical presence; it finds itself always and already caught in the process of dissemination and difference, nomadic and polyvalent. But even more fundamentally, as *Antigone* reminds us, there are two invincible and inescapable powers, unbreakably and fatefully linked: love and death. Heidegger showed how the knowledge of death opens the field of human possibilities in mortal living. The individual discovers her existential specificity by recognising the singularity of her being in relation to death. Nothing and no one underwrites and guarantees existence; no truth, history or ego can recentre a subject that opened herself to the mortal possibility of living. The flight of existence to death forces the individual to get hold of the only properly human being in possibility, the violent forcing of the overpowering. This is the specifically human being-there, *Dasein*, of which the Ode gave Heidegger the best unconcealment: a continuous flight forward in pure, uncharted possibility that is both opened and shattered against the totally other of death.

If death, however, is the limit that gives *Dasein* its human specificity, *Antigone* shows that it is the loving turn to the suffering and unique other that bestows on the individual her own singularity. If death is the external limit that must be brought inside life to put human life into being, the other is the internal limit that in asking and receiving help creates individualities out of *Dasein*. And it is in this sense that the original *nomos* divides and breaks; the paths and byways that destiny opens take their unpredictable directions and map out mortal possibilities because they are signposted by the unique encounters with unrepeatable others who always come before us and impose on us the mystery of an originating 'must'. The law of law, destiny, is always open to an outside, an otherwise than Being, death and the other.

Destiny, the universal force of law, lives and is enforced in singular, unpredictable and forceful manifestations. We can now understand why *moira* and *tychē*, luck, are both necessary and contingent. The other who arises before me and the demand she puts to me are contingent, they happen unpredictably and without warning and could have happened otherwise. But there is an inexorable necessity, a strict legality to this contingency: some other will arise before me and I will have to answer her demand. Indeed my own individual *Dasein* is the necessary opening to the contingent demands of fate that appears to me in the face of the other.

This reading retains the basic insights of Heidegger's ontology. It accepts that the demand for a moral code while indicating the ethical character of the destiny of Being cannot be satisfied without violating the essence of the ethical relation. It affirms the contingent character of human *Dasein*, but insists on the necessarily relational nature of contingency. But the reason why an ethics is not possible is that the human *Dasein* is primordially ethical and that openness to the other is part of the basic design of Being. Acts of destiny are not signs of an essence; they do not re-present an absent cause, fate, nor are they means used to achieve some unknown ends. On the contrary, such acts are the manifestations, the epiphany of destiny.[24] And if destiny is the 'unwritten law' before human and divine, in a more modern and linguistically obsessed terminology, the writing of fate performs. It acts (forces) in speaking and it speaks by killing. In other words, destiny is life open to the call of something beyond self. This beyond is quite specific for Antigone. If she answers its call, she says, she could face her brother as the most beloved of friends and she will lie with him in nocturnal bliss.

Death, eros and the force of the (br)other are the registers of destiny, they put into operation its unwritten and universal law. Its epiphany is always in the singular. Law is force. Both the ethical force of the living, embodied other, entombed in the 'you must' and the destructive force of the other as shrouded corpse and death. Both a force internal to law, that befalls and obligates, binds the 'I' to the law and saves it; and an externally applied force, the sanction and limit of the law, that kills the 'I' to save the law. Law's force: a force that binds and preserves or a force that severs and preserves.

At the mythical moment of its foundation the law is split into divine and human. On the one hand, the madness of a 'must' gets hold of the 'I' with an inestimable force and obliges the ego without any knowledge or calculation, without criteria or evaluation. On the other, the law of the state, the law of universality, of calculation and of uniform application applies its own force and persuasion. *Antigone* teaches that the *nomos* rises on the ground of the polemical symbiosis of female and male, singular and universal, justice and law. Force and form, value and validity are both implicated in the ethical substance of the law, are both parts of law's original 'must'. And launched at the heart of both,

---

[24] This analysis resembles Walter Benjamin's (1978) mythical semiology and his analysis of fate.

encrypted in law's essence, lurks the memory of violence and death.

But the law of the law, destiny, is unknown. We can never know destiny but we must follow it, like Antigone. Fate comes as the other, the dying/dead other who asks us to save or bury him. The force of the 'must' is the force that the most remote and different from self imposes on self. Death as the other of life; the stranger who is left outside the wall of Thebes to be devoured by the dogs; the force of eros as the total transcendence of the world projected by and revolving around self. Fate is the other. We must follow the traces of its apparent extinction on the body of jurisprudence.

Could we not argue then that (unknown) fate is the good (or God)? It stands before the law and it infuses it both with its opposition to Justice and with the superiority of Justice over Law. It is also destiny as the force of the multiplicity of Being (gods as others) that propels the law into being. These are the horizons that shape the genealogy of jurisprudence. Greek philosophy founded ontology and sent out the letter that Heidegger gratefully received. But Greek tragedy, in its sense of tragic destiny, alludes to singularity and otherness, a destructive force and an unmediated duty, that has been always associated with Greek's other, the Jew. This force could be the writing of the dead body or the other. Antigone alludes to both, but she does not give a final answer. 'Who knows what the rules are among the dead?' She leaves it to (s)he who answers the call of the 'must'.

3

Cases of casuistry

The common law and a lost tradition

I

Antigone claimed that the force driving her life was something that had to take priority over the duties placed on the citizen by the rules of the state. She did not deny the commands of Creon's civic community and she agreed that these demands knew no limits: 'To speak and act/ Just as he likes is a king's prerogative' (505–6). Nevertheless, and in apparent contradiction to this acknowledgement, she claims: '[Creon] has no right to keep me from my own' (48). In spite, therefore, of the blunt description by the Chorus of the sovereign's power – 'Your will is law' (215) – there is something else the law ought to recognise notwithstanding its purported universal jurisdiction. The demand to which Antigone responds is that, in the case of her (br)other, the threat of (un)necessary eternal torment must be negated before the mere 'will' of the law-giver is obeyed. In less dramatic, cataclysmic terms, the individual circumstances of the particular subject, to which the law addresses its commands, must be considered alongside the all-powerful will of the commanding body.

Antigone was speaking, however, of a demand based outside of time. Her claim drew on a time before the tradition of the law had established how to cope with any apparently intractably conflict-ing commands. Sophocles' play portrays demands that are not simply based on how things were done before in the lawfulness of authority established by long use, whereas, for the common law, long use is the best-known means of evidencing legitimate title. For whilst *Antigone* contrasts two sets of laws, those before and those after the time of the founding of the authority of laws as such, the common law knows no such divisions. The traditions of the common law, like the law Antigone obeys, have existed since time immemorial, that is, outside of time altogether. In effect, the common law knows no origins[1] and has no need of them, since the tradition itself contains a sufficiently rich heritage to enable it to draw on its own resources for the authority of its decision-making processes. The common law does not require an Antigone to search for valid rules outside of the system, which is why, for the common law, there is simply no outside; just as the law knows no limits[2] of time, so all time comes within its limits. The common law, therefore, sometimes appears to think of itself as a Creon writ large.

Somewhat more prosaically, and in sharp contradiction to the claim of the common law that its knowledge and traditions are based on memory rather than writing, this ability of the common law to claim an origin that returns to a time out of mind relates to the development of the recording of court judgments without which even the mind of a Homer is liable, occasionally, to be curiously forgetful. The writing of the results of important legal decisions probably began in the early thirteenth century (Baker 1979, p. 151; Milsom 1981, p. 5). Semi-organised reporting itself can be dated to the 'year books' around the start of the fourteenth century (Milsom 1981, pp. 44–8). From about this time, the common law formed a complex inheritance which lawyers could be expected to study and know. This inheritance has furthered the development of the operational tension between principles and facts that is a feature of the system. The common law's claim to originality lies, in part, in the creative use of this tension.

In this chapter, we examine English law's development of the balance between principles and fact, alongside another intellectual tradition which also developed around the time the common law began to be written and which operated in a similar manner – casuistry. We try to show a parallel, sometimes inter-related, development between the two, and argue that the common law's largely unacknowledged casuistical method of operation can help

---

[1] The significance of the originless origins of the common law is touched on in Chapter 8.

[2] We explore further what might be said to lie beyond the 'limits' of the common law in Chapter 5.

us formulate an approximate starting place for an ethical theory of justice which can be placed alongside the demands of Antigone that we have just examined.

In essence, casuistry was a method of resolving problems of conscience which involved a religious element. Casuistry is a Church-based, predominantly, but not exclusively, Roman Catholic, form of moral reasoning.[3] Until at least the seventeenth century, most problems of conscience took on religious connotations. Matters such as the relations with one's family or neighbours, or with one's one body and soul, as in the correct attitude to suicide (Aristotle's question [1976, p. 200]: 'Whether a man can treat himself unjustly . . . ?'), how to behave in public, attitudes to sexual matters, to the lending of money at interest and so on, all came within the casuist's scope. Indeed the Catholic Church, assuming the world was *universitas christianorum*, decided that all aspects of conscience came under its jurisdiction. Christian casuistry, designed to help priests resolve borderline conscience problems in a principled yet sensitive manner, reached its height of refinement and influence around the sixteenth and seventeenth centuries. For a time, it became a widely accepted and respected method for the resolution of disputes and problems faced by the all-encompassing Church jurisdiction. Even when casuistry had become predominantly associated with a minority religion, as it did from Elizabethan times in England, it still affected the orthodoxy. Both as something 'other', as a discourse of justice alien to the presumed majority opinion, and, even more insidiously, within the very orthodoxy that seemed to reject entirely the basis of casuistry's jurisdiction and method of operation, casuistry triumphed. For a time, even in Protestant England, it was ubiquitous.

Casuistry fell out of intellectual favour from around 1650. Despite something of a recent revival, casuistry became, and is still now, frequently treated as synonymous with another debased tradition – 'sophistry'. In the sense of unjustifiable reasoning which, its critics claimed, was the sort of reasoning that could justify anything, casuistry was violently attacked, especially by a different group of religious fanatics in France. But it was not only

---

[3] Delumeau (1988, p. 148), though not specifically dealing with casuistry, points to the important similarities between Catholic and early Protestant pedagogy.

in France that casuistry came under fire. One of Milton's celebrated euhemeristic descriptions might well have been inspired by the idea that casuistry could be used to justify almost any extremes of iniquity. Writing as casuistry's reputation was beginning to decline, he described Belial ('A fairer person lost not Heav'n ... ') as someone who: 'though his Tongue/ dropped Manna could make the worse appear/ The better reason, to perplex and dash/ Maturest Counsels' (*Paradise Lost*, Bk II, 110–15).[4] Milton, like many early Puritans, probably had a generally supportive attitude towards casuistry. Indeed, according to Slights: 'The casuistical paradigm pervades almost everything Milton wrote' (1981, p. 247). Nevertheless, Milton's description of Belial's vice represents the cautious approach to casuistry's 'extremes', even from the generally sympathetic by this time. To those who were hostile, this making the worse seem better was utterly abhorred, and it was this view that came to predominate after about 1650.[5]

In the next section of this chapter, we outline the doctrinal similarities between the reasoning processes of casuistry and the common law, and also show how and why the former fell out of favour, whilst the latter thrived. In section III, we give a modern, specific example of common law decision-making, and show how closely this might be seen to resemble the general casuistical tradition. In section IV, we examine the doctrinal twists and turns in one of the most important problems casuistry faced, the question of interest; and in section V we illustrate the remarkably similar about-turns and backslidings of the common law around the same issue. Finally, in section VI we set out a central position of this book, that the casuistical 'basis' of the common law, and the traditions that lie within both forms of reasoning, allows for the possibility of recreating a form of ethical decision-making, and a radical rewriting of our notions of justice. Casuistry, because of its insistence on the individuality of each case, is forced to respect the other of its own pronouncements; as such it provides another way

---

[4] Since at least Plato, this charge was the standard accusation against the rhetoricians by the philosophers; see Kennedy (1963, pp. 25, 31, 45, 140 and passim).

[5] It might be added that it is claimed the fall from grace was probably based more on schisms in the Christian Church than on any fundamental defect in casuistry's method of argumentation; see section II below.

of seeing that the process of judgment does not have to purport to apply blank principles no matter what the cost.

II

To begin with the law: as a system of principles, it drew on three major inter-related sources for its authoritative statements – common law, equity and statute. Although in the twentieth century it is generally assumed that statute is the major source of law, this was not always the case. Statutes were regarded merely as specific examples of state interference in the system of principles as the judges knew them. So far as the early common law was concerned, 'statutes were inferior laws – mere petty regulations rather than grand principles' (Rose 1975, p. 67; and see also Baker 1979, pp. 169–70). These grand principles derived mainly from custom and the memory of previous decisions. They have had their status and authority worked out in a complex process involving much detailed discussion of rather fine, technical and often arcane distinctions: which court, which judge, what was the status of the judge and the court in question? What was the respect in which later ages held him or it? Were there dissenting opinions, and if so by whom? All these questions, the stuff of the self-claimed status of the legal profession as a 'learned' one, were, and still are, a vital element in decision-making. That out of this darkness come principles was never doubted, and it was principles that had to be applied before any dispute that came before the courts could be resolved. The problem generally for common law decision-making was not so much in determining which principles were relevant, but how to rank the various principles that might be deemed applicable in any particular dispute.

Linked to this, indeed the very basis on which the common law stands, is the institutional operation of the case law system itself, the second aspect of the development of the principles of the common law. The common law has traditionally worked its adjudicative processes by comparing facts and circumstances of previous cases and then applying refined judgments drawn from these to the details of the particular facts and circumstances of the instant case. So far as the bulk of civil law is concerned, within the common law system, cases are decided by a complex analysis of the previous decisions that point to a principled solution (or a range of principled solutions) alongside an exacting inquiry into the facts of the particular case. Therefore, the case method is a rigid application of principles to the specific facts. The (eternal) principles of the common law, as expounded in previous cases, are focused on the particular circumstances of any actual dispute, and the precise reasoning of the judges, balancing the principles against the facts, is guaranteed to produce a (correct) result. And if there is no exact previous comparison to guide the judges, then a wise application of analogical reasoning (there is always an analogy in some previous decision, no matter how unusual the facts of the instant case) will solve the problem the court faces. Although the legal 'memory' of previous decisions formed the root of this source of principles even before court proceedings began their haphazard reported history (see Goodrich 1990), it was the writing of the decisions that allowed all lawyers to delve into the sources in a way that enabled previous decisions to become of such importance.

The third source, especially in the jurisdiction of the court of equity, was conscience. Conscience did not mean, and in its modern application does not mean, simply the way the individual justifies his or her behaviour. Conscience is only a valid argument within equity's traditions if the specific conscience before the court fits the tradition's understanding of what 'conscience' means. For the equity courts, conscience is not just a knowledge of wrongdoing: it is a circular matter. As the Court of Appeal once put it: for a claim of conscience to be pleaded successfully, 'it must be shown to have an ancestry founded in history and in the practice and precedent of the courts administering equity jurisdiction' (Re Diplock[6]). Conscience is both principle and individual mental comprehension of the possibility of right action.

Casuistry is the largely forgotten and much derided history which this tripartite intellectual endeavour reflects. Like the common law, casuistry involves a detailed investigation of the facts of any particular situation. In the words of casuistry's modern defenders,

the method of casuistry involved an ordering of cases by paradigm and analogy, appeals to maxims and analysis of circumstances, the qualification of opinions,

---

[6] [1948] Ch. 465.

the accumulation of multiple arguments, and the statement of practical
resolutions of particular moral problems in the light of all these considerations.
(Jonsen and Toulmin 1988, p. 256)

Casuistry is based on general maxims, but these are not 'universal
or invariable, since they hold good with certainty only in the
typical conditions of the agent and the circumstances of action'
(ibid., p. 257). Like the common law, which is full of 'maxims',
especially in its equity branch, casuistry formulated maxims and
carefully applied them to individual situations. Principles were
made to fit the facts.

For the casuists too, principles were derived from three sources:
first, principles came from God. The source of knowledge of these
could be discovered from both revelation and reason, which was
God's way of allowing human beings to partake in divine wisdom.
The obvious starting place, especially for Puritan casuistry, was
the Bible (Bellhouse 1988, p. 66). On this aspect of the casuists'
main source there were few, at the time of casuistry's rise, who
would argue with the declared forms of casuistical authority. But it
was the second aspect at the root of the casuists' wisdom that
caused the most problems: the casuists relied on the opinions of
the learned who had, in the past, written about moral problems
broadly conceived, and whose opinions, like those of the judges of
the superior courts of the common law, had come to be recognised
as authoritative. Since at least the eleventh century (Ullman 1962,
pp. 360–1), the Catholic Church had been wedded to the
importance of 'authority', and the casuists grasped this notion in a
big way. Bishops, priests, doctors, saints, recluses, learned men of
religion of all sorts had written, some of them in exhaustive
quantities, on the detailed results that the confessors and advisers
should reach in coming to conclusions in particular cases.
Although mostly couched in terms of hypotheticals, the discus-
sions were usually based on actual cases that had occurred, in
many instances, many times over. The endless works of casuistry
were intended as a sort of handbook for those involved in day-to-
day 'adjudication' over matters religious and moral (if indeed such
a distinction was a valid one in societas christiana).

Finally, the casuists used 'conscience' as a source for the
determination of particular disputes. Conscience, like equity's
conception of the term, was not merely what the individual
thought on any occasion. 'Conscience' was a complex interweav-

ing of universally valid rules with the individual understanding and application of those rules. Casuistry's attitude to conscience has been described as somewhat paradoxical, in that it presented 'cases of conscience simultaneously as demonstrations of the principle that each human action is unique and as models of decision-making process to be imitated by all men with similar cases of conscience' (Slights 1981, p. 297). Although conscience depended on individual circumstances, it, too, was ultimately determined by those steeped in the tradition, based on their knowledge of the wisdom of past practices.

The reports of legal decisions, which began to be extensively (though never, even now, systematically) compiled from about the fifteenth century, show English law as closely resembling this tradition. Both casuistry and the common law treated the specific facts of any case with great respect; each claimed its decisions were based on principles; each was directly concerned with adjudications over 'consciences', though by the end of the Middle Ages the scope of each jurisdiction's conscience applications had been separated; and finally, each used the method of 'analogy' to deal with troublesome cases for which there was no direct 'precedent'.[7]

The growth of statutory interventions notwithstanding, the common law blossomed, but from about 1650, casuistry as a church art, fell out of favour. It was all too easy to pick out faults in its practice. In some instances, it was not even necessary to invent the charge of 'sophistry': the casuists proclaimed it as a virtue. Priests leaving for England around 1578 were advised by the seminary at Rheims on the following question: 'Howe may the Catholicke convented before heretickes answere without synne sworne or not sworne to the Interrogatores?' The answer was by the use of sophistry: '[w]hen a Catholic is dragged before the heretics he can either refuse to take the oath (which is more prudent) or he can swear sophistically, or he can reply sophistically to their individual questions' (Holmes 1981, p. 52).

In particular, casuistry's opponents charged that casuistry encouraged 'laxity' towards morality and could be used to defend

---

[7] The term 'precedent', certainly so far as the law is concerned, is somewhat anachronistic at this stage, but the comparison still holds.

wrongdoings. Casuistry received a pounding at the hands of its critics because, seemingly, anything, any behaviour, almost no matter how immoral or irreligious, could be justified by the practitioners of the tradition. The best example, the one which probably heaped more scorn on the casuists than anything else, was the notion of 'mental reservation', and the similar doctrine of 'equivocation'. In effect, mental reservation held that it was not lying to make a statement which was known to be untrue, provided the person making the statement mentally, that is, silently, added a further phrase which actually stated the correct position. The idea can probably be traced to Plato, who in *The Symposium* has Socrates say that although he agreed to contribute to the discussion on the praise of Eros, he now regrets his rash consent to do so. He justifies his apparent change of heart by saying that 'it was my tongue that gave the promise, not my mind' (Plato 1951, p. 74). The same idea was expressed by Euripides, who wrote: 'I swore with my tongue, I kept my mind unsworn' (Euripides, 1953, *Hippolytus* 612). The notion was endorsed by Cicero: 'For on the question of keeping faith, you must always think of what you meant, not of what you said' (*De Officiis* I.40).

Whatever its origins, mental reservation filled an important role for the casuists, especially in times of extreme religious persecution. One notorious example of the casuistical practice of mental reservation was of the English Catholic priest who, when asked by the Protestant authorities whether he was a priest, or had ever been overseas, said 'no' to both questions, when in fact the correct answer was 'yes'. But in denying he was a priest, he had mentally added 'of Apollo', and in claiming he had never been across the seas, he had mentally added 'Indian' before 'seas' (Sommerville 1988, p. 160).

Although the doctrine, as in this last example, seems now to be a straight justification for lying, the defenders of casuistry did not take it like that. Leading casuists encouraged mental reservation, sometimes using biblical texts which they claimed were in themselves incomplete without further mental additions (*ibid.*, p. 173). And modern defenders of casuistical practices, such as Sommerville (1988) and Jonsen and Toulmin (1988), do not take the jaundiced attitude of the critics to this strange doctrine. The study by Rose (1975) of the position of Catholics in late Tudor and early Stuart England does illustrate neatly some of the problems that

Catholics faced. What were Catholics living under Elizabeth or James supposed to do in the face of the imposition of a religion of which they strongly disapproved? Flight (especially to America) was becoming a possibility, though it was hardly attractive. If they stayed and openly opposed the authorities, they would, sooner or later, be disposed of; if they stayed and just kept quiet, apart from the fact that for priests in particular this would be pointless, there was the question of conscience: could your conscience justify, in effect, living as a good Protestant? Certainly Catholics living in heretic England in the early 1580s were advised on all sorts of shifts, from running away to bribing guards, escorts or magistrates, in order to escape capture (Holmes 1981, p. 124), all with a good conscience. In other words, mental reservation, when suffering persecution by intolerant religions, might be a good compromise, even though it gave the generally more privileged critics a field day.

Mental reservation did not only have its uses for persecuted priests and recusants. From the lowliest to the highest, casuistry provided a convenient method of saying one thing whilst meaning another, of ensuring, when necessary, that 'legibility and trans-parency of meaning do not coincide' (Gallagher 1991, p. 232, referring to Spenser). This form of reasoning proved especially useful for the monarch herself when she was faced with the delicate problem of the threat posed by her possibly treacherous cousin. In her replies to Parliament on the question of Mary's execution, Elizabeth gave an 'answer answerlesse'. Her two statements 'presented a pattern of unaccountability in language: a word that undid itself, making its meaning the very process of self-erasure' (ibid., p. 56). Casuistry had not only come of age, it had come to power. But this very powerful potential was also partly responsible for the critical onslaught. It was all very well for the very embodiment and emblem of authority to indulge in such fancy games, allowing the execution of her most notorious subject, whilst apparently distancing herself from the responsibility for the event; it was quite another matter to permit those supposedly subjected to power's gaze the same licence. A free conscience was very different from a lax one. Some hundred years before the authorities in Rome took action against 'mental reservation', therefore, Parliament tried to prohibit it by requiring those suspected of non-conformism to promise obedience 'without any dissimulation or any colour or means of any dispensation'. The effect of such proscriptions were limited.

[T]he discourse of conscience exposed the potential of such words to undo themselves, to engage interlocutors in what we might call an infinite spiral of language, a process not only of questioning the use and abuse of words but of confronting the underlying network of social and cultural conditions that frame the very questions posed. (ibid., p. 119)

Parliament on this occasion did not succeed in preventing mental reservation; but it had given a warning against its chief usages and against casuistry in general which was taken seriously in the next century.

Another major doctrine of casuistry, 'probabilism', also gave the critics much room for manoeuvre. Probabilism could be traced to the fundamental Aristotelian distinction between knowledge (epistēmē) and practical wisdom (phronēsis). In scientific matters, it was thought perfectly possible to have exact knowledge; in matters of human wisdom (morals, sexuality, possibly even the organisation of society), things were only likely, and statements could only be 'opinions'. 'Probable certitude was opinion, an assent to one proposition, coupled with the acknowledgement that its opposite might be true' (Jonsen and Toulmin 1988, p. 165). Once this is accepted, then probabilism recognises that in many situations of moral difficulty there might be reasonable doubt as to the correct thing to do. The casuists took the next step of saying that if there were these reasonable doubts, so that two or more forms of not necessarily compatible action seemed possible (generally to be evidenced by the fact that learned or scholastic opinions could be found giving contradictory recommendations), it was acceptable to follow any, either or sometimes just one learned recommendation. As one commentator put it: 'the authority of a single doctor, if he is wise and prudent, renders probable any opinion he maintains' (Sanchez, quoted in ibid., p. 168). Although some casuists, such as John Donne (Shami 1983, p. 58), argued against the acceptability of moral postures based on one authority or one instance, their opponents could argue that the casuists did use (and therefore abuse) the 'one authority' argument.

Both mental reservation and probabilism were attacked mercilessly. Even the Pope could no longer accept such evasions as mental reservation seemed to permit, and the doctrine was officially condemned in 1679. It was also 'unofficially' condemned by Pascal in the 1650s; whether or not individuals might be justified in resorting to mental reservations in times of peril, or perhaps to prevent further unjustifiable harms being done to others (lying to protect priests hiding in 'safe houses' for example), it was too easy for the opposition. Mental reservation was merely the most gross of the examples; no respectable religion, based on biblical teaching, could succeed in a proper defence of aspects of the practice which, in the end, simply permitted lying. So far as probabilism was concerned, this too was subject to easy attack. The casuists, the critics claimed, could never put a foot wrong – if the argument you want is not supported by one authority, simply search through the tradition until you find one which does support it. Two authorities, advising Catholics under the general heading of 'The Resolution of Cases of the English Nation' in around 1582, admitted that there may even be cases when God was a little double-tongued, when 'two divine precepts have a bearing on a particular case and it is necessary to violate one of them'. Their solution was this: 'In such circumstances the more important precept prevails and the other gives way to it, so that, by the observance of the more important precept, the transgression of the less important is made lawful' (Holmes 1981, p. 61). The casuists seemed to cover every possibility. No wonder some critics, more aware of their own fallibility, as well as the supposed infallibility of their religious leader, felt threatened.

Many of the arguments used by the critics were distinctly unfair and exaggerated. Indeed, Pascal's attack on casuistry only suc- ceeded in exposing one corrupting aspect: extreme laxism (Jonsen and Toulmin 1988, p. 246). Whether or not the casuists were guilty of such a fault (and their defenders continue to deny it, e.g. Sommerville 1988), the modern-day casuists argue that the strength of the fundamental reasoning process of the tradition could not be denied. '[Casuistry] was a simple practical exercise directed at attempting a satisfactory resolution of particular moral problems. ... [it] had never been intended as a susbtitute for ethical theory or moral theology' (Jonsen and Toulmin 1988, p. 242). In summary, the critics 'could not destroy the plausibility of "case analysis" as an approach to the resolution of moral problems' (ibid., p. 249).

But whether or not the criticism of casuistry was as 'fair' as it seemed to the critics, there was another development which signalled the end of the casuistical tradition as it had blossomed in early modern Europe. This was the rise of the 'individual' and the need for individual decision-making in cases of moral and legal doubt. The application of universal absolutes to particular difficult choices only by those specifically (and in some cases, perhaps dubiously) qualified to do so fell out of favour, as the emphasis shifted towards the individual and his or her own moral responsibility. In a post-Copernican world, a world retreating from faith into uncertainty, in 'an age of scepticism' (Docherty 1986, p. 47), the individual began to assume greater importance. If individualism was to be effective, it meant that individual decisions on matters of conscience could not just be resolved by an appeal to authority.

As we have indicated, the Aristotelian distinction between science and practical reasoning formed part of the founding wisdom of the casuistical tradition. For Aristotle (1976, p. 207), scientific knowledge was immutable. 'Scientific knowledge consists in forming judgements about things that are universal and necessary' (ibid., p. 210). It was therefore pointless to deliberate, as distinct from trying to learn more about it. But knowledge and reasoning on practical matters were on a different plane. Phronēsis, the exercise of informed and intelligent common sense, operates in 'the sphere of the variable' (ibid., p. 208). It cannot be scientific, because the things with which it is concerned are not the way they are necessarily; like money, they are the result of human arrangement. Phronēsis concerns 'judgements about what is to be done ... prudence is concerned with human goods, i.e. things about which deliberation is possible' (ibid., 213). It was the function of wisdom (sophia) to reason about things, such as morals and the good government of city states, and that reason would be based on 'knowledge of particular facts, which became known from experience'. Not an activity, therefore, for the young, whatever their ability in the (natural) sciences (ibid., p. 215).

For casuistry, then, the natural sciences could be left to look after themselves, as they were, in effect, in the Aristotelian scheme of things, dealing with eternal truths. Matters of conscience, morals, and the political organisation of society generally, demanded careful judgments, based on the wisdom of study, experience and a knowledge of how to handle principles in circumstances where rules might not necessarily apply universally and unproblematically. After all, for Aristotle it would often be necessary to rectify law itself, 'so far as law is defective on account of its generality' (*ibid.*, p. 200). Regarding matters of morality, that is how to behave in public and private, Cicero's cautious reasoning seemed to make sense: 'where other men say that some things are certain and others uncertain, we disagree with them and say rather some things are persuasive and others not' (*De Officiis*, ii.7). In summary, casuistry claimed the ability to perform well this delicate act of balance and rectification so as to take account of all three principles, the mere persuasiveness of moral reasoning and the details of the particular case.

But the distinction between science and almost everything else became suspect. The province of exact reasoning spread, and, for a time, was unbounded. Casuistry became 'obsolete because of the existence of a new connection between reason and moral feeling' (Kittsteiner 1988, p. 190). The philosophical developments this position represented culminated in the individualism of Kant; the casuistical notion of probabilistic reasoning no longer seemed applicable. Morality, too, became a question of science, or something akin to it, and the mere following of an opinion, however unlikely, simply because it was, as it were, there, because one learned doctor of the tradition said it might be all right in some circumstances, seemed a relic of a bygone age. The enlightened, scientific, individualistic, moralistic reasoning of Kant could find no place for such primitive reliance on the unlikely opinions of others. A new conviction stalked Enlightenment thinkers: 'a chief property of a truly moral will was its rationality and the belief that no one, however proper his intentions, could claim rationality for his will, if he was governed by external authority' (Leites 1988, p. 120). History itself became progressive and thus amenable to scientific analysis, and this, combined with increasing reliance on the individual's own responsibility, signalled a hard time ahead for casuistry in the field where it had successfully operated.

Traditional casuistry suffered, but the common law carried on the same sort of reasoning, blithely confident of its own universal *phronēsis*, Kant and other German doctors notwithstanding. The doctrine of mental reservation may have no evident counterpart in the literature of the common law, but the fundamental distinction, in the criminal law, between guilty intents and guilty acts is not totally dissimilar. Even today, when statute has intervened so extensively in the development of the criminal law, in most cases for defendants to be convicted of a crime they must have a 'guilty mind', an intention to do wrong. To take an extreme example, if a defendant can show that although she shot someone, she genuinely thought she was playing with 'a plastic replica or a water pistol'[8] and not a real gun, no crime is committed. Mental reservation is almost the counterpart of the guilty mind requirement. The parallel here may be far-fetched; there is a closer analogy between probabilism and the common law's use of authority. The casuists looked for written, respected, definitive, institutionally backed opinions from the past to judge current conduct; so do the common law judges. And whilst the common law does not specifically admit to the possibility of following any learned opinion of the tradition, in practice, in cases of dispute, it often does so.[9]

But above all, the common law has never rejected the working procedures of casuistry. As we have mentioned, in their writings the casuists had followed the best of 'heathen' authorities. Aristotle had expounded carefully what the different virtues were, and that each had to be understood and applied around a notion of a mean. But, Aristotle had continued, such exposition of principles was insufficient: 'a generalisation of this kind is not enough; we must apply it to particular cases' (1976, p. 103). The casuists took this injunction seriously, and set about detailing how principles should be applied in the vast area faced by Christian

---

[8] The example is taken from one of the judgments in the Court of Appeal in R v. *Secretary of State for the Home Department, ex parte Sivakumaran* and conjoined appeals, [1987] 3 WLR 1053; the case is discussed in detail in Chapter 6.

[9] Our discussion of the shift in the common law's attitude to usury in section v of this chapter may be seen as one of many examples. Our presentation does not specifically focus on this aspect, but some of the cases discussed do involve the acceptance of 'single' or 'minority' or dissenting opinions as against those of the majority; a form of probabalism in action. One famous twentieth-century example is the acceptance by the House of Lords in *Hedley Byrne* v. *Heller* [1964] AC 465 of Denning LJ's minority opinion in *Candler* v. *Crane Christmas* [1951] 2 KB 164.

consciences. The doctors of the Jesuistical-casuistical tradition required the confessors and advisers, the dealers in heavenly approvals and damnable disapprovals, to determine the cases of conscience with which they were presented with a fine attention to the infinite detail of the myriad circumstances which flesh is heir to. And, notwithstanding their opponents and detractors, although they were concerned with principles (just as much as their common law counterparts), they had the wisdom to appreciate that all the principles in the world did not solve any specific problems. They would act as a guide to the conduct of the judge, they would always be relevant, but the final decision depended on the precise circumstances of the individual matter facing the arbitrator and trader in absolutions.

Likewise the common law: the case method which has typified the common law has always been a matter of determining the precise relationship between the general principles to be derived from common law, custom and statute, and the specific facts involved in any particular dispute. Past decisions are both sources of general principle, precedents for future cases, and careful, often lengthy examination of the witnesses, the documents and all 'relevant' surrounding circumstances.

III

Almost any area of the civil side of the common law jurisdiction could be used as an example of this meticulous attention to detail, combined with an acknowledgement of the overarching role of principle. In this section, we outline one current area of importance in English law to show the quasi-casuistical nature of common law adjudication. The area we have chosen is one faced by the House of Lords in the 1980s and which has continued to trouble it in the 1990s: the problem of whether contractual arrangements concerning the occupation of living accommodation created a tenancy (or lease) or a mere licence. Until January 1989 this seemingly trivial, almost purely verbal, quibble could determine whether someone had the right to remain in rented accommodation under the various security of tenure Acts then in force, or whether the property owner (the landlord) could require the court to grant an eviction order once the contractual term of the agreement had expired.[10]

In summary, the common law had always drawn a distinction between leases and licences. The former gave an 'interest in land', whereas the latter did not. The distinction would be fairly meaningless for most tenants were it not for the fact that the social legislation designed to protect tenants, since the First World War, had made it crucial. Until the Conservative government from 1979 started to cut away at it, the major principle in the area of private rented accommodation in the various Rent Acts had been that if someone was a tenant, that is, held the premises under a lease, he or she could not be removed when the contractual term came to an end without the court agreeing that certain fairly limited circumstances applied. In most cases of arrangements between private landlords and tenants, when the contractual period of the tenancy (usually as little as a week or a month) expired, the tenant could remain in possession of the premises under one of the Acts (as a statutory tenant) protected from eviction or excessive rent increases. But the legislation used the old common law distinction: in order for people to obtain the benefits of this social legislation, they had to be tenants or lessees as the common law had defined them, not mere licensees. The common law had used various tests to make this somewhat elusive distinction, but one that had been most resorted to was that of 'exclusive possession'. If the tenant had this metaphysical entity (largely based on whether he or she could or could not exclude the landlord or his or her assistants from the premises during the course of the agreement), the court determined there was a relationship that went beyond mere contractual terms, a relationship concerning land. The occupier was then a tenant. As we have suggested, the distinction might have been of no significance were it not for the fact that according to the judges' interpretation of the law, only tenants could obtain the security of the Rent Acts.

Because of this legislation, landlords and their legal advisers

---

[10] One of the curiosities about the mass of cases that have reached the House of Lords is that the distinctions which they have elaborated so carefully have more or less been swept away by the latest legislation (especially the Housing Act 1988), and that the Lords busied itself with the most careful and fine distinctions at a time when Parliament was deciding to tilt more towards landlords the balance that had been held under housing legislation for so long in favour of tenants.

devised all sorts of schemes (sometimes called 'shams' by the courts) to try to avoid the consequences of the characterisation of their agreements as 'tenancies'. They would include terms under which the occupiers were not entitled to exclusive occupation, the landlords being allowed to enter the premises at any time of the day or night, or entitled to introduce additional occupiers to share the premises with the original contracting parties.[11] Other dodges were used such as forcing the tenant to turn him- or herself into a limited company (the security of tenancy protection only applied to individuals), granting separate agreements to two people who were taking premises together to make it look as though there were separate occupancies with neither having the necessary exclusive occupation, and many others which need not detain us here.

After many false starts by several senior courts, in 1985 the House of Lords, in *Street* v. *Mountford*,[12] finally determined that the courts would not be satisfied with the apparent or formal terms made in the documentation by the parties; what they really wanted to know was what was the *substance* of the arrangements. If in substance the parties (in practical terms, the landlord) merely inserted the clauses denying exclusive occupation in order to defeat the tenant's rights under the protective legislation, the courts were to set aside those clauses and declare that the occupier was actually a tenant and entitled to protection. In a lovely example of judicial, no nonsense, straight talking in *Street*, Lord Templeman said: 'The manufacture of a five-pronged implement for manual digging results in a fork even if the manufacturer, unfamiliar with the English language, insists that he intended to make and has made a spade.'

The point for our present purposes is that the courts were urged to dig out the precise details of the cases. The House of Lords had declared a spade a spade,[13] and the lower courts were then instructed to excavate until they came to the foundations, the real factual substance. A recipe for the law's delays perhaps, but also an injunction that would appeal to the casuistical tradition. The

---

[11] This was often tried in agreements relating to the letting of one room to two people; or where the landlord was (notionally) entitled to possession of the premises for ninety minutes each day, see *Aslam* v. *Murphy* [1989] 3 All ER 130.

[12] [1985] AC 809.

[13] An analogy whose origins, according to Cicero, can be traced to the Stoic Zeno (*Fam.* IX.22).

'factual matrix', as one of the judges put it,[14] became crucial. In numerous cases since *Street*, the courts have been concerned to ensure that every specific factual detail is available before County Courts make decisions.

In *Westminster City Council* v. *Clarke*,[15] the House of Lords was asked to determine whether hostel accommodation provided by the local authority under its statutory duty to house the homeless in general and specifically the especially vulnerable could be deemed a tenancy; that is, whether the rooms let in any particular hostel were exclusive to the use of any particular occupant, or whether in the circumstances where the local authority had to keep control over the rooms for the sake of the mentally or physically disabled occupants, no particular occupant could become a tenant. That the Court of Appeal decided in favour of the former construction and the House of Lords the latter is not particularly important for our purposes. What is significant is the quasi-casuistical injunction from Lord Templeman: 'This is a very special case which depends on the peculiar nature of the hostel maintained by the council, the use of the hostel by the council, the totality, immediacy and objectives of the powers exercisable by the council and the restrictions imposed on Mr Clarke' (p. 703). The 'circumstances' which here made Lord Templeman conclude that 'Mr Clarke has never enjoyed that exclusive possession' necessary for his claim to be entitled to stay in the premises, at least for a time, against the wishes of the local authority, would not necessarily apply in the next case.

Totalities, immediacies, peculiar natures, special cases; this is a description of the practices, almost the very language, of the casuistical tradition. Judgment, the application of the law, demands sensitive attention to the details. Aristotle would have expected no less. Judgment requires not science (the mechanical application of principles) but the knowledge of principles combined with *phronēsis* 'law, being the pronouncement of a kind of practical wisdom or intelligence' (Aristotle 1976, p. 338). The common law is sticking to casuistry's origins. Indeed, it has been suggested that during the period of the start of the decline of

---

[14] *Hadjiloucas* v. *Crean* [1987] 3 All ER 1008.
[15] [1992] 1 All ER 693.

casuistry (in England, around the time of the Interregnum) the lawyers were at one with the casuists: 'In effect, Hale and Davies, along with many other defenders of the common law . . . had claimed that the common lawyers were the casuists of English society, treating of justice in its application to particular cases' (Sampson 1988, p. 80). Somehow general principles have to be made relevant to the impossibly endless facts of any particular instance. When trying a conscience, there was no artificial limit to the potentially relevant circumstances. But whereas sixteenth- and seventeenth-century casuists could write at length with, seemingly, infinite time and patience at their disposal, the law is a process that requires immediate and rushed results. The demands on courts to speed their procedures, to give instant judgments, and to deal with matters expeditiously (and hence cheaply) has been one of the rallying cries of senior lawyers over the last ten years and more. Here, the common lawyers have taken another aspect of Aristotle's teaching even more seriously than the casuists. Lengthy deliberations are all very well, but: 'if one is to deliberate in every case, the process will go on to infinity' (Aristotle 1976, p. 120). Most recent reforms of court procedures stem from this fear of 'infinity' and the recognition of the need to dispose of an increasing case-load as swiftly, simply and cheaply as possible. Hence the need for general principles which the lower courts, minor officials and practising lawyers can simply 'apply'. But against this, as the casuists patiently would have explained, is life's infinite variety, the fact that every court adjudication is, in effect, 'a very special case'. Lord Templeman, in recognising that justice can only be done by taking account of the peculiarities of each case, reaffirms the common law's traditional method of working, the requirement of meticulous attention to detail. Maybe the courts' rather confusing attitude to rented accommodation is simply an example of poor quality reasoning (or bad casuistry) which would make Pascal writhe, but this is the way the common law works. Many other areas of significance that have taxed the courts in recent years might be used to illustrate the point.[16] But the case method, the determination to take account of all 'relevant'

---

[16] The boundaries of the law of tort, that is, who is to be responsible for losses in unplanned circumstances of accidents and the like, is another good recent example.

circumstances in relation to the 'relevant' principles, the hallmark of the English legal system, is not just the child of the common law.

IV

One of the best-known problems the casuists faced was the question of 'interest', or usury as it is more pejoratively known. Aristotle had written of a class who 'go to excess in receiving by taking anything from anybody . . . moneylenders who make small loans at high rates of interest; [they] receive more than is right and from the right source' (1976, p. 148). For the traditional republicans of Roman society (though, curiously, not apparently for Brutus himself) lending money at interest was despicable. Cicero compared it with the activity of fishmongers, butchers, cooks, poulters, fishermen and those who collected harbour dues. He said that Cato, when asked as to the respectability of the activity, replied contemptuously: 'What about killing someone?' (*De Officiis* I.150 and II.89).[17] Medieval Christianity started with the same basic presuppositions: 'That usury is a sin was and is a dogma of the Catholic Church' (Noonan 1957, pp. 2–3). The casuistic development of theological principles from this original position, demanding an entire ban on any lending or borrowing 'upon advantage', to its more refined (as we have seen, 'sophistical' in the view of its opponents) tolerance, gave casuistry's critics one of the simplest targets effectively to lampoon and degrade it. It was almost too easy to suggest that the transformation of the absolute ban on any 'doit of interest' to a smoothed out series of circumstances in which the taking of interest (or its equivalent) would be acceptable to the absolved conscience was a complete degrading of any moral principles. For Pascal, no honest reasoning could result in such abominable shifts in direction. Yet, according to Jonsen and Toulmin, the transformation of the casuists' position

---

[17] Not that such sneering prevented Cicero borrowing heavily for his own needs (Cicero, *Letters to Friends* v.vi.2) just as similar superior sentiments did not prevent English landowners borrowing heavily from moneylenders when it suited their turn, as section v of this chapter illustrates. Not so much 'Neither a borrower nor a lender be', more 'Borrow what you can and treat the lender contemptuously.'

on this question 'reveals not an evasion of morality but its progressive refinement, marking more precisely the grounds and limits of judgment about economic life' (1988, p. 194).

The case of usury, and casuistry's adaptation of religious prescriptions, is paralleled in the common law's attitude to loans at interest. Like the medieval Church, though considerably later, the law was faced with the fact that not only was lending at interest widespread, despite statutory and common law prohibitions, but also the moral-legal opprobrium attaching to it had evaporated. Our argument is that the economic circumstances forcing change in the casuists' position and the reasoning built upon these circumstances were similarly used in the process of the legal shift, as the law abandoned controls over interest rates,[18] though, it goes without saying, the legal arguments never seemed to have acknowledged that their process of tortured reasonings have a striking resemblance to those of the casuists.

To begin with, the casuists argue that the Church's absolute ban on the receipt of any interest (not just excessive amounts) related directly to the economic situation of mainly agricultural communities. 'The usury prohibition made its appearance in an era when the economy of Europe was largely composed of subsistence farming' (ibid., p. 185).[19] Before the development of full-scale commercialism, any taking of interest almost always involved a direct relationship with one's neighbour in which the latter would be exploited. This was for the simple self-evident fact (self-evident, that is, to the makers of religous morality – a self-evidence echoed centuries later, as we shall see, by the common lawyers) that the person who was taking the loan was only doing so because of distressed circumstances. In times of plenty, loans would be

[18] This 'abandonment' was never as complete as the abolition of the usury laws might indicate. In particular, since the repeal of usury laws Parliament has passed Bills of Exchange Acts, Moneylenders Acts, Banking Acts, Building Society Acts, etc. and the Consumer Credit Act 1974 with its strict controls on interest rates and allied matters.

[19] Whilst interest prohibitions were also found in early societies which were not apparently as dominated by agriculture as medieval Europe, so far as the development of the Catholic prohibition on usury is concerned, it was the increasing contrast between agriculturally based economies and the newer forms of mercantile activity that put the matter of interest into sharper focus. This made urgent the resolution of the question of whether it could be deemed lawful.

unnecessary; in times of dearth, loans might be the only way to avoid starvation. '[T]he paradigm for the moral analysis of usury appears to have been aid in times of distress' (ibid., p. 183). In the words of one medieval scholastic authority: 'One ought to lend to one's needy neighbour only for God and principally from charity' (St Raymond, cited in Noonan 1957, p. 33, and see also p. 100). Insofar as those Christians in the early medieval period, such as the large banking communities of northern Italy, who were in moneylending, were able to reconcile their moneylending gains with their religious conciences, they might have done so partly on the basis that, as bankers, their interest dealings were only with the rich, and not the poor (ibid., p. 192).

Even in the exceptional cases, where the scholastics had allowed some receipt of interest payments (for example, where the debtor delayed on repayment, causing loss to the lender), any interest was only licit if the original loan had been granted out of charity. In principle, loans threatened the stability of an agricultural, mainly peasant community. 'Usury was first condemned in situations in which, in a subsistence economy, neighbours took advantage of the misfortunes of the afflicted (notably, poor farmers and peasants) by charging interest on their loans and dispossessing them for nonpayment' (Jonsen and Toulmin 1988, p. 309). On this reasoning, it followed that any taking of interest, any receipt, whether in money or goods, of anything more than the principal lent would involve an immoral gain; it would be the equivalent in moral turpitude of theft, since it would be at the expense of the needy and distressed. An absolute ban on usury therefore seemed easy. Sufficient biblical texts, especially Luke 6.35 and the injunction 'lend freely, hoping nothing thereby', were available to enable the proscription to fit the Christian religion's most esteemed mode of reasoning – the clear word of God linked to irrefutable moral arguments.

But in order to cope with the demands of the time, more specific intellectual distinctions were developed. As the early Renaissance Italian cities commercialised, it became necessary to develop some theoretical defence of the taking of interest. This was especially the case as the Italian city states themselves were large-scale borrowers and payers of interest. As Noonan put it: 'The chief cause leading to the new general attitude [ie a more relaxed view as to taking interest] is the need to justify the financial practices of the Italian city states' (1957, p. 121). By the use of two major arguments, namely that the Italian states forced their citizens to lend them money, and that they only paid a relatively low rate of interest, some apologists for the new attitude to interest-taking opened a chink in the armour of the absolute opponents of usury (*ibid.*, pp. 122–4).

Another development dangerous to the Church's absolute ban was the concept of the 'shared risk' in business. The person who entered into what we would call a partnership was not simply taking advantage of the hard times of a 'brother'; the 'trader' would be sharing a risk and, quite possibly, joining in the work involved. And in these circumstances, the 'partner' would probably not receive any advantage until the joint venture terminated successfully, further justifying the claim that what was received was based on merit rather than exploitation. A *societas* was therefore not usurious.

Roman law had distinguished commercial joint ventures from pure loans and, as early as the eleventh century (*ibid.*, p. 135) Church writers were discussing similar distinctions. With some difficulty, religious authorities struggled towards recognising commercial enterprises as non-usurious, and therefore licit, though for a time the conflicting opinions and false starts appeared, even to the sympathetic, as intellectual 'chaos' (*ibid.*, p. 143). But this simple recognition of commercial trading allowed for much more. As financial activity developed and became important, so it was the case that more opportunities were available for 'investment'. But someone who provided 'capital' for one venture, of necessity, would not have it available for use elsewhere, in other investments or for consumption. The 'lender' would therefore inevitably suffer losses in any transaction, and ought to be entitled to compensation in consequence. A similar way of putting it was to say that when payments were made for lending money this was not interest but compensation to the lender for the time during which no use of the funds could be made. Payments then could be justified if, for example, they were intended to cover the period it took for a merchant to travel from one commercial fair or centre to another or the consequent time taken to change credit documents such as bills of exchange into specie. The common law may, as we have hinted, purport to exist outside of time; for merchants, such attempts to play God were too expensive. The more commercially than religiously acute consciences needed to be accommodated.

In a word, as the economic conditions were transformed, so the tradition on the banning of usury was reworked.

> The scholastics had to take a great risk to admit that interest might be due from the start of a loan. To do this seemed to many of them to abandon the foundation for the usury prohibition, the normal gratuitousness of a loan . . . But the leap was finally taken. (ibid., p. 112)

The casuists, as always, based their 'leap' on 'circumstances'; 'all the circumstances must be carefully specified' (Jonsen and Toulmin 1988, p. 190). Usurers might still be damned, but such a blanket prohibition could not deal with all the facts. Each new case had to be submitted to the casuistical tribunal that examined whether the original reason for the prohibition, the prevention of the taking of advantage of the distressed, was really relevant.

Jonsen and Toulmin inevitably summarise this development as showing the casuists in their best light.

> The casuists did not concoct their novel points merely at the insistence of imperious rulers, avaricious prelates, or greedy bankers: they sought, in the midst of the economic pressures, to bring to light the morally relevant circumstances that would permit meaningful discriminations. [They made] honest efforts to direct the conscience of rulers, prelates and bankers. (ibid., p. 194)

through the use of 'well-reasoned arguments' (ibid., p. 193). In summary, the Church recognised the distinction between usurious loans (that is, loans where unfair advantages were taken) and non-usurious loans (where no such vitiating circumstances operated) (ibid., p. 310). In modern terms, the distinction, especially in law, is often put as that between reasonable and excessive rates of interest.

The 'defence' of the Christian conscience, the development of the interest 'paradigm' as Jonsen and Toulmin repeatedly call it, can be left to defend itself. Our only comment at this stage is to say that to deny the pressures of imperious rulers, avaricious prelates and greedy bankers on moral/religious principles (because their pressures would be illegitimate reasons for change), but to accept that economic pressures can alter moral/religious principles, in summary the Jonsen and Toulmin argument, is really pushing the social irresponsibility of individual agents (at bottom, of all things, a Marxist argument) to extremes. And why economic pressures that cause a struggling poor peasant to borrow from a rich neighbour are unacceptable, but the thousand and one economic pressures that modernity brought are acceptable (with suitable deference to specific circumstances, of course) may need more than their mere statement to convince.[20] After all, as early as the thirteenth century, Pope Innocent IV had recognised that the prohibition on usury was as much related to economic conditions as it was to high-flown notions of justice (Noonan 1957, pp. 48–9), even though in the following century St Bernard made no such concessions (ibid., p. 71). That is, the Church itself had always built an economic aspect into its teaching on this subject. The claim that the change was based on principle looks thin. But our purpose is not to pursue this argument. Instead, very swiftly, we propose to demonstrate how the English common law, centuries later, brought about a similar shift in its attitude to usury, using reasoning remarkably similar to that of the casuists.

V

English law traditionally had a slightly ambiguous attitude to interest on money. In this, it was not that dissimilar from the scholastic tradition upon which most of casuistry's teaching was based, though the defenders of religious doctrines on the subject would no doubt have preferred their somewhat shifty attitudes to be described as 'subtle', or 'nuanced' or 'complex'. Be that as it may, medieval English law had disapproved of interest-taking, but allowed aliens (notably Jews until they were expelled) to charge for loans. Interest-taking as a whole was frowned upon, whilst, at the same time, limits were laid down by Parliament as to the amount of interest that could be charged. But, like the Church rules, successful, wholesale prohibition of interest-taking was clearly out. Just as the medieval Church relied on borrowing, so did the medieval upper sectors of English society, including the Crown. Before the Civil War, the courts were struggling with an

---

[20] This is especially the case in the 1990s when thousands of people are suffering precisely because of their inability to meet repayments on loans from, notably amongst others, 'greedy bankers'.

apparently insatiable demand for the recognition of the legality of
loans at interest, whilst proclaiming a conscience based on a
religion that seemed to demand usury's proscription. A court in
1622 recognised that religion, and indeed even heathens like
Aristotle, disapproved of usury. 'Griping' or 'biting' usury was
condemned, but in other than such extreme cases, the court said,
even the divines were unsure. And apart from this, there was the
question of trade: 'q serra grand impediment al trafficke &
commerce, si ceo de Usury . . . Aliter le Judges ne poent determin,
q chescun usury est illoyal' (in *Sanderson* v. *Warner*[21]). To put it
simply, usury was everywhere. As one writer lamented in 1572: 'I
do not knowe any place in Christiendome so much subiet to thys
foule synne of usurie as the whole realme of England ys at this
present, and hath bene of late yeares' (Wilson 1925, p. 178). The
court in *Sanderson* were only recognising what was going on
around them.

  After the Restoration, statute put interest-taking on a regulated
basis, perhaps because, curiously, the class that most needed to
borrow were the landed aristocracy and gentry; though it did not
yet become respectable. By the eighteenth century, loans, secured
by the venerable English institution of the mortgage, were as
common amongst landowners as pawnbroking became amongst
the poorer sections of society in the following century. Nevertheless, both Parliament and the courts hesitated to abolish fully
controls on usury. There was the lingering religious suspicion that
money was different from goods. Money was there as a substitute
for use, and the notion that it could itself be used for profit seemed,
just as it had seemed to Aristotle, the casuists and scholastics,
somehow to be a form of double counting, and therefore wrong.
Since Aristotle, money had been regarded as sterile. How,
therefore, could it 'earn' anything? Indeed, even Adam Smith had
great doubts about any total abolition of usury controls. It was all
very well to argue that the restrictions on the lending of money
was a violation of 'natural liberty', but some restrictions on natural
liberty, for example, fire regulations, were always necessary
(Smith 1976, p. 24).

---

[21] (1622) 2 Rolle Rep 239. 'It would be a great hindrance to trade and commerce if
usury were prohibited. So the judges were not able to say that every act of usury is
illegal.'

[T]hose exertions of the natural liberty of a few individuals, which might endanger the security of the whole society, are, and ought to be, restrained by the laws of all governments; of the most free, as well as of the most despotical.

On the whole, Smith favoured retaining a maximum legal rate of interest of around 5 per cent, a rate which he considered 'perhaps, as proper as any' (ibid., p. 357).

But Smith's caution was not matched by others. Ricardo thought that interference by states in the rates of interest that could be charged were mainly the results of 'mistaken notions of policy' (1951, p. 296). And he continued by pointing out that even though the maximum legal rate of interest was still the 5 per cent fixed in Queen Anne's reign, even the government had been borrowing at a higher rate (ibid., p. 297). Above all, for Bentham, restrictions on the lending of money made no more sense than any other form of market restrictions. They were all evidence of outdated super-stition and the general incompetence of lawyers and judges to understand what was in the best interests of the community. With his usual supreme confidence, Bentham announced 'at a stroke' a proposition that would demolish all objections to the usury laws:

that no man of ripe years and of sound mind, acting freely and with his eyes wide open, ought to be hindered, with a view to his advantage, from making such bargain, in the way of obtaining money, as he thinks fit: nor, (what is a necessary consequence) any body hindered from supplying him, upon any terms he thinks proper to accede to. (1787, p. 2)

No doubt partly stung into action by the Benthamites, Parliament finally plucked up the courage to abolish the usury laws in 1845. The courts made a more ambivalent meal of it. Traditionally, and no doubt for straight economic reasons which need not detain us, the courts had seen the protection of landed wealth as one of their chief tasks. Landowners may have been sullying the purity of their rent rolls in the grubby world of commerce and industry, but the courts always thought that these moves were out of necessity rather than choice. That is, by a process of reasoning remarkably similar to the casuists, the courts thought that any landowner who borrowed money must have done so out of necessity, and would clearly need court protection from the greedy moneylenders, who stood poised to take over the landowners' estates if the least article of the harsh terms of bonds, deeds and mortgages were not fulfilled to the letter. Like both Blackstone and Adam Smith, the courts assumed that there could be no life more desirable than that of a country gentleman. It was to protect that lifestyle, and the economic privileges that went with it, that, out of the maxims of equity, the Chancery Division developed two of its most remarkable, and, to modern eyes, perhaps strange, doctrines.

The first was the rule that enabled the courts to protect 'expectant heirs'. These people were the poor and deprived eldest sons of rich, often very rich, landowners. They would expect to inherit their father's (occasionally their mother's) estates when, finally, 'the aged patriot groaned and died'. In the meantime, they wanted cash to live according to the standards they expected. If their parents would not or in some cases could not provide the readies, then they turned to moneylenders. The moneylenders (often including big and respectable city institutions and banks, not merely the unscrupulous back-streeters of Victorian fiction) willingly lent the money. But there was a catch – they extracted harsh terms. First, the rates of interest they charged often worked out extraordinarily high, up to 60 per cent in some cases (for example, *Aylesford* v. *Morris* [22]). Second, they took a charge on the 'expectancy'. Because of the flexibility of English landed legal forms, even though these 'expectants' actually owned nothing of substance yet, they could charge or mortgage what they expected, that is, their title to the family estate which they would hope to inherit. In most cases, provided they outlived their parents (usual, but, of course, not guaranteed), and provided no unexpected arrangements or unsuccessful financial dealings by the parents deprived the young hopeful of the inheritance, then they would actually inherit in due course.

When the time came for payment, or even worse, when there was default and the lenders demanded the transfer of the estate itself, the 'unfortunates' rushed to the chancery courts to try to defeat the rapacious money-grabbers. The courts were not slow to respond. In most of the innumerable eighteenth- and especially nineteenth-century cases, the lenders made a strong argument as to why the heirs should be made to stick to the terms of their bonds, a claim based on the changed economic climate, that is, the development of a commercial society (Jonsen and Toulmin's change of paradigm). The first argument was that these loans were

---

[22] (1872) 42 LJ Ch. 146.

inherently risky: the borrowers had no tangible, physical assets to support the loan. Subject to the developing practice of life insurance and some possibly nebulous notion of family honour, if the expectants were to die before they inherited, the lender might get back nothing. Second, these heirs understood what they were doing: they wanted money and knew the terms on which they were getting it. The high rates of interest that were charged were necessary to cover the special risks the lender undertook, the risk of not receiving much or anything back at the termination of the agreement. After all, in a free market for money, no one forced anyone to borrow at high rates; if they could get the money at standard rates of interest, often as low as 2 or 3 per cent, they would have done so. The fact that they regularly took out loans at much higher rates proved that the moneylenders were only asking the market rate and therefore there was no unfairness in the transaction enabling the court to interfere.

The clinching argument, for a Benthamite at least, was that if the courts were to intererefere with the agreements and not allow lenders to enforce them, then the only (market-oriented) result would be that lenders would refuse to lend in these cases, and this would be to the extreme disadvantage of the very class the courts were supposed to be protecting. In a case shortly after the repeal of the usury laws, one counsel for a lender put the new economic orthodoxy quite succinctly:

If the engagements of persons who borrow money, without being able to give any reasonable security, are to be set aside on the ground that the rate of interest is too high, the result will be that persons in that position will be put upon still harder terms in borrowing, since the lender must take into account the risk of a Chancery suit. (in *Croft* v. *Graham*[23])

The court in this case was singularly unimpressed, and supported the old rule with all the vigour of a fifteenth-century scholastic. Knight Bruce LJ said that the lender's claim to a high rate of interest, 'cannot be supported by reasonable argument' (*ibid.*).

That is to say, the traditional paradigm was clear: landowners borrowed out of necessity and lenders always took advantage; the court's job was to protect the weak (the rich weak of course – very few genuinely weak got near a court of equity); clearly these people only borrowed the money at these exorbitant rates and on

---

[23] (1863) 2 De G J & S 155, at p. 336.

such harsh terms because they were forced by necessity to do so; therefore the courts should strike down the bargain. As one eighteenth-century court put it: any loan to an expectant heir would 'not only be looked upon as oppressive in the particular instance and therefore avoided, but as pernicious in principle, and therefore repressed' (in *Gwynne v. Heaton*[24]). But through the nineteenth century, there was a growing sense of unease; although Lord Hardwicke had more or less treated all interest demands against expectant heirs as penalties, and therefore unenforceable, this became more problematic. Like the casuists, the courts generally, and certainly in other areas, had recognised a change in paradigm. Commerce and industry, far from being dishonourable, had become ultra-respectable. It was the source of wealth and prosperity, the courts taking little cognisance of the fact that prosperity for some did not necessarily mean for all, or even that it might mean at the expense of many. The dogma of 'freedom of contract' had more or less become enshrined and only lost its potent hold in the twentieth century (see, for example, Atiyah 1979; Horwitz 1977). Freedom of contract meant that the courts should not interfere in freely negotiated contracts, almost no matter what the circumstances. The question therefore, was virtually identical to that faced by the casuists – how to square the old doctrines and consciences with the new economic climate.

Needless to say, eventually the courts did so. Cases first expressed doubts, then moved to the position of finding ways to enforce bonds without regard to the facts of 'necessity' that had forced the poor unfortunates to enter into them in the first place. Indeed, as with the casuists, the precedents were there. Even in the eighteenth century, the court had occasionally enforced harsh terms and huge rates of interest against hard-pressed landowners or their heirs. One Lord Chancellor, Chelmsford, had accepted an interest rate of 60 per cent, saying he did not think the court had any power to interfere, and a nineteenth-century court found it useful to accept this (*Webster v. Cook* [25]). In the end, of course, expectant heirs as the seventeenth and eighteenth century knew them more or less ceased to be the problem for the courts that they had been. Landowners, and their offspring, especially from the

---

[24] (1778) 1 Bro CC 1.
[25] (1867) 36 LJ Ch. 146.

great agricultural depression in the last quarter of the nineteenth
century through to 1914 and beyond, were eager to sell or mortgage
their lands to anyone who would take them off their hands. The
last thing they wanted was the courts destroying their 'bargains', as
the House of Lords itself recognised in the great settled land case of
Lord Henry Bruce v. *Marquess of Ailesbury*.[26]

But if expectant heirs dropped out of the limelight, another
group of 'embarrassed landowners'[27] did not just go quietly.
Landowners themselves were huge borrowers, as we have said.
Sometimes they borrowed for commercial development, sometimes for agricultural development, sometimes for family reasons
(marriage settlements and the like), sometimes for straight consumption (see, for example, Smith 1976, pp. 350 ff.) but always
they borrowed. And, as landowners, they were welcomed by the
money markets, because they had the actual security the expectant
heirs still lacked, landed estates, often in vast quantities. They
were able, therefore, to borrow on much more favourable terms,
especially as to rates of interest, than their, as yet, less privileged
sons. But they also ran into difficulties: they too often could not or
would not pay. Specifically, their chief problem frequently was
that they could not repay on the exact date stipulated by the
mortgage deed, though they might well be able to do so at some
later time, or at any rate hoped they would be able to do so. They,
too, sought relief from the terms of their agreements from the
equity courts. In the cases of expectant heirs, the courts, when they
felt it right, more or less rewrote the terms of the contract. With
impoverished landowners the courts were more creative: they
rewrote the law. They decided that a mortgage document might
say one thing, but actually mean another. From around the
sixteenth century, and certainly from the Restoration, the courts
decided that no matter what the terms of the agreement actually
stated as to the specified day of repayment, landowners could
ignore it. The document itself would always provide that if
repayment was not made by the specified date, the lands of the
borrower would be forfeited to the lender. The courts said the law

---

[26] (1892) AC 356.
[27] The description is Lord Macnaghten's in *Samuel* v. *Jarrah* [1904] AC 323, at p.
326.

overrode that provision. Provided the landowner could offer repayment at some time prior to a final order, and sometimes even later, the courts would allow the landowners to get back the land.

The actual origins of this remarkable piece of judicial imaginative manipulation are lost, though the Chancery courts were probably rewriting the law of mortgage contracts in the interests of landowners, and on the basis that interest-taking itself was a distinctly dubious act, from at least the fourteenth century. By the seventeenth century, the jurisdiction was routine.[28] But, for very similar reasons to that sketched for expectant heirs, the courts became uncomfortable with the protective blanket they had developed for landowners. What was the point of proclaiming the freedom of parties to create their own contracts, with one hand, whilst, with the other, brazenly rewriting them? With a struggle that was far more intense and commercially significant than that relating to expectant heirs, the courts shifted their arguments in this area also, to meet the requirements of the new 'paradigm'. Eventually, after a string of bitterly fought cases, mainly in the House of Lords in the last decade of the nineteenth century and the first of this, the House of Lords recast the old law in 1914[29]. Freedom of contract was to rule; the interest laws, at least what was left of their medieval form, had been repealed; and it was no longer necessary for the courts to rewrite the terms of contracts entered into by people who were, in effect, businessmen.

As we have suggested, the transformation was curiously close to that undertaken by the casuists and schoolmen. The usury prohibitions had once seemed so plain. The Bible and the interpretations (heathen and Christian) of the problems that were caused by moneylending seemed to authorise both the Church and the law to proscribe all lending at interest. The medieval tradition gradually and subtly worked out a series of exceptions to the blanket prohibition so that not all merchants and traders were doomed for the Devil. It managed to square its conscience partly by some deft intellectual footwork in relation to the interpretation of the two great authorities, Aristotle and Aquinas. In particular, it

---

[28] *Bacon* v. *Bacon* (1693) Tot 133.
[29] *Kreglinger* v. *New Pategonia Meat & Cold Storage Co* [1914] AC 25.

became accepted that as long as the rates of interest were not 'excessive' or 'extortionate' (another ambiguous concept with which English law still struggles[30]) and, more importantly, provided advantage was not being taken of a neighbour, some receipt of money other than the principal advanced would be acceptable, and the burgeoning bourgeois life could tick along pleasantly enough without a population explosion in hell.

The English legal tradition developed similarly. Capitalism was rampant, and both Parliament and the courts embraced commercialism. Certain aspects of the old doctrine, however, did not sit easily, and the lingering afterlife of the usury prohibitions demonstrated Parliament's, and especially the courts', uncomfortable time as they tried to dodge previously proclaimed dogmas. With both expectant heirs, and aspects of mortgage law, the lawmakers found awkward the pressures to bring about change in order to put the law in line with commercial requirements. Like the problem faced by the casuists, the modern-day equivalent of the 'imperious rulers, avaricious prelates and greedy bankers' combined with the very group the usury restrictions were supposed to protect (rich borrowers) to bring about the downfall of the old eternal truths. Like the casuists, the law changed slowly, case by case, holding on to old principles for as long as possible, and then announcing new principles as though they had been there, and obviously there, all the time. Detailed factual inquiries would sometimes show that the cases on which it had been thought principles had been established were in fact 'special' or decided 'on their own facts' only, just like the *Westminster City Council* case. If the object of the exercise is to preserve an intellectual architecture, then it is not surprising that to the casuists' critics, or to the critics of the law's tenuous hold on old doctrines, the process can look shoddy. In Milton's terms, both the casuists and the common lawyers managed to make the worse appear the better reason. Classical casuistry did not appear to survive such exposure; the common law flourished.

---

[30] The term 'extortionate', in the Consumer Credit Act is currently being reconsidered. It might be replaced by the term 'unjust credit'. This would be a nice return to casuistical basics.

VI

Our argument has been that casuistry, like rhetoric (for example, Vickers 1988), has seemingly been so thoroughly debased that it no longer has any intellectual respectability. Yet if we take its strict meaning, freed from its currently overwhelming pejorative connections, casuistry is simply the process of the application of universally known and tested moral principles to individual instances. And when we see it like this, we find, again like rhetoric, it is in operation in many spheres, well beyond that of mere religious conscience. Indeed, according to some critics, since around the seventeenth century, the whole of literature itself has been dominated by casuistical procedures, choices and analysis (Seiden 1990; Slights 1981). It has even been argued that the modern novel starts when casuistry moved from the moral world of religious conscience to the moral world of the fictitious character (Leites 1988, pp. 132–3).

When we turn from literature to life, we find casuistical implications almost everywhere. The example that is currently the most topical and perhaps most intense comes from medicine, and its modern application (see, for example, Brody 1988). Jonsen and Toulmin (1988) repeatedly point to the casuistical problems encountered by doctors as they are faced with standard medical procedures which need adaptation to the particular patient, and the specific mental and physical problems of the body with which they are dealing. The tragic case of Baby J is only one of many recent examples of the necessity of casuistical reasoning.[31]

But a host of other situations, more or less common to daily life in a complex society, are applications of the same process. The allocation of limited housing resources by local authorities to homeless persons based on the principle that 'need' is to govern priorities is one; similar is the making of discretionary welfare payments to social security claimants; likewise, the application for early release by prisoners to parole boards; or disputes revolving around the question of professional ethics (for example, in the case

---

[31] Re J (a minor) [1990] 3 All ER 990. See also the House of Lords decision on the Hillsborough disaster victim, Tony Bland (Airedale NHS Trust v. Bland [1993] 1 All ER 821).

of lawyers, see Luban 1988); or problems about academic merit.[32] But the application of the obvious principle, as Aristotle recognised, is supremely difficult. These problems, however, are no more easy or difficult to solve than, say, the traditional casuistical problem of determining whether it was wrong for a starving man to steal from a rich neighbour or whether, in some extreme circumstances, lying might be justified.

The casuists' greatest claim was that they were supposed to be able to help solve such difficult, day-to-day problems. In the past, their learned men had given more thought to these issues than anyone else, or at least this is the substance of their position. In the modern world, in medical, ethical, employment, social security, academic, etc. circumstances, where decision-makers are trying to apply general principles to individual cases, the casuists would say that what would help them do so, in the best way possible, would be both a clearer understanding of the process by which a good conscience is determined and principles are created, a crucial sensitivity to the particularities of the case and, equally importantly, a better knowledge of the way like or similar instances have been dealt with before. A systematic collection of the opinions of those who have pronounced on these matters, of the great, the good and the wise, would be an enormous help in ensuring that the right decisions could continue to be made; indeed the study of such collations is essential. The opinions of

---

[32] This example might be nearer to home for some readers: the academy is full of casuistical decison-making. The principle that the candidate who produces the better essay or exam paper should get the higher grade is one ripe for casuistical analysis. A clear principle needs applying to specific instances. Likewise, the requirement that the applicant who is the better teacher and researcher should be appointed to the university post is also fraught with casuistical implications. The principle on which applicants should be appointed is easy to state, and indeed obvious, just as it is obvious to state the principle that local authorities should decide which homeless family gets housed first on just principles, or that the better essay gets the higher mark, or that lying is wrong. But, for example, any two or more applicants for any academic post are different, with different merits and defects, and people charged with the delicate task of making appointments somehow have to apply a seemingly simple principle, whilst taking note of the endless differences and individual circumstances. (Is an 'original' paper of fifty pages somehow worth more or less than a derivative book of 500? Is the candidate's underprivileged minority background relevant, etc.) And there are numerous other seemingly equally intractable questions.

the authorities ought to be carefully consulted before decisions
involving complex moral issues are made.

It is, no doubt, easy to exaggerate the potential importance of
casuistical reasoning and start to see it everywhere. But it must be
evident by now that our argument is that the one discipline that
has taken the injunctions of casuistry seriously for centuries, with
only very rare acknowledgements of its close cousin, is the
common law. It does all that the casuists ask of it; it preserves the
opinions of those who have pronounced on particular matters in
the past; it grades these opinions into a strict hierarchy so that
those who come after know, in the event of conflict or doubt,
which opinion is of greater worth, and, in the form of treatises and
textbooks, it tries to organise these decisions so that when the next
complex case has to be decided the decision-maker can turn
swiftly to the relevant authorities before pronouncing. Like the
casuists, it demands that those who are to make decisions are
steeped in the wisdom of the tradition, in this instance the wisdom
of the common law judges, the great, the good and the wise, before
they are empowered to make decisions. The rules of the common
law, especially as operated in England, work so that only those
who have already spent their lives in the tradition are entitled to
make the pronouncements that the tradition will authorise.[33]
Finally, and above all, the common law, like casuistry, has the
possibility inherent within its own operations to consider sensitively the specifics of the person before it, even if, like Antigone's
brother, the particular supplicant seems to be an utter outcast.
Indeed it could be argued that, in many areas, but especially in the
current pressing one of medical decisions around the pained or
dying body (see Douzinas and McVeigh 1992), nothing else is
possible. On the other hand, the common law's frequent failure to
take seriously the possibilities of its own resources is one of the
reasons for the perceived moral failings of its operation.

The common law's potential for recognising the details of
individual cases, of victims, accuseds, accidents, circumstances,
or, in Lord Templeman's language, the totalities, immediacies and
peculiar natures, makes it a prime example of casuistry continuing
to flower after all in the modern world, despite its apparent and
irrevocable decline. This book argues that in recognising the

---

[33] We take this idea further in Chapter 8.

uniqueness of each case, in terms which are explored more
specifically in other chapters, the common law retains the
potential for an ethical application of principles and the development of a radically new notion of justice which is aware of the
requirements of the individual before the court, without descend-
ing into unacceptable 'laxity'. The common law, like casuistry, is
sensitive, or potentially sensitive, to the contingency of decision-
making.

For us, the problem with casuistry in its traditional sense, at
least in part, is simply its basis, Christian ethics.[34] This might
seem like a contradiction in terms – casuistry without Christianity
is unthinkable. What we want to develop here though is just that, a
secular form of casuistical reasoning for use in the law. That is,
within the common law, there are already the resources for turning
to a form of decision-making which is fully cognisant of the needs
of the other, as well as the requirements of principle. Casuistry's
modern defenders (for example, Sommerville 1988, p. 177) deny
that casuistry could be used to justify anything. We would not
underestimate the difficulty of adopting a flexible humane,
philosophical, well-informed approach to justice which does not
lead simply back to where the common law is now, or to a
dangerous 'laxity' that might be even worse. But if questions of
justice and ethics are to be taken seriously, something the common
law claims to do, though generally not getting beyond mere formal
platitudes, then an understanding of one traditional aspect of the
case law system, that it is a system of principle, but its principles
are sensitive, or can be interpreted as sensitive, to the needs of the
individual and the totalities of circumstances in the particular
case, has to be brought to the forefront of legal reasoning. Of
course, the common law's treatment of the 'other' is generally
harsh, and sometimes brutal, as our discussion in Chapter 6
particularly illustrates. There is all the more reason, therefore, to
draw out the possibilities implicit in the common law for arguing
otherwise. The need to acknowledge all the circumstances of the
case without playing either the religious basis of casuistry, or
using its often fairly evidently shifty forms of reasoning without,

---

[34] To an extent, some aspects of the modern revival of casuistry seem designed only
to deploy old Christian dogmas in new settings; for an example of this art, see
Hauerwas (1983).

that is, making the worse appear the better reason, is crucial. A contradictory notion it may be, but a secular from of casuistry, fully aware of the call of the other, itself a potent source of principled action, as our discussion of *Antigone* in the previous chapter illustrates, is where we start. *Antigone* tells us there is more to law than its claim to principled reason, something which stands outside of the rather overplayed traditions of natural law; casuistry tells us how to operate that something else; the common law purports to have the authority to synthesise the two. In the next chapter, we examine in more detail the philosophy which provides the basis for our argument that the law does treat the other in ways that are unacceptable and that it ought to be made to do otherwise.

4

Another justice

In Chapter 1, we alluded to the current moral failures of the law. Whilst the law has been universally acknowledged as the only suitable supreme arbitrator between different social interests, it is an institution that has largely failed to achieve minimal standards of justice in its operation. In this chapter, we first examine the traditions which have permitted and encouraged this disastrous break, and then explain how an alternative philosophical theory might be used to rethink the relationship between law and justice.

There is a whole philosophical tradition that sees the problem of modernity as the problem of law, or more accurately as that of the antinomy of law: the dual exclusion (and we will claim implication) of law and ethics, legality and morality, or of validity and value, form and substance (Rose 1984, 1992). But this modern 'diremption' (Rose 1992, p. xiii) or separation of the two aspects of normativity points to an earlier epoch when the quest for justice had not been split into an institutional-legal and an individual-moral pole and its political and ethical facets were still inextricably linked. Heidegger claims, as we saw, that the epochal split between nature, *physis*, and its overarching order, *dikē*, took place in Greece before the classical age and the Platonic inauguration of western metaphysics. Undoubtedly, such separation is necessary before *dikē* as justice can become a critical concept. To imagine and to demand a just society presupposes an initial estrangement from the world, a dissatisfaction with the current state of things and the hope that some agency – whether human or divine – can intervene and reform man and society. As Heller notes, the initial

formulation of the problem of justice both in the Old Testament
and in Greek philosophy is negative and involves the denunciation of a double injustice:

the world is regarded as unjust, as the very negation of justice, and this
negation of justice must itself be negated . . . men are unjust because they are
corrupt and wicked, rather than righteous, and society (or the body politic) is
unjust because it puts a premium on wickedness and allows the righteous to be
trampled upon and perish. (Heller 1987, p. 54)

The striking characteristic in this ethico-political idea of justice is
the identification of justice with righteousness and of injustice
with wickedness, in other words the close link between justice and
the idea of the good. In the ancient definition of morality, men
have a télos, an aim in life, that places them in the scheme of
physis and dikē. Virtuous action helps them move from what they
are to what they ought to be and to occupy their proper place in the
wider order of cosmos.

Plato's Republic (1955) and Gorgias (1960) are two of the
earliest philosophical attempts to consider the condition of the
just and good city. The quest is conducted in the form of dialogue
and argument between the defender of justice as righteousness,
Socrates, and the Sophists, Callicles and Thrasymachos. Callicles
in Gorgias argues, in a proto-Nietzschean manner, that men are
divided by nature into the strong and the weak and that law and
convention are the creations of inferiors who use the talk of justice
to drag their superiors to their own low level. Thrasymachos' view
in the Republic is more cynical towards the strong: what passes for
'justice' is the expression of the interests of the rulers, the wealthy
and the strong and the truly righteous man will always lose out. It
is in the interest of the virtuous, therefore, to act unjustly and to
promote their own profit since injustice gives more strength,
freedom and mastery than the misnomer 'justice'.

Socrates, as the rational philosopher par excellence, must
combat these arguments by using reason alone. He draws a parallel
between the just state and the just man and argues that the right
constitution leads to a balanced relationship between the three
classes in the city and that a similar harmony between the three
parts of the soul of the citizen makes him virtuous. But Socrates
soon realises that while philosophy is committed to the rule of
reason, reason cannot win the argument. Reason cannot prove that

it is better to suffer injustice than to commit it. Socrates knows with the classical tradition, rediscovered in modernity by Kierkegaard, that, as Ovid put it, *video meliora proboque; deteriora sequor* (I know the good and approve of it, but I follow evil). To win the assent of his audience, Socrates must supplement his rationalistic arguments with a variety of non-rational claims. He puts forward accordingly many unprovable assertions: he claims first that righteousness should be practised because it brings happiness, an argument that can be empirically accepted only by those already righteous; he narrates the myths of Radamanthus and Er to remind his interlocutors the religious threats of divine retribution for evil; he finally admits that while the practice of wisdom and knowledge, philosophy, is the best teacher of conscience and city, the external authority of parents and legislators may be the only practical source available to the many for the instruction of virtue.

But despite the long series of rational and non-rational arguments canvassed, Socrates offers no definition of justice. Justice is first replaced by reason, later by the idea of the good, which is presented as its substance and ultimate value. The good of the individual and of the *polis* provide the necessary criteria for choosing between competing courses of action, but the good itself is not accessible to reason. Similarly with justice: Socrates follows various routes in his quest and repeatedly re-affirms that justice and the good exist and are the highest value. But all attempts to define or describe their content are soon abandoned as the dialogue moves in circles from justice to the good and back. It can be argued that this exemplary use of the dialectic confirms it as the proper method for the education of the philosopher, furthermore that the future just city advocated by Plato is a metaphor for the activity of philosophy itself, coined at its inauguration, by its first 'philosopher king'. And while philosophy, the love (*philia*) of knowledge and wisdom (*sophia*), and reason can only guide us within the domain of knowledge, the good is declared by Socrates to be *epekeina ousias*, beyond Being and essence, at the other side of knowledge and reason. Every time that the dialogue appears to approach an answer to the problem of justice, the position is soon abandoned and the search starts again only to repeat the same procedure. As Plato admits in his seventh Epistle, we can never fully know the good 'for it does not admit of verbal expression like

other branches of knowledge' (Plato, 1973).[1] Justice too, the
political expression of the good, cannot be discovered in laws and
in written treatises either because it has no essence that is open to
philosophical speculation, or because its essence lies beyond
immediate life in the 'city in the sky'. But while it is not open to
the operation of reason, justice exists and reveals itself to
philosophers and law-givers in mysterious ways and through
divine visitation. Thus, quest for justice exemplifies the paradox of
reason, formulated by Socrates 'in the most extreme manner:
reasoning leads to unreason. Faith surfaces three times and in
three forms: faith in other-worldly justice, faith in authority, and
faith in revelation' (Heller 1987: p. 73). The victory of *logos* over
mythos is never complete. On the contrary, *logos* needs the
rhetorical and emotional force of *mythos* to establish its empire.

The Platonic dialogues started western philosophy and have
been read as the first clear statement of rationalism. And yet, the
power of reason in matters of morals and justice appears limited in
many important, almost debilitating, ways. What makes the
meandering dialogues persuasive is Socrates' ultimate argument:
his sacrifice at the altar of a justice that cannot be defined or its
superiority proven rationally but which must be acted upon, even
at the greatest of costs. 'The truth of righteousness is thus
expressed in the gesture which no argument can justify. Socrates
chose to suffer injustice rather than commit it; he justified it
without justifying it; he observed philosophical reason beyond
reason' (*ibid.*, 65). Socrates represents not so much the triumph of
reason but the first clear formulation of the *aporia of justice*: to be
just is to *act justly*, to be committed to a frame of mind and follow a
course of action that must be accepted before any final rational
justification of their desirability or superiority.[2] From the earliest
western denunciations of injustice, philosophy asserted that
people need and possess a sense of justice which unceasingly
creates legal and moral systems, but justice is not fully of this

---

[1] For a full discussion of the Platonic search for the meaning of justice and the good
and his admission of defeat, see Kelsen (1947).
[2] The aporia of reason and justice is even stronger in the Jewish tradition. To be just,
the Jew must obey the law without any reason or justification. For Buber, Jews act in
order to understand while, Levinas denounces what he calls the western 'temptation
of temptation', the – 'Greek' – demand to subordinate every act to knowledge and to
overcome the 'purity' and 'innocence' of the act (Levinas 1990; pp. 30–50).

world. Justice is thus caught in an unceasing movement between knowledge and passion, reason and action, this world and the next, rationalism and metaphysics.

Aristotle takes the rational quest for justice further.[3] He gives virtue a geometrical definition as the mean between excess and defect and identifies justice with the proposition of giving everyone his due. The Aristotelian moral agent is the *phronimos*, who acquires his moral sense and discrimination in the course of a life full of experience. His practical judgment is always situated in the concrete circumstances of the case at hand. Moral knowledge becomes sensitive to context and circumstance and practical judgments involve calculations, tempered by immersion in experience and prudence and guided by the *teloi* inherent in persons and things by their nature. But the twin bond between justice and righteousness and ethics and the city still remains: man is a political animal and it is only in a just *polis* that the individual becomes a virtuous citizen; conversely just men make the city great. Aristotle is the last classical philosopher in whom these links remain strong. By the beginning of modernity, both sets of links have been severed.

There are two broad modern versions of rationalism in ethics: in the first, moral obligation is grounded through an appeal to conscious and rational deliberation and decision which is then implemented by an act of will, or, alternatively, moral duty is created through the subordination of conduct to rules autonomously formulated in Kant or heteronomously but legitimately legislated according to the jurisprudence of modernity. Classical teleology thus turns into modern deontology. The ethical aim of the good (life) is turned from its Platonic status as the supreme virtue into a quantitative problem to be resolved through the scientific calculation of consequences. Theories of justice, too, have veered ever since classical Greece between rationalism and non-rational approaches, between conceptions of justice amenable to the operations of truth and ideals of justice that transcend any possibility of cognitive recognition. Cognition is being asked to provide a rational foundation for the choices of will and the operations of power, but rather than legislating to control power, it often ends up justifying power by declaring the justice of its

---

[3] For a discussion of Aristotle's ethics, see Urmson (1988) and Hardie (1980).

products. The grounds of justice are sought in contracts and negotiations, in the upholding of legal rights and their concomitant duties, but they are too weak or controversial or they appear to undervalue and even disenfranchise too many categories of people to be anything other than a transient and unconvincing legitimatory discourse. And as we stand at the end of modernity with all our traditional critical resources in retreat, the question of ethics and justice becomes a central concern for the politics of postmodernity. The sources of *ēthos* have moved from divine *logos* to the forms of things and from the Christian ethic to its secular heir, human rationality, but all traditional foundations of morality lie weakened. Faced with a pluralism of conflicting moral and legal authorities, we approach the *fin de siècle* with only one of the great intellectual and political inventions of modernity still intact, personal freedom as self-construction and definition. This quest for self-definition within the plethora of partially authoritative authorities invests life-plans and choices with a new ethical emphasis and re-awakens the demand for institutional justice. But can we develop a contemporary critical and reconstructive concept of justice for our legal system after the end of all grand narratives of modernity and all attempts to ground the social bond on a principle of universal application? We need to re-examine modernity's (de)linking of legality and morality.

II

As we saw in Chapter 2, nineteenth-century philosophy, as exemplified by Hegel, was preoccupied with the fragmentation of the social and psychic worlds and the dissolution of community, ushered by modernity. As Alasdair MacIntyre (1981) puts it, modernity has witnessed a profound 'moral catastrophe', a radical breakdown in ethical agreement and the systematic annihilation of communities of value and virtue. This destruction of ethical consensus and the impoverishment of ethical substance persecutes modern ethics and law, the two fields that modernity proposes as substitutes for the classical agreement of value and purpose in private and public life. The modern quest for a just society starts with what Parsons called the 'Hobbesian problem of order', the need to reconcile in political terms society and state, desire and order, self and community, or, in philosophical terms, the claims of practical and theoretical reason, of freedom and necessity. The key problem in this quest is that justice is no longer identified or even associated with righteousness, nor is the link between a just *polis* and the virtuous citizen assumed either as empirical truth or as the promise of future utopia. Modernity radically separated theoretical and practical reason and the domains of legality and morality and was subsequently faced with the (seemingly impossible) task of mediating between them.

The transition in ontology, ethics and aesthetics from their original understanding to their modern versions is long and tortuous (Douzinas and Warrington with McVeigh 1991, Chap. 1; Heidegger 1962; Heller 1987; Kearny 1988). However, it is broadly true to say, following a felicitous and now classical presentation of the move from the ancients to the moderns, that modern man is not conceived any longer as a mirror of some superior and external reality but as a lamp, a source and centre of light illuminating the world. Modern ontology does not understand Being as a product of a divine first cause nor does it approach reality as a copy of a pre-existing original. Being is now seen as productive and man becomes the centre, creator and cause of actions and things and the bestower of meaning upon a profane reality. Similarly, imagination and its creation, art, are no longer conceived as resemblances and imitations of the transcendent world of forms nor is the artist a craftsman who imitates the divine demiurge. The model of the modern artist is the inventor, and imagination, in its ability to coordinate the faculties, becomes itself transcendental. Finally, in the practical realm agency becomes central. The subject is enthroned as a free agent, as the immediate source of activity and the cause of actions that emanate from it. The modern self fulfils itself in what it does, our actions and our work express our true existence and as a result we bear responsibility for the consequences of our activities.

The modern will is always directed towards an outside; action projects the sovereign self onto the world both in its orientation towards others and in its work that bestows value and mastery on nature. The self as agent recognises himself as the centre of decision-making and as the possesser of a power that springs neither from emotions nor from pure intelligence. The power of will is unique; Descartes describes it as the same in us as it is in

God. Modern will knows no theoretical limits only empirical constraints; will is the power of choice between yes and no, an indivisible sovereingty of the self. This power finds its perfect manifestation in decision. In making a decision, self becomes agent, an autonomous and responsible subject, whose sign is found in external manifestations, the actions that can be imputed on him. If there is no self without free-will, similarly there is not action without its agent. 'There can be no agent without this power that links the action to the subject who decides upon it and thereby assumes full responsibility for it' (Vernant and Vidal-Naquet 1990, p. 50).

It is against this background that the classical aporia of justice is reformulated and turns into the 'antinomy of law'. When the good and justice coincide, practical judgments and moral action move in parallel lines. Ethical conflict, the outcome of a fundamental split in the grounding forces of ēthos, is irreconcilable; it inevitably takes tragic dimensions and creates Antigones. But with freedom the main aspiration and achievement of modernity and subjectivity its ontological corollary, the modern subject becomes free to decide what is good for himself and his actions cannot be restricted to the unquestioning application of norms and rules. Modern conscience and free will thus become legislative: the subject can now examine the rules themselves and can reject and replace them if they do not fulfil criteria that may vary according to circumstance and belief. And while the classical link between society and citizen remains, its content changes radically: legislative will can no longer refer to a consensual horizon of shared teloi and must for the first time construct the 'good' almost ex nihilo on two conditions: first, this artificially created 'good' must be acceptable to the newly emancipated bourgeois but at the same time it must have the ability to shape the virtuous citizen of the modern state. Freedom, reason and morality must be combined against the background of a polyphony of values. It is a Sisyphean task that finds its most perfect philosophical solution in the work of Kant.

The genesis of the 'antinomy of law' that closely accompanies the coming of legal modernity and its consciousness, jurisprudence, can be traced back to the Cartesian meditations and their inward turn. Descartes recognised that while the phenomenal world of reality is external to the subject, it can be approached on the analogy of the subject's self-understanding. Behind every *cogito* (I know) there is an *ego* (I), 'the apodictically certain and last basis of judgment upon which all radical philosophy must be grounded' (Husserl 1964, p. 7). After Descartes, philosophy becomes a meditation on the subject and its relationship with its opposite, the object. This coordinated split and the aspiration to transcend the apparent opposition have been at the heart of modern thought and philosophy ever since.

The modern conception of will and its psychological corollary, free will, find in Kant a formulation of great significance for the realm of practical judgment both as law and as morality. The critical philosophy of Kant was the first to bring together subject and object under the reign of reason, and his *Critique of Practical Reason* (1956) is the foundation of modern jurisprudence. In it, Kant sets out to deduce the (moral) law in the same way that he deduces knowledge in the first *Critique*. Kant's starting-point is the experience of personal, social and intellectual fragmentation of early modernity. His interest is both philosophical and political. He wants to show how freedom and reason are inseparable in their common concern to enlighten man and to release him from his self-incurred tutelage and his 'inability to make use of his understanding without direction from another' (*ibid.*, p. 3). Reason accordingly has two forms. In the theoretical domain, the subject acquires knowledge by using a priori forms of intuition (space and time) and categories of understanding (identity/difference, cause/effect, necessity/contingency, substance/accident) to construct the manifold data of experience as coherent and unified. Practical reason, on the other hand, helps unite the personality by subjecting conflicting inclinations and desires to the a priori moral law. In this sense, reason acts as the principle of unity between the subject and the world.

When Kant turns to the (moral) law, he asks it by what right is it the law, where does it derive its authority from, and why should people follow it? The law, like reason, is subjected to a tribunal which will determine its title and legitimacy (G. Rose 1984, Chap. 1). But Kant notices a fundamental asymmetry between the two. In the case of theoretical reason, the critical meta-language that deduces the principles of knowledge – mainly causality – is homologous to the language of its object (the operations of a scientist, for example, who extracts axioms from his observations

and experiments). With law, however, there is no simple homo-
logy. Kantian philosophy asserts a radical dissymmetry between
prescriptive and constative statements. In ethics the object
language of commands and prescriptions ('You must x') and the
meta-language of norms and rules ('It is decreed that in circumstances y, persons of type z should x') are not isomorphic. The
knowledge of a state of affairs cannot be the basis of moral
knowledge and action nor can the principle of law be deduced
from the recitation or examination of particular laws. As the good
is no longer given, it cannot be apprehended in experience nor are
moral judgments the affective reactions of moral agents to
empirical properties. Moral law does not follow causality; on the
contrary morality is itself the cause of acts. In a move that
resembles the operations of the aesthetic in the *Critique of
Judgment*, Kant deduces the ethical command by analogy, *as if* it
were a fact of nature amenable to reason, *as if* it were a 'universal
law of nature'. But if the law cannot be derived, it is a 'fact of
reason' and not of experience, and its principle helps deduce
freedom. The law prescribes through its inscrutable power freedom, which is nothing other than the practical aspect of reason.

These ideas give Kantian practical philosophy its revolutionary
character. Morality is not grounded in some pre-existing idea of
the good nor does it derive from an external source. Classical
theory made the mistake of positing first good and evil and then
fashioning moral law and the object of will accordingly.

The ancients openly revealed this error by devoting their ethical investigation
entirely to the definition of the concept of the highest good and thus posited an
object which they intended subsequently to make the determining ground of
the will in the moral law. (Kant 1956, pp. 66–7)

But in so doing, 'their fundamental principle was always hetero-
nomy, and they came inevitably to empirical conditions for a
moral law' (*ibid.*, p. 66). Kant reverses the procedure; it is not the
concept of the good that posits the law but the moral law that
defines good and evil. Kant searches for the universal preconditions of moral action and discovers them in the free and rational
action of the autonomous agent who follows the law posited in the
categorical imperative out of a pure sense of duty and respect: 'Act
in such a way that the maxim of your will can always be valid as
the principle establishing universal law' (*ibid.*, p. 30); and in its

more Christian formulation 'act so that you treat humanity, whether in your person or in that of an other, always as an end' (*ibid.*, p. 47).

This law is rather strange: it is imperative, a rule (act in such a way . . .); but its command to the will is to follow a pure form, the form of legality (the principle of the action should be always valid, in the form of a universal norm). While it forces and obligates the will, it emanates from it. Kantian autonomy makes modern man the law's *subject* in a double sense: he is the legislator, the subject who gives the law and the legal subject, subjected to the law on condition that he has participated in its legislation. And again as a quasi-law of nature, the moral law appears both as regularity, the universal interconnection of things, and as a purposeful order in the tradition of natural law. All the concepts, conceptual oppositions and strategies of modern jurisprudence and social theory can be traced to this 'foundational' text: form and substance, validity and value, regularity and force, sovereign and subject, law and rule, legality and morality.

The categorical imperative asks me to act as if the maxim of my will can become a principle of universal legislation. The law commands only to follow a pure form, that of universality, which is declared to be a part of reason. But as reason is launched within and legislates upon my will, the moral will is free and finds all its determinations in itself. Modern will, in following the requirement of practical reason, becomes free in a double sense: it obeys the law it discovers in itself, thus becoming autonomous; and second, it is only free people who are subjected to practical reason. But the moral law hurts; to follow its injunction to universalise means abandoning all individual feeling and desire and acting totally disinterestedly, out of a pure sense of duty.

The recognition of will's involvement in action is a typically modern move that distinguishes pure from practical reason. Furthermore, the pronouncement of self as both law-giver and law's subject marks the inauguration of the modern conception of autonomy or self-determination, the other side of will's enthronement. Within the legal system, laws from now on are to be considered just if they are prescribed by those who have to obey them. Duty and respect for the law are equally important for both morality and legality; moral action follows the law of the universal imperative of reason, legality is obedience to the laws of the state.

But only those maxims, rules and norms that meet the criteria of universality are morally binding since all others are contradictory.

When Kant turns to the theory of state, he sees the social contract not as a historical covenant but as a requirement of reason that lies behind state law. It commands the legislator to introduce laws as if they emanated from the will of the people and to treat the subjects as if they had participated in the formation of the law. But this way Rousseau's concrete democratic demands are seriously weakened and Kant is able to accept that the laws of the autocratic Prussian state meet his formal criterion of legality. Thus, freedom as autonomy, reason and morality come together in a perfect philosophical synthesis that appears to solve the aporia of justice in favour of a strict rationalism. For Kant, the metaphysical foundations of morality have no history, although, under this cloak of universality, they seem to meet the condition and needs of modernity. In the process, the classical concept of justice has broken down. Its ethical part, morality, becomes a formal requirement disassociated from any content, community or immediate object. Its political part, on the other hand, is turned into legality; it, too, must meet the criterion of formality which from now on will become the moral substance of positive law.

The Kantian revolution transferred the foundation of meaning and the ground of law from the divine and transcendent to the human and social. This law commands and obliges immediately and absolutely but it is not deduced from a conception of the good nor does it follow empirical or social criteria or other constative propositions established in a theory of society. Moral law is granted to us before we can start questioning its nature or operation. But this radical first step comes to an end in the assertion that we live in a totalisable community of reason. To act on principles that would be acceptable and willed by all rational people is to assume that self's desires and actions are compatible and coherent with those of all others. As we will argue below, this assumption turns morality into an ontological imperialism in the same way that the derivation of moral norms from a theory of the good can turn it into an epistemological one.

We can summarise this critique of Kantian practical philosophy, the implications of which for jurisprudence we will pursue in section IV below, as follows: the solution to the aporia of justice, the synthesis of reason, freedom and the law, passes through the birth of the modern subject; but for this autonomous subject, morality is exclusively obedience to the law while the other makes no independent claims upon my respect and action except as an instance and proof of law's existence. Moreover, the (moral) law appeals for its operation to the horizon of a universal community; but as such a community does not exist and cannot be created, references to it become a rationalising and legitimising device for a state law devoid of any ethical idea of justice. We take up this last point further in the next section.

III

The classical ethico-political conception of justice brought together individual and community and law and ethics. As we have seen, Kantian philosophy distinguished between right and good and abandoned any overarching idea of virtue. In its absence, morality loses its empirical intersubjective basis and must be grounded solely on the isolated subject. Rationalism, however, abhors subjective morality because it smacks of subjectivism and relativism and positions the ethical substance on the universality of the law. The paradoxical outcome of the destruction of local communities of meaning and value is that in modernity universality becomes the true meaning of normative generality. We examined in the previous section the Kantian conception of moral autonomy, the basis of modern ethical discourse. We now turn to the public facet of community and to law.

The secularisation of meaning and authority led inexorably to their relativisation and weakening. Authority must be established now without reference to external principles or law-givers. As a result, modern political theory is preoccupied with the problem of justice and the legitimate exercise of power. But the concept of social justice that survives, after the destruction of the classical ideal and the assignment of ethics to the realm of individual conscience, is severely restricted. The liberal theory of social and political justice is only concerned to secure the rights and property of individuals and makes no claims about the good life, the choice of which is left to individuals acting within the confines of the laws. The content of its prescriptions derives from the form of the moral law and is determined through the operation of the principle of non-contradiction. In this restricted conception, social justice extends its scope to the just distribution of resources, benefits, rewards and punishments, while formal or legal justice concerns exclusively the application of the same rule to all persons who belong to a given category (Perelman 1963). But this dominant modern conception of justice as fairness is only the 'shabby remnant of the "sum total of virtues" that was once called "justice". On the plane of socio-political justice, only *minima moralia* remain' (Heller 1987, p. 93).

The alternative is the contractarian tradition, in which the law is the outcome of a notional or historical agreement of citizens who seek to guarantee their property and security. But can the legitimacy of democratic procedure and law-making give the law its missing moral content within the parameters of Kantian rationalism? The Kantian conception of autonomy depends for its concretisation upon a universalisable and rational community, a *communis rationis*, which acts both as a heuristic principle and as the historical and empirical horizon and limit for the newly enfranchised subject. We are autonomous in the strong sense that we follow the law we give ourselves, but this law must be valid for all. This move, at the basis of all social contract theory, was first conducted by Rousseau. And yet, as de Man's reading of the *Social Contract* has shown, the contractual derivation of authority and of the constitution are as fictional as individual autonomy; they are both based on the rhetorical strategy of *metalepsis* (the reversal of cause and effect) in which what comes after (the legislator) is presented as the source of the law (de Man 1979, pp. 135–302, 1983, pp. 102–41; Douzinas and Warrington 1991; Douzinas and Warrington with McVeigh 1991, Chap. 7; cf. Goodrich 1990, Chap. 5). The contract, this outcome of the pure will of the parties, which establishes civil society and state has, at its core, a performative narrative which itself constitutes the original participants whose pre-contractual existence is necessary for the agreement to be entered. The legislator and subject of the law of freedom is an imposter, a trickster put on stage by the operations of rhetoric. Rousseau's legislator is the outcome of his own parthenogenetic action. But the deception of this retrospective legitimation was soon understood and the first signs of disenchantment with the world according to reason were felt not long after Rousseau. The same foundational move, however, which cyclically founds the founder, is repeated in those instances of interpretation of legal texts, where the act of the interpreter and the meaning of the text are metaleptically attributed and assigned to the intentions of the original author. Here too, the rhetorical operation both allows the hermeneutical enterprise to operate and opens its extravagant claims to semantic transparency to the gambits of deconstructive unpicking. The interpretation debate is interminable and inconclusive because indeterminacy is the precondition of the debate.

But the assumed community of reason introduces a second type of defrauding and exclusion. The 'we' implied by the categorical norm can never be co-extensive with the community that legislates within an actual nation-state. Nation-states are defined through territorial boundaries, which demarcate them from other states and exclude other people and nations from the role of the citizen-legislator. The 'we' of the rational community to which the subject must refer in order to formulate the law and win his autonomy becomes a mirage once any of the empirical characteristics of the historical legislator and subject are added to it. The principle of autonomy is created in the moulding together of the split self and the split community which modernity introduced against the horizon of an alleged universal community. But all empirical law is bound by sovereignty and territory and therefore excludes from the 'we' of its legislator everyone who does not fall within its borders.[4]

To explore this point further, let us refer briefly to recent linguistic philosophy. Ethical or legal commands are prescriptive; they order their addressee to carry out a certain act. Substantive provisions of statutes and legal rules, on the other hand, are formally normative sentences. Norms are the meta-language of commands. Normative sentences can be analysed as prescriptives or commands put in inverted commas that give them authority. The prescription says 'x should carry out y'. Its normative reformulation adds 'it is a norm (or z decrees) that "x should carry out y"'. In a democratic polity, political and legal legitimacy are allegedly bestowed by the fact that the addressor of the norm (the legislator) and the addressee of the command (the legal subjects) are one and the same. The legislation of democratic states is introduced on behalf of the citizens, in 'our name'. 'We decree that x should carry out y.' The essence of political freedom is that the

---

[4] See further Chapter 6 below.

subjects who make law are also law's subjected. As a recent case puts it, 'The first law is the law of the land . . . [T]he final arbitrator of the public interest can only be Parliament . . . [others] may not agree with it, but it is society's answer given through the mouth of Parliament.'[5] We will argue in section v that ethical prescriptions are felt as obligatory without any further authorisation other than the immediate call to obedience they give rise to. But in law, the normative restatement of the various commands in legal form elevates their addressees to legal subjects who are at the same time metaleptically declared to be its legislators and therefore free and equal before the law.

The law of the nation-state, however, despite its generality, excludes from the community of its subjects foreigners, immigrants and refugees. Aliens, who are not within the original addressees of the legal norm, are given notice nevertheless that if they come in contact with the state, the authority of its law will be engaged. A necessary dissymmetry develops, therefore, between the addressees of the law (subjects, citizens, the nation) and those others, its secondary and potential addressees. The first group comprises all those who are subjects in the eyes of the law. The second is a virtual group: it includes those who may come to the gates of the state and put themselves before the law. In such a case, they will be the addressees of the law's commands but not its subjects. The requirement that law's subjects and subjected should coincide cannot be satisfied. There are two types of positive law, however, where the Kantian injunction, that the law should represent the whole rational humankind, appears to be borne out. Human rights and colonial law.

International and supranational law, the international treaties and principles of human rights, are instances of a law that potentially addresses all states and all human persons qua human. Article 1 of the Universal Declaration of Human Rights, which only repeats the universalistic claims of the Declaration de Droits de L'Homme et de Citoyen, states that all 'men are born equal in rights and in dignity'. The Declaration claims that human nature is abstract and universal and is being parcelled out in equal shares to everyone, to all people in all eternity. But as we know, once the

---

[5] We discuss the case from which this quote is taken in Chapter 6.

slightest empirical and historical material is introduced into this abstract human nature, equally shared and equally free, once we move from the legal subject on to the concrete embodied person, human nature with its equality and dignity retreat. In other words, when we move from the abstract legal subject of the Kantian discourse and the declarations of human rights to the concrete human being in the world, the discourse of human rights is seen for what it is: an indeterminate discourse of legitimation or of rebellion that has little purchase as a descriptive tool of society and its bond. The community of human rights is universal but imaginary; the humankind of universal nature does not exist empirically and cannot act philosophically as its necessary principle. We should add that the draughtsmen of the Universal Declaration, suffering from a certain loss of philosophical under-standing and historical sensitivity that characterises the twentieth century, may have believed that they were acting on behalf of the whole humankind; but the French revolutionaries were much more cynical. They knew that only as historical representatives of the French nation were they enunciating the discourse of Universality.

Nations owe their existence and uniqueness to narratives, emblems and symbols. There has never been a nationalism that has successfully based its claim to nationhood and independent state existence on abstract claims of right and universality. Nations owe nothing to humanity, human nature and rights and everything to the repeated narrations of their origins, continuity and tradition. The French Revolutionary Assembly acted as a typical Kantian Legislator. It split itself in two parts: the philosophical part legislated for the whole world, the historical and empirical part for the only territory and people it could, France and its dependen-cies. The gap between the two is also the distance between the generality of state legislation and the universality of the absolute law. The French Assembly did not and could not legislate for the world; what it did was to attempt to make the discourse of universal right part of the foundation myth of modern France. From that point onwards, as Lyotard puts it (1988a, p. 147), it remains unknown whether the law is French or pan-human. A similar analysis could apply to the American revolutionaries and their Declaration of Independence (Derrida 1986b).

A second possibility of reconciliation between state law and its universal claim suggests itself in the French and American Revolutionary moves. The Kantian notion of autonomy is premised upon the power of the national legislature to impose its law upon the universe, the alien, the colonial, the third (world) in the name of the community of reason. The claim that national law represents the national community is as fictional as the assertion that the discourse of human rights represents the universal community. And yet all wars in modernity are in a certain sense imperial wars; they are ongoing battles in the civil war which aims to unite the national legislator with the universal human subject. Imperial law extends its authority beyond the territorial boundaries of nation-state and tries to address an ever-expanding group, to speak *urbi et orbi*. In all these instances, the (potential) audience of the command (you ought to . . .) and of the norm (it is authoritatively decreed that you ought to . . .) become co-extensive, but a huge gap opens between the legislators–subjects and the colonial–subjected. The explicit purpose of the Empire is to expand the community of those subjected to the law of the nation and make it co-extensive with the whole world. But those others or 'thirds', subjected to imperial law, are not and can never become its legislators, they can never be autonomous in a Kantian sense. The other side of the universal legal subject, of equality and autonomy, of law's formalism and its imperative (the categorical command), is the necessary inequality and the lack of autonomy of the alien and the other to nation. The discourse of universality is necessarily a White Mythology: the enthronement of free will as the principle of universal legislation is achieved only through the exclusion, disenfranchisement and subjection without subjecthood of the other (Derrida 1982; Spivak 1987; Young 1990).

In the universal community of reason, which acts as the horizon for the realisation of the law, the other, the alien, the third and unrepresentable is turned into the same, the critical distance between self and other is reduced and the experience of value of moral conscience is grounded solely on the representation of the other by the knowing and willing ego. The alternative is the other's exclusion, banning or forgetting. But the other who approaches me is singular and unique; she cannot be reduced to being solely an instance of the universal concept of the ego nor can she be subsumed as a case or example under a general rule or norm. The law of modernity based on self's right and the subject's empire is strangely immoral as it tries either to assimilate or to exclude the other.

IV

The dissolution of the classical ethico-political conception of justice created the two unrelated components of the modern social bond: morality and legality, or the ethical and the social aspects of justice. Moral philosophy abandons the examination of questions of social organisation, public virtue and the good, withdraws to the realm of private, almost solitary, conscience and concentrates on a largely abstract speculation about individual moral action. Political philosophy and its descendants, sociological theory and political economy, on the other hand, define justice exclusively as a social problem and concentrate on questions of distribution and retribution.[6] The second major component of the modern conception of justice is that of legal or formal justice, the proper concern of jurisprudence, to which we now turn.

If modernity is an era of a profound 'moral catastrophe', modern law, both as an institution and as the theoretical solution to the weakening of authority and of the social bond, has been the field where the abandonment of ethics has been carried out in its most radical form. Jurisprudence has based the specificity of the law in the programmatic exclusion of all considerations of value and substance from its domain. But at the same time, the law is proposed as the main substitute for the absent value consensus and the emptied normative realm. We are well aware of both the de-ethicalisation of law, of the banning of morality from legal operations and of the demand and expectation that law should

---

[6] The single concern that seems to unite many disparate theories of justice is the determination of the right criteria for the social distribution of rewards and benefits. (See Heller 1987, Chap. 1 and passim; Lucas 1980, Chap. 8 and passim; Perelman 1963, pp. 6–7; Rawls 1972; and Rescher 1966.) Our critique of the emphasis placed by modern theory on social justice does not imply that such inquiries are redundant. On the contrary, the importance placed by Marx and the socialist tradition upon the exploitation and suffering that economic conditions can create forms the strong background of our own exploration of justice (see Douzinas and Warrington, 1986). Our concern is to show how the *exclusive* emphasis on social and formal justice has left the law empty of ethical substance and unable to deal with the condition of postmodernity.

become the public face of an absent morality. For the bulk of
modern jurisprudence, the law is public and objective; its posited
rules are structurally homologous to ascertainable 'facts' that can
be found and verified in an 'objective' manner, free from the
vagaries of individual preference, prejudice and ideology. Its
procedures are technical and its personnel neutral. Any con-
tamination of law by value will compromise its ability to turn
social and political conflict into manageable technical disputes
about the meaning and applicability of pre-existing public rules.
Morality as much as politics must be kept at a distance; indeed the
main requirement of the rule of law in its contemporary version of
legality is that all subjective and relative value should be excluded
from the operation of the legal system. This insulation of law from
ethico-political considerations allegedly makes the exercise of
power impersonal and guarantees the equal subjection of citizens
and state officials to the dispassionate requirements of the rule of
rules as opposed to the rule of men. And as adjudication is
presented in common law jurisdictions as the paradigm instance
of law, the demand for justice is equated with the moral
neutralisation of the judicial process. In formal terms, justice
becomes identified with the administration of justice and the
requirements and guarantees of legal procedure, and the 'interests
of justice' are routinely interpreted as the interests of adjudication.[7] In substantive terms, justice loses its critical character.
The identification of justice with legality may have a long
historical pedigree since the coming of modernity; this
institutional-formal conception of justice, however, cannot act as
critique but solely as critical apology for the extant legal system.
Justice has changed from a utopian, even mystical tool of
denunciation of personal and socio-political wickedness into the
key legitimatory theme of modern law.

   In the eyes of jurisprudence, morality is private and subjective,
it is about individual values, norms and preferences which are in
principle incommensurable as no general value agreement exists.
Indeed, even this mutilated and publicly worthless morality is
treated as a second-order legality that is both ineffective and
indeterminate. Morality is about moral codes and the following of

---

[7] See our discussion of the technical term 'the interests of justice' in Chapter 6,
section v.

rules and principles posited either by a divine authority whose claims to universality in a multi-religious society are defunct or, in the various versions of neo-Kantian legal theory, by the autonomous and free subject who must discover in himself the laws of his universal subjection. Moral responsibility is measured according to the heartless subjection to the law and moral success according to criteria of instrumental rationality and conformity to the dictates of utilitarian calculations.

This attitude of legal theory towards ethics was reinforced by a more general tendency in Christian theology and classical political philosophy which assumed that man is naturally immoral and that his ethical ignorance and ineptitude necessitated the introduction of a social power to restrain his excesses. If man is immoral, society must introduce moral rules and norms and police his behaviour and actions through various internal and external devices and mechanisms. Religion and the Church were the first institutions to base their authority on the innate sinfulness of human nature. Liberal political philosophy took up the same theme with enthusiasm. Human nature before society is wild, aggressive, brutal and in need of restraint. The classical theorists were agnostic as to the causes of the predicament and the original sin soon lost its explanatory value. Nevertheless, the social contractarians after Hobbes saw the agreement as an attempt to tame human nature. Pre-social man is immoral or at least morally inept. Society, on the other hand, is the embodiment of morality and the main task of the state and its laws is to impose the restrictions necessary to prevent descent to total chaos.

Kantian practical philosophy and its progeny could be used as further evidence of the thesis of immorality of human nature. The free moral action that practical reason ordains is intensely painful for the subject who must suppress personal inclinations, desires and feelings to follow the moral law. Kant separated the human faculties and put an enormous wager on the power of reason to combat individual interest and inclination; but the reservations of Socrates and classical tradition about the ability of reason to make people choose to suffer rather than commit injustice were vindicated and the classical social theory had to follow where political philosophy had broken off. For Durkheim, the pressure of the collective conscience of society is necessary to restrain the amoral individual. For Freud, too, civilisation is based on the social renunciation of natural instinct and passion. The superego is the internal police which, by restricting untrammelled natural freedom and instinct, endows man with the necessary security. Indeed, one could define 'society' as the medium for and the site of moral restraint of recalcitrant (human) nature.

The jurisprudence of modernity has surreptitiously adopted a similar attitude towards human nature. For Austin (1954), law is the commands of a sovereign habitually obeyed because of the threat of sanctions. Austin's model of normativity as fear of punishment applies not just to the laws of the state but to law *tout court*: even divine and moral law base their obligatory character and effectiveness on threats and coercion. Two assumptions seem to operate here: first that morality has all the characteristics of legality, and second that man becomes moral and law-abiding in the same manner, that is, through fear or calculation of consequences. When Hart (1961) announces, *contra* Austin, that the law is not commands but rules, the main characteristic of which is their normative character, the transition from a morality of personal responsibility to a morality of heteronomous legislation is complete. Hart's concept may have lost the brutal realism of Austin's recognition of the role of power and force for the success of law's aims, but it has achieved the final transition from a morality of value to a legality of norm. The 'internal point of view', the characteristically ethical response of obligation towards the law, is now accorded to the valid accretions of state power in the form of rules which are carefully quarantined from ethical content.

The separation of law and morals means that, for the jurisprudence of orthodoxy, morality has vacated the normative universe, which is now exclusively inhabited by the prescriptions of the legislator and the decrees of the institution. Consequently, the main ethical concept and concern of law and jurisprudence, justice, is not directly involved with moral values. As Lucas puts it, justice is 'set in a somewhat low moral key. . . . I can be just, and yet lack many moral virtues' (1980, pp. 262, 263). Hart, too, accepts that wicked and bad laws are not necessarily unjust nor are good laws necessarily just (1961, pp. 153–4). According to his now classical formulation, justice has two parts, 'a uniform or constant feature, summarised in the precept "Treat like cases alike" and a shifting or varying criterion used in determining when, for any given purpose, cases are alike or different' (*ibid.*, p. 156). Its core is found in the administration of law: justice is identified with formal equality before the law and with the application of the same general rule to the various cases without prejudice or interest. And while conformity to the law is the key to legal justice, the concept includes also a limited 'dynamic' element which allows the critique of the rules determining the relevant resemblances and differences that the law must recognise if it is to treat like cases alike. In this sense, 'justice constitutes one segment of morality primarily concerned not with individual conduct but with the ways in which *classes* of individuals are treated' (*ibid.*, p. 163). But as Hart recognises, this type of critique concerns the distribution of burdens and benefits and is only one aspect of what we called the *social* concept of justice. For other 'realist' positivists, even this concession to an ethico-political conception of justice is too much. Alf Ross, for example, dismissed all non-formal conceptions as 'illusions which excite the emotions by stimulating the suprarenal glands'. There is no hope of a rational foundation of justice, Ross claims, because the concept is ideological and 'biological-emotional' and the science of law should abandon it (1974, p. 275). In the world of law, justice and injustice refer to fairness, the restoration of balance and proportion and the redress of the *status quo* between individuals.

We find the symbol of legal justice outside our civic buildings and courts of law: it is a blindfolded goddess holding the scales of justice or a sword. There is something chilling about the austere image of the scales accurately balancing actions and the sword threatening the punishment of the unjust. Justice is presented as a 'cold virtue, sometimes even a cruel one' (Heller 1987, p. 11). The world of legal justice 'lacks the warmth' of morality (Lucas 1980, p. 263). The standard explanation of the blindfold is that for Justice to be impartial and impersonal, she should not be able to see those she judges. The law should be declared and the wrongdoers punished without fear, prejudice or any consideration for charity, pity or the individual characteristics of the litigant. The judgment of Justice must not be corrupted by the senses and must be discovered within herself, in her bosom. As Anatole France memorably put it, the law in its majesty forbids both rich and poor to steal bread and to sleep under bridges. *Fiat justitia and pereat mundus.*

It should be remembered, however, that the practice of blindfolding justice is modern. In Chapter 2, we saw Antigone coming to the feet of all-seeing Dikē and launching herself to the altar of the goddess. Until the sixteenth century, hundreds of images have Justice with open eyes and without its cruel implements (Curtis and Resnik 1987). Furthermore, the late addition of the blindfold is not without its ambiguity. A blind justice may be an uninformed, uncaring, unjust justice who, as Thrasymachos argued, can be hoodwinked by the wealthy and powerful. Indeed, it can be argued that the initial motivation behind the blindfold was critical; the addition coincided broadly with the creation of centralised legal and judicial systems throughout Europe and it may have indicated to some the removal of the local and caring character of old law and Justice's subsequent inability to see the truth (ibid., pp. 1752–61). Interestingly, the gender of justice remains throughout female; and as Hegel reminded us in his readings of Antigone, the feminine principle is not associated with the cold logic of legal reason nor with the uncaring character of a blind calculation. It could be argued that the blindfold was added as a complaint by early modern art, as a reminder of the blindness of justice and a request for its removal.

The positivistic undermining of ethics was completed in the picture that jurisprudence painted of morality itself. For Hart, morality consists of rules which impose obligations and duties and are in many respects similar to primary legal rules. Moral rules are distinguished from legal rules, on the other hand, because they are important, they are backed by an intense form of moral pressure to conform, they are immune from deliberate change and finally because culpability follows only the voluntary commission of moral offences (Hart 1961, 163–76). The striking characteristic of this depiction of morality is its formal character and the absence of any discussion of its substantive requirements. Hart acknowledges that morality may include certain ideals (those of the hero and the saint) on top of rule-based duties, but he immediately adds that the moral criticism of such ideals should satisfy 'two formal conditions, one of rationality and the other of generality' (ibid., p. 178). Thus, while the law acquires its validity through the formalities of the rule of recognition and its legitimacy through its acceptance by the 'officials of the system', morality, too, appears to acquire its legitimacy through its extreme formalism. Morality has become a second-order legality. Both are based on a few 'truisms' about human nature that Hart discovers in those rules universally recognised and calls the 'minimun content of natural law'. All these truisms refer to the limitations of humankind; limited resources, understanding and vulnerability characterise the human condition. But it is the 'limited altruism' accompanied by the inequality amongst men which necessitate the enactment of restraining moral and legal rules.[8]

Despite the disavowal of all substantive moral theory, positivism inevitably adopts the thesis of moral ineptitude of human nature. The acceptance of this 'axiom of immorality' turns the law into the key institution that will install morality into man. But after the abandonment of the contractarian tradition, the morality of legality is totally heteronomous and operates exclusively through fear of sanctions or the utilitarian calculation of rewards and punishments. The principle of legality bestows legitimacy on the law through its origination in the organised power of the state and acts through the imposition of the 'collective' will upon immoral and anti-social individual instinct. Legality, as the nineteenth-century liberals explained, operates through external coercion. But the paramount legal task of suppressing human wickedness endows the legality of coercion with the ethereal attributes of morality; moral values may not be the provenance or contribution of legal transactions or judgments but the operation of the law as a whole is the only expression and guarantee of ethical power and public virtue that can tame private vice. The very absence of ethical value ensures the morality of the law. This is the basis of the jurisprudential claim that unjust laws should be obeyed because the morality of legality overrides local injustices (Finnis 1980; Fuller 1964). Thus, moral content may have been abstracted from law but the legal enterprise as a whole is blessed with the overall attribute of morality. On the surface, the transition from status to contract is supplemented by a parallel passage from value to norm and from the good to the right. The foundation of meaning and value has been firmly transferred from the transcen-

---

[8] Inequality is euphemistically called 'approximate equality' and this 'more than any other [factor] makes obvious the necessity for a system of mutual forbearance and compromise which is the base of both moral and legal obligation'. Based on these truisms, the setting of sanctions is declared a 'natural necessity' (Hart 1961, pp. 191, 195).

dent to the social; in this transition normativity has forfeited its claim to substance and value and has replaced them with blanket certifications of source and of conformity with form. But at the same time, form acquires moral value in itself and the law becomes the modern repository of a downgraded virtue.

This predominantly positivistic attitude is taken a (sophisticated) step further in the writings of Dworkin (1977, 1983, 1986). The law is no longer just about rules à la Hart, and certainly it is not the outcome of the unlimited will and power of the omnipotent legislator à la Austin. Law's empire includes principles and policies and its operation involves interpretative acts of judges who are invited to construct creatively the 'right answer' to legal problems; to do so judges must develop and apply political and moral theories that should present the law in the best possible light and create an image of the community as integrity. Morality (and moral philosophy) now enters the law and is properly recognised as an inescapable component of judicial hermeneutics. But its task is to legitimise judicial practice by showing the law to be the perfect narrative of a happy community. Morality is no longer a set of subjective and relative values nor is it a critical standard against which acts of legal and judicial power can be judged. The law is assumed to possess an internal integrity and coherence that allows the construction of public and quasi-objective principles of morality which can then be used as its underlying grammar and help resolve 'hard cases'.

Law's morality, as found by the judge with the help of moral philosophy, becomes the guarantee that the law never runs out. If a right answer exists, it can be discovered in every case through the mobilisation of the morality that law's internal criteria of coherence yield. Judges are never left to their own devices; the dreaded supplement of judicial discretion (in other words, the individual morality of the judge) that Hart had reluctantly admitted at the cost of endangering rational completeness, coherence and the closure of law is firmly kept outside. Dworkin seems prepared to reintroduce moral consideration to law. But his theory is the last step in the juridification of morality and in the assertion of the moral legitimacy of legalism, common symptoms of the process of de-ethicalisation of the law. The radical gap in the normative universe created by the strict separation between legality and morality and the reduction of ethics to the private and subjective is filled by the discourse of law, as the lighthouse on the way to universal and objective truth. But for those who want to challenge the dominant political theory; for those unrepresented, unrepresentable and excluded from the 'integrated' community; for those who experience the law not as rationality, rights and justifications but as victims of the exercise of power and as targets of legal force; for all those 'others', law's empire has no place.

The profound scepticism of orthodox jurisprudence towards morality is shared by progressive lawyers and critical legal theory. Their reservations stem historically from the rather muted approach to morality and justice adopted by Marx and Marxist theory. To put it briefly, the writings of Marx are full of outrage and condemnation of the suffering, poverty, oppression and exploitation created by capitalism. According to E. P. Thompson, 'Marx in his wrath and compassion, was a moralist in every stroke of his pen' (1978, p. 363). But at the same time, Marx and later Marxism, as a self-proclaimed scientific theory of society, insist on the transient character of morality, its context-dependence, finally its (immediate or ultimate) determination by the economy and domination by politics. This contradictory attitude led Marxisant lawyers to adopt a rhetoric of moral condemnation and exhortation when faced with the well-documented legal abuses towards women, ethnic minorities or other underprivileged groups. But this was accompanied by an almost universal lack of interest in morality, which was presented as bourgeois, Christian or simply as ineffectual liberal apologetics. Moral concerns were unflinchingly voiced on the streets and in the courts; but they were accompanied by persistent theoretical attempts to demystify their rather weak hold on political imagination. If the orthodox positivist thought and acted morally only outside the law, the radical acted politically both inside and outside, both in law and in morals.

A similar attitude was adopted by Marxism towards justice. A well-known debate amongst political theorists in the 1970s and early 1980s exhaustively considered the contradictory attitudes of Marx himself (Cohen, 1979; Buchanan 1982; Lukes 1985; Geras 1985, 1992). The majority concluded that his frequent references to the unfair nature of capitalism were polemical and pragmatic and that Marx and Marxism have no satisfactory theory of justice. But this attitude was also characteristic of radical lawyers. They denounced justice as 'class justice', while their struggles were aimed at achieving 'social justice'. At the practical level this led to limited successes; but theoretically the field of moral philosophy was abandoned and the few radical responses to the most influential liberal theory of social justice, that of Rawls (1971), remained at the level of general denunciation. In a curious, almost schizophrenic way, progressive lawyers are both for and against justice, fired by moral indignation but unable or uninterested in developing a critical conception of justice.

This lack of – theoretical – interest in questions of morality and justice was seemingly confirmed and strengthened by recent developments in poststructuralist and postmodern theory. One strand associated with Foucault emphasised the death of God and of the subject and virulently attacked the barren moralism of humanism. The subject is no longer seen as the ontologically unified centre of meaning; her consciousness cannot ground the world phenomenologically nor conscience morally. If the subject's soul is the contingent creation of the discourses of knowledge and power and her body the pliant outcome of the operations of the disciplines, any appeal to moral codes based on unalterable characteristics and needs of the human nature is wrong in theory and counter-productive in practice. This type of argument was particularly familiar and well-suited for critical lawyers. After all, it was in law that the first radical critique of the form of (legal) subjectivity was developed and entered the left canon.

The extension of this well-known critique from the legal subject to the subject *tout court*, and from Marx, Pashukanis and Edelman to Foucault and Baudrilliard, seemed quite natural. In what was a rather unprecendented instance, critical theory appeared for once to follow its counterpart in law. But for orthodox jurisprudence, the textual and deconstructive turn are the final attack on reason, morality and humanism. Deconstruction allegedly sees the subject as the outcome of linguistic, semiotic and psychoanalytic codes, which are in principle undecidable and open to the free play and dissemination of the sign. If no ultimate ground for meaning and morality exists, the postmodern intellectual relishes freedom, in a release of *jouissance* and innocence and a Nietzschean affirmation of amorality. The legal proponents of these heresies are derided from the right for nihilism, self-indulgence and immorality and from the left for relativism, lack of political commitment and of any relevance for the concerns of the 'real world'.

Against both the complacency of orthodoxy and the smugness
of early critical theory, postmodern jurisprudence insists that
morality and justice are not identical with legality nor can they be
simply reduced to the following of legal principle and procedures.
Acts of power cannot be criticised solely according to other acts of
power. Justice is either a critical concept or it is totally redundant
if not positively harmful for jurisprudence by encouraging an
unquestioning attitude to law. But is there a critical conception of
justice and morality that can be used to arbitrate between the
various conflicting versions of the good or of ethical action after
the modern attack on the Good and the postmodern attack on the
power of reason?

V

The classical conception of justice linked its ethical and political
aspects through a teleology of the good (life) that could also act as a
standard of critique. Modernity, by secularising the foundations of
authority and meaning, opened the independent normative realms
of morality and legality which, deprived of any overarching point
of exteriority or transcendence, based both the claim to power and
to its critique upon the universalising faculty of reason. Postmodernity recognises the exhaustion of the exalted attempts to
ground action upon cognition, reason or some a priori stipulated
conception of the good and marks the beginnings of a new ethical
awareness. But the relinking of the two realms must pass through a
different, another conception of the good, in a situation where
classical teleology is historically exhausted and religious transcendence is unable to command widespread or uniform acceptance.
We must transform the antinomy of law into the postmodern
aporia of justice; we need a quasi-transcendental ethical principle
that will allow us to criticise our moral and legal practices, while
being firmly placed within our history and experience. Our quest
will take us from Athens to Jerusalem, and from ontology to ethics.
    Emanuel Levinas (1969, 1989, 1991), the Jewish philosopher of
alterity, stands as the figure of the other of Greek archaeology – the
ethics of the *archē*, of principles and origins, and of *logos*, reason
and logic. The ethics of alterity, on the contrary, are based on the
shifting relationships between self and other. It is the unique
encounter with the living other, in her present and unrepresent-

able corporeality, that opens up the field of ethics. Levinas's ethics is a wholly different enterprise from that of traditional moral philosophy and jurisprudence. It calls for the re-ethicalisation of law, but the ethical substance to be reintroduced or reactivated in the body of law has nothing in common with the moralism of moral philosophy that exclusively builds collections of rules and principles.

Levinas argues that western philosophy and ethics share a common attitude towards the world which reduces the distance between self and other and returns the different to the same. Since the time of classical Greece, philosophy has put speculation as to the meaning of Being at the centre of its concerns and has claimed in various forms that the question of Being is governed by the protocols of reason. Universal *logos* reflects and will reveal the structure of reality since the ontological realm follows the demands of theoretical necessity. The traces of this ontological totalitarianism litter the body of philosophy. In its modern version, individual consciousness has become the starting-point of all knowledge and, as a result, what differs from the self-same has turned into a question of epistemology, an exploration of the conditions under which I can know the other's existence and understand her mental life. For phenomenology, the ego acquires knowledge through the intentionality of consciousness and its adequation with the phenomenal world; Husserl asserts the primacy of the perceptions of self and claims that the world discloses itself fully to consciousness. Heidegger, on the other hand, emphasises the historical and social nature of self. Self is not constituted before its implication with others. 'By "Others", we do not only mean everyone else but me – those over against whom the "I" stands out . . . but those among whom one is. . . . The world is always one I share with others' (Heidegger 1962, pp. 144–5). There is no life which is not life with others. Self does not postulate the other in its own image but, in discovering itself, it simultaneously recognises the other.

But Heideggerian ontology, too, by privileging the question of Being, makes the relationship between beings and Being the key concern of philosophy and explicitly abandons ethics in favour of the primordial *ēthos*. For Heidegger, self and the other are equal participants in the 'we' through which we share the world. However, all speculation as to the meaning of Being starts inevitably from the examination of my own being and returns to ontology's preoccupation with self. Sartre, on the other hand, accepts that the other is a subject before me but finds the separation between self and others so radical as to preclude any possibility of genuine knowledge of the other's consciousness. The other fixes her gaze on me and turns me into an object before I can establish myself as a gazing, objectifying subject. The shame of being looked at and judged makes me want to objectify the other in turn and ends by discovering hell in the face of others. The epistemology of modernity also claims that the world corresponds with its representations built by the subject and defines truth as the approximation between private mental images and theories and the world.

When ontological philosophy turns to ethics, it must supplement Being with the postulate of free will, a faculty absent from the empire of pure reason, and then subject freedom to the demands of reason. The universal *logos* thus becomes both necessary and morally obligatory, as it provides the criteria that establish the morally valid nature of action. As we saw, in Kantian moral philosophy it is the subject who legislates the law he obeys, but to do that he must postulate a universal community of beings who are similar if not identical in reason and inclination with the ego. The move from ontology to ethics, which is also a move from the protocols of theoretical necessity to the realm of praxis, must posit freedom and justify it through the universal rationality of form that legislates principles valid for all. To obey the *logos* is therefore to be autonomous (Bernasconi and Critchley 1991; Ciaramelli 1991; Critchley 1992). Reason reveals the structure of reality and subsumes individual cases and moral dilemmas to the imperative of universality, but in doing so it necessarily reduces the singularity of the individual person. The starting and concluding point of this universal moral law is the ego, the knowing and willing subject, who finds within himself all the resources necessary in order to turn the formal injunction to universality into a concrete moral norm.

Respect for the other is the unconditioned bedrock of Kantian morality. But this respect is motivated by the fact that the other, too, obeys the law and thus becomes a facet of my own respect for the law. I perceive the other as a free subject to the extent that she is governed like myself by the moral law and I offer her my respect for her obedience which is also the best available evidence of the operation of the law.

To be sure, I cannot fully know that the other is ruled by the law. But I must believe it, I am obliged to accept that her acts and moves follow the law, that the law rules her even though I have no immediate proof of that; I have to, I need the other's subjection as a 'type', a model of how the particular (act) can exist as an instance of the universal (law). It is the sense of the operation of the law in another that constitutes her as another. (Lingis 1989, p. 179)

I see the operation of the law in the pain 'with which the other rationally reduces his particular – irrationally impulsive – nature into the system of universal nature', I sense 'the mortification with which the universal becomes a motive in his will and intercepts the sensuous attachments from their objects'. (ibid.) The autonomous other becomes the exemplary figure of the law: in her pain and suffering I sense the work of the universal which also afflicts me by reducing all sensual inclination and carnal impulse to passivity. Both I and the other are autonomous as instances of obedience to the law which ordains that 'the particular die before the epiphany of the universal' (ibid., p. 183). The moral subject is as isolated as the epistemological subject and as a consequence morality must be grounded on the most universal and undiscriminating considerations. But as both Heidegger and MacIntyre have argued, the moral agent starts with too little and the search for rules and criteria for moral action cannot succeed for the same reason that the search was launched in the first place, that is, the lack of value consensus as to the purpose and meaning of the world. In all these instances, the movement is from the subject and the inside outwards and to the other, who is presented as an extension of or as a hindrance to the subject. Freedom 'is assurance that no otherness will hinder or prevent the Same and that each sortie into alterity will return to self bearing the prize of comprehension' (Critchley 1992, p. 6).

The ethics of alterity challenges the ontological and epistemological assumptions of traditional philosophy and their application in morals and jurisprudence. It always starts with the other and challenges the various ways in which the other has been reduced to the same. The other is not the self's alter ego, self's extension. Nor is the other the negation of self in a dialectical relation that can be totalised in a future synthesis. Heidegger correctly emphasises

the historical and social nature of self. But the other is not similar
to self; self and other are not equal partners in a Heideggerian 'we'
in which we share our world; nor is it the threatening externality
and radical absence of Sartrian existentialism that turns self into
an object.

The other comes first. (S)he is the condition of existence of
language, of self and of the law. The other always surprises me,
opens a breach in my wall, befalls the ego. The other precedes me
and calls upon me: where do you stand? Where are you now and
not who you are. All 'who' questions have ended in the
foundational moves of (de)ontology. Being, or the I of the Cartesian
cogito and the Kantian transcendental subject, starts with self and
creates other as an *imitatio ego*. In the philosophy of alterity, the
other can never be reduced to the self or the different to the same.
Nor is the other an instance of otherness or of some general
category, an object to a subject that can become a move in
dialectics.

The sign of another is the face. The face is unique. It is neither
the sum total of facial characteristics, an empirical entity, nor the
representation of something hidden: soul, self or subjectivity. The
face does not represent an absent presence, and cannot therefore
become a cognitive datum. Nor is the face the epiphany of a visage,
or the image of a substance. The face eludes every category. It
brings together speech and glance, saying and seeing, in a unity
that escapes the conflict of senses and the arrangement of the
organs. Thought lives in speech, speech is (in) the face, saying is
always addressed to a face. The other is her face. 'Absolutely
present, in his face, the Other – without any metaphor – faces me'
(Levinas quoted in Derrida 1978, p. 100). In its uniqueness, the
face gets hold of me with an ethical grip, I find myself beholden to,
obligated to, in debt to, the other person, prior to any contracts or
agreements about who owes what to whom. To comprehend is to
make something my own. But the face of the other cannot be
domesticated or consumed; alterity remains outside, quasi-
transcendental, unique, frail as the face that demands that I accept
my responsibility. The face is a fundamental ontological fact
which, however, cannot be systematised; in its orientation towards
me the face turns into an ethical fact by addressing me. In the face-
to-face, I am fully, immediately and irrevocably responsible for the
other who faces me. A face in suffering issues a command, a decree

of specific performance: 'Do not kill me', 'Welcome me', 'Give me Sanctuary', 'Feed me'. The only possible answer to the ethical imperative is 'an immediate respect for the other himself ... because it does not pass through the neutral element of the universal, and through respect, in the Kantian sense for the law' (Derrida 1978, p. 96).

The demand of the other that obliges me is the 'essence' of the ethics of alterity. But this 'essence' is based on the non-essence of the other who cannot be turned into the instance of a concept, the application of a law or the particularisation of the universal ego. 'The other arises in my field of perception with the trappings of absolute poverty, without attributes, the other has no place, no time, no essence, the other is nothing but his or her request and my obligation' (Lyotard 1988a, p. 111). As the face of the other turns on me, (s)he becomes my neighbour. But (s)he is not the neighbour of the neighbour principle in law. As absolute difference and otherness, my neighbour is at the same time most strange and foreign. The appeal of the other is direct, concrete and personal; it is addressed to me and I am the only one who can answer it. Against the claims of moral philosophy, this demand does not depend on universal reason or general law but on the concete historical and empirical encounter with the other. It is this situated encounter and unrepeatable, unique demand which assigns me to morality and makes me a bound and ethical subject. Our relationship is necessarily non-symmetrical and non-reciprocal as her unique demand is addressed to me and me alone. Equity is not equality but absolute dissymmetry.

The ontology of alterity, too, is based on the absolute proximity of the most alien. When self comes to constitute itself, before it faces the I, it must face I's relationship with the other. Subjectivity is constituted through this opening. All consciousness is intersubjective and all language is given, but as the other comes first, the nature of (inter)subjectivity is not that between two equal parties nor is the other a projection of self. My *principium individuationis* is my inescapable call to responsibility. My uniqueness is the result of the direct and personal appeal the other makes on me. It is me that the other addresses and not a universal ego or a legalistic personhood, as Antigone discovered. Before my identity and my subjectivity are constituted they have been subjected not to the law but to the other. This radical passivity precedes my

ontological freedom and makes it ethical, turns it into the acceptance of a vocation to which I alone can respond when called. To be
free and to be me is to do what no one else can do in my place.

In the ontology of alterity, the ego is elected; I am always
persecuted by the refugee and seek asylum from the exile, but (s)he
always comes back, always before me, a step behind or a step in
front, the not yet which is the always has been. Closer than the air I
breathe and further away than the starry sky, the other calls on me
but the encounter can never be fully consummated. Against the
concepts and strategies of traditional philosophy, the other is not
only the ground who by calling me to my unique responsibility
assigns me my singular subjecthood, but also the conceptuality
that escapes all systematicity, thus exploding the claims of
traditional philosophy, law and ethics to declare the social closed
upon itself. In this sense, the other has always and already been
within self, (s)he dispossesses and decentres self. The face is a
trace of otherness inscribed on the 'ground' of self. And if such is
the case, all return to self from otherness is exposed to this
exteriority which leaves its trace but can never be fully internalised. Self is always followed by the other's demand, never able to
return home fully, always an internal exile.

After the death of God, transcendence must be situated in
history. The experience of otherness is what lies beyond all totality
and takes us to the point where 'totality breaks up, a situation that
conditions totality'. The other who defines me gives me also
paradoxically the 'gleam of exteriority or of transcendence'
(Levinas 1969, p. 24). This empirico-historical transcendence
becomes the basis of judgment, an invisible judgment that
criticises or replaces the judgments of law and history, when they
forget otherness for the norm or destroy singularity for the
judgment of universal history or reason. The invisible judgment
lies behind subjectivity, the law and politics but it must become
explicit, it must come out from behind its veil. This is then the
basis of another judgment, the judgment of justice against which
the law will be measured.

VI

Let us summarise our argument. Modernity, in destroying any
generally acceptable conception of value or virtue and in disasso-

ciating ethics from law, makes justice a central concern of political
theory and the main area of contention of practical politics. But the
modern conception of justice is no longer that of dikē, the social
face of the ethics of intersubjectivity; it becomes exclusively *social*
justice, an artificial way of organising the social order when all its
traditional bases have been weakened. Justice becomes a key
concern for social theory and secondarily for jurisprudence but it
is no longer about ethics, either in the sense of the good or in the
sense of 'boundedness' to the other. It is either the justice of the
social contract, based on the claim that obligation is binding only
if all subjects rationally agree to it; or, in law, it becomes a
derivative of the morality of the Kantian imperative and combines
self-legislation with the rational form of moral law. While the
quest for social justice has led to some of the most important
improvements in social conditions in the last one hundred years, it
has much greater relevance for politics and economics than for
law; Kantian formalism, on the other hand, ends up in the blatant
assertion that formal legality equals justice and identifies justice
with the administration of justice. We need to reintroduce ethics
in law but traditional moral philosophy has proved insufficient. At
this turning-point, the ethics of Levinas can provide the initial
inspiration for imagining an Other Justice.

The ethics of alterity is a challenge to all attempts to reduce the
other to self and the different to the same. The ethical arises in
relation to a point of exteriority that cannot be included in any of
the totalities and systematicities that philosophy and law build.
Moral consciousness is not an experience of values but the
anarchic (an-archē, without beginning or principle) access to a
domain of responsibility and the obligated answer to the other's
demand. Unlike moral philosophy and applied ethics, the ethics of
alterity is not concerned to legislate moral codes or to discuss and
apply norms of morality. Unlike jurisprudence, it does not attempt
to legitimise the operations of the law but to *just*-ify the law, to
bring it before the altar of justice. This is not the traditional
moralistic ethics of deontologists or the consequential and
calculative morality of utilitarians. Levinasian ethics, somewhat
like the law of Antigone, is an origin before any origin, an ethics of
ethics and the law of law; it is the opening upon which rises
individual and community and which grounds the moral stimulus, the legality of laws and the politics of community.

Political philosophy and jurisprudence have based their theories on the assumption of immorality of human nature. The law, too, as the secular successor of religion and jurisprudence, as the heir to theology, has insisted that pre-legal human nature is morally ignorant, inept or plainly evil while the law is the embodiment of morality. The ethics of alterity, on the other hand, starts from the opposite premise, namely that the ineradicably intersubjective nature of consciousness points to the direction of an innate human ethicity. It may be that the assertion of innate ethicity in the midst of the ravages of the domestic and international scene in the 1990s sounds extravagantly optimistic if not dangerously deluded. Yet the claim of human wickedness too, which dominates political theory and jurisprudence, despite its superficial realism, is itself a quasi-transcendental axiomatic presupposition and not the inevitable conclusion of empirical observation or the reasoned outcome of theoretical practice.

The validity or accuracy of such axioms does not lie in their ability to represent 'social reality'; mimetic epistemologies can no longer innocently sustain the validity of theoretical constucts by simply 'pointing' to their evidence (Feyerabend 1993; Rorty 1979). Such constructs can defend themselves by claiming that they display a systemic consistency of explanation or an organic unity or coherence which can be reproduced in their *explanandum*. The alleged coherence of the theoretical explanation is subsequently and unarguably presented as an attribute of the object. It is accepted without much argument, accordingly, that since much of jurisprudence and political theory assumes the moral deficiency of human nature, man is evil. But theory *tout court* and its axiomatic presuppositions even more are not neutral. Organising paradigms are intensely normative; despite protestations to the contrary, they invariably include sets of values that prescribe certain theoretical paths while prohibiting others. The choice of a particular interpretation, from amongst the many competing in a field, is itself the outcome of an interpretative process and already involves a pre-theoretical election of value. In a field like law and politics, where description and prescription, fact and value, theory and practice are inextricably linked, the choice of interpretative axioms is itself a supreme act of legislation. The hypothesis of human wickedness is a self-authenticating paradigm: it helps establish the paramount significance of social and legal attempts to tame moral deficiency

and at the same time, by denying the moral nature of consciousness, it contributes to its suppression. As Bauman puts it, the
allegation of 'moral deficiency of man, like all self-authenticating
devices, is its own construction and verification' (1990, p. 3).

But while the axiom of natural immorality is the founding
hypothesis of modern jurisprudence, it cannot be denied that legal
rules carry a sense of obligation independent of sanctions. Hart, for
example, claimed that legal rules have an 'internal aspect', that
people 'feel bound' to follow them and that they adopt a 'critical
reflective attitude' towards the behaviour they require; this
attitude of non-coerced obedience is characteristically expressd in
the 'normative terminology of "ought", "must", and "should",
"right" and "wrong" ' (1961, p. 56). A large amount of literature
has unsuccessfully tried to explain the nature of this feeling of
obligation or 'boundedness', which sits rather uncomfortably next
to Hart's emphasis on the positivity of law and its divorce from
morals; various types of psychologism and sociological concepts
such as socialisation, normative internalisation and integration
have been proposed. But they all share Hart's axiom of immorality
and are thus caught in an inescapable circle: if human nature is
morally deficient, all feelings of obligation must be inserted from
the outside by the agent of morality, society, and are only
supplementary to the main device of moral education, that is,
heteronomous legislation and coercion. As Hart himself admits at
the end, the internal point of view towards rule-following is only
necessary for ' "the officials of the system". The private citizen
need only obey legal rules "for his part only" and from any motive
whatever' (ibid., p. 113). Morality has been excluded ex hypothesis; it only re-enters the picture as so many informal societal
impositions and as a supplement and substitute for law.

Yet the intuition of Hart and of the natural law tradition can be
interpreted from the alternative hypothesis of the ethical nature of
human intersubjectivity. It is not the existence or operation of
rules that create feelings of obligation, of 'ought' and 'ought not',
nor is it the normative horizon that generates the 'internal aspect'
of human behaviour. The good is not the outcome of the operation
of the law but precedes all laws, norms and principles. In this
sense, the good is the name for the radical ethical turning of
human consciousness to the other which creates a feeling of duty
before and beyond any rules and norms. It is this ethical attitude

that establishes the possibility of all law and it is the relationship to the other that lies behind its – often unjust – crystallisation in rules. This attitude is characterised by unconditioned concern and care for the other which is not based on calculation of reward or fear of sanction. This disinterested concern resembles the Kantian respect for the law, but unlike the latter, it has the other as its exclusive target. It starts from the other's demand and finishes with its satisfaction. It does not follow the contours of traditional natural law; there is no claim that the world is organised in morally significant ways that allow us to learn our duty through our rational comprehension of its purposeful patterns. No law follows from the observation of nature and no law can be discovered exclusively through even the most elaborate rational deliberation. The concern for the other is innate, it needs no excuse or justification, it allows no choice and asks to be acted upon immediately.

Such is the attitude of Antigone; her momentous actions do not follow any serious contemplation or deliberation, she needs no argument, convincing or explanation and has no doubts or reservations. Her stubbornness has surprised generations of critics. Antigone does not consider the arguments and pleadings of her sister, of Creon or the Chorus. She acts before reasoning and without justification because she needs none; Antigone acts before she knows. Her duty is known to her at once and therefore it is strictly unknown as it does not enter independently the realm of knowledge. This unknown knowledge resembles the operation of language: all knowledge is acquired through and in language but in such manner that language itself becomes invisible. Antigone's attitude of disinterested concern for the other is the basis of self's existence. The social and political aspect of this concern, the law that Antigone follows and inaugurates, can be called ethical justice, or, to avoid terminological difficulties, since the concept of justice has been so strongly identified with fairness and distributive principles, dikē. It is this concept of dikē, the moral face of justice, that must be reintroduced in the law.

But how can we move from the ethics of responsibility to the law? What is the relevance of a discourse that claims pre-ontological and pre-rational status and emphasises the uniqueness of the face for a legality that has universalistic pretensions and bases its empire upon the rationality of judgment and the thematisation of people and circumstances? If the ethical response is based on the contingent appearance of a face in need, can there be a justice that moves beyond the ethicity of the contingent, thus helping the re-ethicalisaton of the law? Can the ethics of alterity be generalised and thus become the justice of the law? Does the justice of the law derive from the unabiding hostility of one for another and the need to restrain violence or does it derive from ethics and responsibilty? These are the key questions that we have to answer.

The ethics of alterity is unequivocal; the sense of responsibility, the 'internal' point of view speaks to me and commands me, the 'should' and 'should not' that lie at the base of all law come from the proximity of one for another, from the fact that we are involved and implicated as we are faced and addressed by the other. In my proximity to the other, within the law or outside of it, I am preoccupied by the absolute asymmetry and I find myself in an irreplaceable and irreversible relation of substitution. The ethical critique of the law has as its main aim to alert law to its ethical significance and to bring it again before the altar of Dikē. The ethical critique of law is conducted in the name of another justice. To be sure, the law is about calculation and systematisation, it regulates and totalises the demands that are put before it.[9] The law translates these requests in the universalisable language of rights, legal entitlements and procedural proprieties and synchronises them, makes them appear contemporaneous and comparable. Almost by definition and necessity the law seems to forget the difference of the different and the otherness of the other. To say, therefore, that the law begins as ethics, as the infinite, non-totalisable and non-regulated moment of the encounter with another, sounds counterfactual. And yet it is on the basis of justice as *dikē* or of the 'legal as ethical' that we can visualise a politics of law that disturbs the totalising tendency of the legal system. Such politics would allow the other to reappear both as the point of exteriority and transcendence that precludes the closure of ontology and as the excluded and unrepresentable of political and legal theory.

We should start with critique. Law and jurisprudence share fully the cognitive and moral attitudes of modernity. Cognitively,

---

[9] See further our discussion in Chapter 5, section II.

the law knows the world to the extent that it subjects it to its regulative operations. For the jurisprudence of modernity, the law and the world are potentially co-extensive. The legal system has all the necessary resources to translate non-legal phenomena into law's arcane discourse and thus exercise its regulative function. Indeed, the so-called 'constitutive' theory of law that found favour in the 1980s amongst American critical scholars repeats in law one of the great foundational myths of modernity, namely that we can know something to the extent that we can create it (Hunt 1986). According to this 'poetic' theory of law, nothing is in principle beyond the reach of the legal institution, which becomes the instrument and metaphor of the Will of modernity, the demiurge that shapes the world. In moral terms, on the other hand, the law is declared free of any ambition and is assigned to the technical administration of the world and of justice. But as we saw this moral indifference or impotence of law results in the central paradox of modern political theory and jurisprudence: ethics is absent from law but social theory becomes obsessed with justice. Ancient and medieval theories linked ethics and the good with the just organisation of the community and thus facilitated the mediation between individual ethical responses and the structures of social power. And as we now move from the certainties of modernity to the postmodern condition, the demand for an ethics becomes the most important theoretical and practical priority.

The second major criticism of law and jurisprudence concerns the form of personhood that the law makes central to its operations. In existential terms, the subject of legal and contractual rights and agreements stands at the centre of the universe and asks the law to enforce his entitlements without great concern for ethical considerations and without empathy for the other. If the legal person is an isolated and narcissistic subject who perceives the world as a hostile place to be either used or fended against through the medium of rights and contracts, (s)he is also disembodied, genderless, a strangely mutilated person. The other as legal subject is a rational being with rights, entitlements and duties like ourselves. We expect to be treated equally with the other and reciprocity of entitlement and obligation is placed at the base of the legal mentality. But this conception of justice as fairness must necessarily reduce the concreteness of the other, it must minimise the differences of need and desire and emphasise the similarities and homologies between the subjects. The moral worthiness of the other's demand is to be sought more in what self and other share than in those differences and specificities that make the other a concrete historical being.

The other of law is not dissimilar in its main characteristics from the Rawlsian moral agent. It would be useful to examine briefly Benhabib's important feminist critique of Rawlsian theory which is of great relevance for law too (Benhabib 1992). The Rawlsian self in the original position is blindfolded, like many artistic representations of justice, by 'the veil of ignorance'. She does not know her class, her status, her fortune and ability or her intelligence and strength, nor does she have any conception of the good or a rational plan of life. Behind this absurd hypothesis lies the concern of moral philosophy for the interests of the other. The – temporary and heuristic – destruction of identity puts self in a position of reversibility with the others, thus enabling the agent to consider their interests while still acting as a rational egoist, since she cannot tell what her exact state in life is. Such a huge abstraction from what a real self is and from how moral argument operates is necessary to sustain the Kantian claim of universality of the moral law. The subject of concern of moral philosophy is a 'generalised other' with whom we relate through public and institutional norms of formal equality and reciprocity. The other is a representative of humankind and as such dignified and worthy of respect as much as self. But as Benhabib notes, while such individuals may have the capacity of agency, they are not human selves at all.

Identity does not refer to my potential for choice alone, but to the actuality of my choices, namely to how I, as a finite, concrete, embodied individual, shape and fashion the circumstances of my birth and family, linguistic, cultural and gender identity into a coherent narrative that stands as my life's story. . . . The self is not a thing, substrate but the protagonist of a life's tale. The conception of selves that can be individuated prior to their moral ends is incoherent. (1992, pp. 161–2)

The proper moral standpoint of the 'concrete other', by contrast, is based on norms of 'equity and complementary reciprocity: each is entitled to expect and to assume from the other forms of behaviour through which the other feels recognised and confirmed as a concrete, individual being with specific needs, talents and capacities' (ibid.). The veil of ignorance and all such generalising

devices, by obscuring the concreteness of the other, destroy her
identity and, as they lack the necessary criteria for individuation,
they cannot distinguish between self and other.

These criticisms are equally valid in law. Legal rules ensure
equality before the law and guarantee the freedom of the parties.
But this equality is only formal: it necessarily ignores the specific
history, motive and need that the litigant brings to the law in order
to administer the calculation of the rule and the application of the
measure. Similarly with legal freedom: it is the freedom to accede
to the available repertoire of legal forms and rights, the freedom to
be what the law has ordained, accompanied by the threat that
opting out is not permitted, that disobedience to a legal norm is
disobedience to the rule of law *tout court* and that life outside the
legal form ceases. We examined above how legal rules and their
mentality are strangely amoral as they promise to replace ethical
responsibility with the mechanical application of predetermined
and morally neutral rules and justice with the administration of
justice. But there is more: moral philosophy in its ontological
imperialism needs and creates the generalised other. The law, on
the other hand, sharing the preoccupation to abstract and
universalise, turns concrete people into generalised legal subjects.
But the legal subject, too, is a fiction and the natural (legal) subject
is infinitely more fictitious than the corporate. The difference
between the fictions of Rawls and those of the law is that the legal
subject is a *persona*, a mask, veil or blindfold put on real people
who, unlike the abstractions of moral philosophy, hurt, feel pain
and suffer. It is doubly important in law and jurisprudence,
therefore, to remove the mask from the face of the subject and the
blindfold from the eyes of justice. But is there an ethical residue in
the law behind the all-concealing veil of formal legality?

In *Otherwise than Being*, Levinas (1991) introduced the distinction between *saying* and *said* as the main metaphor for the
opposing fields of ethics and ontology. The opposition is not
between two aspects of the same phenomenon nor is it a totalisable
dialectical relationship. The two are both connected and radically
separate: every said proceeds from an act of saying radically
turned and addressed to an other. But as soon as saying becomes
said/heard, it takes the form of a constative or descriptive
proposition or judgment in which a subject is assigned to a
predicate (y is z). The constative proposition, Levinas's 'said',

states truth, it is public, generalisable and objective; the said enters
the language of ontology, which is concerned with the meaning of
beings and thematises concepts and entities whose essence belong
to the presence of Being. But ontological philosophy has forgotten
that all speculation on Being and beings in verbal form is always
addressed to other(s). For philosophy, the exclusive domain of
intervention is the said or the text. The act of saying, of speaking/
hearing, the performance which takes place diachronically and
involves at least two in a face-to-face has not been of much
concern. Indeed, structuralist linguistics examines the act of
enunciaton but only after it reduces it to a said, a description of a
state of affairs that has lost its radical nature as a saying that
happens here and now. The time of the said is synchronous,
unified, its order is linear, an orderly succession of past, present
and future points along a continuum. As we explain further in
Chapter 6, this is also the time of (legal) interpretation. The time of
saying, on the other hand, is diachronic: a dispersed arrangement
of unrepeatable moments, the authentic time of the event when it
happens, in its discontinuous, unpredictable seriality. This is the
time of ethics.

Levinas uses the auditory metaphor to emphasise the difference
between an ethics of alterity and western ontology, which has used
the all-seeing eye (*theorein, theoria*: to see, the gaze) as its main
symbol and organ. But the metaphor helps us identify a key area of
law that seems still to acknowledge the importance of alterity. The
law recognises within its own procedures and attempts to impose
to a certain extent upon decision-makers and judges the principle
of speaking/hearing: *audi alteram partem*, let the other speak,
before judging another give her a hearing. This is the first principle
of natural justice and it is also the first principle of *dikē*. The
injunction that the judge should hear the other speak can first be
explained as a requirement of logic. If we look at criminal law and
procedure, intention has been defined as a requirement of foreseeability, of prognosis and acceptance of one's acts. As in all other
areas, here too, the law has eliminated aspects of value and the
good by addressing all such matters as questions of capacity or by
reducing them to the formal question of whether the defendant
acted with the intention to bring about the consequences of his
actions. The criminal subject autonomously calculates, wills and
causes the acts for which he takes responsibility but has no moral

existence that is relevant to the question of guilt. To the extent that
law's theory of action distinguishes between intentional and
unpredictable or unintended consequences, hearing the litigant is
a main prerequisite for categorising his actions and determining
responsibility. Legal procedure cannot operate with the litigant
silent. This requirement may have now turned into a formality as
the civil litigant in particular will be heard in person only rarely;
yet the legitimacy of adjudication is largely based on the oral
character of the procedure.

But, second, the *audi* rule shows the law concerned to hear the
concrete person who comes before it, rather than to calculate and
adjudicate the general qualities and characteristics of the
abstracted legal person. Not to give the other a hearing is to deny
her humanity, to treat her as someone without the basic qualities
of moral worth and capacity. Even more, the demand to hear the
concrete other undermines the persistent claim of the law that
persons must be judged exclusively according to their classification in broad categories and be treated equally as instances of the
application of general rules. The *audi* rule turns the ethical
obligation to treat the other as a full and unique person into a
logical prerequisite of all judgment.

Judgment exists and can be passed only because the primordial
dikē opens the field of its possibility. It is only because self is
unquestionably and unreservedly bound to otherness that the legal
institution comes to existence in the first place. The oldest Greek
courtroom was the *agora*, the oldest judge a *histor* (Homer 1961,
p. 388; cf. G. Rose 1984, p. 66). Rather than the law being the
symptom and proof of man's immorality, in its emphasis on
speaking and hearing, the law appears to come to existence
because of man's morality shown in the natural turn to hear the
other. As Seneca's Medea put it: 'he who decides anything with
the other side unheard, may have reached a just decision, but is
not himself just' (v. 199–200). The law always comes after and is
built upon the clearing opened by ethics.

VII

But can the recognition of the ethical grounding of law help us
approach the demand for justice in the contemporary legal
institution? The ethical relationship concerns the encounter

between self and other. The law, on the other hand, introduces the demands and expectations of the third party. When someone comes to the law, he is already involved in a situation of disagreement or conflict with at least one more person; the judge will often have to balance the conflicting requests of two others. Indeed, the judge himself, seen from the perspective of the litigants, is a third person, whose action removes the dispute from the domain of interpersonal hostility and places it within the confines of the institution. In all instances, the law appears to be concerned not just with 'I' and 'Thou', but with the public aspect of the intersubjective encounter which is mandated by the existence of the third. This public aspect of the ethical relationship is created by the fact that the third party is other than the neighbour, but she is also herself a neighbour and also the neighbour of the other. Even in face-to-face encounters, the third party looks at me through the eyes of the other and puts a distance between me, the other and his contemporary and neighbour. Thus, my ethical response to the other who faces me is also and inevitably an address to the community. 'The other is from the first the brother of all the other men' (Levinas 1991, p. 158). But the co-existence of 'all the other men' places a limit on my infinite responsibility towards the other.

Because the third is always present in my encounter with the other, the law is implicated in every attempt to act morally and the need for *justice* arises.

Justice is necesary, that is, comparison, coexistence, contemporaneousness, assembling, order, the *visibility* of faces, and thus intentionality and the intellect, and in intentionality and the intellect, the intelligibility of a system, and thence also a co-presence on an equal footing as before a court of justice. (*ibid.*, p. 157)

For Levinas, 'law' refers to the Torah, and his Talmudic readings give a moving analysis of the unconditional acceptance Jews owe to the gift of law, an acceptance that precedes any examination and a commitment to action before any understanding or conscious adherence. This specific use of the term 'law' makes Levinas use the word 'justice' to describe the operations of the legal institution. It is justice in Levinas's terminology or the law in ours that limits the infinite responsibility for the other and introduces the element of calculation, representation, synchronisation and thematisation in the asymmetrical ethical encounter. 'In the order of justice, I and the Other can be compared as contemporaries or peers, occupying the same synchronic order. . . . At the level of justice, I and the Other are co-citizens of a common *polis*' (Critchley 1992, p. 232). In a community of equals, I, too, am another like the others, and I, too, am a legitimate claimant and recipient of the other's care. Community, then, is double: first, it is an ethical community of unequal hostages to the other, a network of undetermined but immediate ethical relationships of asymmetry where I am responsible and duty-bound to respond to the other's demand. But community also implies the commonality of law, the calculation of equality, and the symmetry of rights. Here we approach a key contemporary aspect of the *aporia of justice*: to act justly you must treat the other both as equal and as entitled to the symmetrical treatment of norms and as a totally unique person who commands the response of ethical asymmetry.

While the ethical community lives in the synchrony of the here and now expressed in the active mode of saying, the community of law is that of the contemporaneity of the said. The saying creates subjectivity and individuality while the said, by comparing the incomparables, opens the field of representation, reason and consciousness. In justice

everything is together, one can go from the one to the other and from the other to the one, put into relationship, judge, know, ask 'what about . . .?', transform matter. . . . The saying is fixed in a said, is written, becomes a book, law and science. (Levinas 1991, pp. 158–9)

If ethics comes before law and the subject, justice is the ground of representation and substitution, in other words the ground of being. In this precise sense, truth is justice; justice is not the creation or derivation of truth but, as Antigone, too, taught us, the ground upon which all claims to truth and the law arise and are judged.

But do we not betray our responsibility to the other by moving from the saying to the said and from ethics to justice and the law? Is justice possible? What would it mean for justice to be empirically possible? We have already seen that no ethical theory that describes ethical action is possible. Similarly, if we were to define justice as the ethical operation of the law, no theory of justice would be possible nor could we say in advance 'justice is x or y', because that would turn the injunction of ethics into an abstract theory and the command 'be just' to an empty judgmental statement. Justice is not about theories and truth; it does not derive from a true representation of just society. If the law calculates, if it thematises people by turning them into various types of legal subject endowed with rights and entitlements, ethics is a matter of an indeterminate judgment; a judgment without criteria. Justice is the bringing together of the limited calculability and determinacy of law with the infinite openness and contingency of alterity.

The idea of an indeterminate judgment refers us to two seemingly unrelated traditions, Aristotelian practical wisdom and Kantian reflective judgment. To be sure, Aristotelian ethics is criticised by the neo-Kantians for being undetermined by moral principle and therefore open to manipulation through the mas-querading of unbridled decisionism as (non-existent) virtue. Similarly, the principle of reflective judgment has been restricted to aesthetic matters while practical judgment is presented as the determined action of the universal moral law. But the postmodern condition has increased our awareness of the aporia of justice: legal authorities proliferate in a pluralistic, under-regulated manner without the false solace of universal reason or principle that modernity promised, and this pluralism injects decisions with the sense and urgency of ethical responsibility. But at the same time the only principle capable of universalisation is that of personal freedom. In these conditions, the eclectic adoption by law of principles from the traditions of practical wisdom and of reflective aesthetic judgment is imperative.[10]

We have referred to the Aristotelian *phronēsis* repeatedly (see Chapter 3 and Chapter 4, section I, but let us return to this alternative tradition in ethics for the last time. In Aristotle, *phronēsis*, or practical wisdom, can become a coherent theory of judgment because it is inextricably linked with a clear teleology of persons and actions. The aim of ethics is the achievement of the good life, but similarly every practice, profession or engagement is

---

[10] Hannah Arendt was one of the first philosophers of the century to try to combine the practical philosophies of Aristotle and Kant with particular emphasis on the context-dependence and the uniqueness of moral and political judgments. (See Arendt 1958 and 1977; cf. Benhabib 1992, Chap. 4.) The recent writings of Jean-Francois Lyotard (1988a and 1988b), on the other hand, have been concerned to explore the importance of the *Critique of Judgment* for practical judgments.

unified through what MacIntyre calls 'standards of excellence' which allow us to call an orator, or a politician or a carpenter good. The good life is always situated, it is good for us; it involves an ongoing dialogue and adjustment between our actions, aiming at the standards of excellence of the various practices we engage in, and our overall 'life plan', the more or less clear set of ideas, hopes, dreams and expectations that make us believe that our life, through its various episodes, joys and mishaps, is a fulfilled, good, successful one. Against this background, phronēsis is the method of deliberation followed by the prudent in order to arrive at judgments that will help them achieve the standards of excellence of the various practices, as stations of the wider project of enjoying the good life.

Practical wisdom is, then, the virtue of praxis, the achievement of the good in practical matters under our control. The prudent man can deliberate well and can aim 'at the best of goods attainable by man' (Aristotle 1976, VI. 213–14). Practical judgments, unlike theoretical statements, do not deal with essences or with necessary and immutable relations; they have a timely and circumstantial character and depend on a full and detailed understanding of the factual situation. The theoretical sciences examine general principles and the formal connections between phenomena, while practical knowledge deals with the changing and the variable, with 'ultimate particulars', and tries to grasp the situation in its singularity (ibid., 215). Indeed, Aristotle goes as far as to compare the singularity of practical judgment to that of perception (aisthēsis) (ibid., 219–20). Thus, while the evolving knowledge of the aims of good life forms the horizon of Aristotelian ethics, phronēsis recognises that moral norms and values are just that, a horizon. And in his discussion of justice, Aristotle argues that equity (epieikeia) is the rectification of legal justice (nomos) insofar as the law is defective on account of its generalisations. While laws are universal, 'the raw material of human behaviour' is such that it is often impossible to pronounce about it in general terms. Thus 'justice and equity coincide, and both are good, [but] equity is superior' (ibid., v. 199). Aristotle goes on to use the rule as a metaphor for law. But as the object to be regulated has an 'irregular shape', the law should be like the leaden Lesbian rule: 'just as this rule is not rigid but is adapted to the shape of the stone, so the ordinance is framed to fit the circumstances' (*ibid.*, 200). Justice and the variety of circumstances in which practical judgment is exercised require that the prudent go beyond the application of rules. Aristotle did not follow the casuistical route and did not compile lists and classifications of good and bad acts like his medieval followers. But the Aristotelian practical judgment is preoccupied with the specificity of the situation and with the perception, understanding and judging of the singular as singular.

For the Kantian morality of duty, on the other hand, practical judgments are determinant and their task is simply to subsume the particular under the universal law. In contrast to aesthetic judgments, practical judgments follow a *factum rationis*, the law given to practical reason as an a priori transcendental precondition. This formal law gives rise to duty, not to specific duties to do something or other, but to the feeling of duty in general and to the pain of feeling obliged, which must be concretised by the subject. But while the moral law, respect of which leads to the morally good, is 'supersensuous', moral actions belong to the phenomenal world and the senses (Kant, quoted in Benhabib 1992, pp. 130–1). It has been repeatedly observed that the idea of moral law and universal freedom as a fact of reason cannot subsume or direct empirical behaviour. If it belongs to the suprasensible world, the law itself becomes an undetermined concept, a critique of Kantianism that we examined above in a different setting. Thus, free will, to become moral, must be embodied in action as determined by the law but as soon as it becomes concretised, the law loses its pure character and stops being a fact of reason (Benhabib 1992, pp. 131–2; Lyotard 1988b, p. 37). This paradox of practical judgment alerts us to the relevance of the reflective judgment for ethics.

A reflective judgment starts from the particular object that confronts us and functions without pre-existing general rules. Aesthetic judgments make a claim to universality, but their law is unknown, indeed non-existent; it is active in its application and yet always still to come and be formalised. The appeal to the universal makes a promise of community, of a *sensus communis*, and that appeal differentiates aesthetic judgments from contingent or idiosyncratic preferences and tastes. But the community remains virtual; aesthetic judgment alludes to its existence but this republic of taste can never become actual. These strict preconditions and qualities necessarily make the aesthetic a judgment of pure form, uncontaminated by considerations of need, interest, desire or use. While everyone should be able to experience the pleasure of the feeling of beauty in confronting the aesthetic object, the subject cannot formulate the concept or the law that her judgment implies and thus make it accessible to others. Aesthetic judgments are examples in search of their rule, subjective and individual yet in the service of the undetermined universal. As the universal law and the community they imply cannot be actualised, they are only an idea present in each judgment which carries 'the promise of its universalisation as a constitutive feature of its singularity' (Lyotard 1988b, p. 38; cf. Douzinas and Warrington with McVeigh 1991, Chaps 3 and 10; Kant 1973). The aesthetic community is in a continuous state of formation and dissolution; it is the precondition and horizon of judgment but each judgment passed marks the community's end.

This analysis can be of great importance for the revitalisation of justice and ethics in law. The Aristotelian *phronēsis* insists on the importance of situation and context but is predicated upon a teleology that does not exist and cannot be recreated. The judge may be the person closest to the classical model of the *phronimos* in modernity but, in the absence of a shared universe of value, his ethical prudence is strictly circumscribed. We, therefore, must envision new ways of giving the other her due and of returning law to justice. Modern legal *phronēsis* must move between the norm and the event in the same way that reflective judgments find in each particular the mark of an undetermined universal. The morality of legal duty and right produces inevitable and inescapable conflicts and injustices that the legal institution can address only if it returns to the initial intuition of ethics, that practical judgment only works in the context of the good (life). But this universal can no longer be the consensual virtue of the *polis* of classical teleology nor the abstract duty to follow the law of modern deontology. At the end of modernity, the good can only be defined according to the needs and demands of the other, the person in need, but also the self-defining autonomous person whose request asks for the reawakening of the sensitivity to singularity inherent in the sense of justice as *dikē*. The demand that the other be heard as a full person, in other words the demand for ethics, introduces certain minimum communicative and moral requirements for legal procedure as to the type of hearing to be given to the person before the law and the nature of the interpretation and application of the relevant legal rules.[11] The sense of justice returns the law to the other and the good. But we should repeat and conclude: law's inescapable commitment to the rule means that injustice is the inescapable condition of all law.

Laws and judgments are performatives. They perform on the world and they change it. Law's performance subjects people to the norm and makes them instances of a rule. It is predicated on predictability and the subsumption of facts to an authorised repertory of narrative patterns. Its normative formulation makes the law a cognitive field, an object of representation, interpretation and description. As we saw, the 'we' of the norm, the authority that attaches to the law, is based on the elimination, regulation or containment of differences, the thematisation of persons and the generalisation of situations. The law both becomes an object of representation and creates the legal subject, corporate and indi-vidual. But as representable and knowable, the legal system claims to have a referent and the injustice of the silencing of all those who are not representable is inevitable.

Justice, on the other hand, cannot be represented or be turned into a normative sentence. But although we cannot say what justice is, we can attempt to say what would be injustice. The first thing to emphasise is that while legal justice asks the judge to sit in judgment, 'justice is impossible without the one that renders it finding himself in proximity. . . . The judge is not outside the conflict, but the law is in the midst of proximity' (Levinas 1991,

---

[11] Narrative theory (1988) can be of great use in this moral envisioning of legal judgment. Jackson has argued that both the interpretation of the law and the construction of the facts in the judicial syllogism take narrative form. Jackson, in his semiotic ultra-positivism, is uninterested in the ethical aspects of narrativity, or indeed in the political significance of the assumption of roles of narrator/narratee. Ricoeur (1992, p. 88–168) and Benhabib (1992, pp. 121–30) analyse the ethical importance of the narrative construction of life stories; Lyotard (1985, 1989, Chaps 6 and 7) insists that the political imperative of postmodernism is to keep the 'tales in motion and circulation, keep interchanging narrators, narratees and narrated, keep making the judge defendant and the defendant judge' (Douzinas and Warrington with McVeigh 1991, p. 110). An ethically aware theory of legal judgment must combine the narrative nature of law with the recognition that a 'just' decision responds to the demands of the other as put before the law in the story (s)he constructs.

p. 159). The judge is always involved and implicated, called upon to respond to the ethical relationship when he judges. Justice is not a mere legality regulating the subjects or the subsumption of particular cases under general rules. He who judges must compare and calculate, but he remains responsible and always returns to the surplus of his duties over his rights. Injustice would be to forget that the law rises on the ground of responsibility for the other and that ethical proximity and asymmetry overflow the equality of rights. The law can never be the last word. Legal relations of equivalence, comparison and attribution are just only if they recognise 'the impossibility of passing by he who is proximate' (ibid.).

This is another instance of the sense of justice which takes again the form of an aporia: to be just you must both be free *and* follow a rule or a prescription. A just and responsible decision must both conserve and destroy or suspend the law sufficiently in order to reinvent it and rejustify it in each case. Each case is different and requires a unique interpretation which no rule can guarantee absolutely. But at the same time, there is no just decision if the judge does not refer to law or rule, if he suspends his decision before the undecidable or leaves aside all rules. This is why we cannot say that a judgment is just. A decision may be recognised as lawful, in accordance with legal rules and conventions, but it cannot be declared just because justice is the dislocation of the said of the law by the – unrepresentable – saying of ethics. The incalculable justice demands of us to calculate and to make the relationship between calculation and the incalculable central to all judgment. Justice seeks the particular at the moment when the universal runs the risk of turning to its opposite, and as such it has the characteristics of a double bind. The action of justice requires an incessant movement between the general rule and the specific case that has no resting place and finds no point of equilibrium. There is a dislocation, a delay or deferral, between the ever-present time of the law and the always-to-come temporality of ethics. Justice inscribes itself on this imperceptible moment and mobil-ises an open, plural, opaque network of ethical relations which are non-totalisable and where 'the contemporaneity of the multiple is tied around the dia-chrony of the two' (Critchley 1992, p. 225). If there are criteria of justice, they are only momentary, they arise at the point of their application, as the just decision must be both regulated and without regulation. These criteria are local, partial and concrete, they give *justice* body, gender, a place.

We can conclude that justice has the characteristics of a promissory statement. A promise states now something to be performed in the future. Being just is acting justly; it always lies in the future, it is a promise made to the future, a pledge to look into the event and the uniqueness of each situation and to respond to the absolute unrepeatability of the face that will make a demand on me. This promise, like all promises, does not have a present time, a time when you can say there it is, justice is this or that. Suspended between the law and the good in-the-face-of-the-other, justice is always still to come or always already performed. But as the ethical exposure to the other is inevitably and necessarily reduced to the simultaneity of the text, the law and the judge are unavoidably implicated in violence. There is violence in law: the violence of turning the other to an instance of interpretation but also the physical violence that follows every verdict and judgment. Postmodern jurisprudence has to keep disrupting the law in the name of justice and to keep reminding the law of its inescapable violence. A postmodern theory of justice allows otherness to survive and to become a critical space to criticise the operations of the same. The law is necessarily committed to the form of universality and abstract equality; but it must also respect the requests of the contingent, incarnate and concrete other, it must pass through the ethics of alterity in order to respond to its own embeddedness in ethics. In this unceasing movement between the most general and calculating and the most concrete and incalculable, or between the legality of form and subjecthood and the ethics of response to the concrete person, law answers the primordial sense of another justice.

5

Textual authority and the other

Community and beyond in jurisprudence

I

In the previous chapter, we tried to explain the notion of otherness in terms of a philosophical tradition within which we situate our own analysis. Before we move on to our three 'case' studies, in which we examine the implications of our analysis for specific examples of legal, literary-legal and artistic-legal texts, we outline in this chapter two recent works that, at least superficially, appear to speak our language. The two books chosen also talk about the need to consider otherness in law, often implicitly, sometimes explicitly. Our two works are concerned, frequently passionate, ethical pleas to the effect that a legal system that does not take seriously the needs of the stranger forfeits any claim to justice and, hence all respect. We share their commitment, ethical concerns and, we hope, seriousness of intentions. But we need to understand that a philosophy that proposes to recognise the significance of the ethical demand of the other is not simply a question of tolerance and humanistic values, crucial though these are, or some abstract, do-good conception of ethics and justice. That is to say, despite our necessary sympathy, we have doubts about the success of the attempts we analyse here.

A word of caution is needed before we start: we are painfully aware that in setting out the specific reservations we have about our 'targets', we frequently open our own work to criticisms similar to those that we raise and as a minimum a blunt *tu quoque* response would be in order. In effect, this would frequently ask whether we are doing any better than our selected texts. A necessary reservation, therefore, even scepticism concerning our own position, accompanies much of our seemingly somewhat over-harsh reservations.

II

We start with Boyd White (1990).[1] He proposes a notion of justice as translation in order to expound a philosophy that respects the 'other'. He starts with an idea from John Dewey, now a pragmatist's commonplace, that 'democracy begins in conversation' (p. 91). What is required is 'a way of establishing a conversation about who we ought to become' (p. 138). Like other late twentieth-century pragmatists (Rorty is the outstanding example), he sees the world as the result of 'conversations', a polite tea party or perhaps well-ordered undergraduate seminar writ large, in which the most important thing is sensitively to handle the delicate activities of verbal linguistic exchanges. What is needed is a deep commitment to respect the chatter of everyone, as well as one's own, in order to credit 'the ultimate value of the individual person that is necessarily enacted in any sincerely other-recognizing expression' (p. 158). In this superabundance of tittle-tattle, reading and writing are ethical activities because they are 'a way of becoming someone in relation to another ... we invite from our reader one kind of response or another, as we call upon different capacities of mind or feeling' (p. 101).

Now, unfortunately, this is not what generally goes on in the universal banter of the world. Boyd White claims that this is partly because of one of the chief vices of modernism, namely intellectual arrogance. Many disciplines, but especially economics, take other disciplines and linguistic forms and force them into a mould that embodies their own concerns, instead of respecting the uniqueness of the particular conversational forms under examination. The law and economics movement in particular is severely criticised for trying to turn the values of economics, as understood by this particular discipline, into the values of society as a whole as expressed, in part at least, through the law. It is argued that economics, in its current, dominant neo-classical form, is incapable of appreciating anything but the values of a market-driven society, where all human choices are only valid to the

---

[1] All unattributed page numbers in this section are to this text.

extent that they have market effect. This way of thinking 'is to be silent on all the questions of human life' (p. 58).[2]

Instead of the imperialistic arrogance of dominant linguistic forms, each competing for control over other forms, we must appreciate that society is composed of many different language speakers. This is most evident if we compare different countries, races or nationalities, but it is also important to recognise that this applies within countries and cultures too. It is necessary to become sensitive to all the possibilities and the problems that this involves. The thoughts of each person, discipline or nationality have to be transformed into something that can be understood and respected by others. This means that it is unacceptable to absorb others; they have, like Bottom, to be 'translated'. But, for Boyd White, translation is not an exact, positivistic, scientific matter, nor is a Bottomless vision of precise correspondence even possible. The idea that any language merely represents pre-formed universalistic ideas which exist before their linguistic manifestations is dangerous nonsense. Although Boyd White does not spell it out, such a vision of instantaneous perfect translatablity from pre-linguistic thinking to linguistic expression is merely a hangover from our Platonic inheritance. Translation becomes a major philosophical problem,[3] with serious social and political implications.

Even more important than the problematic relation between original conception and linguistic expression is the question of translation of meaning from text to text. Texts, for Boyd White, have meanings determined by communities, not concepts, but in order to be understood, even in their 'original' language, these community-based meanings have to be translated. He takes poetry as a good example: with a poem, there is no such thing as an exact or scientific translation from one language to another. When any text is transposed from one language (here using the term 'language' very broadly) to another, something different results, which is both more and less than the original, and essentially and rightly different. The metaphor of translation is then used to

[2] Why issues of how to make and distribute the produce we need in order to live, the 'proper' subject matter of economics, are not one of the 'questions of human life' is not explained.

[3] Boyd White's work, therefore, can be situated within a broader, current concern, even preoccupation and fascination (for example, Benjamin 1989, p. 9), with the importance and difficulty of translation. See also Derrida (1992b, pp. 256ff.).

illustrate the practice of interpretation. Every interpretation, almost no matter of how simple a text, involves a process of translation.

These rich ideas refer us to the hermeneutical tradition and in particular to the work of Gadamer (see Douzinas and Warrington with McVeigh 1991 and Chapters 3 and 7, this volume). Modern hermeneutics, informed by the linguistic turn in philosophy and epistemology, argues that language mediates our access to the world. This primacy of language challenges both the sovereignty of the subject and his consciousness and the naïve positivistic belief in given external data awaiting their discovery by science. From Nietzsche to Ricoeur, language is held to be the plane in which we apprehend the world in acts of understanding and which mediates between us and the stranger, the other and the alien. Interpretation is always an act of application, where the interpreter relates the text to his/her situation. But if interpretations create the world for us and are always situated in our context and history, they also measure their success and usefulness against a text to which they address their appeal for validity. As Gadamer (1989, p. 31) puts it, text is what resists integration in experience and becomes a 'supposed given' that helps orientate our understanding. Texts are therefore hermeneutical concepts, they have meaning and follow the injunction 'be understood'; they emerge as intermediate points in interpretation when disturbances in the process of dialogical understanding and agreement occur. A text understood belongs neither to author nor to reader but creates a third shared position. The dialogue between text and its tradition and our own tradition makes us understand differently as we come to know the cultural objects in their otherness and make them relevant to our present concerns. Gadamer uses translation as a good metaphor for the process of hermeneutical understanding. The translator steps in when understanding is disturbed, he enters the text and becomes the mediator between the two original positions. His task is to serve the speakers or the reader of the text by conducting a dialogue between them and disappearing as a meeting of minds or a 'fusion of the horizons' of text and reader is achieved. In the process of understanding, the reader is caught up in what the text says and the respective positions merge.

Boyd White follows this model closely. In interpretation, out of two different entities we create something else, a third, which is both faithful to the original and the true expression of the person responsible for the translation. This third is capable of speaking to us, in our context and world. Every interpretation, from interpreting the simplest of desires of another person, to the complexities of the interpretation of, say, the Fourth Amendment of the American Constitution, is always a question of translation. Translation, properly conceived and executed, makes the other (text, institution, society, group or person) intelligible to us, and whilst inevitably creating something new, it respects (or ought to respect) the integrity of the text or other person being interpreted. Translation is an inevitable transforming cultural process, which puts 'two things together in such a way as to make a third' (p. 263), but in doing so, it also 'forces us to respect the other language, the other person, the other text – yet it nonetheless requires us to assert ourselves, and our own languages, in relation to it' (p. xvii).

This welcome integrating process, inevitably involved in almost any encounter in the world, is then used as a model for law, or rather law is a model for it. For it turns out that the best version of what this process should be is the law itself. Here again Boyd White follows Gadamer, who presents the law as the perfect example of the relationship between text and interpreter. The law is the one discipline that is always outside any specific discourse, and yet which has to listen to all. Every court case, every complex or indeed simple interpretation of a statute, involves a difficult process in which the law takes its evidence from outside of itself, from the discourse of the parties, the words of others. For another well-known critic of the law–literature relationship, Judge Richard Posner (1988, p. 18), lawyers' ignorance of other disciplines is a major problem. For Boyd White it is just the reverse. Law is the supreme listening discourse, and that gives it its great potential. When it neglects that potential, it is open to the dangers of appropriation by bureaucreats, economists, original intentionalists, etc. who 'have so nearly captured the law [that] its future is in doubt' (p. 267). Specifically, the writing of legal opinions takes texts of authority from the past and makes them speak to our own world. If this becomes a mere bureaucratic, authoritarian procedure, it is a disaster, because it destroys the other and, consequently, all the values of the community. Law has to recognise the centrality of the unique individual; its main aim is to produce and continue the democratic conversation within the framework that the great achievement of the rule of law has made possible. The art (never the science) of translation, of which law is the greatest example, ensures that we can span the apparently unbridgeable discontinuities between texts, languages and people, between the past, present and future. 'It recognizes the other – the composer of the original text – as a centre of meaning apart from oneself' (p. 257).

This admirable intention to respect the other text, person or institution in the act of (legal) translation, in which the common third meaning emerges, can only work if the text, tradition or community possess a unity or wholeness. The hermeneutical circle can operate and guide interpretation, through the continuous adjustment between the general pre-understanding of a text or tradition and its particular detail and concrete instances, only if the *interpetandum* is endowed with integrity and consistency. Gadamer needs the circle in order to validate certain interpretations as better than others and to avoid the accusation of interpretative relativism. Unless we approach our object with good will, assuming even temporarily its coherence, completeness and unity, its truth and value will escape us. Boyd White is full of the good faith of wholeness. He regrets the fragmentation of disciplines, especially in the academy, and longs for the revival of the Renaissance scholar in whose shadow he sees his own writings. He deprecates the fragmentation of our selves, our lives and our ways of working. But the idea of wholeness, on which his lament is based, is rather suspect.

First, he writes as though there were once communities which really were whole, in the sense that all voices were heard. But apart from some periods in ancient Athens and Rome, to which he does point (perhaps it is otiose to remark that even these whole communities managed to exclude most of their members, that is women, children and slaves, from their wholeness) it is hard to think of any 'authentic' examples of 'communities' in his sense. There is no historical community known to the West that did not exploit and degrade, that did not enthrone greed, power, privilege, place and status and its inevitable correlatives, that did not listen to some voices and ignore most of the others. As we saw in Chapter 4, the quest for justice starts with the experience of unjustifiability of the organisation of the community and this sense of justice is critical of the extant legal and political system.

If we examine next the community Boyd White wishes to recreate, law is to represent the ideal. In order to escape the problems of contemporary fragmentation, and of the failure of law to deliver on its promise of justice,

> we should turn to the traditional constitutional conception of humankind living in a natural world beyond our full comprehension, bound together by law, the first principle of which is the equal value of each human being, under a set of governments that democracy aims to make communities as well. (pp. 81–2)

Law acknowledges the variety of voices within the context of a society of people living together, raising children and existing in some sort of organic relation with the natural world. 'Law as we have traditionally conceived and practiced it – as a rhetorical and cultural activity, as an art of language and of life – has been based upon such a view of human life' (p. 82).

In this and similar formulations, an American variety of Hegelian humanism can be detected in which law incorporates the republican Sittlichkeit without the extravaganza of the world odyssey of the spirit. Against the rigorism of Kantian universalism, Hegel insisted that civil society, with its pluralistic network of institutions, organisations, practices, professions, etc. which develop their own ēthos, is the domain of individuality, human freedom and happiness. The state and its law, on the other hand, incorporates and transcends all particularities and integrates the various subordinate Sitten in the order of the universal. But as no truly universal Sittlichkeit emerged to claim the allegiance of humankind and no pan-human moral bond is likely to evolve, the Hegelian gesture is now restricted to the claim that the universal is evident in its particular guise, the western democratic state, and that the state finds its most perfect manifestation in, indeed can be identified with, its constitution and legal system. Boyd White's interest lies in the combination of this type of poor man's Hegelianism, which is also found in Dworkin, Ackerman, Ely, Rawls and most American liberal political theory, with an attention to the intricacies and richness of the text and an emphasis on respect for otherness.

But the premises of the enterprise are questionable and cannot deliver its commendable aims. The assumption of unity and coherence of tradition, community, self and text is the clearest sign of that type of metaphysical thought which dominates jurisprudence. We have criticised *logonomocentrism* elsewhere at length (Douzinas and Warrington with McVeigh 1991, pp. 27ff. and Chap. 2); what must be emphasised, however, is that hermeneutical humanism cannot sustain its proclaimed respect for the other and cannot therefore become the basis for the theory and practice of justice. The action of the spirit, according to Gadamer, is to recognise itself in the other, and the movement of the hermeneutical circle is a return to self via an excursion to otherness. Self recognises itself in the other and the different and in so doing discovers the moral bond carried in tradition. But this homecoming of the spirit and self can be turned into one more gesture of ontological imperialism as otherness is again devoured and 'enriches' self. For the ethics of alterity, as we saw, the other comes first. (S)he commands self and becomes the master of justice.

We encounter this inattention to the coercive possibilities of hermeneutics in Boyd White's tautological construction of law (Question: 'What is law to be based on?' Answer: 'Law'). Law is to rule after all, and it is to work in the way law traditionally understood has always done things; the result is more of the same authoritarian, power-based discourse with its failure to recognise the sensitivity of the unique individual text or person that comes before the law. Almost everywhere, Boyd White talks about respecting the 'authority' of texts (for example, p. 121), his discussion of the authority of the Constitution being especially significant, in this regard. He is concerned to bring into our world, that is, to translate, 'authorised' texts (p. 246). But why are particular texts authorised, and why does he select the texts he does? Might it be because they fit particular patterns of power, property and hierarchical relations? What about the lost texts, the suppressed texts, the ignored texts, the drowned texts, the unwritten texts (see, for example, Goodrich 1990, Chap. 2)? Are not most authorised texts written by those who are authorised in the first place? Is it not the case that the common law in particular draws its rhetorical power from 'discourses of denunciation directed at outsiders, heretics, iconoclasts' (Goodrich 1992, p. 207)? Boyd White's authorised texts are remarkably similar to those that could be regarded as authorised by any authoritarian republican from Cicero onwards.

This is one more instance of the tendency of jurisprudence to reduce all power relations to relations of authority and to forget the

aspect of power that Weber called domination and the violence
intrinsic in the performative action of law.[4] Arendt (1958, 1977)
has argued that power as authority in a community stems from the
wish of a people to act and live together and survives for as long as
this action in concert reproduces itself as its only aim and end.
Following her seminal analysis, Ricoeur notices that this common
power and wish to live and act as a community becomes invisible
and forgotten, covered by relations of domination. 'This gap
beween domination and power is marked, within the structure of
the state itself, by the dialectic . . . of the *political paradox*, in
which form and force continue to confront each other in the same
agency' (Ricoeur 1992, p. 257). This paradox takes in law one of its
most acute and obvious forms in what we have called the aporia of
justice. And yet hermeneutically orientated jurisprudence
assumes that domination has given way to *auctoritas*, and that the
law is the greatest repository of the common will to live together.
But as Benjamin (1978) reminds us, there is 'something rotten' in
law, both the marks of the violence that accompanied the creation
of all states and scar the surface of the legal system and the daily
mundane violence that sustains the law as a system of domination.[5] Forgetting this simple fact does not make the law any more
legitimate but turns jurisprudence into a naïve and unrealistic, if
not slightly disingenuous, legitimatory discourse.

Boyd White occludes this violence in a contradictory double
move. He argues that our cultures, languages and disciplines are
fractured. At the same time, he claims that there is some whole
self, some whole way of expressing ourselves, a total manner of
'being' which we know 'to be true to ourselves and our minds'
(p. 12). But we are never told what this wholeness is, where we

---

[4] Weber (1978) distinguishes between *Macht* (authority) and *Herrschaft* (domination). The latter characterises politics with its typical separation between rulers and
ruled (*ibid.*, p. 16). In his 'Politics as a Vocation', Weber describes the state as a
relation of domination based on the use of legitimate violence (*ibid.*, pp. 212–25).
This distinction, based on Spinoza's between *potentia* and *potestas*, was also
extensively used by Hannah Arendt.

[5] See Walter Benjamin's superb analysis of legal force that inspired Derrida's 'Force
of Law' (Benjamin 1978; Derrida 1990). We discuss further this neglected aspect of
violence in law in Chapter 6. See also Cover (1986) and Sarat and Kearns (1992). It
can be argued that the inability of jurisprudence to develop an ethical theory of
justice is linked to its almost total forgetfulness of the violent component of legal
action, as we outlined in the previous chapter.

TEXTUAL AUTHORITY AND THE OTHER

could find it and, given Boyd White's thesis that we are completely fractured anyway, how we could possibly know it if we came across it. There is an element of mysticism in humanism, a commitment to a 'common mana' dwelling in us, which makes us 'turn towards each other as we suspend our particular affiliations, without abandoning or resigning them' (Heller and Feher 1988, p. 52). In any event, why we should want to be whole, if indeed we ever were, and what possible benefit this could bring other than a dull sameness is not explained. To recognise difference is to negate the authoritarian myth of wholeness. Under the guise of plurality and tolerance, what we are offered is a patrician view of values in which the authority to speak is limited to the very few, those fully absorbed in the traditions and values that the authorised culture empowers.

Boyd White's search for authenticity ends where it began. We must make explicit, he claims, the language behind language (p. 36) and reinstitute the proper language of reason and justice. 'The essence of rationality is not the manipulation or explication of ideas or concepts, assumed to have extralinguistic reality and force, but using words well in accordance with the conditions of reality' (p. 40), accepting the literary conditions under which we live. His discussion of the judgments in the historic American nineteenth-century slavery cases suggests that the judges, like the legal realists and most of the disciples of law and economics, were guilty of producing reductive fictions: they never reached a 'true grasp of reality ... because all such views wish to erase the complex reality of the text, and the intellectual, ethical and political relations embodied in it' (pp. 136–7). We make no large claims to understand or have access to 'reality' in this work, and sometimes Boyd White does not either. But a consistent hermeneutics must accept that there is a 'true' meaning of every text, even if it is only true for ourselves, that somewhere 'out there' reality is going on. And if we can draw any picture of this reality it is a violent, fragmented world of fragmented individuals, discourses and communities. If the being that can be understood is language, the being our language points to is decentred and our moral intuition is not to try to suture it again but to listen to the cause of our destabilisation, the other.

The unintended result of liberal humanism is to gloss over the distance between authoritative texts and values and a rather

authoritarian legal imperialism. Instead of the language of economics, of 'concepts' and intentionalist fallacies (but why pay so
much respect to the Constitution therefore?), Boyd White wants to
substitute the law. Now it is law as translation, true, which may
not be every authoritarian positivist's Bostonian tea party cup,
though there is little of substance that they would actually need to
disregard. But the hegemonic domination by law, far from being
kept in place, has become universalised. Law's great merit, Boyd
White claims, is that it translates all other 'concepts' (science,
economics, literature, philosophy, the list appears to be endless)
into its own terms. Law 'is a discourse that mediates among
virtually all the discourse of our world, all ways of talking . . . by
the creation of texts that are new compositions' (pp. 261–2). This
translation of everything into legal language has to be handled
sensitively, but law does (or perhaps can) actually do this. Law
listens (apparently) to other discourses and then, it seems, uses
them as 'appropriate'. Instead of law serving the world, the world
serves law, and all experience gets translated into it, as virulent a
form of legal imperialism as any positivist's. And just to enforce
the authoritarian view, certain texts literally become sacred (pp.
267–8). 'It is the genius of the law to provide a place in which
unheard voices can be heard and responded to; it is our task as
lawyers to realize this possibility' (p. 267). Boyd White's text only
gestures in this direction. By translating all experience into law,
Boyd White makes the arrogance of economics, which he so
despises, seem puny in comparison.

Boyd White searches for a way to read that genuinely respects
the authority of tradition, the needs of the individual and the
present-day requirements of a community. To do this, he invents
someone whom every writer would love to find in droves: we need
'to think of the text as creating an Ideal Reader, the version of
himself or herself that it asks each of its readers to become' (p.
100). What is required to read a text is not mere reason, 'as if that
could be segmented off from the rest of experience and the self, but
attunement, or right orientation: the effort to make oneself its ideal
reader' (p. 172).

Here we come to the ultimate impasse of juridical hermeneutics. In the long road between Aristotle's *phronimos* and
Dworkin's Hercules or Boyd White's Ideal Reader, we have lost the
belief both in the ability of texts to carry 'objective', 'true'

meanings and in the *subtillitas legendi* of the reader, his tact and discrimination necessary for teasing the true meaning out of the text. The former loss is linked with the failure of biblical hermeneutics and its secular heir, jurisprudence, to prove beyond (reasonable) doubt the univocal regulative power of their respective texts, an alleged outcome of their divine or semi-sacred nature. The latter loss is a result of the historicist abandonment of the belief in the existence of a permanent human nature. The Aristotelian prudent and wise judge did not need instruction into truth or method, into theories of interpretation or the art of translation. His judgment was part of his nature, indeed the best definition of a prudent judgment was a judgment reached by a prudent man. But Nietzsche taught that one interpretation is more persuasive than another as a result of its rhetorical force, making hermeneutics an instance of the will to power. Gadamer knew, on the other hand, that subtlety and insight, although he himself exercised them, cannot be taught because human nature is the variable creation of its own history. It is against this backgound, and in order to repel the spectre of nihilism, that philosophical hermeneutics builds its edifice. In Gadamer, the problematical concepts of situated truth and of hermeneutical good faith act as a principle of falsification of interpretations. In White and Dworkin, the 'Ideal Reader' or the genius 'Hercules' are devices of stabilisation of textual openness.[6] But we are too late in history to believe that we can rediscover the prudent man on the bench of the Supreme Court. A theory of interpretation based on Boyd White's assumptions is impossible and the search for the modern equivalent of the Aristotelian *phronimos* is futile.

The 'Ideal Reader' (IR) is someone, therefore, whom we would seek to avoid, and whom we do not demand. Instead of IRs, we would ask that readers be allowed to make their own transformations of texts, without the authorially stamped, lawyerly impress of the judicial authority of authorised texts and their academic apologists. But although we therefore distance ourselves from Boyd White's version of otherness, there is still a shared difficulty.

---

[6] For a critique of the role of Hercules in Dworkin's hermeneutics, see Douzinas and Warrington with McVeigh (1991, Chap. 3). For a critique of the ontological and philological presuppositions of contemporary hermeneutics, see Rosen (1987, pp. 210–42).

Even if we reject IRs, we still have to determine the values on which we are to make decisions. Boyd White pleads for the sensitive translation of the needs of others, the requirement of respecting the integrity or at least the wishes of other texts, communities and persons. At this most general level, we are sympathetic and the text of this book is, in some sense, a version of Boyd White's IR. In addition, we would also respect Boyd White's insistence that it is not enough to do this in 'theory' without taking it further. '[F]rom what perspective can the lawyer prefer one language, one person, one set of possibilities over another? How can she make the choices for which she is responsible?' (p. 260).

Boyd White's answer is to suggest that what is at stake is a recognition of the way law works, or ought to work. We, as lawyers, should move 'from the immersion in our world and its languages to a place critical of them, on the margin and then return' (ibid.). We recognise law's centrality and power but also recognise that the law creates new compositions.

> In this sense the law (like the laywer) is both central and marginal at once; it exists at the edge of our discourses, outside all of them, structurally supplementary; yet it is also the discourse of power in our official world. (p. 262)

The only truth that this allows us to recognise is that we all inhabit different languages which cannot be reproduced in each other's terms, and that each of us is distinct and cannot be reduced to the language of an other. 'The one great human universal then is that we all speak languages, none of which can become a universal language; our universal question is how to relate to one another across this fact' (p. 263). As we have seen, Boyd White's answer is to turn everything into law, cram all answers into the process of (respectful) legal translation. The implications of this are disquieting if only because, even within Boyd White's analysis, 'the law' generally is the cause of many of the dysfunctions he is trying to eradicate. In our analysis, the respect for the other of discourse and of life cannot simply be subsumed under some possibly tidied up version of the existing legal process.

We touch on the possible devastating effects of supplements and margins as against the supposed centre in the remaining chapters of this book; at this stage, we might just hint that to accept law's 'structurally supplemental' role involves a simple danger:

that the supplement is never just supplementary, that the margins are never outside, that they are always what makes the centre what it is, or in other words, 'the discouse of power in our official world' can only exist because the margins are there to set it in motion. The official world depends on such trifles as marginalia[7] but at the same time tries violently to banish them.[8] Legal adjudication's 'reality' suggests a more cautious approach to the possibility that the minor marginal discourse of law might entail a truly humanistic recognition of the languages and discourses of the other; a more substantial rethink than the mere sort of 'back to basics' or back to 'law's proper role' that Boyd White suggests is needed.

III

Whilst we therefore reject the starting-point of this particular version of justice as translation, this does not mean that the idea of translating, of going across languages, and therefore possibly beyond particular language constraints in order to appreciate that the other is never the same as self, is not worth further enquiry. Our criticism of Boyd White notwithstanding, it may well be that the notion of justice as translation allows a more positive engagement with the ethical questions involved in legal judgments both in currently existing communities and in relation to their potential transformation. This, in summary, is the view of Cornell (1992),[9] who admirably believes that deconstructive thinking about law must of necessity transcend immediate judicial activities and concerns. 'Deconstruction keeps open the "beyond" of currently unimaginable transformative possibilities precisely in the name of Justice' (p. 182). Like Boyd White, she agrees that, in effect, translation is inevitable as things never speak for themselves in any language; such a plain notion 'is always blocked by the imposition of our language, our meaning. We are always translating, but without the assurance of the presence of the messianic language that makes translation possible' (p. 80). But it is there that the connections with White, and still more with conventionalists and pragmatists like Fish come to an end (see, for

---

[7] In terms of Chapter 8 below, 'ornaments'.

[8] As Chapter 6 below indicates, this banishment is sometimes literal.

[9] All unattributed pages numbers in this section are to this text.

example, Fish 1980, 1989). For the Whitian version of translation, but especially for Fish, any notion of 'transcendence' or a 'beyond'[10] of what we now know, even at the extreme end of feminist or of deconstructive practices, is meaningless. There is no way of going beyond the system, the community, or the *nomos*. By contrast, for Cornell, nothing else is worth the struggle.

In terms largely specific to law and justice, Cornell is concerned with a philosophy of 'the limit', that is, a philosophy that recognises the inevitable nature of the restrictions we face, yet at the same time takes seriously the possibility of transgression. Our aims and even our dreams of a more just set of practices are always limited, whether it is by the community (as in Hegel, and no doubt both Habermas and Rorty), or by the system (as in Luhman), or by the social contract (as in Rawls), or by the permitted terms of the story we are telling (as in Dworkin). (See, for example, Dworkin 1986; Habermas 1984, 1987; Rawls 1971; Rorty 1991.) What Derrida teaches is that there cannot be a limit without a beyond to it. We can only know the limit because we know of the beyond of the limit or at least that there is a beyond that provides the placing of the limit, and indeed allows us to make some sense of it.

Cornell wants to use this position to make two points. First, she claims that the argument of the so-called nihilistic wing of the current critical legal studies movement (and in the eyes of many critics, deconstruction itself), which, simplistically put, asserts that as there is no possible universalistic grounding to meaning, so everything is meaningless, is quite mistaken. Just because there is no method for providing a common support to all systems of belief does not mean that nothing has meaning. More important, second, Cornell wants to demonstrate that the very conventional notion of limit allows us to examine what must exist beyond the limit, and that this is the urgent task in any deconstructive work on the relation between ethics and justice. The philosophy of (the beyond) the limit raises the urgent question of how to achieve justice. Consequently, Cornell continually, and rightly in our opinion, stresses the 'quasi-transcendental' aspects of any discussion of justice. The main difference between orthodox expressions

---

[10] On the other hand, Cornell's use of translation would agree with Andrew Benjamin's description of Walter Benjamin's notion of 'a conception of translation that takes place beyond' (A. Benjamin 1989, p. 86).

of liberal concern about the failure to achieve justice and the deconstructive movement lies 'in their divergent opinions on the desirability and possibility of thoroughgoing social and legal transformation . . . the unerasable moment of utopianism which is inherent in "deconstruction" ' (p. 8). Both in legal analysis, and in terms of the reconstitution of society generally, deconstruction 'understood as the philosophy of the limit, gives us the politics of utopian possibility' (p. 156).

To make good her argument for a transcendental jurisprudence, Cornell pays close attention to the call of the other. Her complex position can be rather crudely summarised as a rejection of Hegel via a Derridean modification of Levinas.[11] Hegel's ethical certainty and his ability to approve legal judgments ultimately depends on linking judgments with the standards of the community. Whilst Cornell does not entirely reject the ideal of the community (p. 56), the danger is that 'the appeal to community ineluctably slides into an appeal to totality' (p. 39). Hegel's community and the values of *Sittlichkeit* supply the element missing in Kant in order to provide the grounding and substance of ethical judgments. But, of course, it does not take a Derrida to point out that the community only exists by what it rejects; the community is a totality in the sense that it excludes those who do not fit – women, ethnic minorities, people whose own social and sexual relations do not conform, refugees (the ultimate late-twentieth-century symbol of the outcast),[12] those that are 'other' to the established norms of the *nomos*.[13] And again, it does not need much philosophical deep thought to appreciate that those who are excluded are on the receiving end of violence, which leads Cornell to consider the claims of those other to the system and Levinas's strong ethical claim that the other, like Polynices to Antigone, calls us before we make ethical decisions. Any ethical relation worth considering indicates 'the aspiration to a nonviolent relationship to the Other, and otherness more generally, that assumes responsibility to guard

---

[11] If this sounds obfuscatory, we hope our discussion in Chapters 2 and especially 4 helps.

[12] See especially Chapter 6 below.

[13] As we have already indicated, it has been claimed that the common law in particular derives its strength by the rhetorical force of its exclusion of others (see Goodrich, 1993).

the Other against the appropriation that would deny her difference
and singularity' (p. 62). By contrast, in order for Hegel to construct
a community with binding ethical standards, it is necessary to
construct a 'logic of identity', a home which, necessarily and
violently, excludes those who do not conform.

Hegel's identification of ethics with the actual exemplifies a
totality which, as we have seen, Levinas wholly rejects. For
Levinas, the face-to-face relation with the other disrupts any
totality and prevents the reduction of the ethical relationship to
any existing actuality. What has to be attended to is what is outside
the system, the remains, the neglected and the rejected. But,
Derrida argues, this is insufficient. There is a danger of a return in
Levinas to the sort of duality (especially of the inside/outside
variety) that deconstruction rejects. 'There is the temptation in
Levinas to turn the excess within history and within totality into
the absolutely Other to totality' (p. 69). Not that Derrida is denying
the excess and the remains; but he is saying that it, too, is not some
absolute universalisable entity, or some entity existing prior to or
beyond the existing known or acknowledged entity. There is no
more a universal 'known' or knowable entity outside the limit than
there is one within the limit. If this 'other' were to exist as a
specific substance, it would be as much liable to deconstruction on
the grounds of what it itself excludes as anything else. Levinas's
temptation towards dualism risks his analysis 'being swept back
into the Hegelian system by postulating "dead" matter as the Other
to the infinite' (p. 69).

Instead of positing the fullness of the absolute other, Derrida
subjects otherness to the same rigorous, ethical enquiry that he
makes of the system and the totality that exclude it in the first
place. Otherness, too, is subject to the difference and deferral that
beset all attempts to produce closed or complete systems of
thought, analysis, politics. The remains are what cannot be pinned
down, defined or drawn together. 'The rest, the remain(s) is
unsayable' (p. 70, quoted from Derrida 1986a). In this uncon-
scious(?) echoing of Hamlet's last line ('The rest is silence'),
Derrida recognises both the inevitability of the exclusion of the
other and the ethical call that this makes on us, and yet resists the
temptation to substitute the totality of the outside for the totality of
the inside. But this does not lead Derrida into some sort of dead-
end nihilism; on the contrary, the ethical task of trying to express

(and act upon) what cannot be said is created by the impossible necessity of the silence and the limit of philosophy. In summary, there cannot be an acceptable ethical priority of otherness or infinity (as in Levinas) as against a Heideggerian commitment to Being.

But though Derrida's distance from Levinas's analysis means that we can never fully know or speak of the other, this does not imply that we stop trying to express in all forms the call that the ethical relation makes on us. Which leads us directly to our own concern, Cornell's intervention in the practice of legal interpretation. Cornell argues that the philosophy of the limit demands that we both interpret the necessary contradictions in legal action, as critical legal studies has always done, and expose the possibility of a transcendental analysis and a vision of something other, a task which critical legal studies has not always approached with the same degree of enthusiasm. In order to go beyond more conventional analysis (especially of the orthodox positivist kind as well as of the critical mode) Cornell reminds us that it is 'the projection of a horizon of the good within the *nomos* of any given legal system, even if reconceived, that is essential to the possibility of legal interpretation' (p. 93). Whilst 'the full realization of the Good' (p. 94) might not be possible, we are still called by our commitment to it in any exercise of legal interpretation. In particular, Derrida's reinterpretation of Levinas makes us see that because there can be no totality of the inside or the outside of the legal system, the necessary interpretation of the legal system (the 'impossible necessity' to distinguish the task from any supposed or ultimate resolution of the problems) is a practical and immediate necessity facing, in Cornell's terms, all judges, academic and practising lawyers (pp. 100, 109). The notion of the inevitable *différance* of meaning, 'the nonfull, nonsimple, and differentiating origin of differences, disrupts the claims of ontology to fill the universe, and more specifically the legal universe' (p. 110). Putting the claim at an even stronger level, Cornell asserts, in effect, that the recogntion of the deferral, dissemination and disruption of meaning not only allows the ethical claims of the other to be taken seriously, 'it is the Other within the *nomos* that invites us to new worlds and reminds us that transformation is not only possible, it is inevitable' (p. 111).

This high-minded, morally serious analysis has much to

commend it. In the rejection of both the orthodox and the
'nihilistic' wing of current critiques, Cornell touches on much
matter that is near to our own concerns. We share her aspirations
both for a 'thoroughgoing' analysis of the ethical imperatives in
legal decision-making and for her rejection of a solipsistic,
anything-goes type of analysis masquerading as deconstruction.
Furthermore, we applaud her deep commitment to the necessity of
a 'beyond', and we accept that the mere 'trashing' of the doctrinal
pretensions of orthodox liberal commentators is no longer sufficient.[14] Her vision, blurred and rather vague though it may be, of
a transformed legal practice, in which we always 'remember that
we are responsible, as we interpret, for the direction of [the] transformation' (p. 115), is an aspiration to reach the moral limits (the
heights) and to expose the moral depravity (the depths). This book
fully shares these ethical, transformative, aspirations. But of
course, as we have already hinted, high-minded aspirations are not
everything; the desparately honest commitment to the good, even
to the Good, may not be sufficient. Whilst it is very hard to go
beyond the dreams that Cornell eloquently sets out, there are
features of the analysis that we feel compelled to question.[15] There
is some fine analysis of positivism, especially in the way she
shows how law specifically excludes those it does not wish to
protect (the best example is probably the splendid reworkings of
the abortion controversy in the Supreme Court) and her straightforward opposition to the current state of affairs so that, for
example, racism in South Africa and elsewhere can be unequivocally condemned (for example, p. 114). So far, so radical. But we
would make two paradoxical points: first, that her rejection of
positivism comes very close to conventionalist analysis if it is not
a straight misunderstanding of what positivism means, at least in
law; and second, that her positive suggestions as to what is to be

---

[14] However, we should beware of the tendency in some poststructuralist writings to
erect a 'deconstructionist' orthodoxy and condemn all those who do not follow the
'canon' with the scholastic rigour of the analytical philosopher. As we have argued
elsewhere, orthodox jurisprudence is fiercely ideological and critiques of its hold
upon the legal imagination may use counter-ideological tools, like 'doctrinal
trashing' to good effect. (See Douzinas and Warrington with McVeigh 1991, Chap. 8.)
[15] We are aware of the all too obvious dangers here, perhaps more than anywhere
else in this work, of making criticisms to which, if valid, we, too, are subject.

done, as distinct from her philosophical analysis,[16] are, at times, simply and depressingly *positivistic*.

To begin with the attack on positivism, much of the analysis seems to misunderstand what positivism argues. The caricatured argument of positivism is that it regards the legal system as a separate functioning entity,[17] the nearest analogy to which is the machine. This analysis is simply wrong. 'Law', Cornell tells us, 'cannot be reduced to a self-generated and self-validating set of *cognitive* norms' (p. 102). We are reminded that 'law cannot be reduced to a set of technical rules, a self-sufficient mechanism that pulls us down the track through each new fact situation' (pp. 101–2). It is a positivist fallacy to think 'that the legal world is just given to us as a self-perpetuating mechanism' (p. 120). But this is hardly news, and would not raise a flicker on the face of the most die-hard of positivists. Legal positivism does not think law is a machine, a 'self-perpetuating mechanism'. It is because law cannot simply feed into the computer and produce a mechanistic response that positivism in law exists. Legal positivism attempts to explain how the very human institution of the law works and how it can justify what it does. The most orthodox of constitutional slogans 'the rule of law' has a certain weight in part because it is creating an impossibility, 'the rule of law not of men'. Laws cannot rule, and the rule of law notion achieves its effect, or at least has its part to play, by making the issue of how rules operate less dramatically offensive. Legal positivism itself arises because the law is seen to be about difficult human choices, or impossibly complex decisions and the need to balance conflicting claims about aspects of the human condition that lead to disputes. By reinforcing the law's claim to neutrality, positivism shows how law can claim to be impartial, even though it is not a machine.

But the problem is not just that Cornell misconstrues the legal positivism she opposes. What we find in her analysis is a return of the positivism the analysis is supposed to exclude. Deconstruction shows how the banished, the repressed and the marginal often return to haunt the centre, and this is what we (un)expectedly find here, just as in Boyd White's other-regarding analysis. Central to Cornell's ambitious aims is a crossing from the orthodox readings

---

[16] Such an un-Derridean distinction must be suspect.

[17] See Luhman's autopoesis system theory, discussed by Cornell in Chapter 5.

and writings of judgments, with all that these mean, to the opening of alternative modes of thought, reading, writing and judgment in law. But instead we get a very familiar set of positivistic prescriptions, with which few orthodox lawyers ought to have any difficulty. What is involved in judging at law? Having damned legal positivism throughout, we are then assured that feminist critical legal scholars would argue as follows: 'Rather than try to replace legal positivism with explicit ethical principles, we should instead simply accept the fallibility of judicial discretion as a better way to respect difference.' And: 'The best the judge can do is to try to sensitively weigh each competing perspective' (p. 103). If her representation of critical feminist legal theory is somewhat one-sided, her descent into a Dworkinian version of positivism becomes moderately explicit. In order to hear the claims of the other, we need 'principles' to guide us through legal interpretations, and the search for justice involves 'the search for a principle' (pp. 105–6). But a principle is not the same thing as a rule:

A principle is instead only a guiding light ... a light that guides us and prevents us from going in the wrong direction. A principle, however, cannot determine the exact route we must take in any particular case; it does not pretend there is only one right answer. (p. 106)

In order to determine which principle to apply in any particular case, we employ '. . . the practical use of *reason* to synchronize the competing demands and perspectives of individuals through the appeal to legal principle' (p. 106). There has to be a reasonable assessment of competing legal principles (p. 107).

This is either positivism simpliciter, or positivism disguised under a Dworkinian notion of sensitivity in the delicate act of balancing competing claims, but either way it has little to distinguish it from the most standard analysis of the problem involved in judgment. Furthermore, the 'hearing' which Cornell is so keen to stress[18] turns out to be a 'seeing', that is, a vision of the very familiar responsibility for the future in the work of judges. Lawyers are called upon to remember the future in their writing of judgments, presumaby executed in the present, on the circum-

---

[18] For a more thorough analysis of hearing, see Docherty (1990).

stances of the past. On the basis of Derrida's analysis, especially in relation to our memory of the past and its implications, she states:

> The judge can never be reduced to the instrument of the system who simply recollects precedent. ... She is responsible for her memory and the future which she promotes in the act of remembrance itself. ... We are responsible precisely because we cannot be reduced to automatons. (pp. 148–9)

One of Derrida's 'remarkable insights' and his unique 'contribution to legal interpretation is to show us why the act of memory in judging involves the seemingly contradictory notion that the judge, in his or her decision, 'remembers the future' (p. 120). Good advice no doubt, but surely Derrida does not have to be invoked to remind the judiciary that a case decided today is always liable to be used as a precedent for a decision taken tomorrow. Positivists would have no great difficulty with these bland suggestions.

Is not Cornell's claim, then, simply sound positivistic analysis of the role of all judges? All judges in a precedent system supposedly recall the decisions of the past; indeed now that legal memory (though not the Aristotelian art of weighing argument) is becoming computerised, that 'supposedly' may itself be unnecessary; likewise they consider the implications of their decision for the future. Despite the sensitivity of Derrida's approach to memory and tradition, it can be argued that the precedent system is the most comprehensive attempt to institutionalise memory[19] in order to try to make decisions applicable (responsible) for the future. '[T]he Derridean deconstruction of the privileging of the present reminds us of the responsibility of judges, lawyers, and law professors for what the law "becomes" ' (p. 120). But are not sensitive positivists, even insensitive ones, aware of their responsibility for what law becomes? Is not this the basis of so many wrangles in the courts?[20] Would any Dworkinian Hercules tremble at such advice?

Now Cornell's chief response would be to suggest that it is specifically the insertion of the 'good' into her analysis that rescues it from orthodoxy. The 'Law of Law demands that we justify our interpretation through an appeal to the Good' (p. 113).

---

[19] See Goodrich (1990) for a discussion of the implications of legal memory.
[20] For example, many of the House of Lords decisions in the 1980s and 1990s on the contract/tort boundaries of negligence, or the recent rulings on nervous shock.

For Cornell the 'Good' remains, always present, as a disruptive element.

We are called to the commitment to the impossible, the full realisation of the Good and to the need to defy the impossible by projecting a horizon of the good embodied in the *nomos*, even if in the form of the classical modern emancipatory ideals within any given legal system. . . . The philosophy of the limit persistently exposes the philosophical fallacy of legal positivism by showing the moment of ethical alterity inherent in any purportedly self-enclosed system, legal or otherwise. (pp. 94, 93)

Our own analysis, too, shows that the ethical moment is part of all legal and moral systems of adjudication; the law arises on the ground of ethical intersubjectivity and expresses the sense of (in)justice that accompanies every attempt to establish a human polity. But the transcendent principle, the 'good' that works the outside of the system beyond 'the limit', cannot be translated into a series of transcendental presuppositions and extant principles that can decide cases in Dworkinian 'rightful' fashion. Indeed, appeals to some conception of the good are not lacking in legal judgments. The 'good' may consist of crude utilitarianism, the need to limit the list of potential claimants, the requirement not to disturb established authority or appeals to the public interest amongst others. None of these can be the 'good beyond the limit', the principle of exteriority from which the legal system can be criticised and its just rearrangement imagined.

The end of the analysis relates not to the good itself, which, as the principle of ethical alterity, is present only in its absence, an unknowable exterior always still to come that erupts within the law not only as the 'echo' of the call of the other, but also to choices about the good. Cornell does not approve most of the judicial decisions that rhetorically utilise the idea of the good. Neither do we; but it looks as if she feels obliged to help with the choice of values that determine what the good shall be. In those instances, however, when she adopts the judicial mantle, Cornell trembles at the thought of devaluing any position whatsoever in case, in so doing, something of merit is lost. Difficult choices must be made, as '[a]ll claims, however, cannot be vindicated even if they must be heard. We need legal principles that guide us through the maze of competing legal interpretations, precisely because all claims cannot be vindicated' (p. 105). The obvious retort at this stage would be both to ask for these competing principles to be enumerated and to point out that 'legal principles' are precisely what orthodox analyses provide in such pitiable profusion. The question is how to choose between these principles. Cornell not only does not provide legal principles, her analysis becomes paralysed at the very point where principles might be provided because she is actually incapable of making choices.

All claims must be heard. But of course, only being heard is not a great deal of comfort for the supporters of principles that are rejected. What is needed from within this principled approach is the grounds for rejecting some principles in favour of others. At this crucial moment, Cornell shies away from grasping the hard choices. It may be the case that claims to ethical superiorty of one system over another may be unfounded. '[O]n the interpretation I am offering here, it would also be unethical to *theoretically* reduce to an inferior position the standing of competing normative perspectives' (p. 109). 'If all ethical thematizations are "equal" in the sense that they cannot claim to be grounded in first principles, then we must always recognize the "equal claim" of competing interpretations to be heard' (p. 108). Cornell, in other words, wants to do justice to all sides, hear all sides,[21] not prefer one side over another, although some sides are to be preferred, some down-graded, as is evident in her strong commitment to feminist analysis and her rejection of, for example, racism. Choices must be made but the only guidance offered is a not very useful reference to respect for the various conflicting interpretations and to the need for principles as guiding lights. Merely hearing all sides is precisely what positivism offers;[22] likewise not 'theoretically' (as distinct from practically – our stories we tell to justify one state of legal affairs over another 'can only be judged practically' [p. 108] she also tells us) reducing disfavoured perspectives to inferior positions. And again the principles envisaged are not different from those offered by hermeneutical jurisprudence, nor is it clear how the commitment to the ethics of alterity will affect their constitution and application. This is the price we fear Cornell has to pay for moving too quickly from her valuable analysis of the role

---

[21] We agree strongly with this argument, as the previous chapter in its discussion of the *audi alterem partem* rule indicates.

[22] As the argument in Chapter 4 above illustrates, however, this crucial ethical position is only a starting-point.

of the good in law, as an absent horizon that calls to justice, to specific prescriptions about legal judgment that necessarily remain at a level of abstraction and generality that resembles much contemporary American jurisprudence.

It is in this light that we can understand the repeated attacks on some feminist and critical legal scholars, the ethical sceptics, who hold to the 'indeterminacy thesis' which has given their work (and allegedly deconstruction more generally) a bad name. The sceptics believe 'there is no institutional meaning, no "real" intelligibility of the legal sentence' (p. 101). As a result, ethical responsibility 'is reduced to an existential choice' (p. 102). But Cornell's liberal humanism, too, calls for all positions to be heard and nothing to be rejected, theoretically at least. But if choice cannot be made on mere subjective grounds, and if legal principles are to be refashioned in order to enable necessary choices to be made, then Cornell appears to marry the aspect of critical legal studies she rejects to the positivism she also rejects in order to produce a positivistic philosophy within the limit she was supposed to reject.

It may be that at this turning-point in our legal civilisation we can only point to the ethical ghost launched in the heart of law without else. It may be that critical legal scholarship must, like Minerva's owl, wait for the completion of the crisis of legal form that postmodernity ushers in before it can start its flight towards a contemporary theory of judgment. Cornell's work can be seen as part of the clearing of the ground and of the reawakening of the ethical sensibility and of the sense of justice. Our work, too, we hope, belongs to the same project and makes the same promise to the good for ever still to come but which has already and always been the genealogy of law and jurisprudence.

6

A well-founded fear of the other

The momentary principle of justice

I

'Does he know his sentence?' 'No', said the officer. 'He doesn't know his own sentence?' 'No', the officer said again; he was still for a moment as if expecting the traveller to volunteer some reason for his question, then he said, 'There would be no sense in telling him. He experiences it on his own body.'

Kafka, *In the Penal Colony*

Legal judgments are statements and deeds. They both interpret the law and act on the world. A conviction and sentence at the end of a criminal trial is the outcome of the judicial act of legal interpretation, but it is also the authorisation and beginning of a variety of violent acts. The defendant is taken away to a place of imprisonment or of execution, acts immediately related to, indeed flowing from, the judicial pronouncement. Again as a result of civil judgments, people lose their homes, their children, their property or they may be sent to a place of persecution and torture.

The recent turn of jurisprudence to hermeneutics, semiotics and literary theory has focused on the word of the judge and forgotten the force of the word.[1] The meaning-seeking and meaning-imposing component of judging is analysed as reasoned or capricious, principled or discretionary, predictable or con-

---

[1] The linguistic and interpretative aspects of the law were always a part of legal theory. They were somewhat neglected during the heyday of legal positivism, but they have been reinstated within jurisprudence. Law is often now seen as an exclusively linguistic and meaningful construct and various types of hermeneutics and literary theory have been adopted to explain and justify the operations of the 'prison house of language'. Within orthodox jurisprudence, Dworkin (1986), Levinson and Mailloux (1988) and Fish (1989) are examples of the linguistic turn.

211

tingent, shared, shareable or open-ended according to the political standpoint of the analyst. But as Cover has reminded us, in our obsession with hermeneutics we forget that 'legal interpretation takes place in a field of pain and death' (1986, p. 1601). The main if not exclusive function of many judgments is to legitimise and trigger past or future acts of violence. The word and the deed, the proposition and the sentence, the constative and the performative are intimately linked.

Legal interpretations and judgments cannot be understood independently of this inescapable imbrication in violent action. In this sense, legal interpretation is a practical activity, other-orientated and designed to lead to effective threats and – often violent – deeds. This violence is evident at each level of the judicial act. The architecture of the courtroom and the choreo-graphy of the trial process converge to restrain and physically subdue the body of the defendant. From the defendant's perspec-tive, the common but fragile façade of civility of the legal process expresses a recognition 'of the overwhelming array of violence ranged against him and of the helplessness of resistance or outcry' (ibid., p. 1607; cf. Sarat and Kearns 1992). But for the judge too, legal interpretation is never free of the need to maintain links with the effective official behaviour that will en-force the statement of the law. Indeed, the expression 'law enforcement' recognises that force and its application lies at the heart of the judicial act. Legal sentences are both propositions of law and acts of sentencing.

Legal interpretation, then, is bonded, bound both to the deeds it triggers off and to the necessary conditions of effective domination within which the sentence of the law will be enforced. Without such a setting that includes a formidable array of institutions, practices, rules and roles – police, prison guards, immigration officers, bailiffs, lawyers, etc. – the judicial word would remain a dead letter. All attempts to understand legal judgments and judicial decision-making as exclusively hermeneutical are there-

---

More critical approaches can be found in Goodrich (1986, 1990), Hutchinson (1988), Carty (1991), Fitzpatrick (1991) and Douzinas and Warrington with McVeigh (1991). Whilst the importation of literary theory and the welcome recognition of the fact that law is, at least in part, a linguistic construct, has done much to revive jurisprudence, this chapter is particularly concerned to stress the violent nature and unjust action that characterise much legal action, something often missing from literary theory's analysis of law.

fore incomplete. Legal interpretations belong both to horizons of meaning and to an economy of force. Whatever else judges do, they deal in fear, pain and death. If this is the case, aspirations to coherent and shared legal meaning are liable to flounder on the inescapable and tragic line that distinguishes those who mete out violence from those who receive it.

This necessary distinction and linkage between the constative and performative aspects of legal judgments has passed without much comment in jurisprudence. Hermeneutically orientated legal theory assumes that the rightness, fairness or justice of the interpretative enterprise will bestow its blessing on the active component of the judgment and justify its violence. Theory and practice, word and deed are seen as belonging to the same field, as successive points on an unproblematic continuum. A just interpretation and statement of the law is accepted without more argument as just action. But is this assumption justified? Does the correct interpretation of the law – if it exists – and the 'right answer' to a legal problem – if we can find it – lead to moral and just praxis? Is the law law because it is just, or is the law just because it is the law? Law and justice? Law or justice? Law against justice? What is the relationship between the promised universality of the law and the – apparent – singularity of justice, justice as judgment, as the justice of the sentence pronounced upon those who come before the law? Can we ever say that the law is just or that its application is just? Can we know what it is to be just? What doorways does justice open or close? We examined these questions from a historical and theoretical perspective above. Here we want to take our discussion a step further by examining a few recent legal judgments in which the question of law's relationship to the other and to ethics, that is the question of justice, was at the heart of the matter. This examination will also help us to start addressing the problem of the practical application of our (non) theory of justice, which we proposed in Chapter 4. But first, as a postscript to our earlier discussion, we want to return briefly to the critique of modernity's de-ethicalisation of the law and the closely linked juridification of morality.

II

In ethics, the field closest to law, the – unquestioned – passage from interpretation to practice or from a logic of propositions to a logic of action lies at the heart of some of the most interesting recent debates. Western ethics has appealed since Plato to the concept of the good, an appeal adopted by some recent postmodernist and feminist writings, as we have seen in Chapter 5. An action is moral if it promotes what counts as good according to the theory. For moralists and deontologists of both the Kantian and Hegelian type, the moral act applies and respects some stipulated conception of rightness in itself. Utilitarians, on the other hand, adjudge the morality of an act in accordance with its consequences.

But a large part of recent moral philosophy accepts that while moral beliefs and judgments are linked with cognitive discourses, they often fail to trigger moral acts. In other words, moral theory does not seem to be either an indispensable or a necessary component of moral action. People may be persuaded by arguments about the superiority of a particular conception of the good but then fail to pursue any particular course of action as a result. If ethics is the field of moral action towards other people, the failure to translate ethical judgments into action is of great concern to moral philosophers. Both MacIntyre (1981) and Nagel (1970) have pointed out that there is no assurance that moral action will necessarily follow even a perfect moral theory. Indeed, Nagel (ibid., pp. 143–5) starts his attempt at refashioning moral philosophy from this very recognition. How could critical theory account for this extraordinary state of affairs?

As constitutively other-orientated *action*, ethics must be distinguished clearly from all types of cognition. According to de Certeau

ethics is articulated through effective operations, and it defines a distance between what is and what ought to be. This distance designates a space where we have something to do. On the other hand dogmatism is authorised by a reality that it claims to represent and in the name of this reality it imposes laws. (1986, p. 199)

In this definition, the space of ethics is suspended between – cognitive and moral – theory and the call to action. The moment of moral action, the 'something' we have to do, is not co-extensive with 'what is' (cognition) and does not simply follow 'what ought to be' (moral philosophy). In this sense, the pragmatic critique of MacIntyre and Nagel is only a starting-point.

Moral action is a response to an ethical stimulus. Furthermore,

as Heidegger's (1977) ontological critique of the modern technolo-
gical Being has shown, theory is involved in an endless pursuit of
control. The identification of truth with logic in modern technolo-
gical reason turns the 'real' into a system of causal links, infinitely
calculable and manipulable. People, too, are treated as 'homogeneous units that lend themselves to abstraction and formulaic
manipulation based on the principle of parsimony' (Wyschogord
1990, p. 135).

Moral philosophy is not innocent of Heidegger's indictment.
Even those theories that emphasise practice, like Nagel's, cannot
avoid the ontological condition of modernity steeped in the dream
of total control. Both the means/ends distinction in Kantian ethics
and the calculus of happiness, utility and equitable distribution in
utilitarianism and Rawls (1964) belong to the modern horizon of
manipulable Being. The metaphysical identification of Being with
the good since Plato and the 'idea of the Good [as] the basic
determination of all order, of all that belongs together' (Heidegger
1961, p. 116), finds its most disturbing expression in the transformation of the good into aspiration of control over Being.

Recently, Lyotard has renewed the attack on traditional moral
philosophy. Lyotard has attempted throughout his career to
theorise the particular as particular; his recent work, inspired by
Levinas and linguistic philosophy, presents the event as a unique
phenomenon whose unrepeatability is akin to that of the sentence.
Lyotard claims that a morality that derives from theoretical
propositions is cognitively illegitimate and politically unjust. The
linguistic mode of ethics is the imperative, or, in Lyotard's
terminology, the prescriptive sentence (Lyotard 1988a).[2] An
ethical command cannot be derived from a theory, a concept or a
descriptive sentence nor from a general prescription or law, like
the Kantian categorical imperative. The demand 'Welcome me' of
a stranger asks me to act but offers no criteria of choice. The
specificity of the ethical moment is that the self feels obligated,

---

[2] The sentence is for Lyotard the basic unit of discourse and action, the minimun
building block of the world. Sentences are pure happenings that combine to create
meanings and the world. The translator of The Differend (Lyotard 1980) chooses the
English word 'phrase' to translate its French homonym. We prefer the word
'sentence', which, in its ambiguously legal character, captures Lyotard's ambition to
theorise the irreducibly unique. On sentences between grammar and the law, see
Douzinas and Warrington with McVeigh (1991, Chap. 12).

and acts in response to an inescapable order: 'You must.' I must
act, I am not free not to act, I cannot do otherwise. Criteria of
judgment, on the other hand, follow theoretical and deductive
models and attempt to ground ethical action either on the
description of a state of affairs to be achieved or on a calculation of
the consequences of action.[3]

The specificity and urgency of the ethical command, however,
befalls and obligates me before any possibility of refusal and
without any need for reasons or justifications, as Antigone argued.
Indeed for Lyotard, every sentence is a unique event that happens
now. When it occurs, the sentence–event presents a 'universe'
upon which its four poles or instances and their unique relationship, their 'situation', are placed: a sentence presents, first, its
referent, that of which it is about; second, the meaning of the case
which the sentence presents; third, that to which or to whom this
meaning is addressed (the receiver); and finally those in whose
name the meaning signifies (the sender). Thus sentences position
both subjects and realities and open up worlds of possibilities.
Sentences belong to various incommensurable 'regimes': they are
descriptive, prescriptive, normative, interrogative, etc. Sentences
from the various regimes link together and create 'genres' of
discourse – science, philosophy, poetry, law, etc. Every sentence is
a radically unique occurrence but it is always followed by another
sentence. Linking between sentences is necessary but what type of
linking actually occurs is contingent. Genres act like a gravita-
tional force: they try to attract sentences towards those linkages
that promote the function of the genre, for example to know,
persuade, seduce, amuse, be just, etc. 'One will not link unto *To
Arms!* with *You have just formulated a prescription*, if the stakes
are to make someone act with urgency. One will do it if the stakes
are to make someone laugh' (Lyotard 1988a, p. 84).

The characteristic of descriptive sentences is that their sender
and addressee are potentially interchangeable. They find themselves in a position of equivalence because the referent of the
sentence is 'reality'. Prescriptives, on the other hand, place
addresser and addressee in a situation of radical dissymmetry. An
ethical command turns the 'I' of the receiver into its 'you', as the
sender of the command becomes master and takes the other's 'I'

hostage. Self experiences this displacement into the receiver's pole, the 'you', that the command imposes, as a loss of freedom, knowledge and pleasure. The 'I' is tempted to explain or justify its dispossession. New sentences are produced that will transport the 'I' back to the sender position; their stake will be to give persuasive reasons for the command and the obedience. For the ethics of alterity, this urge to explain is due to the blindess of the 'I', ego's infatuation with knowledge which, as we saw, presents the other as symmetrical to self. 'The blindness or transcendental illusion resides in the pretension to found the good or the just upon the true, or what ought to be upon what is' (Lyotard 1989, p. 290). But this epistemological narcissism has no object. The 'I' cannot put itself in the position of the other and discover her intentions or deduce them from the sense of the command. To be obligated by an order because self can understand its sense would be a crime against ethics. It would both reduce the other into self and would violate the autonomous underived sense of obligation that ethical prescriptives create. More generally, no theory of the good society or account of justice can furnish criteria for ethical action. Theories are descriptions of determinate states of affairs while the ethical response is indeterminate, something to be done rather than something said.

The philosophy of sentences and the ethics of alterity refute these assumptions. The Kantian injunction to distinguish will from reason becomes pointless, when good will is only the will which adheres to clear ideas, or which makes decisions only out of respect for the universal. Similarly the split 'we' of legislator/ subject cannot become the horizon of the ethical relationship between self and other. The other cannot be turned into an integral element of a totality or into a monad of an empirical consensus. Ethical obligation cannot be derived or explained cognitively, nor is it the outcome of autonomy willing the universal law. The morality of modernity seems to veer between a formal and empty injunction to universalise and a universe of rules and norms built upon the cognitive and ontological omnipotence of the ego. Morality has become rational and is fully immanent. But the retreat of the transcendent from the social leaves no room for otherness, exteriority, or a space to mount a critique of the law. And as morality becomes form and individual will, the justice of the law is reduced to the formality of legality. Boxed between theory as logic that can represent but cannot act and a praxis that can only act as technique, calculation and control, ethics seems to veer violently between an incapacitating subjectivism of will and a cynical objectivism of value.

But is this not the charge levied against postmodernism? Can postmodern jurisprudence help us to introduce and act the aporia of justice in law or is it even more guilty of moral insensibility than traditional jurisprudence? Postmodernism and deconstruction have been repeatedly accused of moral agnosticism, of cognitive relativism and of a political indifference that borders on reaction. In a somewhat unlikely linkage, both law and deconstruction have attracted doubts as to their attitude towards ethics and justice. Law, justice and deconstruction or the universal, the singular and what affirms and denies universality and uniqueness; do they have anything in common? To do justice to such questions we have turned to some paradigmatic texts and examine three judgments from the higher courts of the United Kingdom in order to expose the 'limits' of the practice of justice within the law. While we cannot positively state a theory of justice, we can and should, following the tradition, criticise and condemn the instances where injustice is done to the other.

III

The first two cases are similar.[4] They involved a number of Tamils seeking asylum in Britain. The refugees were fleeing Sri Lanka in 1987 as a result of an offensive by the majority Sinhalese government and the Indian army against the guerrilla Tamil forces in the north of the islands.[5] According to the court, parts of the country

---

[4] R v. Secretary of State for the Home Department, ex parte Sivakumaran and conjoined appeals ([1988] 1 All ER 193, House of Lords, henceforth cited as '1' followed by page reference); Bugdaycay v. Secretary of State for the Home Department and related appeals ([1987] 1 All ER 940, House of Lords, henceforth cited as '2' followed by page reference).

[5] An Amnesty International report paints a harrowing picture of many thousands of extra-judicial executions and disappearances and of extensive torture of Tamils in recent years (see Amnesty International, 1990a). But despite the well-documented evidence of persecution against Tamils, the British government adopted a hostile approach towards Tamil refugees in 1987, describing their claims as 'manifestly bogus', Tory MPs calling them 'criminals' (Hansard, 17.2.1987). The political resolve of the government to refuse asylum was also evident in the tough legal tactics

have been in a serious state of civil disorder, amounting at times to civil war. The authorities have taken steps [which] have naturally resulted in painful and distressing experiences for many persons innocently caught up in the troubles . . . [The] Tamils are the people who have suffered most. (1: 198)

In both cases, the applicants were refused asylum by the immigration authorities and challenged the refusal in proceedings for judicial review. In the first case, the material question was under what circumstances is someone a refugee entitled to asylum; in the second, what can one do to challenge the decision that refuses the applicant refugee status. Crucial here is Article 1 of the UN Convention on the Status of Refugees; under this, a refugee is someone who,

owing to well-founded fear of being persecuted for reasons of race, religion, nationality, membership of a particular social group or political opinions, is outside the country of his nationality and is unable or, owing to such fear, is unwilling to avail himself of the protection of that country.

In the first case, the sole point for consideration before the House of Lords was the proper basis for the determination of a 'well-founded fear of persecution'. The Court of Appeal held that the test for determining that a 'well-founded fear' existed was largely subjective. It would be satisfied by showing (a) actual fear and (b) good reason for this fear, looking at the situation from the point of view of one of reasonable courage. Unless an applicant's fear could be dismissed as 'paranoid', 'fear is clearly an entirely subjective state and should be judged accordingly' (1: 195).

The House of Lords reversed, reinstated the immigration decision and as a result the refugees were sent back to Sri Lanka. The Court held that a genuine fear of persecution could not suffice. The fears should have an 'objective basis' which could be 'objectively determined' (1: 196). Such fears, to be justified, should be based on 'true', 'objective facts' that could be ascertained by an

---

adopted. In February 1987, for example, Mrs Thatcher announced that airlines could be penalised for carrying immigrants into the country without proper documentation, and in March of the same year the government introduced the Immigration (Carrier's Liability) Act. Furthermore, under new arrangements, the government severely restricted the right of refugees to seek independent legal advice and limited the traditional power of MPs to intervene in individual cases in favour of immigrants (see Amnesty International, 1990b; Burgess, 1991).

objective observer like the Home Secretary or the immigration officers and not solely 'on the basis of the facts known to the applicant, or believed by him to be true' (1: 200). Once that was accepted, the Secretary of the State was entitled to have regard to facts 'unknown to the applicant' in order to assess whether 'subjective fear was objectively justified' (1: 202). The Secretary of State indeed had taken into account 'unknown facts', such as reports of the refugee unit of the department compiled from press articles, 'journals and Amnesty International publications, and also information supplied by the Foreign Office and as a result of recent visits to Sri Lanka by ministers' (1: 198). He had concluded the army activities 'that amounted to civil war' and 'occurred principally in areas inhabited by Tamils ... do not constitute evidence of persecution of Tamils as such ... nor any group of Tamils' (1: 199). As no 'real risk' of persecution of the group in general existed, or no risk 'on the balance of possibilities', the Home Secretary went on to conclude that none of the applicants had been or was likely to be subjected to persecution.

Lord Goff rounded off by assuring the UN High Commissioner for Refugees, who had intervened in favour of the applicants, that he need have

no well founded fear that, in this country, the authorities will feel in any way inhibited from carrying out the United Kingdom's obligations under the convention by reason of their having to make objective assessments of conditions prevailing in other countries overseas. (1:203)

The United Kingdom would continue to apply the law and give sanctuary to refugees. The objective test was necessary to ensure that this country – regarded as 'a suitable haven by many applicants for refugee status' – would not be 'flooded' with persons who, objectively considered, had no fear of persecution (1: 201).

The second case involved four applicants who were refused asylum by the immigration authorities and wanted to challenge that decision. They claimed that they met the criteria for asylum and that they should not be removed to a country where they feared persecution unless they had exercised a right of appeal against the initial refusal. Under the Immigration Act 1971, illegal entrants and those refused leave at a port of entry have a right of appeal against refusal to the immigration adjudicator and further to the Immigration Appeals Tribunal but only after they have left the country. With the beginning of the troubles in Sri Lanka, a visa requirement was imposed upon all those arriving from that country.[6] Both those without visa and those refused refugee status at a port of entry should leave the country and appeal against the refusal from abroad. The Act's remarkable assumption that people fleeing persecution will not experience some difficulty in carrying out this procedure paves the way for the courts' subsequent actions.

The appellants had been designated illegal entrants because they had obtained temporary leave to enter on various grounds and later applied for refugee status. They claimed that under the *UN High Comission for Refugees Handbook on Procedures for Determining Refugee Status* they had a right to appeal against refusal and that their removal – a precondition for appealing under the Act – would frustrate that right. The House of Lords ruled first that the *Handbook* had 'no binding force in either municipal or international law' (2: 946). It then went on to endorse the applicants' designation as illegal entrants. At the time of arrival, they had misrepresented to the immigration authorities the 'true nature and purpose of their visit . . . by making statements – which they knew to be false or did not believe to be true' (2: 947). Such being the case, to allow the applicants to stay, while all visitors denied leave to enter could only appeal after leaving, would be 'plainly untenable' (*ibid.*). It was prohibited by law and it would discriminate in favour of illegal entrants.

---

[6] Visa requirements were introduced in 1985 for Sri Lankans and, somewhat piecemeal, for more nationalities since. The Immigration (Carrier's Liability) Act 1990 imposed on airlines a fine of £1,000 per passenger brought into the United Kingdom without proper documentation. As the visa requirements and carrier sanctions do not distinguish between refugees and what the government calls 'economic migrants', it is hard to imagine how a refugee could ever legally reach this country. Schiemann J resisted the further step of the government which argued that six Lebanese had used fraud to travel to the United Kingdom and claim asylum while in transit. The judge aptly described the catch-22 facing refugees: 'He who wishes to obtain asylumn in this country, short of prior contact with the Home Secretary offering him asylum, has the option of lying to the UK authorities in [his] country in order to obtain a tourist or some other visa; obtaining a credible forgery of a visa; or obtaining an airline ticket to a third country with a stopover in the UK.' (*R v. Secretary of State for the Home Department, ex parte Yassine and others, The Times*, 6 March 1990.)

IV

1

Before the Law stands a doorkeeper. To this doorkeeper there comes a man
from the country who begs admittance to the Law. But the doorkeeper says that
he cannot admit the man at the moment. The man, on reflection, asks if he will
be allowed, then, to enter later. 'It is possible', answers the doorkeeper, 'but not
at this moment.'   Kafka, 'Before the law'

The Tamils' cases are (legal) judgments on (administrative)
judgments. Are the judgments just? Can we judge their justice? Can
we ever be just when facing the refugee, the other of all others?

A foreigner comes to the house of the law. He says: 'I am in fear'.
He asks to be admitted and to be given sanctuary. The immigration
officer or judge demands: 'Justify your fear, give reasons for it.' He
answers: 'My father has been killed by the police of my country.
My two sisters have been harassed. One of my cousins was
arrested, and taken to a barracks where he died of injuries. Before
dying he gave particulars of my friends and relatives including
myself. My other cousin has since been arrested and killed'.[7] 'Ah!',
the judge says, 'I must insist that fear is valid when it is based on
facts. And facts being what they are I can find them out as well as
you can, if not better. I know the true facts from my newspapers
and from reports by my agents and informers. I can base these on
the "current political, social and law and order position at present
pertaining in your country" (see 2: 949). Let us have a look at the
facts. People are being killed in your part of the world, some
Tamils in particular. But then people are always being killed in
your part of the world. On the basis of the true facts as I know them

---

[7] This is taken, almost verbatim, from the second refugee case. It describes the
experience of a Ugandan refugee who had been refused asylum and was being
deported to Kenya, a 'safe country', whence he had arrived in the United Kingdom.
The House of Lords quashed the decision on what are called by lawyers *Wednesbury*
grounds (see *Associated Provincial Picture Houses Ltd* v. *Wednesbury Corporation*
[1948] 1 KB 223), accepting that the Home Secretary had not taken into account the
fact that Kenya had returned Ugandan dissidents to Uganda in the past, despite
serious fears for their safety. This is the only instance in the cases discussed in
which an appellant won, and, interestingly, it is also the only instance in which the
House of Lords discussed the evidence produced by a refugee to support the claim
that he was a victim of persecution.

I can find no systematic persecution of Tamils or of any group amongst you. There is no objective basis for your fear as you are under no "real and substantial risk". It is possible you will gain entry, "but not at this moment"'.

In this encounter with the refugee, the role of the judge has gradually changed. He started as the recipient of the refugee's request, but in asking for grounds and reasons and in stating the facts he now claims to be on the same plane as the refugee, able to understand his predicament. In other words, the past pain of the refugee and his fear of future torture have been translated into an interpretable, understandable reality that, like all reality, is potentially shareable by judge and victim. But if interpretation is the possibility of constructing interpersonal realities in language, pain, death and their fear bring interpretations to an end.

For the person in pain [or fear of pain], so incontestably and unnegotiably present is it that 'having pain [or fear of pain]' may come to be thought as the most vibrant example of what it is 'to have certainty'; while for the other person it is so elusive that hearing about pain [or its fear] may exist as the primary model of what it is to 'have doubt'. Thus pain [and fear of pain] comes unshareably into our midst as at once that which cannot be denied and that which cannot be confirmed. Whatever pain [and its fear] achieves, it achieves through its unshareability, and it ensures this unshareability in part through its resistance to language. (Scarry, 1987, p. 4)

The claim that fear and pain can be rationalised through the shared understanding of their cause puts the victim in a double bind. Either he is in fear or he is not. If he is, he should be able to give facts and reasons for it which, as they belong to the genre of truth, should match the assessment of the judge; if they do not, the refugee is lying. If, on the other hand, he cannot give 'objective' justifications for his fear, the refugee is again lying. Similarly, when the refugee is inarticulate and cannot explain the 'objective basis' of his fear, he is not in fear. But when he can do so, the immigration officer

formed the view that the Applicant, who appeared in good health, was alert and confident at interview [and] was moving away from [his country] because a better life awaited him somewhere else and that this was not a genuine application for asylum. (2: 949)

In the idiom of cognition, fear is either reasonable and can be understood by the judge, or is unreasonable and therefore non-existent as non-reason is the very thing the law does not recognise. In the first instance, it is the excess of knowledge and reason on the part of the judge that disqualifies the fear, in the second it is the excess of fear that disqualifies itself. But this translation of fear into knowledge and of the *sylē* (the act and the right of seizure, of plundering and reprisals)[8] into reasons and causes assumes that the judge can occupy the place of the refugee and share the pain. Fear, pain and death, however, are radically singular; they resist and at the limit destroy language and its ability to construct shared worlds. Lyotard has called this violent double bind an *ethical tort* (*differend*); it is an extreme form of injustice in which the injury suffered by the victim is accompanied by a deprivation of the means to prove it.

This is the case if the victim is deprived of life, or of all liberties, or of the freedom to make his or her ideas or opinions public, or simply of the right to testify to the damage, or even more simply if the testifying phrase is itself deprived of authority. . . . Should the victim seek to by-pass this impossibility and testify anyway to the wrong done to her, she comes up against the following argumentation, either the damages you complain about never took place, and your testimony is false; or else they took place, and since you are able to testify to them, it is not an ethical tort that has been done to you. (Lyotard 1988a, p. 5)

When an ethical tort has been committed, the conflict between the parties cannot be decided equitably because no rule of judgment exists that could be applied to both arguments. The genre and the rules used to judge such cases will not be those of the genre judged and the outcome will necessarily be unjust. In such instances, language reaches its limit as no common language can be found to express both sides. For the refugee, the legal judgment is a performative; it acts violently upon body and feelings. From his perspective, the interpretative moment is of secondary importance. In the universe opened by the legal sentence, the role of the judge is structurally closer to that of the persecutor rather than that of the victim. The refugee suffers fear and violence, first in the hands of the torturer and second in the administrative/judicial claim that his intimate fear can be translated into shareable

---

[8] In Greek, *asylos* is someone not subjected to *sylē*, not stripped of his arms, possessions and due. Asylum, the place that offers sanctuary to the *asylos*, is usually associated with temples and other religious premises.

knowledge. For the law, this translation of the unique feelings into knowable realities is necessary. It restores its ability to pass sentences which was temporarily disturbed by the encounter with reason's other (feeling, pain, death) and cognition's other (the refugee). But at the same time this translation is unjust.

The violence of injustice begins when the judge and the judged do not share a language or idiom. It continues when all traces of particularity and otherness are reduced to a register of sameness and cognition mastered by the judge. Indeed all legal interpretation and judgment presuppose that the other, the victim of language's injustice, is capable of language in general, is man as a speaking animal, in the sense that is given to the word language. And as Derrida reminds us, 'there was a time, not long ago and not yet over, in which "we men" meant "we adult white male Europeans, carnivorous and capable of sacrifice" ' (1990, p. 951). But our communities have long lost any aspirations to a common idiom. We should not forget, therefore, that justice may turn out to be impossible, just a shibboleth (Douzinas and Warrington with McVeigh 1991, Chapter 11).

2

The Law, the man from the Country thinks, should be accessible for every man and at all times, but when he looks more closely at the doorkeeper in his furred robe, with his huge, pointed nose and long, thin, Tartar beard, he decides that he had better wait until he gets permission to enter. The doorkeeper often engages him in brief conversation, asking him about his home and about other matters, but the questions are put quite impersonally, as great men put questions, and always conclude with the statement that the man cannot be allowed to enter yet.   Kafka, 'Before the law'

The first type of injustice reduced the feeling of fear and pain of the other to objective facts which the judge can, allegedly, ascertain. A different form of injustice accompanies the Kantian assertion that the principle of morality is to be discovered in the universalisable maxim of the will of the rational agent. We examined above (Chapter 4, III) how under the promise of the universal national law excludes non-nationals from the community of its addressees and reduces them to a subordinate pole, as barbarians to the 'Greeks', alien, non-patrial, refugees, people who have no claims under the law, or who are exempted from its protection, but may be arraigned before it.

In immigration law, the philosophical limitations of human rights find their clearest empirical expression. The subject of human rights stands at the centre of the universe and asks the law to enforce his entitlements without great concern for ethical considerations and without empathy for the other. This conception of the subject meets the modern need for universalisation, where the function of commonality, of the shared attributes of humanity, can no longer be played by objective essences or divine impositions but is found in the ability to act on and change the world. The subject, as the site of philosophical introspection, as the outcome of genealogical development and as the vehicle of legal rights, is the mediator between abstract human nature, parcelled out equally to all human beings at birth, and the concrete human being who travels life creating his own unique narratives. The (legal) subject is what gives the person solidity and stability, what makes him present to himself and links him to consciousness and history. Above all, the subject, as the link between human nature and self, is what subjects self to the law, particularly to the law that the subject himself has legislated. The recognition of legal personhood is our accession to a public sphere of legal rights, limitations and duties, all based on the assumption of a shared, abstract and equal essence and of a calculating, antagonistic and fearful existence. The legal person is a persona, a mask, veil or blindfold put on real people who, unlike the abstractions of moral philosophy and jurisprudence, hurt, pain and suffer.

When we move from the legal subject to the concrete human being in the world, the abstractness of human rights discourse can be proved of little use against the concrete claims of power. The community of human rights is universal but imaginary; it does not exist empirically outside Geneva and New York and it has limited value as a transcendental principle. In the universal community of reason which acts as the horizon for the realisation of the law, the other, the alien, the third and unrepresentable can easily be turned into the same; the critical distance between self and other can be reduced and the experience of value of moral conscience can be grounded solely on the representation of the other by the knowing and willing ego. But the other, the victim, is singular and unique; she cannot be reduced to being solely an instance of the universal concept of the ego nor can she be subsumed as a case or example under a general rule or norm. The universality of the law was the formal precondition for the reconciliation of will and reason, but it is universality too that hinders the passage to the concrete human being. Let us follow this process of universalisation and exclusion in the refugee cases.

National law is demarcated both from international law and from the principles of human rights. The UN High Commission for Refugees Handbook on Procedures for Determining Refugee Status 'is of no binding force in either municipal or international law' (2: 946). Domestic law does not give a right of appeal to refugees refused asylum. The invocation of international law and the requests under it that decisions should be reached with the cooperation and approval of the High Commission are therefore 'plainly untenable' (2: 947). Furthermore, whilst the Court admits that 'the most fundamental of all human rights is the individual's right to life' (2: 952), it adds that applications for refugee status 'do not in general raise justiciable issues. Decisions under the [Immigration] Act are administrative and discretionary rather than judicial and imperative' (2: 955). But, at the same time, the Court asserts for the national system the legitimacy of the supranational law, whose validity, however, is denied. The authorities of the United Kingdom, which is regarded as 'a suitable haven by many applicants for refugee status . . . will [not] feel in any way inhibited from carrying out the United Kingdom's obligations under the [international refugees] convention' (1: 201, 203).

Immigration law is a prime and symbolic space for the construction of the asymmetrical relationship between 'we' and the 'others'. The 'we' of 'we decree as a norm' and as 'society's answer' and the 'you' of the 'you ought to obey' are radically external to each other. The 'you' can never become 'we' because it never enters into a dialogue with the 'I'. The other is used to underpin the superiority of the law (and) of belonging. The fairness, worth and justice of this law is proved and its attractiveness 'as a haven' justified even when – especially when? – it turns the refugee away and sends him back to his fate. 'Where the result of a flawed decision may imperil life or liberty a special responsibility lies on the court in the examination of the decision-making process' (2: 956; emphasis added). The dignity of the process should be protected at all costs. Its integrity will both defend those inside and explain why those outside remain other to the national law.

Immigration law, then, acts as a passage from the international to the national, from the universal to the general, as a line of closure and of opening, a boundary like the borders, the checkpoints and the patrols that await immigrants and refugees. To come to the law, the refugee comes to the port of entry, the physical space of entrance into the country but also the metaphorical door of the law. But to face the law and challenge the legality of the refusal to grant asylum, the refugee must leave both the country and its law. In order to come before the law, the refugee must depart. The coming foreshadows the going, the law is present and makes its presence felt only to the absent. The refugee is brought to the law by being removed.[9] This removal is doubly violent: it both shuts the door on the face of the refugee and it may send him 'to the country where, contrary to the view formed by the Secretary of State, he is in fact in danger of persecution' (2: 956). In

---

[9] The extraordinary legal odyssey of the five applicants in the first case did not come to an end with their defeat in the House of Lords. Following their expulsion to Sri Lanka in February 1988 their lawyers commenced an appeal. On their return to Sri Lanka, three of the five were subjected to torture and the Adjudicator found that all five were entitled to asylum, directing that they should be returned to the United Kingdom with minimum delay. The Home Office appealed but the Immigration Appeals Tribunal upheld the findings of the Adjudicator (*Secretary of State for the Home Department* v. *Sivakumaran and others* (1988) Imm AR 147). Not disheartened, the Home Office sought judicial review of the ruling but eventually, after more defeats (R v. *Immigration Appeals Tribunal and Immigration Appeals Adjudicator ex parte the Secretary of State for the Home Department* (1990) Imm AR 429) the five were returned to the United Kingdom in 1989. In the meantime, their lawyers brought an application at the European Commission of Human Rights, alleging violations of Article 3 (torture and inhuman or degrading treatment) and Article 13 (lack of effective remedies to challenge the asylum refusal) of the European Convention. The Commission found no breach of Article 3 on the President's casting vote, but by 13–1 a breach of Article 13. The Commission ruled that 'in matters as vital as asylum questions it is essential to have a fully effective remedy providing the guarantees of a certain independence of the parties, a binding decision-making power and a thorough review of the reasonableness of the asylum seeker's fear of persecution.' Judicial review of asylum refugees is not an adequate remedy, since the courts 'are concerned with the way in which a decision is taken and not with the merits of the decision (*Vilvarajah and others* v. *UK* [8 May 1990, Appl No 13163/87]). The European Court of Human rights, however, found no violation of the Convention. For a more recent case of sacrifice of a refugee, see *M.* v. *The Home Office* [1992] 2 WLR 73 and Goodrich (1992).

doing so, the judgment suspends the need for legal interpretation. The refugee may appeal to the law from the country of his potential persecution, but is unlikely to be able to do so.

And if, as jurisprudence claims, it is the interpretative moment of judgments which belongs to the horizon of justice, the Tamils' cases show that the time of justice is never fully present, but always still to come in a promised but deferred future. If a legal judgment is both word and deed, constative and performative, in this instance the act precedes the interpretation and endlessly defers it. It may be objected, of course, that this precedence of violent performance over legal interpretation is rather exceptional. But it is exactly this 'exception' that indicates the nature of normal cases. In every act of judging, there is a moment of saying and a moment of doing and justice cannot be identified exclusively with what is said.

In the refugees' cases, the deferral ensures that the law will not come face to face with the other. Could it be that one of the reasons for the exclusion of the refugee from the process of law is to avoid the call we outlined in Chapter 4, the call of the face? A face in fear or pain[10] cannot be explained by 'true facts' or be reduced to 'objective reasons'. It cannot be subsumed to the generality of the norm or the uniformity of application that asks immigrants to leave before they can come before the law. Being neither the object of cognition nor the instance of a rule, the face of suffering comes, in its singularity, to haunt its neighbours as much as its persecutors. Is not this the reason why the firing squad blindfolds its victim? The executioner covers the head of the executed as a defence against the face upon which suffering gets indelibly and indescribably inscribed and which, after disposal or death, persecutes the persecutor.

Similarly, the face of the refugee in fear calls for a singular, underived and undesirable answer to its call.

An expression like Welcome the alien must be able to be valid, not because it can be inferred from statements previously admitted, not because it conforms to older statements, but by the sole fact that it is an order having in itself its own authority. (Lyotard 1988a, p. 286; original emphasis)

And yet the law, in its generality, can only answer by subjecting

---

[10] See also our discussion in Chapter 8 on the face in pain.

the fear to procedures of truth, or by subsuming the alien under categories and concepts or finally by applying the norm. 'Neither Tamils generally nor any group of Tamils were being subjected to persecution' (1: 199). Despite the recognition that a 'flawed decision may imperil life or liberty' (*ibid.*), no mention whatsoever is made of the circumstances of the individual applicants. The arguments and objections of the refugees to the conclusions of the immigration officers are not dealt with judicially, but are summarily dismissed: 'It appears that the Secretary of State . . . considered whether any individual applicant had been subjected [to persecution] and decided that none of them had been' (*ibid.*). Even when he comes to the law, the refugee is treated as a faceless entity.

From the applicant to groups of Tamils to Tamils generally – in this process of abstraction and generalisation the individual is sacrificed to the concept in a display of another common type of violence that the law and judgments deal in. The law is about rules and universals. Its categories and concepts, self-enclosed and auto-referential, form a normative grammar that multiplies endlessly according to its internal logic. But the justice of the abstract code must be tested in its applications. The non-referential code must create its own instances of application and be seen to work on the world. In its performative aspect, the judgment abstracts the particular, generalises the event, calculates and assesses individuals and distributes them along normative and normal(ised) paths under a rule that subjects the different to the same and the other to the self.

The most tenacious subjection of difference is undoubtedly that maintained by categories. . . . Categories organise the play of affirmations and negations, establish the legitimacy of resemblances within representation, and guarantee the objectivity and operations of concepts. They suppress the anarchy of difference, divide differences into zones, delimit their rights, and prescribe their task of specification with respect to individual beings. . . . They appear as an archaic morality, the ancient decalogue that the identical imposed upon difference. (Foucault 1977, p. 186)

This ancient decalogue that denies difference lies at the heart of law. The gist of the rule of law, the modern concept of legality *par excellence*, is a demand for equality in abstraction and for repetition. Concrete individuals are turned into legal subjects, unique and changeable characteristics are subsumed under (ideal?) types and roles, singular and contingent events are metamorphosed into model 'facts' and scenes in impoverished narratives constructed according to the limited imagination of evidence and procedure. And as the law ascribes fixed and repeatable identities and transparent and calculable intentions to those brought before it, it necessarily negates the singularity of the other.

Within law we are fated to be 'unfaithful' to otherness, as we are forced to make comparisons which inevitably call for an analogy of the unlike to the same. Law classifies, establishes the norms by which difference is judged. If classification in and of itself is thought to be violence against singularity, then law inevitably perpetuates that violence. (Cornell 1988, p. 1591)

Kant had realised that applying a rule to a particular case or example would be to act legally but not necessarily in accordance with justice. In such a case, the justice of the decision would depend on the justice of the rule. But to determine that, one would have to turn to the origins of the rule and of the law, a process that would be all the more loyal to its aim the more removed it would be from the immediate call to justice of the case in hand. The justice of a straightforward rule-application resembles the efforts of the refugee and of Kafka's man of the country to come before the law. The closer you come to your end, the further away you find yourself from it. But as Derrida reminds us, in his apophantic tenor, the aporia of justice goes further:

If I were content to apply a just rule, without a spirit of justice and without in some way inventing the rule and the example for each case, I might be protected by law, my action corresponding to objective law, but I would not be just. I would act, Kant would say, *in conformity* with Duty, but not *through* duty or *out of respect* for the law. (Derrida 1990, p. 949; original emphasis)

Justice needs to address the other as irreplaceably unique, to judge refugees in their own language and idiom.

How are we to reconcile the act of justice that must always concern singularity, individuals, irreplaceable groups and lives, the other or myself *as* other, in a unique situation, with rule, norm, value or the imperative of justice which necessarily have a general form, even if this generality prescribes a singular application in each case? (*ibid.*; original emphasis)[11]

If law is similarity and repetition, justice is dissymmetry, inequality and contingency. As we saw, the violence of injustice

---

[11] A formulation that seems to summarise the problem the casuists faced, as we saw in Chapter 3. See also Chapter 4 for the theoretical basis of our discussion here.

begins at the point when a community does not share a common language. It survives in every legal act in which the language of the judge is imposed upon the judged, and similarity upon difference. The Kantian identification of morality with the maxims of the self-determining community and its empirical manifestation in the law of the democratic polity finds its limits in immigration law. Legal rules – the Lyotardian normative sentences – distinguish radically between those they present as their addressees and others. Indeed their very existence and action is based on this distinction.

Immigration law, then, in policing the borders and marking the property and propriety of the inside, repeats endlessly the violence of exclusion and silencing. And if the law needs this exclusion in order to present and demarcate its own territory and subjects, the principle of exclusion stands in and before the law alongside the ethical principle. It is the founding violence upon which every legal system rests, what Benjamin (1978) calls the 'mystical foundation of authority'. This violence is none other than the exclusion, de-portation, the *sylein* of the refugee. It attempts to silence the call to responsibility of the other, erase the trace of the face, deny refuge. In sending the refugee back to the place of (possible) persecution, the judge hopes to be released from the other's all-embracing demand to do justice. But as the Court insisted in both cases, the issues arising are neither 'justiciable' nor 'judicial'. And if this approach is not completely misguided, we should be able to find traces of the fear of the other throughout the law.

3

Anyway the machine still works and is its own justification.

Kafka, 'Before the Law'

Nothing could be more removed from the world of refugees than that of the protagonist of our third case.[12] From Sri Lanka to the Square Mile, from fear and torture to high finance and insider information, from the demands of sanctuary from persecution to those of personal honour and professional deontology, the difference is total. And as it was the world of the City that

---

[12]   *X Ltd v. Morgan-Grampian (Publishers) Ltd and others* ([1990] 1 All ER 616 at pp. 622 and 623; the case is cited hereafter as '3' followed by page references).

exemplified the cultural – postmodern – moment of the 1980s, it is no wonder that the Court came to consider and expound its theory of ethics and justice in this case.

Mr Goodwin, the second defendant, a journalist with a specialist magazine owned by the first defendants, was given confidential information by an unidentified source on the business plans of the plaintiff company. There was a suggestion that the information was based on a draft plan stolen from the company. When Mr Goodwin contacted the plaintiffs in order to check the information before writing an article about them, he was faced with a deluge of legal actions. *Ex parte* injunctions were issued against the magazine restraining them from publishing the information and ordering the journalist to disclose his source of information. The Court of Appeal varied the order, asking the journalist to disclose the notes of his conversation with the source which would help the plaintiffs identify that source and take action against him. The journalist refused to comply with the order and he and the publishers appealed.

For the Master of the Rolls the case was about the relationship between personal and professional ethics and the rule of law. Goodwin's refusal to reveal his sources was based either on an explicit promise given to that effect or, more generally, on professional deontology and the National Union of Journalists' code of journalistic conduct that ensures the protection of the sources of investigative journalism. Lord Donaldson's resolution of the 'conflict' was logically quite neat and simple – almost simplistic. He started from a rather bland reiteration of outdated constitutional doctrine:

Parliament makes the law and it is a duty of the Courts to enforce the law, whether or not they agree with it. . . . That is what parliamentary democracy and the rule of law is all about. . . . [The law] is society's answer given through the mouth of Parliament, and who are journalists, victims or judges to set themselves up as knowing better? In a parliamentary democracy personal and professional honour surely equates with the acceptance of and obedience to the rule of law. (3: 621, 622)

Through a series of synonyms and metonymies, society is equated with Parliament, Parliament with law, the law with the courts that 'enforce' it and finally individual morality and honour with the duty to obey the courts.

What is the place and force of ethics against this all-encompassing edifice? The Court accepted that occasionally conflicts arise between 'the first law [which] is the law of the land' and 'the second [which] is a moral imperative, usually, but not always of religious origin' (3: 623). But the moral imperative does not excuse breaches of the law and anyone who contemplates such a course 'would be well-advised to re-examine his conscience'. The judge could not 'over-emphasize the rarity of the moral imperative' (ibid.). If the journalist's moral dilemma was the result of his own promise to the source 'it is of his own making [and] he is deserving of no sympathy'. If, on the other hand, it was the result of his professional ethics, there is 'more honour and morality in conforming to the democratically evolved laws of the land rather than to the private self-imposed rule of the profession to which he belongs' (3: 624).

While the 'rare' moral imperative is often attributable to religious feelings, it is the law that resembles religion most: 'If any secular relationship is analogous to that between priest and penitent, it is that between lawyer and client' (3: 622). The imagery of the law as the 'mouthpiece' of society's wishes and the embodiment of social interests now moves onto a quasi-divine plane. Law's representatives, the courts, are not just the repositories of legality but the arbiters of morality as well. When those rare conflicts between law and ethics arise, 'the answer must be [with] the Courts' (3: 621).

Goodwin's claim to decide the moral dilemma for himself is therefore a challenge to morality and justice. 'The administration of justice in a parliamentary democracy depends in the last analysis on a general acceptance of the authority of the Courts as representing society as a whole. No challenge to that authority can be ignored' (3: 625). Goodwin's challenge was so fundamental that in an unprecedented move the Court denied Goodwin and his arguments a hearing for this contempt of its order (3: 624–5).[13]

---

[13] On appeal, the House of Lords accepted that courts have a discretion to decline to entertain the appeal of contemnors who defy the court's authority. But in the present case, according to the Lords, the Court of Appeal was incongruous. It allowed Goodwin's appeal to be presented, declined to hear his arguments, found against him and gave leave to appeal to the House of Lords. The House of Lords heard the argument from Goodwin's counsel but disssmissed the appeal ([1990] 2 All ER 1 at p. 12). The case is now being examined by the European Commission on Human Rights.

In this display of semi-priestly power that the judges asserted for themselves, the rebellious penitent is silenced and removed from the proceedings. Although more civil than those well-known instances of physical gagging of defendants by American courts,[14] the Court of Appeal's action is as effective. If the body of those arraigned before the law is under the control of the court, their faculty of speech, too, is law's gift to be withdrawn from dissidents and contemnors. The journalist's insistence on acting ethically in the only possible way, that is according to his own lights, makes 'his interests not worthy of consideration' (ibid.). Like the refugees and Kafka's man from the country, the journalist comes to the law and is kept outside its doorway. Access to the law, law's (in)accessibility, appears to be implicated in all our cases. But law's (in)accessibility has always been associated with justice. Let us have a final look at the relationship between law and justice as evidenced in our cases.

The Court of Appeal judgment is more unusual for its effects than for its reasoning and may be critically analysed[15] from a number of perspectives. What interests us here is the way it links law with ethics. The law as expounded by the courts is proclaimed to be the main, if not the exclusive, source of moral duty. Ethics is consistently underrated and is referred to in a series of derisory paraphrases and epithets: 'professional ethics', 'personal and professional honour', 'rare moral imperative', 'quaintly called "iniquities" ', 'self-made moral dilemmas deserving of no sympathy'. The tenor and rhetoric of the judgment keeps repeating that ethics is secondary, that its demands are valid only if formally legislated and that it is for the Court and not the individual to resolve according to the law any conflict between legality and morality.

The argument of the Court resembles a well-known philosophical gambit associated with Hegelian metaphysics. As we have seen, society, the 'real', and law, the 'normative', are presented as co-eval or homologous through a succession of substitutions.

---

[14] The best-known instance is that of Bobby Seale, one of the defendants in the Chicago Six trial, who was bound and gagged during proceedings (Illinois v. Allen, 397 US 337 (1970)).

[15] As was done, at least to a small extent, implicitly by the House of Lords, though not, of course, from the vantage-point we are suggesting.

Society speaks through Parliament, Parliament speaks through law, the law speaks through the courts, the courts define morality and individuals must accept their definition. And as society is the all-inclusive figure of reality, the law, too, is actual and total. If society is ever-present, society's mouthpiece, the law, is fully synchronised with society and matches it as a re-presentation of society's presence. But the law is also a totality; it brings together and unifies legality and ethics, is and ought, the subject and moral duty. There is no outside of law, as law and reality are co-extensive. What exists is legal and what contradicts the law cannot be real and does not count. The law 'imposes its sentence by proclaiming itself as a totality, which informs its own truth and by so doing makes itself a fact' (Cornell 1990, p. 1693).

The truth of the law, which, according to Lord Donaldson's simple equation, is revealed in judicial pronouncements is, at the same time, the essence of ethics. When the legal system has so expanded its empire as to encompass society totally and to fill itself with the myth of presence, the legally correct answer and ethical action coincide. Any person or act that strays beyond or outside legal representation cannot be comprehended by law's mouthpiece. But as Levinas and Derrida have reminded us, there is always a remainder, 'something' that cannot be assimilated by the system of representation and objectification.[16] It may be the otherness of ethics or the face of the refugee, but the remain(s) will deny and endlessly defer the promised closure of the (legal) system.

V

'What do you want to know now?' asks the doorkeeper, 'you are insatiable.' 'Everyone strives to attain the Law', answers the man, 'how does it come about, then, that in all these years no one has come seeking admittance but me?' The doorkeeper perceives that the man is nearing his end and his hearing is failing, so he bellows in his ear: 'No one but you could gain admittance through this door, since this door was intended for you. I am now going to shut it.'

Kafka, 'Before the law'

In the decisions we have examined in this chapter, the law

---

[16] For an exquisite reading of the remain(s) in Hegel, see Derrida (1986a); see also our discussion in Chapters 4 and 5.

imposed its own order on the other. It reduced difference to sameness and it proclaimed the Being of what it alone recognised as the only truth which it is reasonable to operate. Its own whole truth was the truth of the whole which, necessarily, embodied the sort of good we saw Cornell striving towards in our discussion of her work in Chapter 5. The results of such wild, imperialistic self-aggrandisement – silence, deportation and death – were not permitted to disturb the serene countenance of the common law.

Yet, as we saw in Chapter 4, after the 'hermeneutic turn' in jurisprudence, crude positivism is no longer dominant. The hermeneutic approaches emphasise practical reasoning and the principled and interpretative nature of legal decision-making. In so doing, they open legal judgments to considerations and materials, including moral philosophy, not immediately available or ascertainable from within the strict confines of legal rules. The aim, however, is still only to present legal *interpretation* as more creative, or more flexible, or as value orientated. Legal hermeneutics addresses exclusively the constative part of the legal sentence and judges its justice according to the 'rightness' of the expanded conception of what it is to interpret. The field from which the 'right answer' is to emerge has been considerably and admirably extended; but it is still from within this past field of law-worked-by-principle and its interpretation that the sentence will act upon the other. The translation from theory (the right answer according to legal facts and principles) to ethics (the demand for and performance of just action) remains unquestioned and unperformed. Our analysis does not deny the interpretative nature of legal judgment, but questions the automatic identification of its ethical and just character with the 'correct' interpretation of the law. Law's claim to represent reality and to impose judgments and order in its name may still be a kind of dogmatism even though reality now appears larger or more nuanced, open-ended and principled. We saw a virulent instance of this dogmatism in the cases we examined above.

We can conclude that the justice of a judgment is inscribed and suspended in the space between the statement of the law (what *exists* legally) and the invocation of an ideal state of affairs (what *ought to be* according to some principles or conception of morality). It is the space where the other brought before the law is acted upon, where justice is done or violence is inflicted.

For a decision to be just and responsible, it must, in its proper moment if there is one, be both regulated and without regulation: it must conserve the law and also destroy it or suspend it enough to have to reinvent it in each case, rejustify it, at least reinvent it in the reaffirmation and the new and free confirmation of its principle. (Derrida 1990, p. 961)

The operation of the judgment can be compared with the formal structure of performative speech acts. The performative says and does, saying what it does by doing what it says. I say 'I thee wed', 'the meeting is declared open', 'war is declared' and so it happens. Similarly, every judgment is implicated with force: the force of the interpretation which turns the singular and unique into an instance of the norm and a particular to the universal and the physical force that constrains and shapes the body. The 'rightness' of the judgment depends on the institutional felicity of the interpretation of law, and in hermeneutical jurisprudence, on its accord with some moral standard. But its justice can only be judged according to the way it acts. Its action is neither the continuation of legal interpretation nor its opposite. In many key respects, *logos* and *kratos*, discourse and force, differ.

First, the time of justice differs from the time of interpretation. Interpretation turns to the past or measures up to the future as they inhabit the ever-present. Interpretation's time is synchronic. The time of action – violence or justice – on the other hand, is diachronic. It addresses the other here and now in each here and now, and answers or denies the call. This is the pure ethical time, the time of what Levinas calls 'il y a' – it is happening. Interestingly, the two opposing conceptions of time were discussed by the courts in the first refugees case. It will be recalled that the Court of Appeal had adopted a subjective definition of fear. The Master of the Rolls illustrated the text by means of an allegory.

A bank cashier confronted with a masked man who points a revolver at him and demands the contents of the till could without doubt claim to have experienced a 'well-founded fear'. His fears would have been no less well-founded if, one minute later, it emerged that the revolver was a plastic replica or a water pistol.[17]

---

[17] [1987] 3 WLR 1053. As is well known, Hart (1961) uses the gunman analogy repeatedly to distinguish the meaning of 'being obliged' from that of 'having an obligation'. Only the latter is supposed to be the correct response to normative, specifically legal, commands. Lord Donaldson, in accepting that the fear is

The House of Lords, however, dismissed the analogy in summary fashion. An 'objective observer' of the robbery would accept the cashier's fear as well-founded only until he discovered the fact that the firearm was fake. Before that, he could not have been an 'objective' observer in any case. While he was still defrauded, he was in exactly the same state as the cashier, possibly in fear but certainly not seeing the truth. The objective observer must reserve judgment until such time as all relevant facts are in. According to the Lords, immigration officers and judges should also act as objective observers. From that position, the refugees' fears were not 'of instant personal danger arising out of an immediate predicament' and the official response should be determined after 'examining the *actual* state of affairs in [the refugees'] country' (1: 196, 197; emphasis added).

We can draw a parallel here between the time of fear and pain and the time of justice. When fear, pain or justice are dealt with as 'real' entities that can be verified or falsified according to objective criteria, their time or the time of the response to them is the time of constancy and omnitemporality of descriptions, theories and institutions. Truth is atemporal and theory is all-seeing. Fear and pain, on the other hand, are individual feelings experienced as temporal responses to stimuli. In treating the time of fear as non-instant and non-immediate, the House of Lords is also violating the time of ethics. To remind ourselves of the biblical story, God, who knows that Ishmael will in the future shed innocent blood, still gives him water now because he is dying of thirst and therefore suffering injustice now. 'I judge each for what he is now and not for what he will become', God tells the protesting Angel.

Violence or justice can only happen at the moment of their occurrence. They are the performative aspects of the legal judgment. Nothing that happened earlier – a reading of the law or a commitment to principle – and nothing that anticipates the future – a promise or a vision of what should happen – can account fully or pre-empt the uniqueness of the response. And, as in the robbery

---

necessarily an individual and unshareable feeling and in responding to it, is, in this instance, following the principle of justice of the ethics of alterity. His judgment in case 3, on the other hand, shows that this principle is momentary. It is neither a generalisable rule nor does it derive from the consistent and coherent action of a prudent judge.

analogy, the response of the person obligated can only be instant and immediate. We can now understand why, for Derrida, the instant of the just decision is a madness and has an urgency that obstructs knowledge. Justice, like the robber and the fear he created, cannot wait for all relevant facts. Even if the addressee of justice had all the information and all the time in the world, 'the moment of decision, as such, always remains a finite moment of urgency and precipitation . . . since it always marks the interruption of the juridico- or ethico- or politico-cognitive deliberation that precedes it' (Derrida 1990, p. 967).

The tension between the urgency of the call to justice and the omnitemporality of law reminds us that there is an imperceptible fall from interpretation to action, that an invisible line both fissures and joins the legal sentence as the (grammatical) sentence of the legal text and the (forcible) sentence of the legal verdict. This trait conjoins and separates the constative from the performative. But at the same time as the space and time of action and of the encounter with the other, the trace is where the interpretative part of the judgment is brought before the law of its performance. This trace is justice. A judgment is just if it follows and creates its momentary principle. The paradox of a 'momentary principle' best paraphrases just action which, *qua* action, resists and denies all paraphrase. The trace is a *principle* insofar as it answers the call of the suffering other, who is one among many, in a community of ethical sensibility which, like Kant's *sensus communis*, acts as the regulative principle always still to come; but it is only a *momentary* and transient principle, as the encounter with the other is always concrete and unrepeatable. Justice is the momentary and principled response to the other's concrete generality. This is the law of justice, of

whose subject we can never say, 'there it is', it is here or there. It is neither natural nor institutional; one can never attain to her, and she never arrives on the grounds of an original and proper taking place. (Derrida 1989, p. 141)

This momentary principle of justice, inscribed at the heart of the judgment but always before the law, is what turns force into justice and force that does not heed its call into violence. Its principled character links with the legal community of generality and equality, its momentary action with the ethical network of asymmetrical hostages to the others.

Finally, can we aspire with Cornell to discover this principle in the legal system? We should not be surprised to find instances where the 'right' legal answer violates – the momentary principle of – justice. The refugee cases are clearly such examples. But in other instances the performative part of judgments can be seen to act ethically against the grain of the interpretative moment. Cases involving juries who acted against clear judicial instructions come to mind in this respect. The courts themselves came to consider the role of justice in legal proceedings in our third case. The technical context of the discussion was s. 10 of the Contempt of Court Act 1981 under which a court may not force journalists to disclose their sources unless it is necessary in the interest of justice. Lord Donaldson visualised the 'interests of justice' as a doorway, law's door, and judges as the doorkeepers. Plaintiffs must 'squeeze' or 'barge through' before they can get law's protection. But when the Court came to discuss the 'shape, colour and dimensions' of this doorway, it repeated that justice 'is not used in a general sense as the antonym of "injustice" but in the technical sense of the administration of justice in the course of legal proceedings in a court of law' (3: 9).[18] It is just to say that justice can only be talked about in figures, paraphrases, allegories, justice's 'antonyms'. But in immediately identifying justice with court procedure, the Court, like Kafka's doorkeeper, shuts the door. Could this not be judged a well-founded fear of justice?

---

[18] While broadly agreeing with Lord Donaldson, the House of Lords slightly extended the definition of 'interests of justice' to mean that 'persons should be enabled to exercise important legal rights and to protect themselves from serious legal wrongs whether or not resort to legal proceedings in a court of law will be necessary to attain these objectives' ([1992] 2 All ER at p. 13). The identification of a wider concept of the law with justice is, however, still upheld.

7

'As a dream doth flatter'

Law (love, life and literature) in Sonnet no. 87

I

In the first chapter of this book, we drew attention to the fact that despite the common perception of legal work as extremely practical, day-to-day activity, much of what lawyers are called on to do can be seen as closely resembling the activities of literary critics. Both practitioners and academics in law start from the 'text', that is, for lawyers, statutes, cases and the documents and oral arrangements made by parties. Whilst it may be true that working lawyers often do not see their roles as specialised *littérateurs*, or possibly, as our discussion in Chapter 5 might have indicated, *littérateurs* at large, academic lawyers inevitably spend their lives rereading already given written materials.

Despite this evident relation between the academic and the working lawyer which blurs the easy and generally simplistic distinctions between theory and practice, at least in law, academics of all kinds, including academic lawyers, are used to the jibe that they are not involved in day-to-day 'political events', that they are on the 'fringes' of 'real activity' and that the interpretation of texts is somehow not as significant as 'practical action'. All these rather glib phrases, of course, assume that there is some distinction between 'real' and 'unreal' activity, or that there is a difference between practical and 'impractical' action and furthermore that one can be valued higher than the other. If nothing else, Derrida's work has taught the dangers of accepting these simplistic oppositions, and that the clichéd, apparent bipolarities, such as central/marginal, are always included in, rather than excluded out of, each other.[1] But the inside/outside entanglement involves respecting and recognising both the conjunction and the separation of text and world. When it comes to the relation between textual analysis and political action, the complex interweaving of these two opposites has to be acknowledged. As one sympathetic critic put it,

> Derrida seems to understand what he is, a philosopher who speaks and writes about texts. Nowhere in his work can one find any trace of a simple confusion between such activity and political action *per se*, which remain . . . related but resistant categories. (Harpham 1991, p. 396)

At stake in this resistant relation is a question whose obvious banality is only matched by its ludicrous impossibility: what is meant by textual analysis? Does it involve an 'ethical-political' stance which can link the ethical considerations we are endeavouring to raise in this book with legal-political applications? We can start by taking seriously Derrida's often cited remark: 'There is nothing outside of the text' (1974, p. 158). Again, for lawyers, no matter how close to the realities of real life their work must be, this infamous iteration should not really cause the panic that it has raised in certain quarters; in law, the question of the text and what it means to interpret it, is always crucial. Taking the text (not necessarily merely the mean *Writ*-ten of particular forms, but of course including other texts which provide necessary contexts such as the historical and the economic etc., the fact that texts necessarily consist of the combination and reintegration of

---

[1] Derrida's notion of *différance* presents the possibility of this rather strange 'inexclusion'. *Différance* marks 'that the movement of signification is possible only if each so-called "present" element, each element appearing on the scene of presence, is related to something other than itself, thereby keeping within itself the mark of the past element and already letting itself be vitiated by the mark of its relation to the future element, this trace being related no less to what is called the future than to what is called the past, and constituting what is called the present by means of this relation to what is not: what it absolutely is not, not even a past or a future as a modified present' (Derrida 1982, p. 13). Much of our discussion in this book implicitly works on the basis that what is excluded always remains to haunt the excluders (see in particular Chapter 6 and our short discussion of supplements in Chapter 8).

reiterated fragments[2]) is frequently the way analysis must start, if only because there is nothing else. Derrida has elaborated that this starting from texts does not mean an avoidance of the real, or of the practical problems that everyone is concerned to tackle. On the contrary, starting from the text not only acknowledges the totality of any interpretative exercise, but also recognises the unavoidable nature of the process of interpretation itself.

We *can* only start by looking at texts, insofar as they separate themselves from us at the begining of, or rather before, any inquiry.

We could not do otherwise even if we wished to do so or thought to do so. We are no longer credulous enough to believe that we are setting out from things themselves by avoiding 'texts' simply by avoiding quotation or the appearance of 'commentary'. The most apparently direct writing, the most directly concrete personal writing which is supposedly in direct contact with the 'thing itself', this writing is 'on credit': subject to the authority of a commentary or a re-editing that it is not even capable of reading. (Derrida 1992a, p. 100)

Social activity, political relations, critical commentary, all involve the interpretative process that mostly we take for granted. The fact that interpretation is frequently done in a thoughtless manner, no doubt out of necessity, does not mean that we are not always involved in a process of trying to determine the meaning of a text. And the question of textual meaning cannot be dismissed as a deviation from political meaning – politics itself is about trying to make some meanings of texts more effective than others.

If politically concerned academic lawyers have to face the rather tiresome criticism that somehow what they do is not proper, not politically respectable, then those involved with study of literature must find themselves subject to it all the time.[3] At least lawyers can point to some rather vague, usually all too easily assumed, reference to an ultimate real when they argue for a new statute or interpretation in a particular area: the interpretation may or will be taken up by a case, applied to the parties before it, and then determine conduct for all others in similar situations, etc. or

---

[2] Derrida's standard work on iteration is Derrida (1988). See also Derrida (1992b, p. 63): iterability is related to the structure of texts, the inevitablity of 'iterability, which both puts down roots in the unity of a context and immediately opens this non-saturable context onto a recontextualization'.

[3] Evans (1989, for example, p. 97) suggests that much Shakespeare criticism tends to repress the political implications of its analysis.

so the argument goes. But in literary criticism the notion of starting from the text might be all too obvious and might seem all too literal (in at least two senses) a requirement and therefore all too self-evidently not concerned with the real world. Reading another book and writing yet another article on it can easily be portrayed, maliciously, as an irrelevant form of social activity. Yet perhaps precisely because of this 'soft target' nature of the Eng. lit. enterprise, members of its community who regard political interventions as important have no difficulty in justifying their textual work,[4] even if they do not accept the complex interweaving between text, analysis and the world implied by Derrida.

Shakespeare studies, in particular, are often the site of intense battles over the 'politically correct' position. It is because Shakespeare has become *the* cultural icon of the English world (and beyond), a process to which the current Conservative administration seems inclined to add the weight of statutory authority, that the politically motivated literary critics keep returning to the text of the plays. If in each generation the literary establishment finds it necessary to reaffirm the (impossibly) sacred[5] nature of the texts of Shakespeare,[6] it seems that, at the least, they have doubts about the effectivity of the enterprise, and, at the most, more can be done by challenging the received readings of Shakespeare than through almost any other form of literary critique. Commenting on Shakespeare's characters and the impossible situations they frequently confront, Sinfield asserts that 'the complexity of the social formation combines with the multi-accentuality of language to produce an inevitable excess of meaning, as implications that arise coherently enough at one point cannot altogether be accommodated at another' (1992, p. 76). This

---

[4] A good example is Eagleton, who claims that Shakespeare's plays demonstrate, in part, the 'illusion' of trying to reconcile the conflicting strands of feudalism and capitalism. 'Feudalism and capitalism did not, of course, prove amenable to judicious synthesis', he writes and the resulting conflict expressed in the plays 'can be read as an allegory of class struggle' (1986, p. 99). See also Evans (1989).

[5] As Norris put it: 'Any notion of the sacrosanct literary text – whether as an object of scholarly or critical attention – is rendered problematic by the instance of Shakespeare' (1985, p. 56).

[6] Texts which, according to Barker and Hulme (1985, p. 191) are deemed by many critics to portray 'a past which is picturesque, familiar and untroubled'; by implication for these critics, the same is true of the modern world.

excess represents the 'unbounded potential' that Shakespearian interpretation seems to offer as a substitute for the bland, humanistic, patronising, patriarchal, sexist,[7] colonial and post-colonial[8] approaches to Shakespeare that the political critics are anxious to replace.

What is at stake, therefore, in any vigorous rereading of Shakespeare is more than the repeated assertion that there is no limit to the interpretative possibilities within Shakespearian criticism; as Sinfield elegantly and comprehensively puts it: 'Shakespeare, notoriously, has a way of anticipating all possibilities' (ibid., p. 107). What does unite, in a rather loose way, the different theoretical criticisms is the recognition that the texts of Shakespeare are not simply 'there' – that their 'thereness', their elevation into the canon,[9] is the result of a complex process of construction in which certain ends and influences produce a series of readings with particular social and political effects.

Reading works by Shakespeare, then, becomes an activity that recognises one of the most creative aspects of the plays, their serious questioning of the ways meanings are created in any complex social process and the political possibilities this opens. The plays have such scope for misrepresentation and rereading (though again, these distinctions are suspect) because they actually point continually to our own inability to read or to decipher the signs that the plots and characters give out in our vain attempts to determine a given, once-for-all meaning. For one critic at least, the comedies specifically

---

[7] According to Freedman (1991, esp. pp. 114–16), modern feminist theory is committed to 'subverting the structure of [sexual] difference as opposition.' As to how to do this, Freedman suggests: 'The answer provided by avant-garde feminism, then, is that woman does not take (a) place but, rather, re-visions positionality itself' (p. 116). When applied to Shakespearian texts, feminism has been extremely suggestive and has been able to reinterpret even the most assumed misogynist of the plays, The Taming of the Shrew, as something other than a violent reimposition of male domination (ibid., pp. 118–53). 'Even in the most misogynist of dramatic narratives, then, we may discover a subversive strain characterised by a disruptive gaze that never rests secure' (ibid., p. 144). See also French (1981), Jardine (1983), J. Rose (1985) and Belsey (1985).

[8] See Hawkes (1986), Greenblatt (1988), Evans (1989) and Sinfield (1992, esp. pp. 1–28 and 252). Shakespeare has been used to preserve more than the British Empire. For example, Sinfield (ibid., p. 267) remarks: 'Imperial Shakespeare [even] seems to heal the split in the concept of US man'.

[9] On the construction and deconstruction of the canon, see Brown (1993).

function as optical devices for staging distortions and blind spots [and therefore] we can use them to subvert the place of our own look. . . . The end result [of reinterpreting the comedies] is a series of readings that question the possibility of reading as mastery. (Freedman 1991, p. 5)

Freedman claims that the apparent mastery appropriated by actor, director, audience, reader and critic in the interpretative strategies brought to the plays is bound to fail. Just as the main characters in *The Comedy of Errors*, regularly misread the signs before them, so 'we can never hope to read the play correctly' (*ibid.*, p. 84). The search for some organic unity shows that the self, the ego, 'is neither master in his home nor his own master' (*ibid.*, p. 85). The same applies to reader or audience observing the weird goings on in *The Comedy* and, by implication (or at least hope), will apply to heavy-handed attempts by government agencies to reimpose a particular hierarchy on the force-feeders of authorised texts.

But like most good things, new, potentially different, resistant readings must be worked for. Our argument is that literary interpretation can reveal to us more than the various – literary and legal – orthodoxies see in the relationship between law and literature and can help us explore the link between ethics, law and politics.[10] The simple piece of literature we analyse, a love poem, entangles legal meaning in the very attempt to transcend the petty restrictions that law throws upon every aspect of life, even on what literature itself considers the most basic of human emotions. In offering a linked series of commentaries on one piece of work by Shakespeare in this chapter, we try to indicate both the dangers of orthodox legal interpretation and the possibility of exploring the ethical significance of the other in literature and law. If the Shakespeare industry is part of the fabric of society, then by virtue of a non-virtuous circle the law is something that is frequently used to create the apparently non-legal aspect of the fabric. The law's 'suspect'[11] 'respected'[12] place helps interpretations of the works of poets, playwrights and, as our final chapter indicates, even painters establish the legitimacy of what is. We question the

---

[10] We also have the excuse that the particular work chosen for analysis seems to gravitate towards the law, though we are aware that this of itself does not distinguish our object of analysis from much of Shakespeare's other work, where legal metaphors, analogies, characters and settings abound.

[11] *Much Ado About Nothing* IV.2.72–3.

[12] *Measure for Measure* II.1.156–68.

legitimacy of that law by trying to articulate its lack of concern for the preontological call of the other that our discussion of the priorities of Antigone highlighted. Our contention that 'other' readings are always available allows us to make explicit our ethical concerns to respect the other that reading otherwise makes possible.

II

Law, as a process of interpretation, inevitably relates to many of the traditions of interpretative practices carried on outside of law, in particular hermeneutics. As the art of determining the meaning of any and every cultural tradition from pregiven texts, hermeneutics promises much to every person who finds him/herself faced with the question of interpretation. To take the most obvious examples, we appreciate the beauty of a statue from classical Athens, a painting from Renaissance Italy ('the modern framed picture that is not tied to a particular place and offers itself entirely by itself' [Gadamer 1975, p. 119]) and a piece of music from nineteenth-century Vienna. All these works appear to speak to us across the vast chasms of time and culture that separate the modern world of the spaceship from its predecessors by a space that seems to fill an infinite number of worlds. How do they speak to us? Why do we appreciate their beauty still? What is there in the relation between the work and ourselves that moves us now? Why do we still thrill, or at least admire, as much now as then, the cut of a body on Athenian stone, or the line of a face on canvas from fifteenth-century Florence, or the interval between two notes from almost two hundred years ago? All cultural works appear to be solely of their age. How can they, in Gadamer's terms, bring their 'hidden history into every age' (ibid., p. 143)?

We find similar problems with the literature of law, when interpreting a law report, statute or official decree. We may all recognise that the injunction not to drive at more than a certain speed is irreducibly modern, and can speak to us directly without the need to cope with vast distances of interpretative time, but so much law has more to it. To use some random examples: the modern law of negligence takes many of its concepts from a world of horse-drawn transport, inn-keepers under duties of hospitality, and problems arising out of streets which were as dark as a lover's night. The law of contract has rules about the making of contracts by the posting of letters. These rules speak of a society where the mail was the latest, most wonderful invention of the Crown, where delivery was an act personally authorised by the sovereign. Property law still governs its organising formal notions via feudal concepts of estates and tenures. In this field, such basic notions as rights of way depend on fictious grants ('revolting fictions', as one nineteenth-century judge called them) that everyone knows were never made, and yet which are treated by modern judges as though they were made and which oblige the judges to give instructions to juries (which are no longer used in this type of case anyway) to treat the non-existent as though it did exist. Similarly, something as common and everyday as a mortgage depends for its operation on the solemn incorporation into the mortgage document of a crucial binding statement that everyone knows is to have no binding force at all. How can all these strange wonders of a previous age still have meaning for us?

Hermeneutics claims, if not exactly to solve these problems, then at least to lead us towards ways of making sense of earlier texts. In Gadamer's terms, truth can speak out of tradition so that we can understand artifacts that appear only to be relevant to a different age. For we have no difficulty in coping with the nature of scientific knowledge, and making sense of the truths with which, say, Galileo so gravely offended the orthodox tradition of the time. Gadamer argues that, similarly, there can be a truth we can extract from art, music, paintings and the laws of a former age. But it is crucial to comprehend the type of truth claim that is at stake. Connections can be made which make the truth of a previous understanding say something truthful and important to us.

Is there to be no knowledge in art? Does not the experience of art contain a claim to truth which is certainly different from that of science, but equally certainly is not inferior to it? And is not the task of the aesthetic precisely to provide a basis for the fact that the artistic experience is a mode of knowledge of a unique kind, certainly different from that sensory knowledge which provides science with the data from which it constructs the knowledge of nature, and certainly different from all moral rational knowledge and indeed from all conceptual knowledge, but still knowledge, ie the transmission of truth? (ibid., p. 87)

For Gadamer, then, there is in human existence the possibility of continuity and of self-understanding (ibid., pp. 86–7) which permits the artistic, literary and philosophical truths of a former age to be brought down to the present, to make a truth for us. The works of the past can be made to speak so that their beauty and worth can add to our lives by becoming part of them. We can fuse our understandings of our world with the things that have come down to it from previous worlds, and thus start to make a certain sense of our own lives which otherwise would appear to be absolutely formless, reasonless and without point. We cannot appear in the world without inheriting the remains of the world before us; and we cannot start to make changes and improvements without understanding the possibilities provided by the past out of which we have arrived.

In this chapter we present an analysis of Shakespeare's Sonnet no. 87 in which, rather crudely, we pit a 'classic' hermeneutic analysis of the Sonnet, against an equally 'classic' critical analysis which might come out of the Habermasian school of rationalistic thought. Whilst an element of our presentation of these two analyses borders on the parodic, our intention is to contrast them with a third.[13] Starting from our own disciplinary base of the law, we counter both the hermeneutical and critical reading with a legal analysis of the poem's strategies. The disciplinary certainties of a legal terminology through which the poem expresses itself point to an authoritarianism of legal language which tends to destroy the very terrain of the love poetry the Sonnet appears to inhabit.

III

Perhaps by a curious form of conditioning, as we come to literacy or, in Habermas's terms, communicative competence, we know that there will be many works of literature that will speak to us out of their own tradition, and yet which we can somehow make our own. We acquire this perception almost without effort, frequently

---

[13] As a justification for this exercise, we would repeat Felperin's question of the Sonnets: 'Is there any pre-modern text better suited to serve as a test case for deconstruction?' (1990, p. 56). As to whether lawyers should attempt to analyse a Shakespearian Sonnet, see Fried (1988); Fried, though, puts the sonnet he analyses (no. 65) to a very different use from that attempted here.

without understanding. Literature may exist from a previous age but, as Gadamer puts it, 'even then, the normative sense contained in the idea of world literature means that works that belong to world literature remain eloquent although the world to which they speak is quite different' (*ibid.*, p. 144). How is this so? The text we will use is certainly familiar to 'world literature' (whatever that might be):

> Farewell! Thou art too dear for my possessing,
> And like enough thou know'st thy estimate.
> The charter of thy worth gives thee releasing;
> My bonds in thee are all determinate.
> For how do I hold thee but by thy granting?
> And for that riches where is my deserving?
> The cause of this fair gift in me is wanting,
> And so my patent back again is swerving.
> Thyself thou gav'st, thy own worth then not knowing,
> Or me, to whom thou gav'st it, else mistaking;
> So thy great gift, upon misprision growing,
> Comes home again, on better judgment making.
> > Thus have I had thee, as a dream doth flatter:
> > In sleep a king, but waking no such matter.

To begin with, then, we shall follow Gadamer's injunction; we shall see how the horizon of the poem can be fused with the horizons that create and limit our own world, and that the two together can make sense of this artifact from the former age, in a way that will help us understand our own.

The poem, like most poems, and in effect all the sonnets of the sequence, is about love, that is, about strongly felt desires and emotions for one person by another, in this case the other being the poet. But, again like many love poems, it is a poem about a love that is not working towards a satisfactory ending. It is a song of farewell, in which the poet tries to prove how much his love was genuine by a double act of, on the one hand, self-denigration and, on the other, seemingly extravagant praise of the person loved. And there is no doubt that both sides of the equation are overstated. It will almost certainly be the case that the poet is nothing like as unworthy as the poem appears to make out; 'too dear for my possessing', 'where is my deserving', 'The cause . . . in me is wanting', 'Or me . . . else mistaking'. Equally, the person praised and addressed, who has clearly cooled towards the poet, almost certainly is nothing like as worthy as the poet is suggesting. The great gift, the riches, the worth, the estimate, the fair gift of the addressee of the poem is also someone who both 'know'st thy estimate' and who also mistakes both her/his own worth ('thy own worth then not knowing') and the merits of the poet ('Or me . . . else mistaking'). A tension is created between a convention of love poetry in which the loved object is always unattainable or cannot be kept because it is too fine (even though the fine object's worth is itself suspect) and the fact that the poet-lover is himself not worth anything anyway, even if the object of admiration were not so wonderful. The worth of the poem itself comes from a combination of the beauty of the language, the apparent creating of a fairly conventional cross-relationship, and the ability at the same time to question whether that relationship, that series of opposites, value against worthlessness, can ever really be as simple as all that. The good is never completely good, no one really good 'know'st thy estimate' in the way that the poet suggests entitles her/him to disvalue the other. And there is always more to the bad; the mistaking is also of one who, in marked contrast to the object addressed, is all too ready to acknowledge his own defects. In reading of the poet's own 'wanting', we are continually reminded of his incomparable struggle towards immortality, of the poet's own worth.

The poem then tells us about moderation, an Aristotelian ideal. Exaggeration of the merits of others and the demerits of ourselves both lead to severe (no doubt justified) disappointments. The goal of knowledge of self and of others depends on a steady apprecia- tion of personal attributes. Literary excess leads to lived failure. Life is to be conducted outside of literary extravagances; realistic appreciation enables love to understand imperfections and inabil- ities. Life is the fuller and better in consequence. Human relationships can only reach a satisfactory level when this ideal of a reasonable mean between the two extremes of the poem is understood.

So much for conventional analysis; it is heremeutical in the sense that it brings the poem of another age down to concerns of our own, it tell us things about our own world. Reading Shakespeare's Sonnets in a way that takes account of the nuances of the discourse of the age is always a complex process (see, for example, Barrell 1986, esp. pp. 18–44). As indicated, we now propose to complicate matters a little further by reading the poem for and as lawyers, concerned with the ethics and justice of social relations. And as we do so, we realise that a further fusion of horizons is possible, that the poem speaks to us as lawyers, for, rather surprisingly, we find that we have a lawyerly poem. The love of the poet, the story of the coming rejection, the parting that takes place or is anticipated, are all expressed in strong law-like forms. A poem of love turns into a poem that treats love in terms of law. Life, the poem tells us, imitates law, is expressed through law and is broken or destroyed at the command of law. And in this way, we come to learn more about what the poem can tell us, how indeed a sixteenth-century artifact can speak to us, and how, in the merging of the understandings that come together, we produce a new form of Gadamer's truth for 'us'.

What is going on in this poem is an address to lawyers, or perhaps by a lawyer, to a world where, apparently, everything takes legal form, where the common law has indeed achieved that consummation devoutly prayed for and become gapless; it has taken over all aspects of social interaction, including love. The poem is about possession, charters, releases, bonds which are determinate, grants, gifts, patents and, crucially, the reciprocal relationship of contracts. The central image that summarises all this is the common law of contract itself. The poet claims that his worth is not equal to that of the addressee, and therefore the relationship fails. In law, contracts are a process of exchange. When contracts are made, each party subjectively decides on the value of the consideration that is to be given for the legal relationship to come into existence. The startling thing about this particular contract, which makes it a love poem (albeit one determined by law) rather than a legal treatise, is that one of the parties (the poet) takes the unusual step of disvaluing his or her own offering. In contract, the law itself does not determine the actual value of the consideration that is exchanged through the legal process. This is purely a matter for the parties themselves. It is subjective, as the judges say. But there must be an exchange of values of some sort; mere gifts have no contractual effects and cannot be enforced legally. So that although contract law does not purport to take on itself the task of measuring the adequacy of each party's contribution to the legal relationship, there is little doubt, within conventional wisdom at least, that an exchange of (rough) equality is more likely to grow and prosper in law and love than an exchange of gross inequalities.

What we see here is how unequal relationships break down. The exchange itself is unequal; the gift of one is not matched by any equivalent, no matter how small, from the other. The author of the Sonnet claims to be worthless, without deserving, whereas the object of the poem has a charter of worth, and the inequality between the two is sufficient to bring to an end, that is, to determine, the bonds and to give the releasing that otherwise would continue to bind the parties.

Looked at in this light, the poem then falls into place, and we can start to appreciate how it speaks to us, and has meaning four hundred years after its composition. The poem creates a picture which can be seen to speak via the law. The poem cancels bonds of love and law, bonds that previously had been in place. The poet starts with a 'Farewell', a word that rings through the ages, but is indeed the expression of a parting that every severance of a contract expresses. But the first line more specifically states the problem of the lack of reciprocity that leads to an inevitable downfall: 'too dear for my possessing'; precisely the circumstances in which contractual relationships ought not to come into being. Furthermore, the other party knows 'thy estimate'; knows that the relationship has not been one of equality. Indeed, the worth of the loved object is enrolled in law, via a 'charter of thy worth'. The charter, a privilege but also a formal grant, denotes the undoubted value of the loved one. The lover-poet has no choice but to surrender the contract for the court to cancel the deed: 'My bonds in thee are all determinate.' Bonds that are no longer valid in a court of law, that have gone beyond their due date, are determinate. In the next quatrain, the author looks back to the relationship before determination, and sees with the eye not of the party to the transaction, but of the judge. Personal relationships, just like contracts in the commercial discourse in which the poem is swathed, are purely voluntary arrangements. (Indeed, in due course, the whole of politics and the political settlement itself will be seen to absorb this basis of personal life in the consummation of the personal in the political.) The Sonnet says that granting has first to be based on some notion of reciprocity. The riches of the grant, and the validity that goes with it, can only work on the basis that the grantee has some deserving, that is, has given contractually valid consideration. In fact the cause of the gift of love (beauty, ability, compatibility, natural sympathy) is 'wanting' in the grantee, and therefore the patent, the privilege (again – but here the mirror of the grant or charter in line 3) 'back again is swerving'; that is, it is returned to the grantor from whom it should never have issued.

The final quatrain confirms this. The transaction has been based on a mistake of so serious a nature that the whole contractual relationship is to be treated as void *ab initio*. When the transaction commenced, the grantor did not realise 'thy own worth'. Alternatively, there had been a mistake in the identity or worth of the recipient: 'Or me to whom thou gavest it, else mistaking.' Either way, the gift was based on 'misprision', or mistake, and so 'comes home again', returns to the grantor, once the mistake has been realised, 'on better judgment making'. The final couplet merely states the moral for lovers and laywers: in dreams, the lamb lies down with the lion, the beggar with the rich man, and the unworthy is loved by the worthy. In life, love and law the poem says, we must appreciate the delicate nature of relationships that depend not on abstract ideals of selfless love, but on practical day-to-day matters such as reciprocity, affinity and mutual equality and regard.

Here, then, is a potentially hermeneutical, lawyerly reading. A poem about love turns out to be readable (has meaning for 'us') by an analysis around law through which the poem is actually written.[14] Love turns out to be an expression of the law, and for it to work successfully, certain constraints have to be observed. The lawyer reads of love and finds his/her love of law making sense of what might otherwise be insensible, dead, lost to us. Life and love must take particular forms in any complex society. The tradition of poetry in which love appears to be beyond all rules is shown to be false; love, too, works within a social structure of ordered forms of relationships. Love is no more free to make up its own rules than any other aspect of life. Law makes all of social life, including love, possible. In doing so, it gives meaning to our lives; it shows how

---

[14] Other sonnets are liable to the same subjugation: Sonnet no. 46, for example, speaks of the war of love between eye and heart in terms of bars, pleas, defendants, titles, juries' verdicts, dues rights and tenants. Many other sonnets flirt with legal metaphors, for example 35, 49 and 139.

the art world of the past can make sense of the social world of the present. Hermeneutics demonstrates how we can indeed find meaning speaking to us out of the past, and in doing so make sense of our world.

IV

We do not propose here to outline in full what might be characterised as a 'critical' (for want of a better term) approach in the Habermasian or neo-Marxist sense to Sonnet no. 87. But we can very summarily state the way that an approach that rejects a (mock) Gadamerian, over-confident and in the end dangerously complacent analysis might tackle the problem of bringing the Sonnet to our own age and political understanding.

Critique might start by saying that one of the things that is at stake in the Sonnet is the ability of human beings freely to express themselves and their relationship with others. In an ideal world, critique argues, language used by competent proponents of its tools and resources gives us not only the possibility of complex thought processes but also our ability to communicate with others. Our 'rational competencies' in an 'ideal speech' situation would enable us to communicate as near absolutely successfully as we are likely to need to do in almost all situations. But, of course, tragically, we have never reached such ideal speech situations. Our communications are distorted. Some people have more linguistic competencies than others; power relations are imbalanced, we are not equal in our ability, our material resources, our access to other people and possibilities. Those that are in this sense stronger have greater control, greater ability to impose themselves, their interpretations and their desires on others (see, for example, Habermas, 1984).

The Sonnet discusses these ideas not in the somewhat vague terms we have used so far, but in the specifics of the inter-relation and antagonism of law and love based on a larger Habermasian scheme. The poem anticipates what Habermas terms the two different spheres, that is, the sphere of the systems and that of the life-world that emerged out of the Enlightenment. It strongly expresses the dangers that Habermas is at pains to point out when the two spheres come into conflict. The world of the 'system', the market and impersonal relations (in general including law) took their own rational path separately from the order and needs of the (ordinary) life-world (*ibid.*). The result, for Habermas, is that the rationality of the instrumentalism of the marketplace will almost always take priority over the different rationality of the moral, aesthetic or interpersonal sphere, here specifically the sphere of relations of love.

This confrontation between law and life is outlined in the Sonnet. The free and equal expression of intense relationships are always liable to be thrown by the power that legal forms insidiously intertwine around what one assumes is the most natural of social interactions. Law, in more general terms, the control of the social sphere, takes over, indeed smothers love in this Sonnet. For love to work, law has to be evicted from loving relationships. Just as for a truly free, egalitarian society it is necessary to reach a stage where linguistic abilities are not available for some at the expense of others, so for love to work, for any possibility of genuine and satisfactory human relations, it is necessary for law (here, in part at least, an instrument of distortion and repression) to be expelled from the relation. The poem thus yields a meaning about love in the loveless setting of a court of law.

In a brilliant Shakespearian doubling of language the Sonnet is shown to make two contradictory assertions: first that love is born in and through known and respected but authoritarian forms of contractual relationship (for which, no doubt, arranged marriages are but one strong example). The exchange of equals that is the best guarantee of satisfactory contractual consummation applies in all spheres including relations of love. Charters, bonds, grantings, patents and so on are features both of the world of contractual efficiency and of interpersonal relations, and also the best guarantor of lasting and satisfactory arrangements in each sphere. But second, the Sonnet is denying these hopes of legal, lawlike love, portraying them as false. In its sorrow and parting it is expressing the repression, personal frustration and despair that will result when law, a particular and manifest form of (in)equality, determines the outcome of personal relationships. This double meaning is a particular literary device, but there is no doubt that, so far as critique is concerned, what is at stake is the insidious result of repressive and inegalitarian forms of social ordering which inevitably disturb and blight people's lives. The Sonnet emphasises the difficulty in overcoming these disturbances, yet at the same time it is urging us to make the strenuous but necessary efforts to do so. Propelled by the Enlightenment's necessary and continuing 'epistemological impetus' (Docherty 1990, p. 51), we can strive to make sense of the law–love contradiction which the Sonnet reveals.

V

The two approaches caricatured here have both argued that meaning can be produced, that meaning is what interpretation seeks, and that this can be found. We have techniques, modes of understanding and communication, even quasi-scientific methods that can be used to make sense of a previous world. In doing so, we enrich our own world and, within a Habermasian critique, suggest possibilities for an improvement of the state of things. But these two positions abolish the major problem by assuming what is actually the question in hand, whether meanings can be achieved and ultimately agreed upon. They both assume that meaning is there, waiting to be prised from the text. But suppose, as some of the texts mentioned in section I indicate, that we do not accept these unproven assumptions. Suppose that the Sonnet is not trying to produce meaning in the senses so far discussed at all but merely comments, elliptically, at times bitterly, but always suspiciously on the very result that hermeneutics and critique both assume can be achieved? Suppose this sixteenth-century trifle has already anticipated and gone beyond twentieth-century sophistication?

It has been argued that Shakespeare's Sonnets create a new form of poetic language and indeed inaugurate the poetic subjectivity that has dominated literature ever since (Fineman 1986). The Sonnets, whether in praise of the young man, or dispraise of the dark lady, are concerned with the act of seeing rather than what is seen. What is emphasised is the language of vision. Shakespeare takes from Dante and Petrarch in particular, but also from the English tradition, a dying, if not dead, form, the Sonnet in praise of a loved one, specifically a mistress, and transforms it by use of visual motives. The result is the creation of a 'specifically specular language . . . [which] produces a discourse whose referential truth is tautologically or autologically confirmed because such language is the thing of which it speaks' (ibid., p. 13). In the use of specular language, the emphasis moves from what is seen towards the means used to re-tell the image.[15] This inevitably turns the focus of the Sonnets towards language but, in an almost Platonic sense, language as 'corruptingly linguistic', 'language as duplicitously verbal as opposed to something visual' (*ibid.*, p. 15).

Language reproduces vision in words, the only form it knows, but the linguistic repetition can never be true. The duplicitous nature of language expresses itself at the surface in an immediate, convincing, yet utterly treacherous fashion. 'I have sworn thee fair, and thought thee bright/ Who art as black as hell, as dark as night' (Sonnet no. 147); or 'When my love swears that she is made of truth'/ I do believe her though I know she lies' (Sonnet no. 138). There is thus the more insidious threat – that language can never be relied on absolutely. Fineman claims that in the Sonnets Shakespeare pushes the danger of a seemingly innocent specular vision to the stage where language, 'stressing itself as language, truly demonstrates, effectively instantiates, rather than merely asserts, the fact that it is false' (1986, p. 35). Whilst for our purposes this utter and total despair in the tools that Shakespeare must use may be unnecessary, the emphasis on the dangerous nature of the endeavour is a salutary reminder that hermeneutics (despite Gadamer's sensitivity to the linguistic nature of his own interpretative work) and critique (despite Habermas's acknowledgement of the distorting perspective from which language users are forced to speak) may both be making unwarranted assumptions as to the nature of linguisitic expression.[16]

If we return now to Sonnet no. 87 itself, we can start by asking the most simple question, the answer to which both hermeneutics and critique take for granted: to whom is the poem addressed? Who is the 'thou' on line 1? Both traditions assume this to be the poet's lover. Yet there is nothing in the text itself (as distinct from the surrounding context of the other sonnets of the sequence) to indicate any such thing. There is nothing in the poem that gives any description of the addressee, no mention of human personality, no description of face or body, no indication even of the sex of

---

[15] The implications of this emphasis on vision for the interpretation of Shakespeare within theatres themselves are formidably staged by Freedman (1991).

[16] For a more sustained critique of the understanding of language in Gadamer and Habermas, see Douzinas and Warrington with McVeigh (1991, Chap. 2).

the object being addressed.[17] If we are to take the textual indications seriously, if we are to read carefully as hermeneutics, critique and indeed the tradition of law would urge us to do, then as lawyers we find no evidence of the basis of the hermeneutical argument.

Instead, the 'thou' draws attention to meaning rather than a person and the 'Farewell' with which the Sonnet hauntingly opens signals a farewell to something that is too dear – the unified, attainable, once and for all (at least for now) definitive meaning. Too dear indeed because it is purchased at too great a cost both in the literal terms of the poem's all too easily accepted addressee, but more generally in terms of the dangerous overdetermination of meaning that heremeneutics appears to produce. When texts are put together by the requirement to find a single, universal meaning that tells us definitively how it is, too much is lost. Meaning in that sense is too dear for this poet (and by implication, any poet, any person) to possess. Meaning knows its own estimate; it knows it is highly valued, but also that it is a snare or at least a delusion. It is given its releasing because the charter of its worth is not worth the keeping; the poet then declares the bonds determinate because there is nothing to hold on to. Maybe it would be nice were it otherwise, if the world were like the hermeneutician claimed, or if it were one where rational competencies could deliberate, argue and decide. But it was not, and it is not, the poem says. The bonds themselves only work in terms of something that can be bonded, that is fixed, and knowable in some unique sense, even if, in the hermeneutic tradition, only for now, for us.

The second quatrain expresses the realisation for which the opening had paved the way in terms of pain and pleasure. Meaning can only be held on to by its own granting. And we are not only unworthy of such a gift, 'for that riches where is my deserving', we also search in ourselves for its own meaning and

---

[17] Indeed, were we to take the context argument seriously, the poem might also be seen to abolish sexual difference and sexuality itself – the poem's location in the series between the praise of the man, and the dispraise of the false loved woman indicates that at this stage no person is intended at all; the poems in context are more about words than things, impossible meanings rather than impossible persons. Hence Sonnet no. 76: 'O, know sweet love, I always write of you,/ And you and love are still my argument./ So all my best is dressing old words new,/ Spending again what is already spent.' But we are not qualified to take this argument further.

start to question whether, if we could achieve it, it would be worth having. It is in the 'me' of the poet that the gift is wanting; the poet, like the gift, suggests such absolutes are wanting, and sends packing the idea of absolute meaning, or rather the struggle to achieve one: 'my patent back again is swerving.' The final quatrain is then free to express the release from meaning, with a sadness that is quite appropriate – definitive meanings might be a good thing to achieve, though they might not – but either way, 'on better judgment making' the poet is released from this 'mistaking'. And the sense of relief tinges the sadness; the release is given by the very meaning that turns out not to be there. The gift of meaning that hermeneutics and critique both offer is something that the recipient does not appreciate, but which the poet has struggled to work out, or at least the dangers of which he has learned to appreciate. The final couplet then fits into place not just as a lament, but also as an awakening from the dream of which it speaks. In the flattering sleep of a king, meaning had been trapped, fixed, defined and put in its place ready for lawyers to make their own in the destruction of lovers. Love and life are controlled by law as law seizes the dangerous and false assertion (but not dangerous because false) that meanings can be defined in that most precise and definitive of discourses, the law. In the waking world, there is no such matter. If we allow meanings to be acted upon by law in the way that the poem illustrates, so much the worse for love, so much the worse for 'us'. At the least, who can say which version of the meaning of meaning would be better? The advantages of the hermeneutic or critical fixing of meaning are not all certain.

Meaning, then, becomes open to possibilities beyond the restrictions of the hermeneutician for whom the impositions and the narrow interpretations that lawyers place on charters are exemplary; and beyond the ideal situations that critique thinks we ought to strive towards in some indefinable, utopian, Enlightened consummation, whilst in the meantime loves and lives are destroyed. Seeing meaning as something that can be defined is a dream and a mistaking. Texts are always open to saying more and less than they appear to intend. They speak down the ages to us not, as Gadamer and the hermeneuticians would have us believe, because there is a truth that speaks out of tradition, but because a tradition has arisen that seems to require that meanings can be determined. A judge needs to know what a case or precedent meant in order to indulge in the hermeneutical process of application; the lawyer will always try to fix a meaning, in the sense of bending it into shape for the particular purposes of client advancement. Meaning, the poem now appears to be saying, is also something else; it is a promise without a performance, a dream that flatters the clients of the lawyers. The poem asks us about our daily practices of reading, as lawyers and lovers. And as we read, it tells us that those practices, natural and inevitable though they have come to seem, are actually dangerous; the great gift of meaning is 'upon misprision growing'. The poem forces us to address this question. What meaning is left or open to us when meaning does not mean what it seems?

As we have said, the Sonnet sequence as a whole is strongly permeated by metaphors of sight and the question of vision. This is an obvious metaphor both for Elizabethan poetry generally and for Shakespeare in particular, for whom 'seeming' was always a central problem.[18] The final couplet of no. 87 is in one sense mere convention; dreams are not real, in waking one realises that one is not a king. But the substitution of sight for substance of the Sonnets refers also to the sight of the reader, the fact that in reading literature or painting or sculpture one can only read the surfaces, the representations on the wall of Plato's cave. There is nothing else that can be read. Writing is a series of symbols, and can never be more. But if so, hermeneutical appropriation is simply another shadow, a form. Hermeneutics, especially of the lawyerly type, acts with all the confidence it has allowed itself to appropriate. Despite all Gadamer's emphasis on play, that confidence is based on the ability to convince that readings can be true in some sense, provisional and bounded by time though everything is. Both Gadamer and the legal hermeneutician Dworkin (1986) assert a form of right interpretation that, although not absolute, goes well beyond what Sonnet no. 87 would warrant. Sonnet no. 87 says not only is it time to part with such readings, but also that such partings are possible, since it is only we that produce the

---

[18] 'Seems, madam? Nay, it is. I know not "seems" ', proclaims Hamlet (I.ii.76), who then spends the rest of the play showing what seems is actually what is, and what is only seems.

appearance to the contrary: 'For how do I hold thee but by thy granting?'

Meanings are only what we create; we can try to recreate them, change them, alter or improve them. A deconstructive reading says such creative rereadings are urgent and essential. As with all metaphors of sight and sound, there is more to them than meets the eye; in the words of one critic, we have to try to ' "hear" what is not there in the text – and then try to criticise it' (Docherty 1990, p. 61). The (in)justice of interpersonal relationships, of friendship and love, depends on our ability to recreate each time the worth of the other without the folly of exaggeration or the delusion of fixed, definitive meanings that can send out unequivocal messages through time. The Sonnet says we hold on to meaning by our own granting, that is, by our own actions. These actions appear to come down to us in controlled inevitable forms. And there is no doubt that we can never approach a text in a neutral, unbiased fashion (see, for example, Ricoeur 1983). But this hermeneutical truism does not mean we merely have to accept the received orthodox interpretations that time has apparently encrusted on to the texts that make up the context of our lives. The task of freeing ourselves from the orthodox was never more necessary than now, as we survey the blank injustices which sophisticated or not hermeneut-ical interpretations permit, especially in law. Both hermeneutics and critique try to determine a place of literature, to specify the limits to interpretable possibility, to tell us what is and what is not permitted. But literature itself, and the interpretative strategies that are possible in spite of the rules of interpretation that traditions of literature legally establish, ought not to permit such easy, and therefore suspect, resolutions. '[I]n this century the experience of literature crosses all the "deconstructive" seisms shaking the authority and pertinence of the question "What is ... ?" and all the associated regimes of essence or truth' (Derrida 1992b, p. 48). Sonnet no. 87 shows why this is necessary, why this is (still) open.

In other words, and setting about the question without confining its possibilities within the restrictions that ought to accompany the limited nature of the analysis that we have presented, Sonnet no. 87 asks us to think about the momentous issues that questions of 'justice' both hide and expose. We ourselves, like texts, are neither fully open, nor fully closed. The

sonnet that we have here used (and abused) urges us to re-examine
both the supposed fixity, unity and givenness of ourselves and the
assumed justice of the social arrangements that go to make up what
we consider to be our inevitable, legally dominated, world.

VI

The ethical claim to consider the other before, or at least alongside,
the supposed needs of the self demands that the orthodox
understanding of the law, which, put crudely, accepts the
Enlightenment placing of the self as the centre of knowledge,
interest and legal personality, needs to be rethought. Sonnet no. 87
can be seen to articulate the danger of allowing the domination of
the self to emerge in some rather vulgar fashion in the law. The
law's consideration of self, the privileging of the individual, the
very notion of a trial by combat, where two individuals are pitted
against each other,[19] where the winner takes all, shows that the
common law is committed to the notion of the preservation of the
self no matter what the cost to the other, or to any others. Sonnet
no. 87 suggests that not only does this profoundly unethical stance
of the law destroy the other, it also destroys the self at precisely the
moment the Enlightnement thought it had made men (and to a
certain extent women) most able to overcome the mystical 'bonds'
that had enslaved them hitherto, most individually capable and
responsible, and most personally free. The enthroning of the self at
the expense of the community, of other members of society,
destabilises the flattering kingdom of individual autonomy's
worldly-wise ability to ignore the call of the other. Liberalism's
rule of the self promises ultimate personal liberty, but turns out to
be 'no such matter'.

In the final chapter we examine how a discourse concerned
with establishing a charter of the worth of a particular artistic form
can destroy the ability to consider the other and otherness,
especially when this discourse entangles itself, possibly 'accident-
ally', in a legal framework.

---

[19] Cases are still written by lawyers as 'x v. y'.

8

'The most perfect beauty in its most perfect state'

Sir Joshua Reynolds and an aesthetic of the spirit of the laws

I

The common law, as a case law system, operates by application. When it comes to actual decision-making, the day-to-day activity of courts, there is an assumption that a precedent exits that can be adapted and applied to the dispute in hand. But common law has never operated only on this mundane basis. Since the common law was conscious of itself, its practitioners and apologists, or if no one else its critics (see, for example, Goodrich 1990, p. 18), have assumed there was more to it, at least in times of crisis. There is something beyond the individual resolution of disputes connected with principles of justice which, if not necessarily eternal and universal in its scope and existence, was at least there to stand over and above each particular practitioner's daily grind. Were the common law not thought to contain the justifying principles of ideas many years old, even though it was not necessary to articulate them on a regular basis, it is difficult to see how it could have justified its right to rule.

To take Blackstone as the obvious example, his reputation rests on his huge task of systematising the unsystematisable, 'to extract the theory of law from a mass of indigested learning' (1979, p. 31). Sense had to be made of the apparently senseless, that is, of a collection of cases (precedents) whose only justification was that they were 'there'. A system that threatened to dissolve into the barbarity of mere minutiae was not something that could be justified. This is why Blackstone felt it necessary to do more than enable lawyers (and later commentators) to understand the details of the laws by ordering them into an acceptable series of formulas so that the professional and indeed the concerned layperson (JP, MP and landowner) could use them. He was also deeply concerned with the common law relationship between the earthly and the eternal. Blackstone gave the hope, if not the promise, that out of the heroic labours involving the organisation of the precedents and memories of the common law into a coherent body of detailed principles something more could be glimpsed: divine purpose, eternal standards, right reason or some other equally important justification for the system as a whole. The detailed exposition merely confirms what is sometimes lost to view, that the architecture of the common law, within which individual decisions and rights are expressed, is not merely a random series of repetitions of what might have been done before. England, for Blackstone, was '[a] land, perhaps the only one in the universe, in which political or civil liberty is the very end and scope of the constitution' (ibid., p. 6). Unless lawyers were properly instructed in general principles, all they would know would be mere practice. And as well as being a shame to the nation's natural ruler,[1] such a state of ignorance would be dangerous. Rulers and judges in this state could 'seldom expect to comprehend any argument drawn a priori, from the spirit of the laws and the natural foundations of justice' (ibid., p. 32; our emphasis).

Although Blackstone's well-known flirtation with natural law (ibid., pp. 38ff.) exposed him to some fairly cheap and easy attacks (see Lieberman 1989, pp. 226ff.), it was actually more prescient than his critics acknowledged. Without some natural or ethical basis, the system he was defending was as arbitrary as, say, Newton's laws. Human reason was connected to something more, and it was important for the good health of the common law that this was not forgotten.

At roughly the same time as the common law, spurred on by Blackstone, was busy draping itself in the clothes of modernity, Sir Joshua Reynolds was addressing problems in artistic interpreta-

---

[1] A warning that had also been given by Cicero (De Oratore I.xvii.78). The importance of Cicero to Reynolds's argument will become clear as this chapter progresses. Reynolds's reliance on Cicero, mostly implicitly, is very great, though this is hardly surprising given Cicero's influence in the eighteenth century generally (see Wood 1988). But for Reynolds, Cicero seems particularly apt; as rhetorician, philosopher, poet, politician, man of action, stoic, but above all as lawyer, Cicero often expounded views that would have appeared the pinnacle of sense to Reynolds.

tion, where he was to propose answers which were also concerned with the spirit of the laws and which, we will argue in this chapter, are not that dissimilar from those undertaken by the common lawyers. His solutions can be seen as closely related to a common law 'mind-set' (Sugarman 1986) that was in the process of establishing itself. Reynolds set himself the task of demarcating the proper boundaries of the art of painting. In a series of *Discourses* delivered annually between 1769 and 1790, he developed an argument to enable student painters at the newly founded 'Academy', and artists more generally, to understand the 'nature' of their art. Reynolds elaborated an aesthetics of art that tried to maintain the delicate balance between, on the one side, the privileged artist in the heat of artistic creation producing great works, a sort of total artistic licence which was unacceptable, and, on the other side, the subjugation of the individual painter to rules, forms and order which, to the extent that the subjugation might inhibit genius, would be equally unbearable.

The importance of the establishment of a rigorous dogmatics for the common law, at a time when new forms of commercial order were developing, can be taken for granted. But the relation between art and commercialism required that artistic endeavour was also put on a rational ordered basis; similarly with new forms of creating, criticising and selling art which were developing. As Reynolds himself put it:

it is . . . necessary to the happiness of individuals and still more necessary to the security of society, that the mind should be elevated to the idea of general beauty, and the contemplation of general truth: by this pursuit the mind is always carried forward in search of something more excellent than it finds, and obtains its proper superiority over the common sense of life. (p. 150)[2]

As a justification for the eighteenth-century surge in scientific and technical developments, which themselves helped open cognitive areas, Reynolds's assumptions seemed as convincing as any. Indeed at a time of imperial expansion, Reynolds merely states that the establishment by the Crown of an institution such as the Academy needs no justification other than the intrinsic public

---

[2] Unattributed page references in this chapter are to Reynolds (1966), first delivered as a series of lectures. We have not updated Reynolds's own spelling and punctuation.

interest such a project should create in the whole nation. And it was only the 'slow progression of things' (an idea of some significance for Reynolds) that caused 'an empire like that of BRITAIN . . . so long [to] have wanted an ornament so suitable to its greatness' (p. 19).[3] Reynolds came to argue that rules in art, and their justification, depended not exclusively on aesthetic considerations, or on the social position of the artist, but also on his place and genealogy within the institution: 'a question of placement and of the power of the place within the logic of descent' (Goodrich 1990, p. 302). In the late eighteenth century the need to enable the individual to exercise her freedom in the instant creative act and the right of the community to require compliance with known rules and procedures before work could be certified as 'art', or art of the highest quality, is not that dissimilar from the task the lawyers faced in 'rationalising' the common law. For art, unlike law, the institution had to be created, and there was no better model available than the law. Once established, Reynolds took it upon himself to speak for it and mark out its intellectual boundaries.

Reynolds therefore attempted to outline the space between law and freedom, order and art, the spirit of artistic laws and the law of the spirit of the artist. Inevitably he produced a text that has many contradictory elements. In the interests of pedagogy and in the attempt to give students a coherent plan of study, he moved from one extreme to another, from the extreme of order to (almost) its opposite. In this chapter, however, we attempt to show the relationship in Reynolds's text between his aesthetic of painting and what might somewhat loosely be termed an aesthetic conception of common law, and how both tend to exclude any consideration of 'otherness'. This somewhat unexpected relationship is expressed by Reynolds as he struggled to produce both a coherent and eternal system of rules and to hold on to the idea of the creative individual and the just application of the rule in particular instances which seem to go far beyond any mechanical

---

[3] According to Barrell (1986, p. 64), the establishment of the Academy singularly failed to achieve some of the purposes Reynolds thought it would attain. By the end of the eighteenth century, there was 'no sign that the Academy had succeeded in encouraging the development of a school of history painting worthy of a great and free nation'. For a summary of the relation between artistic expression and the public sphere in contemporary USA, see Hoffman (1991).

'legal' order. That is to say, Reynolds's lectures turn to law to try to
establish the nature of a rule-governed procedure which is not
rule-governed. Reynolds's text points to the same problem that
faced the common law: general ideals are necessary for any system
to be worthy of respect. But general ideals may not always appear
to fit the requirements of those who take upon themselves the right
to pronounce the ideals and set the standards. Furthermore, the
application of general rules in specific cases by those empowered
to pronounce on their validity often falls far short of the standards
to which the system appeals for its justificatory force. The gap
between the (frequently assumed) aspiration and the application
confounds common law attempts to produce justice, despite the
supposed high ideals. Likewise for Reynolds: he either has to stick
to his rules and sacrifice the creative instance, or he sacrifices the
rules entirely in the interests of the particular case, that is, the case
of the genius, or, in more general terms, those who do not fit. To
put it in Reynolds's words, for aesthetic appreciation (and for the
common law) there is both 'a just idea of beautiful forms' (p. 46)
based on principles which 'I have proved to be metaphysically
just' (p. 55), and the need to sacrifice the individual, the instance
case, the detail of particular suffering which must not be allowed
to affect the nature of the rules or the practice as a whole: 'All
smaller things, however perfect in their way, are to be sacrificed
without mercy to the greater' (p. 56). The painter of genius, with
whom Reynolds is ultimately concerned, will not 'waste a moment
upon those smaller objects, which only serve to catch the sense, to
divide the attention, and to counteract his great design of speaking
to the heart' (pp. 50–1). This balance between the general and the
particular was a need of Reynolds's artistic system and of the
common law, one which, as Chapter 3 illustrated, also created the
struggles of the casuists. The argument of this chapter is that in
speaking 'to the heart', that is, to the universal, the individual (and
the application to her of justice) becomes a matter which the
painter can sacrifice without mercy, as the common lawyers have
sacrificed those who do not fit – outsiders, seekers after sanctuary,
those who are *heteroi* (others) to the narrow conception of the *dikē*
the system operates.

   In section II we give a short and selective account of Reynolds's
theory of the aesthetic as expounded in his *Discourses*. The
following section shows how this theory is related to a conception

of the common law. Section IV suggests Reynolds frequently reverses his own arguments, and examines the political implications and rhetorical nature of his work, as well as showing further the influence of the common law on the argument. Finally, we suggest some conclusions for this book which can be derived out of Reynolds's highly variable common law-inspired aesthetic.

II

Reynolds gave himself the task of defining the aesthetic of the art of painting in the context of a specifically English setting in which national pride needs both a new and grand institution (the Academy), and sound reasons and rules to say that English painting was as good as anything from the contemporary Italian, Dutch or French schools. In a world where commercialism was to play a greater part, art had to have its price too, which meant valuing it according to principles and rules. For without a proper definition:

> The arts would lie open for ever to caprice and casualty, if those who are to judge of their excellencies had no settled principles by which they are to regulate their decisions, and the merit or defect of performances were to be determined by unguided fancy. (p. 111)

Reynolds's attempt to establish the authenticity of English art is most explicit in his praise of Gainsborough. Gainsborough's genius in the lower ranks of art is to be preferred to the insipidity of the best Italian paintings of Reynolds's age (p. 219). Gainsborough could be praised exceptionally because 'his landscapes [and portraits][4] achieve the end of elevating a lower genre by a concentration on general effect and by the exclusion of mere imitation' (Barrell 1986, p. 120). But as with all high artistic endeavour, the authenticity of English art is to be established by its manifest relationship with the universal standards or rules of art. These can be discovered by a thorough immersion in the works of the

---

[4] Reynolds was bound to run into a certain amount of difficulty in portraits in particular, because as a portrait painter himself, 'his own honour was engaged in the status of the art' (Barrell 1986 pp. 123 and 123–4). See also Sambrook: 'Reynolds made it his life's work to raise portraiture to the expression of great and general ideas' (1986, p. 152).

classical period and Renaissance Italy, especially of 'Michael Angelo' and 'Raffaelle'.

Reynolds's starting-point was that true art relates to a specific 'Nature', not artifice. Nature provides the key to understanding both great art itself and the 'mind' or 'reason' which are the vehicles for the creation and appreciation of great art. Truth in art is not a matter of taste or opinion but of sound judgment, which, as it is based on eternal standards given by the very nature of existence, can be determined with sufficient exactitutde for all practical critical purposes,[5] like any other set of rules. Nature and truth are here synthesised into a universal, discoverable, unity.[6]

Reynolds's audience was the student body at the Academy, usually at the 'Distribution of the Prizes' each year. His concern was therefore at first not only to establish the universal truths of art, but to explain them in a manner that students could understand and realistically strive to reproduce. And, partly for reasons we have already mentioned, and partly for the sake of those that might not be able readily to distinguish the true from the false, Reynolds started with rules. There was, it seemed, no other way to ensure the validity of the enterprise, not to mention the serious matter of determining the financial worth of different products. Compliance with rules was therefore not the antithesis of artistic creation, but appeared to be the guarantor of the truth or the worth of any particular painter's endeavour. In the very first *Discourse*, Reynolds insists 'that an implicit obedience to the Rules of Art, as established by the practice of the great MASTERS, should be exacted from the young Students' (p. 21). The emphasis on 'young' does allow Reynolds to make exceptions for geniuses, but even here the exemptions are not total. Geniuses also obey

---

[5] Even painters who apparently had very different theories from Reynolds seem to want to hold to universal standards. 'For Barry, as for Reynolds, there is only one idea of beauty: it admits, according to Barry, no "diference" or "variety" and is, like truth, a point' (Barrell 1986, pp. 173–4).

[6] The old idea of the relation between truth and beauty was famously taken to poetic perfection not long after Reynolds by Keats: ' "Beauty is truth, truth beauty," – that is all/Ye know on earth, and all ye need to know.' According to White (1987, pp. 18 and also 80), some of Keats's later work complicated this pure idea, just as Reynolds later complicated some of his 'pure' ideas, as we shall see. 'When it comes to *Lamia* we find Keats himself questioning the doctrine that "beauty is truth".' On the question of truth in Reynolds, see section IV.3 of this chapter, see likewise on the connection in Reynolds's *Discourses* between art and poetry.

rules. It is just that geniuses (and the educated) can distinguish true from false rules. 'Genius begins not where rules abstractedly taken end but where known vulgar and trite rules have no longer any place . . . even works of Genius, like every other effect . . . must likewise have their rules' (p. 89).

If the young, and the old who are not geniuses, have to go by the rules, then the next question is how to establish the rules of painting. The answer is to study the great works of others. Reynolds nowhere considers the tautological nature of this advice (until you know the rules how can you be certain that the pictures you are studying are truly great?[7]) but advances it with unrelenting fervour: 'Study therefore the great works of the great masters for ever' (p. 101). Reynolds urges the students to greater efforts in their attempts to determine what are the rules that make greatness great. The investigations required of the student are painful: nevertheless 'I know but of one method of shortening the road; this is, by a careful study of the works of the ancient sculptors' (p. 46), and the 'great masters' of the Italian Renaissance.

In terms of practical activity, after the rules have been elaborated, the studying done, and the student actually wants to lay hand on brush, then the next stage is imitation. Instead of being seen as poor quality work, having little to do with true art, imitation is lauded, provided it is of the right type, that is, imitation of the great masters. Furthermore, unlike later nineteenth-century obsessions, there is no danger of imitation enfeebling the true artist. It can be indulged in safely for the whole of the artist's creative life, provided, as always, the right rules (of the great masters that is) are being followed. For Reynolds was

very much disposed to maintain the absolute necessity of imitation in the first stages of the art . . . [which] may be extended throughout our whole lives, without any danger . . . of enfeebling the mind, or preventing us from giving that original air which every work undoubtedly ought always to have. (p. 87)[8]

---

[7] As to how to know what was great, see section III below.

[8] The source of this idea most probably was Plato, though possibly via Longinus, a respected edition of his treatise becoming available in the latter part of the seventeenth century. Longinus appeared to argue that much of Plato's greatness came from his ability to copy and absorb the style of the masters of Greek prose that had come before him. 'Plato illustrates . . . the way of imitation and emulation of great writers of the past. . . . Plato . . . diverted to himself countless rills from the Homeric spring. . . . In all this process there is no plagiarism. It resembles rather the

Even genius, it seems, is 'the child of imitation' (ibid.). In short: 'The daily food and nourishment of the mind of an Artist is found in the great works of his predecessors. There is no other way for him to become great himself' (p. 191).

The purpose of these huge imitative labours demanded of the student of art is the representation of 'Nature'. The artists to be followed are those who understand the principles of nature and who can produce artistic creations which faithfully reflect a true understanding of the eternal but verifiable principles or forms of nature.[9] Reynolds's praise of Gainsborough, as we have already indicated, is based on this painter's understanding of 'the great school of nature' (p. 223). But Gainsborough is a relatively rare exception in Reynolds's catalogue of the great who might be followed. This is because Gainsborough's choice of subjects, were it not for his 'native' genius, would be somewhat suspect. For the ancients and the Renaissance masters used subjects already determined upon by history, myth or religion, which themselves set the artist on the right road. These subjects are particularly evident for Reynolds and his contemporaries in Renaissance work with its emphasis on 'istoria', the subject as part of a historical, mythological or scriptural tableau,[10] itself symbolic of a greater truth than pictures of other subjects could portray. In any event, painters, for Reynolds, do not decide on 'subjects'. Subjects are already given for them by their character as emblematic of

---

reproduction of good character in statutes and works of art . . . great figures, presented to us as objects of emulation and, as it were, shining before our gaze, will somehow elevate our minds to the greatness of which we form a mental image' (Longinus 1989, pp. 158–9). This description of Plato as an imitator is somewhat odd, given Plato's own disparaging remarks about imitation in The Republic (Plato 1955). Plato downgraded the notion of the artist and poet to the status of mere second-rate copier. Aristotle was more sympathetic, and made imitation a central notion of his exposition of poetry and drama. As is so often the case with Reynolds, however, his formulations appear to draw most directly on Cicero: 'let this then be my first counsel, that we show the student whom to copy, to copy in such a way as to strive with all possible care to attain the most excellent qualities of his model' (De Oratore, II.xxi.90). Like Reynolds, Cicero modified this idea slightly (ibid., II.xxii.92, II.xxiii.98). The notion of art as imitation became a commonplace; it applied to dramatic verse (for example, Girard 1991, p. 37), to all music (Neubauer 1986, p. 62) and, in a sense, to all understanding of written forms (Derrida 1974).

[9] Blake's concern with the relation between art, nature and imagination was more complex (see Barrell 1986, pp. 226 and 244).

[10] For the Renaissance emphasis on 'istoria', see Beardsley (1966, p. 123).

universal ideas where, according to Barrell (1986, p. 100), the specific story being represented becomes almost irrelevant. Greek and Roman fables, events and characters are 'so popularly known in those countries where our Art is in request that they may be considered as sufficiently general for our purposes . . . without being degraded by the vulgarism of ordinary life in any country' (p. 55). The same is true for scriptural history. Historical and mythical figures best represent man according to a true natural end.

But if this stage of Reynolds's grand scheme is to come to grips with nature through art, the next step is to understand that nature cannot simply be appropriated by the artist: 'taking nature as [the painter] found it seldom produced beauty' (p. 65). What is at stake is a form of ideal beauty which is not an exact copy of nature and may even be superior to it (p. 44), an idea that 'was, or was believed to be, almost as old as the art itself' (Barrell 1986, p. 86). In a clear manifesto-like remark, Reynolds instructs students: 'Nature herself is not to be too closely copied. There are excellencies in the art of painting beyond what is commonly called the imitation of nature' (p. 43). Just as other arts are removed from nature, poetry, for example (see section IV below), so too is painting. The great painters are not nature's translators.

So far therefore is servile imitation from being necessary that whatever is familiar, or in any way remains of what we see and hear every day, perhaps does not belong to the higher provinces of art, either in poetry or painting. (p. 207)

'This is an art/ Which does mend Nature, change it rather; but/ The art itself is Nature' (*The Winter's Tale* I.iv.95–7). This 'mending' of nature, the turning of it into art, is, for Reynolds, a process based on the rules that nature gives us, which we learn from observing nature as it is reproduced and translated into the art of the great masters, but is not simple copying. Nature stands behind all worthwhile artistic endeavour and provides the rules and means for evaluation. But painting is not mere gardening,[11] as Reynolds

---

[11] For the relationship between gardening and its transformation in the eighteenth-century country garden, developing capitalism, nature and language, see Pugh (1988). 'The country looks forward to the metropolis and back to the self-yielding classless bounty of the Golden Age' (*ibid.*, p. 23). 'The garden is one way to contain "raw" nature, to possess and control it, even to "cook" it' (*ibid.*, p. 55). The garden

himself notes (pp. 210–11), and would be so much the worse if it were. Painting is an art, a transforming gardening, and art always has in it something more than nature, possibly even something 'deceptive'. 'Painting is not only to be considered as an imitation operating by deception, but that it is and ought to be . . . strictly speaking, no imitation at all of external nature' (p. 204).[12]

The work of the great painters, then, instructs us that 'we must depart from nature for a greater advantage' (p. 143). This greater advantage is the production of artistic worth which can speak beyond the 'ignorant present' (p. 207) and beyond the understanding of the ignorant multitude. The purpose is to express a pure form. The painter 'is to exhibit distinctly and with precision, the general forms of things' (p. 52). In an argument that follows this refined displacing of nature, and that, despite the occasional best endeavours, is very close to Plato,[13] Reynolds claims that the pure forms of things which the painter strives to understand and realise are not based on any actual representation in nature. The aim is the highest excellencies (p. 71), perfect beauty: 'to preserve the most perfect beauty in its most perfect state' (p. 72), a state which does not actually exist in nature. On the contrary, actual states of nature are observed to be distinctly imperfect, if not deformed. The student is urged to learn from nature, but told that merely reproducing nature will not do. If this is a conundrum it is

---

and gardening also left the age of innocence and nature. The importance of the development of gardening as an art is stressed by Sambrook: 'the garden made a greater contribution to landscape art in [the eighteenth century] than the studio. In an international context the landscape garden was, indeed, eighteenth-century England's most notable contribution to the arts' (1986, p. 154).

[12] According to Barrell (1986, pp. 82–6), although Reynolds does claim at one point that the aim of painting is deception, at other stages he says this is only acceptable in the lower branches of the art. Whilst this may therefore be yet another example of Reynolds's about-turns (see sections 3 and 4 of this chapter), the question of deception may be more central than this. If painting, for Reynolds, is about the representation of nature and its rules, in forms that are radically different from those that actually appear in nature, then it can be argued that deception comes very near to Reynolds's meaning of art. (The objection by Reynolds that painting is not deception because art is not imitation of nature after all is discussed shortly in the text.)

[13] Plato also argued that the distortion was necessary to make true art, the most famous examples being of columns on temples. To look equal, the columns must actually be wider at the top (see further, Beardsley 1966, p. 36).

dissolved in a flash,[14] or, as Reynolds is fond of observing of the effect of painting generally, 'at one blow' (p. 129).[15] The student will ask: 'Is not art . . . an imitation of nature? Must he not therefore who imitates with the greatest fidelity be the best artist?' The answer is 'no', otherwise 'Rembrandt has a higher place than Raffaelle. But a very little reflection will serve to shew us that these particularities cannot be nature: for how can that be the nature of man, in which no two individuals are the same?' (p. 111). If the aim is to produce a (Platonic) view of nature and its forms beyond any specific exemplification in nature, then clearly any particular expression in nature itself, in some exact, botanically accurate reproduction, will not do. The forms of different things, classes as Reynolds calls them, differ, though each has its own common idea and central governing concept, an idea clearly traceable to Plato (p. 47). There will be, for example, a proper form for age and for childhood even though different from each other. But as far as specific forms are concerned, each 'is the more perfect as it is remote from all peculiarities' (p. 48), from actual, living nature.

The reason for this is that particular manifestations can only exhibit a form that is clearly imperfect. 'An History-painter paints man in general: a Portrait-Painter, a particular man, and consequently a defective model' (p. 66). Thus portrait painting deals in the trivia of individual defects. By contrast, Reynolds, like Cicero in his depiction of 'The Orator', is looking for someone 'from whom every blemish has been taken away' (De Oratore, I.xxv.118). The great, true and universal forms can only be represented by the type of transhistorical subject which, as already mentioned, Reynolds thinks proper for the expression of the truths of the universal forms of nature. The arts of antiquity received their

---

[14] As we saw, Antigone appreciated her duty before she thought about it, at least before she had articulated the reasons for her overwhelming 'must'. Reynolds also claims an immediate, instant understanding is possible, as it were, prior to detailed thought. But whereas Antigone uses her instincts to protect the most vulnerable, to proclaim a law that safeguards those outside of law's recognised remit, Reynolds uses his insight to get the law to destroy the very vulnerable values he appears to respect, as section v of this chapter tries to show.

[15] This idea was not unique to Reynolds. For Rousseau, the effect of sound was something that had to be appreciated in succession, whereas, for colours and paintings: 'Everything is taken in at first glance' (1966, p. 62). This, for Rousseau, was a recognition that 'each sense has its proper domain' (ibid.), a sentiment that might have appealed to Reynolds.

perfection 'from an ideal beauty, superior to what is to be found in individual nature' (p. 44). Truth itself is expressed via the artistic imagination following known rules of great painters who painted from nature in a way that went beyond nature without breaking its rules. The student who aspires to these astonishing heights creates a higher form of nature, that is, the truth as human beings through natural reason understand or discover it. And the argument is completed by bringing it back to its natural origins. In inquiring after truth in painting we merely return to nature, to the source of art itself: 'The natural appetite or taste of the human mind is for Truth' (p. 109).

The human mind becomes the ultimate arbitrator of artistic standards, again a notion not far removed from Plato (Beardsley 1966, pp. 39–46). The aim of all true artistic endeavour is to please the mind. Painting, although Reynolds frequently referred to it as a work or labour, is not something for which the hand is truly responsible. Painting both addresses the mind and is a work of the mind. This means that painting is not just a question of sight (p. 62). But the mind itself is as much related to nature as anything else; it is certainly not arbitrary in its judgments when those judgments are soundly made, no more than, say, taste is merely a matter of opinion (pp. 108–9, 113 and 116). True judgment, like taste, is fixed in the nature of things (p. 119). The real test of great art, of the grand as distinct from the merely splendid or ornamental style in history paintings, is the extent to which the mind, rightly in tune with reason and nature, is gratified. Imagination and feeling must be correctly impressed. '[T]he true test of all the arts is not solely whether the production is a true copy of nature, but whether it answers the end of art, which is to produce a pleasing effect upon the mind' (p. 211). The intellect, in tune with the discoverable rules of nature, rules the rules of producing a transformed nature and reproducing art.

III

The main object of Reynolds's theory was to justify the ways of art. For Reynolds, art is no longer to be treated as the wayward and arbitrary child of great but unknowable geniuses. Art, too, is a science of sorts, though clearly one that differed from the burgeoning natural sciences. But if scientific rules are the order of the day and the necesssary requirement for respectablity, place and honour, then, despite the scepticism of those 'wise and learned men' who only accept what may be proved by 'mathematical demonstrations', art has a place (p. 114). Reynolds's great achievement, according to Reynolds himself, was that 'I have succeeded in establishing the rules and principles of our Art on a more firm and lasting foundation than that on which they had formerly been placed' (p. 237). Just because art is not one of the natural sciences did not mean that the validation of the rules on which it operated was not capable of an exactitude sufficient to establish its claims to truth, in the great aim of the art of transforming nature. '[T]he acquisition of this knowledge requires as much circumspection and sagacity as is necessary to attain those truths which are more capable of demonstration' (p. 114). The use of universal reason, at times something other than mere common sense, when properly guided by rules as Reynolds has enumerated them, can lead to the great truths of art. What we suggest in this section is that this establishment of rules of art actually relies on a common law form of analysis, sometimes explicitly, more often implicitly. The attempt to legislate artistic rules relies on an aesthetic conception of common law rules.

Reynolds starts with a system of rules which the student is urged to acquire before setting out on the practice of art. But, not surprisingly, Reynolds does not manage to hold on to a system of rules for art. Instead, he turns from rules to hermeneutics, from the rule of law to the laws of those who understand the true Blackstonian spirit of the laws and can operate them accordingly. Laws of art and taste, and how and when to apply them, like the common law, are known by those who know, the highest practitioners of the art, the formers of taste and opinion, upon which the rules depend. The fixed immutable laws of nature and reason, with which the *Discourses* so confidently start, turn out to be no such thing. Taste and the prejudice of the initiated, time and place of application, the sound common sense of those who are entitled to voice opinion, all these openly subvert Reynolds's intentions of guiding students of art via rules.

The common law was not dissimilar. Initiation rites, ceremonies of passage, the common sense of the closed community, especially of those men of genius who have achieved its highest ranks, the learning of previous ages always definitionally superior to present opinion, the practices derived from time immemorial and correspondingly only knowable by immemorial study and immersion in these practices – all these are recognisable traits of the common law system and were perceived as necessary for its operation.

To take a simple example, by the eighteenth century custom was treated as subsidiary to the common law. 'Custom in derogation of the common law, must be controlled strictly' (Blackstone 1979, p. 78). Common law applied to the whole kingdom; universal and representational of the highest form of reasoning, it had long more or less assumed the right to govern all the Crown's subjects. Similarly for Reynolds, local custom ('prejudices') become 'more and more fantastical; recedes from real science' (p. 110). What counts is the same universally applicable reason derived from nature which the common law tries to achieve.

Custom's virtue is that it appears, like God, to exist before it is created; it stands outside of time. By the eighteenth century, the fact that the common law is created and invented also seems to be forgotten. Although, technically, it is custom that exists from time immemorial, the fact that common law was a specific judicial product does not seem to affect the status it derived from age. As Blackstone, neatly adding the immemorial nature of custom to the respectability of the common law, put it: 'That ancient collection of unwritten maxims and customs, which is called the common law, however compounded or from whatever fountains derived, had subsisted immemorially in this kingdom' (1979, p. 17). Similarly, age gives Reynolds the justification for his aesthetic rules. New rules, or new fashions and trends in art, although they might have some merit, cannot be the equal in beauty or worth of what is old. Even if creations of equal beauty were possible 'they would not please ... since the old has the advantage of having custom [not in the technical legal sense here] and prejudice on its side.' By contrast: 'Ancient ornaments, having the right of possession ought not to be removed'. Even if of the same intrinsic merit as the old, innovation will always bring 'evil and confusion' (p. 124).

The art of painting itself, like the art of common law and the true rules of both, are not to be learned in Reynolds's analysis by a narrowly defined conception of rules. Both depend on the veneration to be accorded to age, or, in common law terms, 'precedent', and, anyway, in the end, rules are too difficult to enumerate and apply. Instead, one learns both as painter and lawyer by initiation, by repetition of ceremonies, by absorbing the received wisdom of the community. When one has done this, one is certified fit to practise as lawyer or painter, and eventually, when one can prove an addiction to those standards which have not only stood the test of time, but which also continue to merit the approval of the leaders of the community, then one can be certified as practitioner, judge or, ultimately, genius.

A double move is required here: to begin with, common or vulgar opinion must be excluded; and second, the learning process has to take place by a process of absorption which involves living contact with those who know, a process of osmosis to which the Bar stuck until change was forced upon it in the nineteenth and twentieth centuries.[16] To take common opinion first: if the appreciation of the critic (which also concerned Reynolds) as well as the execution of the practitioner is simply a question of rules, then it ought to be relatively easy to make the rules known, a process which, despite his earlier confidence, Reynolds finds harder and harder to elaborate. But, more significantly, if rules were identifiable, they might fall into the wrong hands. The expression of a great truth in a few lines or touches is the proper work of the great painter. But the ignorant in art do not appreciate this; their opinion is seduced 'by some false notion of what they ought to see in a picture' (pp. 178 and elsewhere).

But, second, even if Reynolds did not feel the need to exclude common opinion from his explication of rules, his lectures still turn not towards rules but towards the expression of opinion of the chosen few which the student does not learn so much as absorb. This is because the student actually encounters the rules and protocols in a very different manner from any mechanical learning of rules. There is a known community, with an 'institution', an Inn

---

[16] Not that the changes have been that great; as is well known, to qualify at the Bar, students still have to join one of the ancient Inns of Court, and as well as passing exams have to go through the elaborate rituals of formal dinners; practitioners (of both sexes) still must wear the garb of an eighteenth-century gentleman in court, a costume which Reynolds would have found familiar; as with the dress, so with the modes of address, which are specific to the traditions of hierarchical authority which the law clings to with, as Byron put it, 'a pertinacity that's rather rare.'

of Court or an Academy, and students join it in order to come into contact with

the conversation of learned and ingenious men. . . . There, without formal teaching, they will insensibly come to feel and reason like those they live with, and find a rational and systematick taste imperceptibly formed in their minds, which they will know how to reduce to a standard, by applying general truth to their own purposes, better perhaps than those to whom they owed the original sentiment. (p. 106)[17]

Formal learning of rules has been replaced by the rule of the community where there are no rules, merely feelings, sense and knowledge based on the way it was done before, acquired by a process of observation and repetition. Besides, the formal teaching of the 'dancing-masters, hair-dressers and tailors, in their various schools of deformity' have only given us a false picture, causing the student to 'mistake the capricious changeling for the genuine offspring of nature' (p. 49). The true artists, the ancients, were never formally taught, and their works are so much the better in consequence. Although reading is permitted, and indeed often encouraged, for even Raffaelle read and learned from philosophy and the works of his predecessors and contemporaries (pp. 190 and 105), the key is instinctive feeling and intuition which is absorbed from mixing in the right company, not mechanically taught and learned in the schools. Right reason, by which alone true art can be appreciated and produced, and as necessary in art as in 'the commerce of life', does not appear by any mechanical process, by

the slow progress of deduction . . . [It] goes at once, by what appears a kind of intuition, to the conclusion. A man endowed with this faculty, feels and acknowledges the truth, though it is not always in his power, perhaps, to give a reason for it. . . . This impression is the result of the accumulated experience of our whole life, and has been collected, we do not always know how, or when. If we were obliged to enter into a theoretical deliberation on every occasion, before we act, life would be at a stand, and Art would be impracticable. (p. 202)

Unlike the ancients, who learned their arts naturally, just by their being part of that community where the natural arts flourished:

---

[17] The 'sentiment' is properly Ciceronian: 'can your Civil Law be learned from books? There are any number of them, but they need a teacher and experience' (Cicero 1982, p. 205).

'We are constrained, in these later days, to have recourse to a sort of Grammar and Dictionary, as the only means of recovering a dead language' (p. 244). Formal learning is, therefore, a poor second best, even possibly a mistake (an interesting doctrine to expound to students).

Reynolds uses the imagery of the common law to bolster the idea that true artistic procedure and judgment is something to be found in the known opinions of the community empowered to make them. And in an unguarded moment, he admits that his (legal) protestation of the worth of opinions, the truths of the authorised community, is irrespective of any intrinsic merit. What matters is their preservation and handing on:

OPINIONS generally received and floating in the world, whether true or false, we naturally adopt and make our own; they may be considered as a kind of inheritance to which we succeed and are tenants for life, and which we leave to our posterity very nearly in the condition in which we receive it; it not being in any one man's power either to impair or improve it. The greatest part of these opinions, like current coin in its circulation, we are used to take without weighing or examining. (pp. 107–8)

The imagery of the tenant for life gives a flavour of Reynolds's method of inculcating artistic sensibility amongst his listeners, something which is not the same as expounding rules which are simply to be followed. Assuming that the 'Gentlemen' to whom all his *Discourses* are addressed are indeed 'Gentlemen' (the same Gentleman students that Blackstone had been addressing), or more accurately 'Gentry',[18] that is, as a minimum, men who have sufficient landed income to enable then to live without work, then the strict settlement controlled by a life tenant would have been a familiar legal concept. After the Restoration, it became the major form of upper-class landholding, and Reynolds's conception of it is legally accurate and metaphorically telling. The legal tenant

---

[18] For the definition of the gentry, see Mingay (1976). For Shaftesbury, 'the *real fine* Gentlemen had to have a knowledge of Customs of European nations, antiquity and records, police laws and constitutions, as well as having studied the arts' (Barrell 1986, p. 17 original emphasis). Barrell adds: 'To this identity the leisure derived from a sustantial unearned income is indispensable' (and see also *ibid.*, p. 77). The eventual 'customers' of the students Reynolds was addressing were as likely to be aristocracy as gentry, but the republic of taste he wished to create distinctly consisted of bourgeois, gentry and above.

Reynolds mentions is actually only the owner for life and would usually be under a legal duty to hand on the property or, by the nineteenth century at the latest, the value of the property, 'very nearly in the condition in which' he received it; just like opinions generally received and floating in the world. Improvements were always permissible, but the overwhelming requirement was not to diminish the value of the inheritance, not to alter what came before. The community of the sons of landowners to whom Reynolds and Blackstone were talking, and the respective, respected Establishment institutions that these Gentlemen were urged to join, must behave in a lawyer-like fashion, preserving existing rights of property and propriety, learning the accumulated wisdom of the specific community in order to leave everything 'very nearly in the condition in which we receive it'.

Reynolds's *Discourses* are in part a lament for a lost world where the proper standards of art did not have to be expounded by the Professors of the Academy. Once nature's rules were learned naturally. It is a matter of great regret that matters have gone into such decline that the lost world of the ancients and the Renaissance masters has to be rediscovered and learned. 'THAT THE ART has been in a gradual state of decline, from the age of Michael Angelo to the present, must be acknowledged' (p. 246).[19] And the cause of this decline is 'indolence'. Like the common law, there was once a golden age (Merrie England perhaps, or Renaiassance Italy) where apprentices and practitioners were not indolent, unlike the present, when practitioners are 'not taking the same pains as our great predecessors took'. This golden age of painting produced the great works we know are great. But given the decline, the loss can only be remedied by the teachers returning to the standards that they know are there, but which have either been ignored or forgotten, just as Blackstone urged Gentlemen to reaquaint themselves with the standards of the common law. This is not to suggest anything but the proper appreciation of the standards that already exist. For Reynolds has not lent his

---

[19] The argument that standards were declining is one that probably goes back to a very lawyerly time immemorial. Certainly by Roman times it was assumed that standards in public life, oratory, eloquence, etc. were not what they once were (see Tacitus 1989). Indeed, for one of Tacitus's speakers, even the standards of the Greeks had declined (*ibid.*, p. 121).

'assistance to foster newly-hatched unfledged opinions, or endeavoured to support paradoxes, however tempting may have been their novelty . . . I have pursued a plain and honest method' (p. 236). Modestly he disclaims any new inventions, and merely says he has established the rules of art on a firmer basis than he found them by absorbing 'discoveries which others have made by their own intuitive good sense and native rectitude of judgment' (pp. 236–7). Like the common law, art, wisdom and truth come from the past, from those with intuitive good sense and judgment. It is disturbed at our peril.

The intuitive good sense is counterposed to the rules Reynolds apparently had set out to expound. Reynolds's concern initially turned him to the law in order to build up an aesthetic series of rules. He used the model of the common law in order to find a system that also incorporated something higher than everyday rules. Law in some higher sense is the supporter of the aesthetic standard, an absolute immutable reflection of all knowing nature, as exemplified specifically in the work of the 'divine' Michael Angelo, or the Blackstonian natural law basis of the common law. At the same time, it is also the rather lower spirit of the community, that is, the legal profession or the Academy.

Reynolds discovered that rules altered to reflect changing circumstances (p. 136) just as he acknowledged taste and standards in art did. This means that rule enunciation is not the relatively straightforward matter implicit in the opening numbers of the Discourses. Remarking on the relation between poverty and luxury, or simplicity versus excess, in great painting, and the need to find a true medium between the two, Reynolds started to despair:

It is not easy to give a rule which may fix this just and correct medium; because when we think we have fixed, or nearly fixed, the middle point, taken as a general principle, circumstances may oblige us to depart from it, either on the side of Simplicity, or on that of Variety or Decoration. (p. 136)

There is only one answer to the problem: throw out the rules altogether and rely on the spirit learned or rather absorbed by the process Reynolds recommends and the Bar practices. By knowing the general purpose and meaning of rules, the painter 'will often find that he need not confine himself to the literal sense, it will be sufficient if he preserve the spirit of the law' (pp. 137–8).

The immutable standards of nature, and the rules that go with them, are turned into the spirit of the community. Once they are spiritual, rather than material, access to the rules can be the prerogative of those who know, those who have the prejudices in tune with the standards that are accepted. The descent from the eternal regions to the prejudices of the great is a device that the method of development and articulation of the common law teaches. The aesthetic postures of the common law are not just eternal, but are also related to Montesquieu's *spirit*, the spirit of a particular society with its own customs and prejudices. The standards of art can likewise be plucked from the skies to the ground. The rather elegant search for the immutable becomes a more grubby justification of the existing modes of discourse and linguistic usages that the authorised community allows. Cicero claimed that 'the cardinal sin' was 'to depart from the language of everyday life and the usage approved by the sense of the community' (*De Oratore*, I.iii.12), a very Reynolds-like position. But the issues then switch from standards in art; they become instead questions of who is authorised to speak on behalf of the community, and which speeches are going to be effective. It is to these questions that we turn in the next section.

IV

1

There has been some rather loose talk in deconstructive writings of works as exemplary deconstructive texts. We have been guilty of such extravagant phrases ourselves (Douzinas and Warrington with McVeigh 1991, Chap. 4). Texts, of course, neither construct nor deconstruct themselves, nor are texts exemplary of anything till they are made so. Texts are complex organisations of signifiers and signifieds expressed in particular forms which are then subject to all sorts of strange actions (not necessarily just by the people who actually interpret them), some of which appear to have little relation to the actual words or pictures that appear on the page or canvas. Howsoever that may be, we have illustrated already some of the most important ways Reynolds's text asserts a series of propositions, often with great vigour, only to renege on them at a later stage as the initial purity of the intentions cannot be retained.[20] For our purpose, the most interesting failure relates to his use of rules and his faith in them. But it is only by virtually reversing his position on law during his lectures that Reynolds is able to achieve what appears a satisfactory compromise; he can worship the genius, and appear to found the science of artistic appreciation, criticism and creative actions.

Fluctuations of position result in the delightful habit of Reynolds pulling down his own delicate edifices. And this is not just true of his use of law. Many of the central notions that Reynolds seemed to set such store by are soon deliberately or inadvertently thrown out. In this part, we indicate some of the main areas where Reynolds appears to turn round his own argument.

We can start by listing some of the central notions that Reynolds did not seem to find necessary to keep in their original form. As we have seen, Reynolds moves, apparently quite comfortably, from a rule of rules to a spirit of the community in which it would be a devil of a job for those outside to have a clue what the rules are. His *Discourses* make it virtually impossible for the uninitiated to acquire a knowledge of the rules even though they are supposedly designed to enable the outsider, the uninitiated young apprentice, to learn the correct route to artistic merit and, ultimately, genius. Genius itself appears to be subject to rules, and not subject to rules. Every judgment is governed by the natural law of reason except that Reynolds cheerfully allows that our feelings (especially of the genius, of the divine Michael Angelo) are, where appropriate, to determine our reason (p. 206).

---

[20] The argument as to whether Reynolds's shifts of position were only apparent (Reynolds merely revealing his hand in stages) or real (the change from the persuasive rhetoric in the tradition of civic humanism to a new political opinion in which the issue becomes one of the ability to abstract general ideas from the raw data of experience) is summarised by Barrell (1986, esp. at pp. 70–2). As will be evident by now, in this chapter, we are, for once at least, on the side of the 'realists'. Sambrook has a different explanation for Reynolds's shifts of position: the contradictions are to be explained either as the result of the long period of time over which the lectures were delivered, or by the fact that 'Reynolds's audience included students of very different ages and degrees of advancement in painting' (1986, p. 127). Neither explanation is very convincing; the first ignored Reynolds's own acutely articulated awareness of his own shifts of position as the years passed. The second explanation appears to ignore the fact that the *Discourses* are meant to give a method to all painters, students and 'graduates'; the rules are really only relaxed for the genius, as we have indicated.

He clearly also has some trouble with notions of copying and imitation. As we have indicated, students are told to learn from the great masters and copy them, but the age of invention must allow for natural genius. And just to copy what was done before cannot be all that is required from the great artist. Reynolds's ingenious solution is to allow copying to be an inventive process, provided certain guidelines or 'rules' are complied with, such as a suitable sensitivity as to which works are to be copied, thus curiously anticipating some very ultra-postmodern ideas (Douzinas and Warrington with McVeigh, 1991, Chap. 12). But copying itself remains both respectable and disreputable.

One further small series of examples: Reynolds has to deal with the question of ornaments, smaller objects, additions generally, matters of dress ('drapery') and the like. His initial position, as is to be expected, is one of deep suspicion even hostility to such trivia. Reynolds again develops an old idea: Cicero had said that for a man to appear to possess the quality of 'seemliness' he should 'remove from his person every unworthy adornment' (*De Officiis* I.130). What matters is the general form, the overall impression, again a fairly conventional Renaissance idea (Beardsley 1966, p. 125). Genius is not interested in smaller objects (pp. 50–1). Nor is the mind to which great art addresses itself concerned with the minute matter of dress. Ornaments or dress in traditional deconstructive scholarship are supplements; that is, ideas that are additions, unnecessary extras, not important for the major concerns of the text being analysed. They are treated as both almost virtually irrelevant, and yet equally unavoidably part of the text's concern, usually to the supposed embarrassment of the argument of the text. Needless to say, the same is true of Reynolds's position on ornaments. They become central. But Reynolds's text is not in the least embarrassed. Having discovered that one of the difficulties of rules is that they are often inconsistent with each other, making coherent exposition for students distinctly tricky (pp. 235–6), Reynolds is totally un-ashamed of the fact that he cannot retain his position on ornaments, dress and the 'meaner mixtures' that go into painting. He cheerfully acknowledged his inability to hold to his pure line. Ornamental style, contrary to the opinion given in the lecture of the previous year, is not wholly unworthy of students' attention after all (p. 73); drapery, instead of being almost irrelevant, requires 'the nicest judgment' (p. 59); his earlier lectures were too dismissive of such matters as ornaments (p. 136). Ornaments are of central concern to the artist.[21] Perhaps texts can self-deconstruct after all.

To avoid simply listing further examples, we can say that two lines of explanation are now open to us: the first is Barrell's excellent political situating and explaining of the strange events in Reynolds's text; and the second is to suggest that Reynolds's most significant moves are contained in his theory and practice of rhetoric. Whilst the two lines of argument are clearly connected, both being concerned with the way arguments seek to persuade, where and why, that is both are really political arguments, it will be helpful to summarise Barrell's more overt political moves first.

2

According to Barrell (1986), Reynolds starts his *Discourses* from within the civic humanist tradition. Writing from within the dominant *Ciceronian* ethic of what has been called the 'Ciceronian century' (Wood 1988, p. 3) in which he was working, Reynolds claimed that art, and the setting of its aims, like politics, was a subject for those who had the leisure to devote themselves to the study of their proper forms, that is basically the landed aristocracy and gentry, and to an extent those immediately below them. They would be obliged to use their knowledge and ability in the interests of civic virtue, governing in politics and declaring standards of aesthetic appreciation in line with the highest aspirations of human nature abstracted from society in general. These abstractions would transcend the limitations of the necess-

---

[21] One response that might be made is that it is all a question of the balance between purity and addition. Hume neatly resolved the problem in a formula designed to combine purity and excess by making ornaments a part of nature: 'Nothing can please persons of taste, but nature drawn with all her graces and ornaments' (1963, p. 196). But this solution to the problem of how to represent nature does not seem to provide much of an advance for the student-painter struggling to make sense of the requirements defined by Reynolds. If ornaments are part of nature ('her graces and ornaments'), then this means that natural adornments are to be included in artistic representation. This is merely requiring the reproduction of nature whole; which is not what Reynolds, and the artistic tradition on which he draws, seemed to want, as we have indicated.

ary imperfect institutions they would see around them, just as we have seen Reynolds argue that painters must ignore the defects of necessarily imperfect individual human models.

But with the dramatic change the eighteenth century was witnessing, around the seventh lecture (given at the end of the not insignificant year of 1776) Reynolds starts a halting shift,

by which the ideal of a civic republic of taste founded on the unattributable principles of human nature begins to be converted into the notion of . . . a 'community' of taste, conceived as a national community, bound together by custom and justifiable prejudice. (Barrell 1986, p. 136)

Civic humanism, acceptable in a more traditional and stable society, may not work well in the interests of order in the more dynamic late eighteenth century, where the public virtue, responsible for artistic standards, can no longer take place automatically in the public sphere. 'The possibility of a public art was therefore understood to be threatened in the late eighteenth and early nineteenth centuries, by what was perceived as a process by which society was being privatised' (ibid., p. 308 and passim).

The change in emphasis is of immediate significance. Reynolds had begun to be influenced by writers who had started to raise not universal principles but particular customs of specific nations in order to counter the spreading but subversive Lockian principles that, ultimately, might allow legitimate governments and standards in taste to be overthrown. These writers (eventually the most important was Burke) argued that the customs of a nation were 'second nature' and

a frank prejudice in favour of established . . . practices were the expression of the collective spirit of the nation . . . and no nation would be constituted . . . by theories of government which, because 'rational', and framed for the use of 'rational' men, could be recommended to any nation whatsoever, without thought for its national character. (ibid., p. 138).

The task Reynolds faced during the Discourses came to be to protect not the republic of taste, but the mixed consitution of the English political settlement, which civic humanism alone would not do. This necessitated the reconciliation of universal with particular national customs. Reynolds did not always find this easy (he had called the local 'fantastical', as we have seen), but there was a way out, at least as a first step. This was to distinguish between true universal customs, those that have indeed become second nature, and customs and habits that are merely local or transient (*ibid.*, p. 143). Thus Reynolds can accept the role of (some) local customs on the grounds that they are based on supra-national ideals, and, surprisingly enough, English customs particularly represent more than the fantastical. Reynolds's theory of art becomes a theory of society (*ibid.*, p. 145) as it can now be reconciled with the defence of a particular society. English law and custom, as developed by the limited franchise of the mixed constitution, can claim the specific allegiance of the political theorists. Artistic theory can be adapted (or even altered, jettisoned or deconstructed we might say) to fit into the new theory. Ornament, the minutiae, drapery, the local, the private (though presumably not the fantastical) 'may, in certain circumstances, be represented by the artist' (*ibid.*, p. 147). Ornaments, for example, which exhibit the characteristic mark of national taste 'may be encouraged . . . if the accidents of nationality do not conceal the substance of the universal as, in the earlier addresses, [that is, Reynolds's earlier lectures] they were bound to do' (*ibid.*, p. 149).

The discourse of custom has therefore, Barrell argues, inserted a third political term, purporting to reconcile the standards of the universal with the recognition of the local. The link here with the common law can be made fairly explicit. According to Blackstone, local customs were to be sacrificed, but the general customs of the realm (that is, the common law) were to be cultivated for the convenience of one uniform and universal system of common laws. A customary aesthetic follows similar principles. The customary system of common law, thought to be so different from its continental counterpart, could incorporate those elements of the local whose very Englishness could be described as entailing universal laws.

But the establishment of this new form of a true republic of taste takes time. Ornaments and the sensual can draw an audience into artistic appreciation. Presumably something similar happens to local customs as they get absorbed into the national system of laws, that is why a national community of taste, or, we add, law, could then be seen as a first step. The appreciation of the truly universalistic aspects of art and the laws of humankind could take over gradually as the purely local and inferior aspects are dropped.

Drawing on Reynolds's unpublished work, Barrell (*ibid.*, p. 155) finds him struggling to reconcile the two different principles of aesthetics that can be seen to be at work in his thinking and suggests he slowly manages to move towards an aesthetic of the rules of an established community, his own, which consists of the 'few' rather than the many (ibid., p. 159). This is a limited community safeguarded by its actual knowledge, rather than universalistic values which, in principle, the mass could strive towards with consequences to which the American Declaration of Independence and eventually the French Revolution led. 'Rules can be drawn up, as they are in the eighth discourse, to prescribe not just how the novel and sensual should be kept in check, but how their legitimate interests may be protected' (ibid., p. 157). Reynolds's new code of aesthetics can establish the legitimacy of the Englishness of English art, just as the lawyers were establishing the legitimacy of the Englishness of English law, or as Cicero had declared the 'local' Roman law superior to all others.[22] The pure occasional and the local and transitory site of a fable can be taken account of in painting, and in law, for example Blackstone's denunciation of corrupting continental influences on English purity,[23] without, seemingly, compromising the universalistic claims of art or the common law. The politics of aesthetic standards, as they are transposed, fit the claims of the specific community with which Reynolds identifies.

3

The cautious abandonment by Reynolds of the civic tradition is expressed in the field of language. He starts with a natural society, in which virtue and standards in politics and art are present almost without the asking, where the forms are just there, Plato-like, waiting to be articulated by the natural leaders and makers of opinion. He moves from this society to his artificial (spirit of the) community. In doing so, he confronts a linguistic problem: what is

---

[22] 'For it is incredible how disorded and well nigh absurd, is all national law other than our own' (De Oratore, I.xliii.197).

[23] 'But the common law of England, being not committed to writing, but only handed down by tradition, use and experience, was not so heartily relished by the foreign clergy; who came over hither in shoals during the reign of the conqueror and his two sons, and were utter strangers to our constitution as well as our language' (Blackstone 1979, p. 19).

the effect of his lectures? Our analysis here, therefore, moves from overt politics, from persuasion in the public sphere of the mixed constitution, to the different public sphere of reading and writing that Reynolds has entered. What is at issue, at least in part, is the truth-telling claims of Reynolds's *Discourses*. In order to understand what happens to these we suggest that it is Reynolds's art of rhetoric, rather than his rhetoric of art, that has to be understood.[24] But it is also politics by another name. And lurking in Reynolds's politics are images of law.

Legal arguments tend to be flexible or, as every law student knows, at least two-sided. This unfortuntate (or convenient) necessity is also a part of Reynolds's aesthetic. As we saw, the great events of history are the legitimate subjects for the great painter. But just as nature has to be transformed, touched up by the make-up artist to become true art, so, too, does the truth itself, when expressed in painting. The truth becomes flexible. The artist must 'sometimes deviate from the vulgar and strict historical truth, in pursuing the grandeur of his design' (p. 57). 'With us, History is made to bend and conform to [the] great idea of Art' (p. 214). No doubt, but the problem is that Reynolds (appeared) to want to hold on to some near absolute notion of truth, and to establish the rules that guaranteed its achievement. In Reynolds's work, truth started as a Ciceronian notion, that there cannot be more than one truth or form of justice existing at different times and different places.[25] Reynolds finds he cannot maintain this position. Truth, like the law, bends to custom and prejudice, and in this context to that art

---

[24] James Barry, lecturing contemporaneously with and shortly after Reynolds perhaps can be seen also to be talking more about rhetoric than painting, though Barrell (1986, pp. 188–9) does not go so far. Barry put forward a much more democratic Christian potential for painting than Reynolds. For Barrell's view on the relation between painting and rhetoric more generally, see *ibid.*, pp. 23–7.

[25] This basic position in Cicero's *Republic* is now familiar: 'And there will not be different laws at Rome and at Athens, or different laws now and in the future, but one eternal and unchangeable law will be valid for all nations and all times' (III.xxi.33). This particular formulation, however, would have been unknown to Reynolds, as *The Republic* was not rediscovered until 1820. But similar views were expressed in other works by Cicero that were then available, such as *De Legibus* (for example, I.vi.19, I.xv.43, I.iv.8). Presumably Reynolds would also have been aware of the Platonic origins of this idea, even though, like many other eighteenth-century thinkers, he probably knew Plato via Cicero.

which is addressed not to the gross senses, 'but to the desire of the mind, to that spark of divinity which we have within, impatient of being circumscribed and pent up by the world which is about us' (p. 214). The spark of divinity, a distinctly human creation in Reynolds's analysis, is different from the natural truth and our desire for it, which is also supposed to motivate us. Sparks, presumably the prerogative of the genius, like other parts of Reynolds's argument, are (contra Cicero) 'different in different times and places' (p. 88). Maybe; but if so, there are no absolute standards of beauty, truth, rules, taste or nature either. Despite earlier protestations, Reynolds agrees: there is real truth, and apparent truth (pp. 109–10), there are greater truths and lesser truths (p. 236).

In order to make the move from absolute to variable or apparent truth, Reynolds turns once again to the common law. 'With regard to real truth, when it is known, the taste which conforms to it is, and must be, uniform.' This sort of truth can probably never be 'known'; but this is not necessarily the case with other truths (legal truths for example): 'With regard to the second sort of truth, which may be called truth upon sufferance, or truth by c[o]urtesy, it is not fixed but variable. However . . . they operate as truth' (p. 110). Sufferances and curtesies are forms of tenancies, that is, holdings of land, well known to Reynolds's audiences, especially, perhaps, curtesies, which specifically were available only to widowers.[26] Holdings in law are also the most significant portion of a judicial pronouncement, the statement of the rule or rules that the judges *hold* determine the legal outcome of a case when the marginal aspects, the particular facts and individuals concerned (the supplements, and the supplicants to the law, or, in Reynolds's terminology, the fantastical), have been stripped away. The holding is the nearest thing to truth the common law knows. As forms of holdings, entitlements to property, or truths, curtesy and

---

[26] The whole tribe of restoration playwrights with their gallery of younger sons searching for a good inheritance depended on legal notions such as widowers. For example, Vanbrugh, himself no slouch with the pencil, and mentioned approvingly by Reynolds (p. 213), claimed of fashionable London: 'widows swarm my boy, the town's infected with 'em' (*The Relapse*, I.iii.195–6). 'Young Fashions', with their inheritance spent, needed (rich) widows out of whom to claim, amongst other goodies, curtesy.

sufferance have their problems. Tenancies by the curtesy were subject to strict conditions and limitations, and a tenancy by sufferance is simply a holding over without the landlord's consent and can be brought to an end at any time. '[I]t is strictly incorrect to call it "tenancy" at all' (Megarry and Wade 1984, p. 655). Like Reynolds's truth, these holdings may or may not hold, it may be 'strictly incorrect' to call them truths at all. As with other eighteenth-century products, truth, in its artistic and legal context, has become something to be manufactured by those who know and are authorised to make it. Once trial by ordeal is abandoned, courts dealt in the 'second' sort of truth: truth beyond reasonable doubt, or merely on the balance of probabilities. The common law rejected truth itself, and so does Reynolds's rhetoric of art.

But although Reynolds starts to bend the concept of truth to fit the new purposes of his *Discourses* as he perceives them, he still has to struggle with the linguistic forms of expression that his move from painting to speaking/writing demands. Reynolds hesitatingly turns from a rhetoric of painting to a rhetoric of words which have little to do with the actual marks on canvas that are supposed to be the object of the analysis; and the main outlines of the two systems have much in common. In a word, Reynolds begins with the claim that the true forms should be expressed without the clutter of ornaments and rhetorical excess. As he moves to a language involved in metaphors of law, he first expounds a similar doctrine for language itself. He finds that he then has to reject both positions in the perceived interests of politcs, art, law, rhetoric, the established order of things, and in the interests of a representationally created nature.

To start with painting, as a practitioner Reynolds can express himself, apparently, beyond language, beyond even the poetic fancies that he admires. Barrell (1986, p. 97) suggests that Reynolds evidences reluctance to be too definitive on the potential persuasive effect of art because 'of the nature of painting itself, which cannot argue, or demonstrate, but can only represent the forms of nature' (1986, p. 97). But it can be suggested that Reynolds's position changes as soon as he starts to articulate in writing the effect of art, rather than simply allowing paintings to speak for themselves, in paint. In any event, when he turns to writing/speaking itself, he notes that he faces a medium that, in comparison with painting, is inadequate. At first this inadequacy is merely inconvenient. Referring to standards in 'Taste', 'that act of the mind by which we like or dislike, whatever be the subject', Reynolds laments that the same term is also employed for our judgments upon an 'airy nothing, a fancy which has no foundation'. But, with a shrug, he adds that this is the way things are: 'we are obliged to take words as we find them' (p. 109). In the sphere of teaching and judgment (here referring specifically to poetry), we must 'generally rest contented with mere words' (p. 107). On the face of things, on the canvas, it should have been different.

But his position gets more complex and superficially hostile as the (inevitable) failures of language burst through his best endeavours. Art has a complex relation with some notion of an eternal view of nature, as we have seen. But the ideas expressed in painting, in their pure essence, are, in their source, no different from those expressed in language. Both are merely the means used to represent the idea. Sometimes, however, like painting, language is simply inadequate.[27] Reynolds uses himself as an example as he modestly (or perhaps here not quite so modestly) laments: 'I am truly sensible how unequal I have been to the expression of my own ideas' (p. 234, and similarly p. 109). In painting and in poetry and prose, ideas drawn from nature come first. Paints, pencils and pens merely express them, well or ill, as the case may be. And it cannot be expected that the use of language by the artist is as felicitous as that of, say, the poet. For, says Reynolds, 'a man perpetually occupied in the use of the pencil and pallet' cannot always translate ideas into linguistic form. The fault is both personal and indicative of the inadequacies of representation in prose, but not necessarily for Reynolds in painting (or, of course, were Reynolds to take the example, in music).

The difficulty starts to get more intense as Reynolds realises that there is more to it than his own, or indeed any writer's, personal inability to control satisfactorily both the potential and the dangers of language. This is partly because there is a familiar 'second'-order problem, that language has been 'misused'. If we cannot do

---

[27] Reynolds might even have agreed with Derrida; in a passage that summarises much of his own work, Derrida claims: 'Language gives one to think but it also steals, spirits away from us, whispers to us, and withdraws the responsibility that it seems to inaugurate; it carries off the property of our own thoughts even before we have appropriated them' (1992a, p. 80).

without it, as painters and musicians apparently can, we must at least try to make the best, unspoilt use of it. We ought to strive towards purity in painting and should do the same for language. Language could express our meaning, if only it were not ruined by excess, ornament and flowery speech, the same sorts of defects that beset lesser paintings. In other words, Reynolds is here taking the traditional Neoplatonic view (Vickers 1988, pp. 18 and 84ff.) that rhetoric is a debased form of expression, an unnecessary addition to natural language (part of a long and familiar argument of declining standards generally). Excess ruins speech, just as it ruins painting. Indeed the decline of Art itself since Michael Angelo can be compared to the similar corruption of eloquence (p. 246), just as the art of rhetoric declined in Rome (Vickers 1988, pp. 46–7, 53–4).

But then there is poetry, which Reynolds frequently uses[28] to make his points. And here he again makes one of his endearing about-turns. At one stage (p. 157), he suggests poetry uses signs which are arbitrary, whereas the sculptor purports to represent 'the thing itself', but he does not maintain this distinction. Poetry is actually like painting, because it addresses itself to the same faculties, that is, the mind. But in order to be poetry, almost to construct its essence it, too, has to deviate from actual nature, that is, presumably, from a language that reflects naturally the natural order. '[Poetry] sets out with a language in the highest degree artificial, a construction of measured words, such as never is, nor never was used by man . . . removed from nature and equally a

---

[28] It has been no part of our intention to try to trace all the many unacknowledged formative influences on Reynolds's essays, though we have, inevitably, alluded to the essential, unavoidable, all-pervasive presence of Cicero. But one possible source that is perhaps worth mentioning is Pope's An Essay on Criticism. Many of Reynolds's arguments on Nature, the copying of the Ancients and the proper subjects of admiration, excess and others seem to come straight from Pope's poem. But the link is strongest on the relationship between poetry and art. It is difficult not to think that Pope's denunciation would not have gone straight to Reynolds's heart:
   Poets like painters, thus unskill'd to trace
   The naked nature and the living grace,
   With gold and jewels cover ev'ry part,
   And hide with ornaments their want of art.
   (An Essay on Criticism, 293–6).
On the relation between poetics and literature in postmodernism, see Hutcheon (1988).

violation of common speech' (pp. 205–6).[29] Indeed, poetry is distinguished from oratory by an even greater degree of artificiality. Oratory only uses a 'more liberal, though chaste use of those ornaments which go under the name of figurative and metaphorical expressions; [whereas] poetry distinguishes itself from oratory by words and expressions still more ardent and glowing' (p. 21 and elsewhere). That is, oratory and poetry are either praised now precisely because they have abandoned natural language, or, if this abandonment is not a matter of praise, then they are lauded because it simply has to be recognised that their lack of simplicity is a necessity, just as the same necessity and excess is finally recognised as essential in painting.

Reynolds shifts his position on persuasion and rhetorical excess because he is faced with the inadequacy of his system. If he is to preserve his own community's right to rule, a rhetoric of 'simple' rules does not work. There are no workable rules. He has to have a different persuasive strategy, but as he enquires into the possibilities that this might involve, he finds a form (language) that is itself inherently unreliable. Language does not behave; it is as dangerously unruly as painting. The way out is quietly to slip into the meanings of the community, to resort to the spirit of the rules, as Blackstone recommends, and to the never-failing, omnipresent 'discourses' of the common law.

Which is why Reynolds's attitude to linguistic usages and standards is as shifting as his attitude to the art of painting. In part he wants to denigrate many uses of language entirely. Writers must

---

[29] Once again, Reynolds's formulation here is similar to Cicero's: 'The truth is that the poet is a very near kinsman of the orator, rather more heavily fettered as regards rhythm, but with ampler freedom in his choice of words, while in the use of many sorts of ornaments his is his ally and almost his counterpart' (De Oratore, I.xv.70); 'poets being the next of kin to orators' (ibid., III.vii.27). In one of his letters (Cicero 1982, pp. 97–109, esp. pp. 107–8), Cicero specifically links writing, oratory and poetry; and he states his preference for these activities over practical politics. Cicero's shadow notwithstanding, Longinus put the matter more conventionally, trying to separate the role of the orator from that of the poet: 'The poetic examples have a quality of exaggeration which belongs to fable and goes far beyond credibility. In an orator's visualizations, on the other hand, it is the element of fact and truth which makes for success' (Longinus 1989, p. 161, also p. 159). Reynolds, like Cicero, wants to join the effective powers of well-formed speech with the truth-telling claims of great literature, a combination that Plato would have found somewhat implausible.

be encouraged to return to true, that is, natural, forms of speech without the interference of unnecessary ornaments, a strict language of rules purged of rhetorical excess. Yet he knows this is impossible, and indeed he frequently indulges in passages of overplay, occasionally bordering on the outrageous.[30] Like so many painters, and certainly writers,[31] Reynolds is deeply suspicious of excess in all its forms, and, at the same time, cannot resist it. His *Discourses* are as much a theory or practice of rhetoric as of painting. Excess, rhetoric, is good and bad, to be removed from true art and absolutely necessary for any expression.

This gives a slightly different perspective on where 'Nature' fits in Reynolds's system. In a claim that Kant was to develop (Beardsley 1966, p. 211), Reynolds refers to nature properly understood as a realm of 'perfect freedom' (p. 197). The artist, for Reynolds, has to be free; he also has to be bound by rules.[32] He is above language, and is caught by it. Language is both freedom and necessity. Reynolds's rules were designed to make the earthly paradise of freedom achievable for the artist, the free gentleman; just as the common law was meant to make freedom achievable for the free citizen, another type of free gentleman. In fact, as Reynolds and the later Romantics discover, rules are a barrier to this end, and Reynolds, almost in spite of himself, rhetorically anticipates the freedom from restraint that was to be one of the calls of Romanticism itself. By the end of the eighteenth century, the notion of rules in art was downgraded as Romanticism (in its many forms) took over the philosophical and aesthetic high ground. In a curious way, Reynolds's equivocal defence of rules paves the way for a system where untrammelled genius, searching for the inexpressible beauty of natural art, has no need of rules.

---

[30] His denunciation of certain artists is not untypical: artists who have quit the service of nature, putting themselves 'under the direction of I know not what capricious fantastical mistress . . . from whose dominion there are no hopes of their being ever reclaimed . . . [and who have] no reason to complain of the shortness of life, and the extent of art; since life is so much longer than is wanted for their improvement' (p. 197).

[31] His contemporary, Adam Smith (1983), is a good example.

[32] Beardsley also says that Kant, in his concern to establish understandings of beauty, thought formal rules had little value; to seek for them, in Kant's terms, was a 'fruitless trouble'. Kant's concern with distinguishing the beautiful from everything else 'does not mean that there can be an objective formal rule that will distinguish beautiful objects from those that are not' (Beardsley 1966, p. 217).

In the meantime, in Reynolds's analysis, nature is, and can only be, a figure of speech. Nature is Reynolds's rhetorical and, in the context of oral lectures, oratorical stand-in for the impossible, indefinable realm of the free-necessity of those necessarily declared to be free. The use of nature, a classic rhetorical move (Vickers 1988, pp. 2–3), is a form of substitution, where causes are exchanged and, in particular, remote causes substituted for immediate ones (*metalepsis*, cf. Douzinas and Warrington 1991). At times, Reynolds appears to create plausible arguments by pure invention (*inventio*)[33] sometimes seemingly out of little or nothing, even though based on a well-known tradition. The immediate cause of standards, that is, politics-law, commercial drives, professional jealousy, whim, sales-figures, professorial, pontificatorial necessity are replaced by a remote, shadowy, yet traditionally utterly persuasive cause, nature. This cause is beyond human control (naturally), almost beyond human comprehension, certainly beyond human argument. Who can quarrel with nature, or object to her dispositions (*dispositio*) of figures in paintings, backgrounds, places of ornaments, etc.? Nature is a standard, and yet suspect, metaphorical displacement, which Reynolds uses brilliantly to entice his audience into a security based on thousands of years of hermeneutically sage nodding. Its ability to persuade depends on a willing suspension of disbelief in human creativity and inventiveness; or if that is too strongly put, given the place of nature in arguments that have been deemed convincing since Plato then, in a Nietzschean move, the use of nature has become so familiar that it is the last part of the discourse to be questioned. To object to standards of nature in painting would simply be silly; for we know that objection is out of bounds. For Reynolds and his audience, to question the place of nature, if it would or could occur to them, would seem pointless.

In summary, as is to be expected, language in general, as well as its specific use (defining great art), becomes another classic supplement. In Reynolds's case, it is a necessary supplement to a non-linguistic medium. It wrecks the purity of his vision. It is the very nature of language, language as the ultimate, total, but fallen

---

[33] For Cicero, inventive arguments were to be 'discovered' rather than 'created': 'Invention is the discovery of valid or seemingly valid arguments to render one's cause plausible' (Cicero, *De Inventione*, I.vi.9).

vehicle, that gets in the way of his best intentions. The immediate, first glance, view is that language is either unnecessary for art, or a 'mere' supplement. According to Plato, arts such as painting and sculpture 'have little or no need of speech.' (1960, p. 24). What Reynolds discovers is that, contrary to this common-sense view, paintings cannot after all speak for themselves. Despite his dreams of artistic purity and immediate communication with the mind in tune with the highest aspirations, the great masters also need expositing. And if this is the case for the creators of all-time standards, how much more so is it for those humble mortals who merely follow in their footsteps, even though Reynolds does suggest, again in a somewhat self-defeating manner, that the apprentice can overtake the master. Language extracts its overly predictable penalty (Hillis Miller 1987) and deconstructs Reynolds's attempt to reason by selected rules and rule by selected reason.

And in this whirl of words, what of the main artistic justification of Reynolds's lectures? What has happened to the truth which Reynolds deemed so important? Reynolds appeared to promise a truth in painting,[34] perhaps the truth in painting, and thought to achieve it through a practical exposition of rules which started to dally, rather dangerously, with the absolute nature of truth itself. In order to get to the truth in painting, Reynolds translated painting into a different medium. But perhaps the whole exercise is futile. Reynolds cites the possibility of translatability from language to language as the key to the intrinsic worth of a text. Texts (or ideas in them) which cannot be translated are, we might say for Reynolds, not worth the translating.[35] But perhaps this common enough test only applies to inter-linguistic exchanges, which is, of course, the way Reynolds uses it. Perhaps in Reynolds's work it can have no place when the issue is the

---

[34] See Derrida (1987). Like Derrida's Cézanne, Reynolds seems to owe us the truth in painting; he offers it to us. 'But must we take a painter literally once he starts to speak?' (ibid., p. 8).

[35] Expounding Walter Benjamin's essay on translation, Andrew Benjamin remarks: 'The essential is re-expressed in terms of translatability . . . in terms of after life/ survival; the capacity of the work to live on' (1989, p. 90). The Platonic notion of an essence, which forms the often unspoken premise of much of Reynolds's text, is both proved and disproved by the possibility and impossibility of translation.

translation from one medium to another.[36] There is nothing in Reynolds's *Discourses* to indicate it has any relevance for the move from art to language. The lectures may, therefore, not be what they seem. Perhaps the truth in painting or music can only speak in painting or music. Reynolds simply follows, or appears to follow, a tradition of trying to make an impossible translation. And perhaps[37] the lectures are a disguised warning against the facility of commentators who have done nothing but make this false translation for centuries. The *Discourses* are their own perfect double – they indicate not the truth in painting, but that this truth, if it exists, is not available in non-plastic forms. But the forms of non-linguistic expression, like painting and sculpture, which most concern Reynolds only flatter to deceive; despite their apparent freedom from the perils of language, they also need linguistic expressions in order to safeguard their very status as aspects of the highest endeavours of human beings in non-linguistic forms. But the very un/necessary translation into language destroys the potential of art to represent the highest forms of truth. Reynolds therefore cannot decide whether he needs language or not. A destructive circle is complete and the supposed rule-bound unity of his *Discourses* disintegrates.

If so, the result is a recognition that truth, far from being the expression of a natural form, is a political, institutional and rhetorical-legal product, in which art may serve and rule or at least serve the rulers, but not in the interest of a Platonic-Ciceronian truth. For Reynolds, the practice of art has fallen from its classical and Renaissance ideals; the fall, like that of Lucifer, may be eternal. Reynolds's *Discourses*, in their own beautiful, tortured way, may be acknowledging this when they tremblingly reveal that the absolute truth that Reynolds sought is as lost as Lucifer. Truth becomes what Reynolds rhetorically produced, not what nature, or God, ordained.

---

[36] Just as for Vickers (1988, p. 365) language and music 'derive from fundamentally different resources', so too with language and painting (on which see *ibid.*, pp. 341–60).

[37] 'Perhaps' we can take comfort from Derrida's similar hesitancy: after nearly two hundred pages of incredibly detailed, almost tortured analysis of a story only just long enought to fill a page ('Which is as brief as I have known a' story), he comments on the result of his own work: 'We are still saying *perhaps*' (1992a, p. 170; emphasis in the original).

V

1

Reynolds had tried to fix the rules for the proper appreciation and creation of art. As we have seen, in an uncharacteristically immodest aside he thought he had succeeded, at least in part. The measure of his success can be related to the extent to which he brought the creation of his artistic rules into line with an understanding of the way the common law was developing. For Reynolds, law or the legal commmunity stood as the guard between the false and the true.[38] Reynolds might have been disappointed by his law's descent from norm to normality, by its failure to provide clear guidelines for students, artists, critics and customers. The failure, partly the result of the linguistic difficulties encountered, nevertheless did not prevent him establishing a legitimacy for the section of the community with which he identified. This was achieved by accepting a different form of law from that with which he started.

Reynolds's analysis, and its comparison with the common law, can be generalised. Our argument in this book is that even accepting that some of the best ideals of justice and eternal truths are incorporated into a legal system, and indeed the common law does embody some of them, when it comes to practical applications the high ideals remain high. There is a difference between the truth-telling utterances of the law, and its aspirations to deliver justice, and its performances when individuals are brought before it. We have illustrated law's inability fully to take account of the concrete, material individual victim, of those 'before the law', and suggested that in the guise of arguments about some of the most fundamental human values, valuable human lives are simply ignored. In particular, we have argued that law takes a neo-Kantian view in which it assumes that other people are always the same as us; that if one person (a judge) feels or thinks certain courses of actions are acceptable, it is permissible to assume everyone will do

---

[38] And although he said that Vitruvius's suggestion, that an architect ought to be well skilled in the civil law 'that he might not be cheated in the title of the ground he builds on' (p. 105), might be carrying the 'point too far', a suspicion remains that the fixing of rules in art, and in the law, as to who can appropriate artistic products has more to it than aesthetic, 'Academic' pretensions.

so. The destruction of the individual concerned is then not noticed. 'The face of the other', what makes the other distinct, makes her otherness, makes her a feeling, suffering person precisely because she is not the same as the judge, is disregarded at the very moment when high ideals of justice and ethical conduct are most necessary. What is needed instead of this suffocating, totalising and totalitarianising reduction of the other to the self is a 'kind of flight . . . one which will not murder or destroy the Other by reducing it to the principles of the Same or to identity' (Docherty 1990, p. 173). All we can do at this stage is provide in a summary demonstration of what we have argued so far, how it is that Reynolds's text, in its proper concern with standards of beauty, nature, taste and truth, paves the way for the near disastrous treatment of these worthy ideals. Our argument is that, by implication at least, the common law is involved in a similar process, as this book has tried to show.

2

In his concern with perfect beauty, Reynolds tried to demarcate what the young student or even the mature master can reasonably be expected to attempt. In Discourse 5, Reynolds started by expressing one of his many self-doubts, that he may have been misunderstood in his previous lecture. What concerned him was the proper place of the various 'excellencies' in art. Everything has its proper place and it is wrong to imagine that you can put an object of esteem higher than that to which it is suited. His main advice for the aspiring great artist was to concentrate on the higher excellencies. When these have been mastered, the great artist can, if he so wishes, turn his attention to 'subordinate qualifications' (p. 71).

This general advice needed illustration, and Reynolds outlined some misguided attempts, even by fine artists, to unite excellencies of a 'discordant nature'. Uniting contrary excellencies in a single figure either degenerates into the monstrous or sinks into the insipid (pp. 71–2). The chief example deals with the 'passions'. And we can now complete the sentence, partly quoted earlier, and which provides the first part of the title to this chapter: 'If you mean to preserve the most perfect beauty in its most perfect state, you cannot express the passions, all of which produce distortions and deformity, more or less, in the most beautiful faces' (p. 72). Cicero had warned 'that one must guard against passions' (*De Officiis* I.172) and Reynolds translated this injunction into his artistic ethic. Passion and compassion, the very things that Reynolds's highest aspirations might have been seen as striving towards, an aesthetic of the highest moral standards, have to be ruled out. The law of art and the art of law cannot cope with passions and faces that are spoilt by suffering.[39] These faces are 'distorted'[40] and must not be allowed to disturb the serenity of the standards of great art. For Reynolds, to retain an inscrutable expression was one of the necessities of the civic, stoic virtue that Cicero exemplified, and he sought to instil in his Academy audience. 'It is a splendid achievement to face all of life with equanimity, never altering the expression of one's face . . .' (*De Officiis*, I.90 and also 102). Reynolds defines beautiful faces as those that are not distorted by suffering, and it is only the beautiful that gain admittance to his Academy. To put it in terms of our discussion in Chapter 4, because the demands of the face of the other are to be considered prior to, or at least alongside, the demands of the self, and since these claims are inherently unstable, possibly threatening, and since we never know in advance the extent of another's claim, Reynolds solves the jurisprudential and philosophical problem 'at one blow' by excluding considerations of the other entirely. The judges of the refugee cases could not have managed things better. All faces demanding our compassion and understanding (such as it can be) are liable to be distorted. In the best traditions of the lawyers whom he has joined, Reynolds therefore declares any claims the suffering face may have to be illegitimate. The argument solves the problem Levinas raises by not allowing the problem to be expressed.

---

[39] Barrell (1986, pp. 110–12) takes a more complex view of Reynolds's attitude to the expression of passion than we are stating here. He argues that Reynolds both denies the possibility of the depiction of the passionate subject and is aware this the passionate subject is liable to be insipid. On the other hand, mixed passion leaves too much doubt for debate and cannot properly instruct.

[40] The idea was hardly new, and already beautifully satirised by Vanbrugh: 'Don't be in a passion Tam; for passion is the most unbecoming thing in the world – to the face' (*The Relapse*, III.i.98–9). On the other hand, no matter how awful the circumstances, 'a philosophical air is the most becoming thing in the world to the face of a person of quality' (*ibid.*, V.v.247–9).

In his concern with fame, Reynolds distinguishes artists who seek to satisfy present opinion which may be vulgar or plain wrong, from those seeking true fame, fame that is eternal. Works that are based on particular customs or habits are not like those that are built upon general nature, which live for ever. 'Present time and future may be considered as rivals, and he who solicits the one must expect to be discounted by the other' (p. 68). What matters are the eternal standards; present applications, individual suffering, the case in hand, the distorted or suffering face before the artist or the judge, are to be 'discounted' if they disturb the all-time standards of the law. The artist must ensure 'in finishing the parts he is not destroying the general effect' (p. 177). The surface, the effect, the commitment to the ideals remain, whilst the application of these ideals is deemed impossible or impermissible. The law commits itself to the highest, most beautiful ideal, and then refuses to have any dealing with this ideal when it is faced with faces that distort, that do not conform to its own established definition of the beautiful.

Reynolds expresses himself in this way partly for straight 'artistic' reasons: passionate subjects are difficult to represent in all artistic endeavours. But there is more to it than sheer artistic difficulty, which, in any event, genius might be expected to transcend. Reynolds's view of the suffering face depends on his relatively straightforward assumption that what I feel, you feel; the view of the judges in the immigration cases for example. Reynolds acknowledges that 'we must regulate our affections of every kind by that of others' (p. 118). In particular, we accept the discipline of the public voice. But this public voice is from a very limited constituency. Besides, this potential softening of position is suspect because Reynolds has already pronounced the common-sense view that we can appeal to commonsense. And when we do so we find that the other thinks like us, acts like us, and can be assumed to have no differences from us that are crucial. Just as the eternal forms are available to all with the leisure and capacity to study, if we work hard enough to find them, so, too, our minds. In a repeat of a direct, Platonic position (Plato 1960, p. 75) Reynolds asserts: 'We have no reason to suspect that there is a greater difference between our minds than between our forms' (p. 117). The other is us, where us is the knowing community, the community of those who can make the rules because they are the people possessed with the 'intuitive good sense' (p. 236) that enables them to do so. Any attempt at a true understanding of the outsider, those with faces which might not fit, ideas about art that do not conform, seems to be impossible. Reynolds's analysis, a celebration of his own declaration of what the community thinks best, is, therefore, an exclusion. Great standards do not seem to work for those who are not worth the attention of the authorised communities in art and, as we have shown, in law. Reynolds's theory, if by now it can be called such, 'must always assume a fundamental normativity which makes the Other the same as the Self' (Docherty 1990, p. 218); in doing so, it can define standards without committing itself to anything the authorised community does not want to accept.

Reynolds's rhetoric seems to break down completely when, instead of the rhetorical excess that he had both condemned and used, he finds himself silenced by his own *Discourses*. His last lecture is partly devoted to a celebration of the divine, his beloved Michael Angelo. But what rules or standards the student or anyone else can draw from such Angelic work (apart from further exhortation to 'diligence'), other than an equally breathless admiration, an admiration that in the end becomes unspeakable, is unclear. Right at the end of the final Discourse, Reynolds half-acknowledges that even with his favourite (or perhaps especially with him), there is nothing that can be said. Reynolds faces difficulties in expressing himself because in his last and moving paean of praise to Michael Angelo he sets the seal on his inability to do what he set out to do. Taste, passion, individual feeling, lawless subjective sense, govern everything in art. Despite his best endeavours, Reynolds finds there is nothing left for the would-be instructor to do but tell students to be equally passionate (provided, of course, they do not try to put their passions on canvas). Reynolds, meanwhile, despairing of language, can say nothing except repeat Michael Angelo's name as his literal last word (pp. 247–8). In the meantime, the standards he strove to achieve not only fail as unworkable; there is nothing that can be said about them, just as nothing can be said about those who are not an accepted part of the community.

As we have seen, Reynolds writes that paintings are to be appreciated by the mind at once, 'at one blow' (p. 62; similarly pp. 113, 129, 172). In taking up this Renaissance idea (Beardsley

1966, pp. 125ff.), Reynolds is setting the seal on his about-turn on
the rule of rules in artistic creation and appreciation. If paintings
are to be appreciated immediately, without pause or reflection,
then there is little room for rules or their application. Rulers rule
by rules which are measured. Measuring and application take
time; thought and reflection are essential. If art is a matter of instantaneous, instinctive appreciation, there is no room for rules.
Instinctive appreciation is learned from the association with the
closed community of knowledge. Admission is a matter of birth,
breeding and influence; this is how judgments are legitimised.
Rules are for the others, the outsiders, those expressing suffering
and passions, those that are to be measured, weighed, ruled and
dispatched.

3

In general terms, Reynolds's text is such a complex and curious
mixture of assertion and counter-assertion, proposition and
denial, that it is not difficult to suggest that it can be pulled in
many different directions. The one that interests us here relates to
the place of the rules of art and law in a society increasingly
concerned with order in a formal sense. We are suggesting in this
book that the rules of law do not achieve some of the high aims
without which a legal system cannot justify itself. Legal systems
can exist in all sorts of circumstances, including sheer terror, but if
they are going to maintain some allegiance (Hart 1961), as the
common law has always tried to do, a presentation of the system as
aspiring to justice is essential.
    Reynolds tries to justify his system of rules and standards by
linking it to a universalistic conception of artistic appreciation, the
values of which are meant to be beyond question. But the falling
apart of his systematic exposition suggests that the object of the
exercise cannot be achieved. Reynolds struggled to come to terms
with what this means for his rules of art. His solution was to
maintain the highest ideals by concentrating on essentials of form
at the expense of the subsidiary, marginal, supplementary elements, those elements that might need most protecting, and
which, in law at least, tend to decentre his essentials.
    In one of the passages where Reynolds consciously articulates
the problems of maintaining a consistent position between

preserving and disvaluing the margins, he freely admits that he probably went too far in previous lectures in downplaying the ornamental as against the sublime style in painting. But, nevertheless, he said what he thought was right at the time. If he had exaggerated it was to a purpose: '[We] did as we do in making what is crooked straight, by bending it the contrary way, in order that it may remain straight at last' (p. 136). To make what is crooked straight is indeed a worthy and necessary task, especially when dealing with laws. But Reynolds failed to make the crooked straight. Straight lines are drawn with the very rules of art that Reynolds seems to have abandoned. And rules, even when used, are never as straight as Reynolds seemed to suppose at the start of the *Discourses*. Rules that do exist, however, are frequently bent in many ways so that the approved community of rulers can operate them. In fact, what Reynolds seems to have proved for himself is similar to what Fineman seems to show Shakespeare revealing in the Sonnets: he has made the worse appear the better reason. Instead of some vague notion of the possibility of purity in art, he has found that he has to rely on the devilish impurity of speech, with some pretty dreadful consequences. No wonder his final Discourse has to retreat into a void. Reynolds has moved from the rules of art, via the art of rules, to the rules of language which deprive the artist of speech. As we have seen in our earlier discussion,[41] though for Reynolds rather literally, 'The rest is silence.'

Jurisprudence has spent much time following Reynolds's pedagogical precept, with notable success, in making the crooked appear straight. Reynolds was both concerned with appearances and wanted to get beyond them.[42] He insisted that the heroes artists were urged to paint were to look like great men, even though the painter could not make them talk as such (p. 58). Art was supposed to be about something more than mere appearance. Our exposition suggests that he ended indicating how crooked rules of

---

[41] See Chapter 5.

[42] Reynolds's prioritising of the sense of sight, a fairly obvious position for a painter, is something on which we have not elaborated. It is probably connected with his theory of art 'at one blow'. The priority given to the sense of sight (also prioritised by Locke) is similarly stated by Cicero: 'the keenest of all our sense is the sense of sight' (*De Oratore*, II.l.xxxvii.357, and the following passages where sight is linked to memory). Beardsley (1966, p. 102) explains the importance attached by other thinkers, such as Aquinas, to the sense of sight.

art had to be in order to work the 'deceptions' that he himself said were the object of the exercise, and at the same time maintain appearances. By contrast, we are, in part, concerned to let the crooked remain crooked, to show what is at stake when such high ideals as those of Reynolds, and of the common law, are sacrificed for an aesthetic conception of perfection which does not allow its general straight appearance to be disturbed by the marginal, ornamental drapery of the application of just rules to particular cases.

Reynolds tried to set out a definitive theory of neoclassical art (Beardsley 1966, p. 149). But its definitive nature was short-lived. Romanticism, Hegelianism, Marxism, theories of the will and many others challenged the pure Neoplatonism of systems like those of Reynolds (even though it might be said that Plato still haunts much later discussion). But that fashions in interpretation and art change wildly is not the main theme of this book. Our argument is that expected, received or authorised interpretations of texts can be challenged.[43] Despite later developments, the work of Reynolds as a great artistic practitioner makes his voice as an interpreter doubly authoritative. And one reading of his *Discourses* would indicate, authoritatively, a definitive laying down of artistic standards. Another tradition, heterodox and repressed, whose traces, however, litter the body of law, would say that such laying down of the law, even in legal discourse, even in the final judgment, is not as definitive as it would claim. It may not be so easy to make the crooked straight.

Postmodern jurisprudence attempts to deregulate the authority of the texts of law, to show that there are other ways, more liberating and creative, of reading texts as important as those of law. If texts make us what we are, if we are the product of authorised readings, unauthorised but perfectly possible readings open the possibility of new forms of living. In order to make a start on this task, we are searching for a paradox, the recognition of the ethical non-foundational foundation of the law. While the other can never be a substance, a failure to strive towards the recognition of otherness is the greatest injustice and the most violent oppression of the law. Justice miscarries when it denies the other.

---

[43] The same, we know, is also true of this text.

Bibliography

Aeschylus (1953) *Oresteia* (trans. R. Lattimore), Chicago: University of Chicago Press

Amnesty International (1990a) *Sri Lanka*, London: Amnesty International

Amnesty International (1990b) *UK: Deficient policy and practice for the protection of asylum seekers*, London: Amnesty International

Arendt, H. (1958) *The Human Condition*, Chicago: University of Chicago Press

Arendt, H. (1977) *The Life of the Mind. Vol. 1: Thinking*, New York: Harcourt Brace Jovanovich

Aristotle (1920) *The Art of Poetry* (trans. I. Bywater), Oxford: Oxford University Press

Aristotle (1950) *Politics*, in *Collected Works* (ed. W. D. Ross), Oxford: Oxford University Press

Aristotle (1976) *Ethics* (trans. J. A. K. Thomson), London: Penguin Books

Aristotle (1984) *The Complete Works* (ed. J. Barnes), Princeton: Princeton University Press

Aristotle (1991) *The Art of Rhetoric* (trans. H. C. Lawson-Tancred), London: Penguin

Atiyah, P. S. (1979) *The Rise and Fall of Freedom of Contract*, Oxford: Clarendon Press

Austin, J. (1954) *The Province of Jurisprudence Determined*, London: Weidenfeld & Nicolson

Baker, J. H. (1979) *An Introduction to English Legal History* (2nd edn), London: Butterworth

Barker, F. and Hulme, P. (1985) 'Nymphs and reapers heavily vanish: the discursive context of *The Tempest*', in J. Drakakis (ed.), *Alternative Shakespeares*, London: Methuen

Barrell, J. (1986) *The Political Theory of Painting: From Reynolds to Hazlitt*, New Haven, CT: Yale University Press

Barrell, J. (1988) *Poetry, Language and Politics*, Manchester: Manchester University Press

Barrell, J. (1990) 'Sir Joshua Reynolds and the Englishness of English art', in H. Bhabha (ed.), *Nation and Narration*, London: Routledge

Bauman, Z. (1990) 'Effacing the face: on the social management of moral proximity', *Theory, Culture & Society*, 7, pp. 1–34

Beardsley, M. C. (1966) *Aesthetics from Classical Greece to the Present*, Tuscaloosa, Alabama and London: University of Alabama Press

Bellhouse, D. R. (1988) 'Probability in the sixteenth and seventeenth centuries: an analysis of Puritan casuistry', *International Statistical Review*, 56, pp. 63–88

Belsey, C. (1985) 'Disrupting sexual difference: meaning and gender in the comedies', in J. Drakakis (ed.), *Alternative Shakespeares*, London: Methuen

Benhabib, S. (1992) *Situating the Self: Gender, community and postmodernism in contemporary ethics*, Cambridge: Polity

Benjamin, A. (1989) *Translation and the Nature of Philosophy: A new theory of words*, London: Routledge

Benjamin, W. (1978) *Reflections* (trans. E. Jephcott), New York: Schocken Books

Bentham, J. (1787) *Defence of Usury: Showing the impolicy of the present legal restraints on the terms of pecuniary bargains etc.* London: T. Payne & Sons

Bernasconi, R. (1987), 'Deconstruction and the possibility of ethics', in J. Sallis (ed.), *Deconstruction and Philosophy*, Chicago: Chicago University Press

Bernasconi, R. and Critchley, S. (1991) *Re-reading Levinas*, London: Athlone

Blackstone, W. (1979) *Commentaries on the Laws of England*, Chicago: University of Chicago Press

Bowra, C. M. (1944) *Sophoclean Tragedy*, Oxford: Clarendon

Boyd White, J. (1990) *Justice as Translation*, Chicago: University of Chicago Press

Brody, B. (1988) *Life and Death Decision-Making*, Oxford: Oxford University Press

Brown, V. (1993) 'Decanonising discourses: textual analysis and the history of economic thought', in W. Henderson, T. Dudley-Evans and R. Backhouse (eds), *Economics and Language*, London: Routledge

Buchanan, A. (1982) *Marx and Justice*, London: Methuen

Burgess, D. (1991) 'Asylum by ordeal', *New Law Journal*, 18 Jan., pp. 50–1

Caputo, J. (1987) *Radical Hermeneutics*, Bloomington: Indiana University Press

Carty, A. (1991) *Postmodern Law*, Edinburgh: Edinburgh University Press

Certeau, M. de (1986) *Heterologies: Discourse on the Other* (trans. B. Massumi), Minneapolis: University of Minnesota Press

Chanter, T. (1991) 'Antigone's dilemma', in R. Bernasconi and S. Critchley (eds), *Re-reading Levinas*, London: Athlone

Ciaramelli, F. (1991) 'Levinas's ethical discourse between individuation and universality', in R. Bernasconi and S. Critchley (eds), *Re-reading Levinas*, London: Athlone

Cicero, M. T.: References to Cicero, unless followed by a date, are given by the standard abbreviation by which the particular work referenced is known, as published in the Loeb Classical Library with parallel translations (28 vols), Cambridge, MA, and London: Harvard University Press

Cicero, M. T. (1982) *Selected Letters*, Harmondsworth: Penguin

Cohen, G. (ed.) (1979) *Marx, Justice and History*, Princeton, NJ: Princeton University Press

Cornell, D. (1988) 'Post-structuralism, the ethical relation and law', *Cardozo Law Review*, 9, pp. 1587–1621

Cornell, D. (1990) 'From the lighthouse: the promise of redemption and the possibility of legal interpretation', *Cardozo Law Review*, pp. 1689–1714

Cornell, D. (1992) *The Philosophy of the Limit*, London: Routledge

Cornell, D., Rosenfeld, M. and Carlson, D. (eds) (1992) *Deconstruction and the Possibility of Justice*, London: Routledge

Cotterrell, R. (1992) 'Law's community: legal theory and the image of legality', *Journal of Law and Society*, 19, pp. 405–22

Cover, R. (1986) 'Violence and the word', *Yale Law Journal*, 95, pp. 1601–29

Critchley, S. (1992) *The Ethics of Deconstruction: Derrida and Levinas*, Oxford: Blackwell

Curtis, D. and Resnik, J. (1987) 'Images of justice', *Yale Law Journal*, 96, pp. 1727–72

Delumeau, J. (1988) 'Prescription and reality', in E. Leites (ed.), *Conscience and Casuistry in Early Modern Europe*, Cambridge: Cambridge University Press

de Man, P. (1979) *Allegories of Reading: Figural language in Rousseau, Nietzshce, Rilke and Proust*, New Haven, CN: Yale University Press

de Man, P. (1983) *Blindness and Insight*, London: Methuen

D'Éntreves, A. (1970) *Natural Law*, London: Hutchinson

Derrida, J. (1974) *Of Grammatology* (trans. G. Spivak), Baltimore: Johns Hopkins University Press

Derrida, J. (1978) *Writing and Difference* (trans. A. Bass), London: Routledge

Derrida, J. (1982) *Margins of Philosophy* (trans. A. Bass) Brighton: Harvester Press

Derrida, J. (1986a) *Glas* (trans. J. Leavey and R. Rand), Lincoln: University of Nebraska Press

Derrida, J. (1986b) 'Declarations of independence' (trans. T. Keenan and T. Pepper), *New Political Science*, 15, pp. 7–15

Derrida, J. (1987) *The Truth in Painting* (trans. G. Bennington and I. McLeod), Chicago: University of Chicago Press

Derrida, J. (1988) *Limited Inc.* (ed. G. Graff; trans. S. Weber and J. Mehlman), Evanston, IL: Northwestern University Press

Derrida, J. (1989) 'Devant la loi', in A. Edoff (ed.), *Kafka and the Contemporary Critical Performance: Centenary readings*, Bloomington: Indiana University Press

Derrida, J. (1990) 'The force of law: the "mystical foundation of authority" ',
Cardozo Law Review, 11, pp. 919–1046

Derrida, J. (1992a) Given Time: 1. Counterfeit Money (trans. P. Kamuf),
Chicago: University of Chicago Press

Derrida, J. (1992b) Acts of Literature (ed. D. Attridge), London: Routledge

Derrida. J. (1992c) The Other Heading (trans. P.-A. Brault and M. Naas),
Bloomington: Indiana University Press

Docherty, T. (1986) John Donne, Undone, London: Methuen

Docherty, T. (1990) After Theory, London: Routledge

Dodds, E. R. (1951) The Greeks and the Irrational, Berkeley: University of
California Press

Douzinas, C. and McVeigh, S. (1992) 'The tragic body: the inscription of
autonomy in medical ethics and law', in S. McVeigh and S. Wheeler (eds),
Law, Health and Medical Regulation, Aldershot: Dartmouth

Douzinas, C. and Warrington, R. (1986) 'Domination, exploitation and
suffering: Marxism and the opening of closed systems', Research Journal of
the American Bar Foundation, 4, pp. 801–28

Douzinas, C. and Warrington, R. (1991) 'Posting the law: social contracts and
the postal rule's grammatology', International Journal for the Semiotics of
Law, IV(11), pp. 115–35

Douzinas, C. and Warrington, R. with McVeigh, S. (1991) Postmodern
Jurisprudence: The law of text in the texts of law, London: Routledge

Dworkin, R. (1977) Taking Rights Seriously, London: Duckworth

Dworkin, R. (1983) 'Law as interpretation', in W. J. T. Mitchell (ed.), The
Politics of Interpretation, Chicago: University of Chicago Press

Dworkin, R. (1986) Law's Empire, London: Fontana

Eagleton, T. (1986) William Shakespeare, Oxford: Blackwell

Euripides (1953) Alkestis and Other Plays (trans. P. Vellacott), London:
Penguin

Euripides (1963) Medea, Hecabe, Electra, Heracles (trans. P. Vellacott),
London: Penguin

Euripides (1971) Bacchae, Ion, Women of Troy, Helen (trans. P. Vellacott),
London: Penguin

Evans, M. (1989) Signifying Nothing: Truth's true context in Shakespeare's
text, Hemel Hempstead: Harvester Wheatsheaf

Feyerabend, P. (1993) Farewell to Reason (3rd edn), London: Verso

Felperin, H. (1990) The Uses of the Canon: Elizabethan literature and
contemporary theory, Oxford: Clarendon Press

Fineman, J. (1986) Shakespeare's Perjured Eye: The invention of subjectivity in
the Sonnets, Berkeley: University of California Press

Finnis, J. (1980) Natural Law and Natural Rights, Oxford: Clarendon Press

Fish, S. (1980) Is There a Text in This Class? The authority of interpretative
communities, Cambridge, MA: Harvard University Press

Fish, S. (1989) *Doing What Comes Naturally: Change, rhetoric and the practice of theory in literary and legal studies*, Oxford: Clarendon Press

Fitzpatrick, P. (ed.) (1991) *Dangerous Supplements*, London: Pluto Press

Foster, H. (1985) 'Postmodernism: a preface', in H. Foster (ed.), *Postmodern Culture*, London: Pluto

Foucault, M. (1977) *Language, Counter-Memory, Practice* (ed. D. Bouchard; trans. D. Bouchard and S. Simon), Oxford: Blackwell

Foucault, M. (1979) *Power, Truth, Strategy* (eds M. Morris and P. Patton), Sydney: Feral Publications

Freedman, B. (1991) *Staging the Gaze: Postmodernism, psychoanalysis and Shakesperean comedy*, Ithaca: Cornell University Press

French, M. (1981) *Shakespeare's Division of Experience*, London: Jonathan Cape

Fried, C. (1988) 'Sonnet LXV and the "black ink" of the framers' intention', in S. Levinson and S. Mailloux (eds), *Interpreting Law and Literature: A hermeneutics reader*, Evanston, IL: Northwestern University Press

Fuller, L. L. (1964) *The Morality of Law*, New Haven, CT: Yale University Press

Gadamer, H-G. (1975) *Truth and Method* (trans. G. Barden and J. Cummings), New York: Seabury

Gadamer, G. (1989) 'Text and interpretation', in D. Michenfeld and R. Palmer (eds), *Dialogue and Deconstruction: The Gadamer–Derrida encounter*, New York: State University of New York Press

Gallagher, L. (1991) *Medusa's Gaze: Casuistry and conscience in the Renaissance*, Stanford, CA: Stanford University Press

Geras, N. (1985) 'The controversy about Marx and justice', *New Left Review*, 150, p. 47

Geras, N. (1992) 'Bringing Marx to justice', *New Left Review*, 162, p. 37

Girard, R. (1991) *A Theatre of Envy: William Shakespeare*, Oxford: Oxford University Press

Goheen, R. F. (1951) *The Imagery of Sophocles' Antigone*, Princeton, NJ: Princeton University Press

Goodrich, P. (1986) *Reading the Law*, Oxford: Blackwell

Goodrich, P. (1990) *Languages of Law: From logics of memory to nomadic masks*, London: Weidenfeld & Nicolson

Goodrich, P. (1992) 'The continuance of the antirrhetic', *Cardozo Studies in Law and Literature*, 4, pp. 207–23

Goodrich, P. (1994) 'Antirrhesis: the polemical structures of common law thought', in A. Sarat and T. Kearns (eds), *Law and Rhetoric*, Ann Arbor: Michigan University Press

Greenblatt, S. (1988) *Shakespearean Negotiations: The circulation of social energy in Renaissance England*, Oxford: Clarendon Press

Habermas, J. (1984) *The Theory of Communicative Action. Vol. 1: Reason and rationalization of society*, Boston: Beacon

Habermas, J. (1985) 'Modernity – an incomplete project', in H. Foster (ed.), *Postmodern Culture*, London: Pluto

Habermas, J. (1987) *The Philosophical Discourses of Modernity* (trans. F. Lawrence), Cambridge, MA: MIT Press

Hardie, W. F. R. (1980) *Aristotle's Ethical Theory*, Oxford: Oxford University Press

Harpham, G. G. (1991) 'Derrida and the ethics of criticism', *Textual Practice*, 5, pp. 383–408

Harrison, J. (1977) *Themis: A study of the social origins of Greek religion*, London: Merlin Press

Harrison, R. B. (1975) *Hölderlin and Greek Literature*, Oxford: Oxford University Press

Hart, H. L. A. (1961) *The Concept of Law*, Oxford: Clarendon Press

Hauerwas, S. (1983) 'Casuistry as a narrative art', *Interpretation*, 37, pp. 377–88

Havelock, E. A. (1978) *The Greek Concept of Justice*, Cambridge, MA: Harvard University Press

Hawkes, T. (1986) *That Shakespeherian Rag: Essays on a critical process*, London: Methuen

Hegel, G. W. F. (1967) *Philosophy of Right* (trans. T. M. Knox), Oxford: Oxford University Press

Hegel, G. W. F. (1975a) *Natural Law* (trans. T. M. Knox), Philadelphia: University of Pennsylvania Press

Hegel, G. W. F. (1975b) *Aesthetics* (trans. F. P. B. Osmaston), New York: Hacker

Hegel, G. W. F. (1977) *Phenomenology of Spirit* (trans. A. V. Miller), Oxford: Oxford University Press

Hegel, G. W. F (1988) *Lectures on the Philosophy of Religion* (ed. P. Hodgson, trans. P. Hodgson et al.), Berkeley: University of California Press

Heidegger, M. (1961) *An Introduction to Metaphysics* (trans. R. Mannheim), New York: Doubleday Anchor

Heidegger, M. (1962) *Being and Time* (trans. J. Macquarrie and E. Robinson), New York: Harper & Row

Heidegger, M. (1977) *Basic Writings*, New York: Harper Collins

Heller, A. (1987) *Beyond Justice*, Oxford: Blackwell

Heller, A. and Feher, F. (1988) *The Postmodern Political Condition*, Oxford: Blackwell

Hesiod (1973) *Works and Days* (trans. D. Wender), London: Penguin

Hillis Miller, J. (1987) *The Ethics of Reading*, New York: Columbia University Press

Hoffman, B. (1991) 'Law for art's sake in the public realm', *Critical Inquiry*, 17, pp. 540–63

Holmes, P. J. (1981) *Elizabethan Casuistry*, Catholic Record Society

Homer (1961) *Iliad* (trans. E. V. Rieu), Chicago: University of Chicago Press

Horwitz, M. J. (1977) *The Transformation of American Law, 1780–1860*, Cambridge, MA: Harvard University Press

Hume, D. (1963) *Essays, Moral, Political and Literary*, Oxford: Oxford University Press

Hunt, A. (1986) 'The theory of critical legal studies', *Oxford Journal of Legal Studies*, 6, pp. 1–45

Husserl, E. (1967) *The Paris Lectures* (ed. P. Koestenbaum), The Hague: Martinus Nijhoff

Hutcheon, L. (1988) *A Poetics of Postmodernism: History, theory, fiction*, London: Routledge

Hutchinson, A. (1988) *Dwelling on the Threshold. Critical essays on modern legal thought*, Toronto: The Carswell Company Ltd

Irigaray, L. (1985) *Speculum of the Other Woman* (trans. G. Gill), Ithaca, NY: Cornell University Press

Jaeger, W. (1947) 'In praise of law', in P. Sayre (ed.), *Interpretations of Modern Legal Philosophies*, New York: Oxford University Press

Jackson, B. (1988) *Law, Fact and Narrative Coherence*, Liverpool: Deborah Charles Publications

Jardine, L. (1983) *Still Harping on Daughters: Women and drama in the age of Shakespeare*, Brighton: Harvester

Jebb, R. (1966) *The Antigone of Sophocles*, Cambridge: Cambridge University Press

Jonsen, A. R. and Toulmin, S. (1988) *The Abuse of Casuistry: A history of moral reasoning*, Berkeley: University of California Press.

Kant, I. (1956) *Critique of Practical Reason* (trans. L. W. Beck), London: Macmillan

Kant, I. (1964) *Critique of Pure Reason* (trans. H. K. Smith), London: Macmillan

Kant, I. (1973) *Critique of Judgment* (trans. J. C. Meredith), Oxford: Oxford University Press

Kearny, R. (1988) *The Wake of Imagination*, London: Hutchinson

Kelsen, H. (1947) 'The metamorphoses of the idea of justice', in P. Sayre (ed.), *Interpretations of Modern Legal Philosophies*, New York: Oxford University Press

Kennedy, G. (1963) *The Art of Persuasion in Greece*, Princeton, NJ: Princeton University Press

Kierkegaard, S. (1978) *Either/Or* (ed. H. Hong; trans. E. Hong), Princeton, NJ: Princeton University Press

Kittsteiner, H. D. (1988) 'Kant and casuistry', in E. Leites (ed.), *Conscience and Casuistry in Early Modern Europe*, Cambridge: Cambridge University Press

Knox, B. (1984) 'Introduction to *Antigone*' in Sophocles, *The Three Theban Plays* (trans. R. Fagles), Harmondsworth: Penguin

Kojève, A. (1969) *Introduction to the Reading of Hegel: Lectures on the*

Phenomenology of Spirit (ed. A. Bloom, trans. J. Nichols), Ithaca, NY: Cornell University Press

Lacan, J. (1992) *The Ethics of Psychoanalysis* (ed. J.-A. Miller, trans. D. Potter), London: Routledge

Lacoue-Labarthe, P. (1978) *Hölderlin: L'Antigone de Sophocle*, Paris: Flammarion

Lacoue-Labarthe, P. (1990) *Heidegger, Art and Politics* (trans. C. Turner), Oxford: Blackwell

Leites, E. (1988) 'Casuistry and character', in E. Leites (ed.), *Conscience and Casuistry in Early Modern Europe*, Cambridge: Cambridge University Press

Levinas, E. (1969) *Totality and Infinity* (trans. A. Lingis), Pittsburgh: Duquesne University Press

Levinas, E. (1989) *The Levinas Reader* (ed. S. Hand), Oxford: Blackwell

Levinas, E. (1990) *Nine Talmudic Readings* (trans. A. Aronowicz), Bloomington: Indiana University Press

Levinas, E. (1991) *Otherwise Than Being or Beyond Essence* (trans. A. Lingis), London: Kluwer

Levinson, S. and Mailloux, S. (eds) (1988) *Interpreting Law and Literature: A hermeneutics reader*, Evanston, IL: Northwestern University Press

Lierberman, D. (1989) *The Province of Legislation Determined: Legal theory in eighteenth-century Britain*, Cambridge; Cambridge University Press

Lingis, A. (1989) *Deathbound Subjectivity*, Bloomington: Indiana University Press

Lloyd, D. and Freeman, M. D. A. (1985) *Introduction to Jurisprudence* (5th edn), London: Stevens

Lloyd-Jones, H. (1971) *Justice of Zeus*, Berkeley: University of California Press

Longinus (1989) 'On the sublime' (attrib. Longinus), in D. A. Russell and M. Winterbottom (eds), *Classical Literary Criticism*, Oxford: Oxford University Press

Luban, D. (1988) *Lawyers and Justice: An ethical study*, Princeton, NJ: Princeton University Press

Lucas, J. R. (1980) *On Justice*, Oxford: Clarendon Press

Lukes, S. (1985) *Marxism and Morality*, Oxford: Clarendon Press

Lyotard, J.-F. (1985) *Just Gaming* (trans. W. Godzich), Manchester: Manchester University Press

Lyotard, J.-F. (1988a) *The Differend: Phrases in dispute* (trans. G. Van Den Abbeele), Manchester: Manchester University Press

Lyotard. J.-F. (1988b) *Peregrinations: Law, form, event*, New York: Columbia University Press

Lyotard, J.-F. (1989) *The Lyotard Reader* (ed. A. Benjamin), Oxford: Blackwell

Lyotard, J.-F. (1990) *Heidegger and 'the jews'* (trans. A. Michel and M. Roberts), Minneapolis: University of Minnesota Press.

MacIntyre, A. (1981) *After Virtue: A study in moral theory*, London: Duckworth

Megarry, R. and Wade, H. W. R. (1984) *The Law of Real Property* (5th edn), London: Stevens

Milsom, S. F. C. (1981) *Historical foundations of the common law* (2nd edn), London: Butterworth

Mingay, G. E. (1976) *The Gentry: The rise and fall of a ruling class*, London: Longman

Moretti, F. (1987) *The Way of the World: The Bildungsroman in European culture*, London: Verso.

Nagel, T. (1970) *The Possibility of Altruism*, Princeton, NJ: Princeton University Press

Neubauer, J. (1986) *The Emancipation of Music from Language: Departure from mimesis in eighteenth century aesthetics*, New Haven, CT: Yale University Press

Noonan, J. T. Jr (1957) *The Scholastic Analysis of Usury*, Cambridge, MA: Harvard University Press

Norris, C. (1985) 'Post-structuralist Shakespeare: text and ideology', in J. Drakakis (ed.), *Alternative Shakespeares*, London: Methuen

Norris, C. (1988) 'Law, deconstruction and the resistance to theory', *Journal of Law and Society*, 15, pp. 166–87

Ostwald, M. (1969) *Nomos and the Beginning of Athenian Democracy*, Oxford: Oxford University Press

Perelman, C. (1963) *The Idea of Justice and the Problem of Argument*, London: Routledge & Kegan Paul

Pietercil, R. (1978) 'Antigone and Hegel', *International Philosophical Quarterly*, 18, pp. 289–310

Plato (1951) *The Symposium* (trans. W. Hamilton), London: Penguin

Plato (1960) *Gorgias* (trans. W. Hamilton), London: Penguin

Plato (1969) *Crito*, in *The Last Days of Socrates* (trans. H. Tredennick), London: Penguin

Plato (1973) *Phaedrus and Epistles VII and VIII* (trans. W. Hamilton), London: Penguin

Plato (1974) *The Republic* (trans. D. Lee), London: Penguin

Plato (1981) *Protagoras and Meno* (trans. W. K. C. Guthrie), London: Penguin

Posner, R. (1988) *Law and Literature*, Cambridge, MA: Harvard University Press

Prior, W. (1991) *Virtue and Knowledge*, London: Routledge

Pugh, S. (1988) *Garden–Nature–Language*, Manchester: Manchester University Press

Rawls, J. (1971) *A Theory of Justice*, Oxford: Oxford University Press

Rescher, N. (1966) *Distributive Justice*, Indianapolis: Bobbs-Merrill

Reynolds, J. (1966) *Discourses on Art*, London: Collier-Macmillan

Ricardo, M. (1951) *On the Principles of Political Economy and Taxation* (ed. P. Sraffa and M. Dobb), Cambridge: Cambridge University Press

Ricoeur, P. (1983) 'On interpretation', in A. Montefiori (ed.), *Philosophy in France Today*, Cambridge: Cambridge University Press

Ricoeur, P. (1992) *Oneself as Another*, Chicago: University of Chicago Press

Rorty, R. (1979) *Philosophy and the Mirror of Nature*, Princeton, NJ: Princeton University Press

Rorty, R. (1991) *Essays on Heidegger and Others: Philosophical Papers, Vol. 2*, Cambridge: Cambridge University Press

Rose, E. (1975) *Alternatives Open to Recusants and Puritans under Elizabeth I and James I*, Cambridge: Cambridge University Press

Rose, G. (1984) *Dialectics of Nihilism: Poststructuralism and law*, Oxford: Blackwell

Rose, G. (1992) *The Broken Middle*, Oxford: Blackwell

Rose, J. (1985) 'Sexuality in the reading of Shakespeare: *Hamlet* and *Measure for Measure*', in J. Drakakis (ed.), *Alternative Shakespeares*, London: Methuen

Rosen, S. (1987) 'The limits of interpretation', in A. Cascardi (ed.), *Literature and the Question of Philosophy*, Baltimore: Johns Hopkins University Press

Ross, A. (1958) *On Law and Justice*, London: Stevens

Rousseau, J.-J. (1966) *On the Origin of Language* (trans. J. Moran and A. Gode), Chicago: University of Chicago Press

Sallis, J. (1991) *Crossings: Nietzsche and the space of tragedy*, Chicago: University of Chicago Press

Sambrook, J. (1986) *The Eighteenth Century: The intellectual context of English literature 1700–1789*, London and New York: Longman

Sampson, M. (1988) 'Laxity and liberty in seventeenth-century English political thought', in E. Leites (ed.), *Conscience and Casuistry in Early Modern Europe*, Cambridge: Cambridge University Press

Santirocco, M. (1986) 'Justice in Sophocles' *Antigone*', *Philosophy and Literature*, pp. 180–97

Sarat, A. and Kearns, T. (1992) 'A journey through forgetting: toward a jurisprudence of violence', in A. Sarat and T. Kearns (eds), *The Fate of Law*, Ann Arbor: University of Michigan Press

Scarry, E. (1987) *The Body in Pain*, Oxford: Oxford University Press

Segal, C. (1964) 'Sophocles's in praise of men and the conflicts of *Antigone*', *Arion*, 3, pp. 46–66

Segal, C. (1981) *Tragedy and Civilization: An interpretation of Sophocles*, Cambridge, MA: Harvard University Press

Segal, C. (1986) *Myth, Poetry, Text*, Ithaca: Cornell University Press

Seiden, M. (1990) *Measure for Measure: Casuistry and artistry*, Washington, DC: The Catholic University of America Press

Shami, J. M. (1983) 'Donne's Protestant casuistry: cases of conscience in the *Sermons*', *Studies in Philology*, 80, pp. 53–66

Sinfield, A. (1992) *Faultlines: Cultural materialism and the politics of dissident reading*, Oxford: Clarendon Press

Smith, A. (1976) *An Inquiry into the Nature and Causes of the Wealth of Nations, Vol. 1*, Oxford: Oxford University Press.

Smith, A. (1983) *Lectures on Rhetoric and Belles Lettres*, Oxford: Oxford University Press

Slights, C. W. (1981) *The Casuistical Tradition in Shakespeare, Donne, Herbert and Milton*, Princeton, NJ: Princeton University Press

Sommerville, J. P. (1988) 'The "new art of lying": equivocation, mental reservation, and casuistry', in E. Leites (ed.), *Conscience and Casuistry in Early Modern Europe*, Cambridge: Cambridge University Press

Sophocles (1984) *The Three Theban Plays* (trans. R. Fagles with an introduction by B. Knox), London: Penguin

Spivak, G. (1987) *In Other Worlds*, London: Routledge

Steiner, G. (1986) *Antigones: The Antigone myth in western literature, art and thought*, Oxford: Clarendon Press

Sugarman, D. (1986) 'Legal theory, the common law mind and the making of the textbook tradition', in W. Twining (ed.), *Legal Theory and Common Law*, Oxford: Blackwell

Tacitus (1989) 'Dialogue on orators', in D. A. Russell and M. Winterbottom (eds), *Classical Literary Criticism*, Oxford: Oxford University Press

Taylor, C. (1977) *Hegel*, Cambridge: Cambridge University Press

Thompson, E. P. (1978) *The Poverty of Theory and Other Essays*, London: Merlin Press

Ullman, W. (1962) *The Growth of Papal Government in the Middle Ages*, London: Methuen

Urmson, J. O. (1988) *Aristotle's Ethics*, Oxford: Blackwell

Vernant, J. P. and Vidal-Naquet, P. (1990) *Myth and Tragedy in Ancient Greece*, New York: Zone Books

Vickers, B. (1988) *In Defence of Rhetoric*, Oxford: Clarendon Press

Weber, M. (1978) 'Politics as vocation', in Max Weber, *Selections in Translation* (trans. E. Matthews), Cambridge: Cambridge University Press

Weinreb, L. (1987) *Natural Law and Justice*, Cambridge, MA: Harvard University Press

White, R. S. (1987) *Keats as a Reader of Shakespeare*, London: Athlone

Whitman, C. (1951) *Sophocles: A study in heroic humanism*, Cambridge, MA: Harvard University Press

Wilson, T. (1925) *A Discourse upon Usury* (ed. R. H. Tawney), London: C. Bell & Sons

Winnington-Ingram, R. P. (1980) *Sophocles: An interpretation*, Cambridge: Cambridge University Press

Wood, A. (1990) *Hegel's Ethical Thought*, Cambridge: Cambridge University Press